MW00777203

A HISTORY OF KOREAN CHRISTIANITY

With a third of South Koreans now identifying themselves as Christian, Christian churches play an increasingly prominent role in the social and political events of the Korean peninsula. Sebastian C. H. Kim and Kirsteen Kim's comprehensive and timely history of different Christian denominations in Korea includes surveys of the Catholic, Orthodox and Protestant traditions as well as new church movements. They examine the Korean Christian diaspora and missionary movements from South Korea and also give cutting-edge insights into North Korea. This book, the first recent one-volume history and analysis of Korean Christianity in English, highlights the challenges faced by the Christian churches in view of Korea's distinctive and multireligious cultural heritage, South Korea's rapid rise in global economic power and the precarious state of North Korea, which threatens global peace. This history will be an important resource for all students of world Christianity, Korean studies and mission studies.

SEBASTIAN C. H. KIM holds the Chair in Theology and Public Life in the faculty of education and theology at York St John University. He is the author of *In Search of Identity: Debates on Religious Conversion in India* (2003) and *Theology in the Public Sphere* (2011) and the editor of a number of books, including *Christian Theology in Asia* (2008).

KIRSTEEN KIM, Professor of Theology and World Christianity at Leeds Trinity University, is the author of *The Holy Spirit in the World* (2007) and *Joining in with the Spirit* (2012) and the co-author, with Sebastian C. H. Kim, of *Christianity as a World Religion* (2008). She is also the co-editor of several books, including *The New Evangelization: Faith, People, Context and Practice* (with Paul Grogan, 2014).

To Jonathan Jae-young and Lydia Sun-young

A HISTORY OF KOREAN CHRISTIANITY

SEBASTIAN C. H. KIM

York St John University

KIRSTEEN KIM

Leeds Trinity University

CAMBRIDGE
UNIVERSITY PRESS

32 Avenue of the Americas, New York, NY 10013-2473, USA

Cambridge University Press is part of the University of Cambridge.

It furthers the University's mission by disseminating knowledge in the pursuit of
education, learning and research at the highest international levels of excellence.

www.cambridge.org
Information on this title: www.cambridge.org/9780521196383

First published 2015

Printed in the United States of America

A catalog record for this publication is available from the British Library.

Library of Congress Cataloging in Publication Data
Kim, Sebastian C. H.
A history of Korean Christianity / Sebastian C. H. Kim, Kirsteen Kim.
pages   cm
Includes bibliographical references.
ISBN 978-0-521-19638-3 (hardback)
1. Korea – Church history.   I. Kim, Kirsteen.   II. Title.
BR1325.K565   2014
275.19–dc23   2014021773

ISBN 978-0-521-19638-3 Hardback

Contents

Illustrations

vii

Acknowledgements

There are many people who have made this project possible and to whom we would like to express our sincere thanks and appreciation. First, we wish to acknowledge the support of our respective institutions, especially Professor Julian Stern and other staff at the Faculty of Education and Theology at York St John University and Professor Maureen Meikle and colleagues in the Department of Humanities at Leeds Trinity University.

Second, we wish to thank experts at several institutions in Seoul: the Presbyterian College and Theological Seminary, the Korean Christian Museum at Soongsil University, the Institute of the History of Christianity in Korea, the National Organization of the Korean Presbyterian Women and Sogang University. We express our gratitude to members of the following networks and organisations: the British Association for Korean Studies, the Korean Religions Group at the American Academy of Religions, the *Journal of Korean Religions*, the Global Network for Public Theology, the International Association for Mission Studies, the Commission on World Mission and Evangelism of the World Council of Churches, the Yale-Edinburgh Group for the history of world Christianity and the Munich-Freising Conferences on World Christianity.

We would also like to give our grateful thanks to the following individuals for their support: Rev. Dr Paul Kiman Choi, Rev. Dr Park Chong-soon, Rev. Dr Kim Sam-whan, Rev. Dr Kwang Sun Rhee and Rev. Dr Lee Chul-shin. And we would like to acknowledge the help of Rev. Dr Jooseop Keum, Rev. Dr Andrew Chung Yoube Ha and the members of the Korean Catholicism hub at Leeds Trinity University: the late Peter Corbishley, Jung Soo Cho and Dr Andrew Finch.

And finally, we both wish to express our gratitude to the staff at Cambridge University Press, especially our editor Laura Morris, for all their hard work to prepare this book for publication.

Abbreviations

ACTS	Asian Center for Theological Studies and Mission
AKCSNA	Association of Korean Christian Scholars in North America
BFBS	British and Foreign Bible Society
BFMMEC	Board of Foreign Mission of the Methodist Episcopal Church
CBS	Christian Broadcasting System
CCC	Campus Crusade for Christ
CCF	Chosŏn Christian Federation
CCK	Christian Council of Korea
CEMK	Christian Ethics Movement of Korea
CPAJ	Catholic Priests' Association for Justice
CPCK	Council of Presbyterian Churches in Korea
CPKI	Committee for the Preparation of Korean Independence
CRS	Catholic Relief Services
CTCCCA	Commission on Theological Concerns of the Christian Conference of Asia
CWS	Church World Service
DAGA	Documentation Centre for Action Groups in Asia
DMZ	Demilitarized Zone
FBO	Faith-Based Organisation
IBMR	*International Bulletin of Missionary Research*
IHCK	Institute of the History of Christianity in Korea
IKCH	Institute of Korean Church History
IKCHS	Institute of Korean Church History Studies
IMC	International Missionary Council
IRM	*International Review of Mission*
JOC	Jeunesse Ouvrière Chrétienne
KCIA	Korean Central Intelligence Agency
KDF	Korea Democracy Foundation

KDP	Korean Democratic Party
KMF	*Korea Mission Field*
KPPS	Korean Products Promotion Society
KPR	Korean People's Republic
KSCF	Korean Student Christian Fellowship
KSCM	Korean Student Christian Movement
KWMA	Korea World Missions Association
MEP	Paris Foreign Mission (Société des Missions Étrangères de Paris)
NAA	National Association of Evangelicals
NCCK	National Council of Churches in Korea
NFDYS	National Federation of Democratic Youth and Students
NGO	Non-governmental Organisation
NKRPC	North Korean Refugees Presbyterian Commissioners
OECD	Organisation for Economic Cooperation and Development
OMS	Oriental Missionary Society
PCUSA	Presbyterian Church in the United States of America
POW	Prisoner of War
RFKCH	Research Foundation of Korean Church History
ROK	Republic of Korea
SCKCM	Special Committee of Korean Christian Ministers
SPG	Society for the Propagation of the Gospel
SVM	Student Volunteer Movement
TEAM	The Evangelical Alliance Mission
UIM	Urban and Industrial Mission
WCC	World Council of Churches
WMC	World Missionary Conference
YFGC	Yoido Full Gospel Church
YMCA	Young Men's Christian Association
YWCA	Young Women's Christian Association

1 East Asia region (contemporary)

Hamgyeong-do

Uiju

Pyeongan-do

Hamheung

Pyongyang

Wonsan

EAST SEA

Hwanghae-do

Haeju

Gangwon-do

Seoul

Gyeonggi-do

Wonju

YELLOW SEA

Chungcheong-do

Gongju

Gyeongsang-do

Jeonju

Daegu

Jeolla-do

Gwangju

Busan

2 Late Joseon Korea, showing provinces and selected cities

CHAPTER I

Introduction

Korea is crucial in North-east Asia both strategically as the chief crossing between China and Japan and politically as the nexus of interest of China, Japan, Russia and the United States (Map 1). In its current state of division, Korea is a serious threat to global stability and a potential source of widespread conflict. Yet this key component in North-east Asian relations is under-researched and neglected compared to the study of China and Japan. Furthermore, the religious dimensions of Korea's history have tended to be obscured by political readings (Wells 2009:60–80). Surprisingly for a country with long Confucian and Buddhist traditions, within the span of 250 years, Christianity – in various forms – has had a deep impact on Korea and Koreans, including in what is now North Korea. It has played a prominent role in social and political events in the last two centuries; it continues to be a major factor in public life in the South; and it is conspicuous by its suppression in the North. Therefore the study of Korean Christianity and its history is vital for a proper understanding of recent Korean history and for any attempt to resolve the conflict between the Koreas.

From the point of view of the study of religions, Korea presents a rare example in which a substantial proportion of the population has converted to Christianity in a country where other world religions are already established. The planting of Christianity among the ancient religions of Korea and its rapid growth to 30 per cent of the population in South Korea is without parallel in Asia in modern times and demands explanation. In this process, the faith has been shaped by the Korean context and accommodated itself to Korean culture in ways which shed new light on the nature of Christianity and its relation to other religions and spiritualities. The interaction of Christianity with the religious plurality of contemporary South Korea is also a fruitful field for investigation.

However, in the study of world Christianity, South Korea is not only a matter of missiological or ethno-religious interest. With nearly fourteen million mostly middle- and upper-class adherents, Korean Christianity is emerging as a major player in the global church. Its wealth, extensive diaspora and vibrant world mission movements are able to impact developments in other parts of the world (S. C. H. Kim and Kim 2008).

This book analyses the dynamics and aspirations of Christianity within the wider historical context of modern Korea. It asks why Christianity took hold in Korea to a much greater extent than it did in almost any other Asian country. What is the nature of Korean Christianity, and why is it so? How, and to what extent, has Christianity impacted events and developments on the Korean peninsula over the past two or three centuries? What role might the Korean churches – in Korea and abroad – play in the future, especially with regard to relations between the two Koreas?

RESEARCHING KOREAN CHRISTIANITY

As its title suggests, this book focuses on the relationship between Christianity and its Korean context. It seeks to analyse a Christianity that has been shaped by that context and is in some sense Korean. This task is challenging. First, much of the early recorded history of the Korean churches is colonial mission history, that is, the story of Western missionary initiatives towards Korea rather than about Korean reception of the gospel and agency in its spread. Both the main nineteenth-century source on Catholic history by Charles Dallet (1874a, 1874b) and the early Protestant histories by Paik Lak-geoon (Lakgeoon George Paik) (1970 [1929]) and Allen D. Clark (1971) used mainly mission sources, although Paik was often critical of mission work. Recent Korean scholars, however, notably Yu Hong-ryeol, Choi Seok-u and Yi Won-sun for Catholicism and Min Kyoung-bae and Yi Mahn-yol for Protestantism, emphasise that Koreans themselves took the initiative in bringing Christianity to their homeland, either by their own activities or by inviting missionaries in. These and subsequent historians have recovered documents, used Korean sources whenever possible and read between the lines of the mission accounts. Researchers and institutions such as the Institute of Korean Church History (Catholic; established in 1964) and the Institute of the History of Christianity in Korea (Protestant; 1982) have gathered archives of Korean materials, and the Korean Christian Museum was established at Soongsil University, Seoul, in 1954. (It was originally founded by Kim Yang-sun in 1948.) More recently, online collections have been developed (e.g. at the Center for Korean Studies, UCLA). Our aim is a history of the Korean church and of evangelisation rather than a history of foreign missions. From this perspective, Christianity is the latest in a series of religious and cultural influences on Korea. Because Christianity was received within the the world-view and culture created by earlier ways of life and philosophies, this study is informed by studies of the wider context of Korean religions (notably, Grayson 2002; D. Baker 2008).

A second challenge is that much Christian history is a history of the church as an institution rather than of the Christian community. While these works are valuable and necessary, a history of Korean Christianity must include the perspectives and activities of the people, that is, the laity – women as well as men. Christianity became Korean during two centuries of tremendous social and political upheaval in which institutional church life was impossible for many years at a time. During these periods it was obvious that the church subsisted in the lay community. The Catholic Church emphasises this in the attention that its official compendiums give to martyrs (MEP 1924; J. Kim and Chung 1964). Similarly, from the 1970s, Protestant historians draw attention to grassroots activities, especially in the works of Yi Mahn-yol and in the three-volume history produced by his institute (IKCHS 1989, 1990; IKCH 2009). Attention to lay concerns increased the integration of Christian history with the people's history and the study of the relationship of churches to nationalist and social movements. A study of Korean Christianity should be set within Korean history in general, particularly social history, and it should go beyond official church histories to discover the stories and views of Korean Christians.

Third, by writing about Korean Christianity as a whole we hope to overcome denominational divides that have blighted historiography. The most obvious challenge here is that there appears to be not one but two Christian histories in Korea: Catholic and Protestant. It is true that the origins, political experiences and institutional histories of these two parts of the Christian church in Korea are quite distinct. Catholic missionaries mostly had little to do with Protestants, who had a heritage of resistance to Catholic influence. Another reason that the recorded histories are separate is that early Catholic mission historians wrote mostly in French and other continental European languages, whereas Protestants generally used English. Consequently, Catholic histories do not usually refer to Protestant history; it is as if Catholicism is the only form of Christianity to be found in Korea (J. Kim and Chung 1964 is an exception here). For their part, Protestant histories either disregard the Catholic Church altogether as discontinuous with the Protestant movement (e.g. Lee Eok-ju 2010) or they record the early martyr history of Catholicism as a precursor to the

Protestant story, and even 'the seed of the church' (e.g. A. Clark 1971); but after that they largely ignore the continuing Catholic presence and growth, giving the impression that Catholicism is now superseded by a new and more dynamic movement. Even more misleading, in Korea Protestants are generally referred to as 'Christians' but this term is not applied to Catholics, who are known as 'Catholic'. A Protestant historian of 'Christianity' is thus under no sense of obligation to include Catholicism.

Since the late 1980s, some historians have attempted to tell about the development of Protestantism and Catholicism in the same volume or in the same article but they continue to treat them in parallel, not intertwined, thus perpetuating the division (D. Clark 1986; Yu Chai-shin 2004; Buswell and Lee 2006; Grayson 2006). It is true that institutionally there was no overlap between them; moreover, successive governments treated them separately and the census lists them as two different religions. However, both Christian communities operated within the same social and religious context, and in practice there was significant contact and collaboration between the two groups, especially in periods of national crisis. Their encounters were sometimes constructive and at other times antagonistic. Furthermore, the two forms of Christianity in Korea exhibited a 'sibling rivalry' (D. Baker 2006b). The fierce competition between them was not only over their comparative growth figures. Protestants demonstrated their awareness of Catholic history when, for instance, they identified Protestant martyrs and stressed the vernacular nature of Protestant churches. Similarly, Catholic historians responded to Protestant activity and were sensitive to criticism, such as the accusation in the 1970s that they lacked social concern. Our aim is to integrate Catholic and Protestant histories into one complex story, using the word 'Christian' to cover all strands of the religion.

Korean Catholic history has become much more accessible through the series by the Institute of Korean Church History (2009 onwards) for which nine volumes are projected. However, Protestant historiography is very fragmented, with many separate denominational histories (e.g. Lee Jae-jeong 1990; Ryu Dong-sik 2005a, 2005b). When it is used in general, the term 'Protestant' sometimes means only the Presbyterians and Methodists whose missions entered together in 1885 and the union activities that they encouraged. More often it is extended to include other groups such as Holiness, Baptist and Salvation Army, but sometimes it refers only to the Presbyterians who are the dominant group. The bifurcation into Catholic and Protestant histories not only neglects the extent to which they are interlinked but also tends to obscure what is a complicated ecclesiastical situation. It excludes the Orthodox Church altogether; Anglicans in Korea, who are Anglo-Catholic, do not fit in either category; and Protestants have not always wanted to include Pentecostals and some evangelical churches under the Protestant umbrella. Moreover, Protestant–Catholic duality and Protestant denominationalism have led to the neglect of ecumenical and interdenominational organisations and activities. We include, as far as possible, all forms of Christianity in Korea. We shall use 'Protestant' to include all the post-Reformation denominations, although sometimes Pentecostals and Anglicans are specified separately.

Korean Christianity is wider than Christianity in Korea and this presents a fourth challenge: to consider diaspora and mission movements. The oppression and instability of the Korean peninsula from the 1860s onwards produced migration movements and a large Korean population outside the peninsula. From the early twentieth century onwards, this diaspora was largely Protestant and there was a reciprocal relationship between the churches inside and outside Korea. Since the late 1980s, the Protestant overseas missionary movement has ranked among the largest globally and is in many respects integrated into the diaspora. We shall treat diaspora congregations, denominations and missionary movements as an integral part of Korean Christianity.

A fifth challenge is the dualisms which polarise Korean Christianity and bias historical perspectives – of which Catholic–Protestant may be considered one. Gender relations is an important interpretative framework for Korean society whose significance for historiography is overlooked (Wells 1999). Most Korean churches, like Korean society, are separated into men's and women's spheres, but histories of Korean Christianity – like most history, and for reasons which are well known – tell the story mainly from male perspectives. We aim as far as possible to bring in women's history, the records of which may need to be found in other sources. Moreover, the partition of Korea, the Korean War and the Cold War polarised Korea ideologically. As far as possible, this is a history of the whole of Korean Christianity, including in North Korea, but since after 1945 the church communities in the north were largely destroyed and North Korea has been closed to historical enquiry, the history of the South is inevitably given greater attention. The stand-off between the Communist North and the liberal-democratic South which continues today produced leftist and rightist theologies. For example, in Protestant churches in the 1970s and 1980s particularly, two different histories were being told: one presented South Korean Protestant history as a narrative of successful church growth by the efforts of missionaries and Koreans, and by the use of certain methods (Ro Bong-rin and Nelson 1983). The other portrayed

Christians as a socially active minority suffering at the hands of colonists and dictators for the sake of the oppressed minjung or masses (Kim Yong-bock 1981a). We intend to show how these views were responses by different actors to a common set of circumstances. They constitute one example of the perennial division among Christians according to their response to cultural change: conservative and progressive. For late twentieth-century Protestants this division was often termed 'evangelical' and 'liberal', respectively; for Catholics it was defined by their resistance to, or embrace of, the reforms of the Second Vatican Council. While these distinctions are relevant, we hope to demonstrate that the complexity and diversity of Korean Christianity and Korean culture transcends such simple classifications.

There is a growing body of literature on Korean history and Korean Christianity. We have tried our best to read as widely as possible and to consult both primary and secondary sources in Korean, English and, occasionally, French. A list of sources cited is given in the Bibliography, and Harvard-system references are used to verify, amplify or qualify the discussion. A technical challenge for Korean historiography is the multiple systems of romanisation for Korean script. There is no perfect system for romanisation; each has advantages and disadvantages. We have chosen to follow the system adopted by the South Korean Ministry of Culture in 2000.[1] The McCune-Reischauer system is the most widely used in Korean studies but is difficult for the non-specialist because it uses diacritical marks and has to be specially learnt. The Ministry of Culture system can be read by anyone immediately and those who have mastered McCune-Reischauer can easily understand what is intended, although it may look unfamiliar at first. The new system is increasingly used by younger scholars, and scholars in South Korea are strongly encouraged to adopt it. It is also the most widely used on the Internet, especially because inputting diacritical marks into search engines is awkward. As Koreans define their own history, we envisage that this system will prevail, and its use in this volume signifies the contemporary approach of our book. An exception to our use of the Ministry of Culture system is where the reference is to a published work in Korean which includes English details. In this case, the spelling of an author's name has been retained, and similarly for the Anglicised names of public figures. As the system allows, we also make exceptions for common surnames such as Cheong, Kim, Suh, Yi and Lee and for internationally known places, terms and figures (e.g. Pyongyang, Hangul and Park Chung-hee). We choose to use a hyphen between the syllables of personal names to clarify pronunciation.

---

[1] Japanese romanisation is according to the Hepburn system, and Pinyin is used for Chinese words.

In all names of individuals, following Korean practice, the surname appears first to avoid confusion. When first used, the baptismal or Christian names of Koreans (where known) are given in brackets, as are the Western-style names by which they may be more commonly known (such as Syngman Rhee). There are relatively few Korean family names so, to avoid confusion, Korean names are given in full in the references. Also in the bibliography, where the publication is in Korean we give the title of the book or article in Korean script (Hangul) with an English translation, giving preference to that of the author. Finally, we have chosen not to use italics for Korean or other foreign-language terms, since these occur frequently in this volume.

Six chronological chapters follow this introduction. Since we are discussing Korean Christianity in all its forms, the period divisions are according to national history and do not correspond with dates significant for any particular church. Chapter 2 deals with the first century of Christian presence, which was in the form of Catholicism. Chapter 3 takes up the story from the opening of Korea by Japan until its annexation by the same in 1910, during which time Protestantism entered. Chapter 4 covers the period of colonial rule until Korea's liberation by Soviet and Allied forces in 1945. Chapter 5 deals with the development of the churches in the South before and after the Korean War until the turn of the 1960s, and with the fate of the churches in the North. Chapter 6 covers the three decades of military dictatorship in South Korea during which the economy and the churches both experienced spectacular growth and Christian-led movements for human rights and democracy eventually overthrew the dictatorship in 1987. Chapter 7 brings the story up to the present. It covers developments with respect to the North, changes in the church scene in the South, the Christian diaspora and missionary movements.

PERTINENT FEATURES OF 'TRADITIONAL KOREA'

For the remainder of this chapter, we set early Korean Christianity within its Korean context by drawing attention to key features of Korea's religious history before the arrival of Christianity and make a few salient remarks about Korea's 'traditional' culture. Readers familiar with premodern Korea may wish to go straight to Chapter 2.

The overall religious history of Korea is of state endorsement of a series of distinct religions – indigenous Korean religion, Buddhism, Confucianism – and of popular practice which in many cases utilised whichever rituals were perceived to be of most practical help. Religions out of favour were suppressed and even persecuted by the state (Grayson 2002; D. Baker 2007a).

Prehistoric Korean peoples believed in a world of 'spirits' with which certain unusual persons, known as shamans, were able to communicate through 'techniques of ecstasy', including exorcisms known as gut (Hogarth 1999). This practice was part of a folk religion concerned with obtaining the power of the gods, dealing with harassment by aggrieved spirits, assuaging the greed of the ancestors and creating harmony within conflicting forces.

From the fourth and fifth centuries, the people of the Korean peninsula came increasingly under the influence of China, and the kingdoms of Korea adopted a Sino-centric world-view. This was expressed ritualistically as sadae, 'serving the great', and by a tribute relationship which reached its height in the late fourteenth and early fifteenth centuries (Fairbank 1968). China did not generally interfere with Korea's internal affairs, but Korea's filiality limited its foreign relations, which partly accounts for its relative seclusion (D. Kang 2010). The annual mission which travelled from Seoul to Beijing via a well-defined route became acquainted with the latest developments in China and the known world. Korea's only other bilateral relationship was with Japan, which involved warfare as well as diplomacy and trade, and the nature of which in the premodern period is contested. Through its orientation to China, Chinese religions – including Confucianism, Taoism and Mahayana Buddhism – entered Korea in combination. But by the end of the sixth century it was the Buddhists, who also claimed a direct link with India, who were patronised by the rulers of each of the three kingdoms of Korea. Buddhism was adopted by the unified kingdom of Goryeo (918–1392) as the national ideology in the belief that its practice would protect the nation and cure the land. It held sway in cultural and political circles for the better part of a millennium (Grayson 1985:16–62). Korean Buddhists developed Seon, or meditative Buddhism, which in Korea is text centred and has a highly developed doctrine. Alongside this elite form of the religion, popular Buddhism also accommodated aspects of traditional Korean religion. It thrived in a form heavily influenced by the shamanistic emphasis on intercession for the people's prosperity and happiness and by the recognition of various buddhas, bodhisattvas and other supernatural beings that appealed to the people. Devotion was directed particularly to the Amitabha (Amita) Buddha of the Pure Land, the Healing Buddha (Yaksa Yeorae), the Maitreya (Mireuk) or Future Buddha and the Avalokitesvara (Gwanseeum), the goddess of compassion (R. Robinson, Johnson and Thanissaro 2005:220–34; Mitchell 2008:245–74).

Under Mongol domination, a number of myths surfaced about the heavenly origins of the Korean people. The most well known, which appeared around 1280, told how Hwanung, the son of the heavenly being

Hwanin, descended from heaven onto Mount Taebaek and mated with a bear-woman (Ung-nyeo), producing a son, Dangun Wanggeom, who in 2333 BCE set up a capital at Pyongyang and founded the nation of Joseon. Dangun was an important deity in shamanistic practices and was one of a trinity of gods (Samsin), together with Hwanin and Hwanung. The myth served a convenient political purpose at the time it emerged – helping Koreans to unite and throw off the Mongol yoke (Hogarth 1999:257–72; Jorgensen 1998) – and it reappeared later in ethnic nationalism.

After nearly five centuries, in 1392 the kingdom of Goryeo was supplanted by the kingdom of Joseon under the Yi dynasty, which lasted another half a millennium, and Buddhism was replaced as the preferred religion of state by neo-Confucianism. The folk religion was despised publically as superstition by both Buddhist and Confucian elites. Its practice was marginalised, and it became mainly an activity of women specialists who could sometimes exercise power on wider Korean society this way. However, its thought-world of spirits remained pervasive in Korean society. The mudang (shaman) – generally female – either inherited her role or was identified after prolonged suffering or 'disease of the spirit' (sinbyeong) which compelled her to recognise the demands of the spirits (Hogarth 1999:45–62). She used forms of divination to tell fortunes and discern the spirits, gave practical or medical advice and made offerings to the gods. If matters were serious, she communicated with angry or playful spirits in a trance-like state and exorcised or placated them through ecstatic dancing to the beat of drums (Kendall 1985; Kim Chong-ho 2003).

As a rationalist reform movement following the school of the Chinese philosopher Zhu Xi, neo-Confucians expressed the basis for the moral living and sage-hood that had been central to the teachings of Confucius as conformity with the Ultimate Reality. By introducing a metaphysical dimension into what had until then been largely an ethical and practical philosophy in Korea, they provoked a clash with Buddhism, which offered a different metaphysic (Grayson 2002:100–104). They rejected Buddhism as superstition and blamed its focus on self-enlightenment and belief in life after death for a loss of social order in Korea (Deuchler 1992:103–4). They deemed Buddhist monks lower class (cheonmin), accused them of corruption, exiled them and banned their temples from cities and centres of power.

The new dynasty imposed neo-Confucianism as the ideological basis for its polity and societal norms. Through its balance of power with the centralised monarchy, which was the main reason for 'the extraordinary stability' of Joseon (Palais 1975:272), the neo-Confucian aristocratic elite launched possibly 'the most ambitious and creative reform experiment in the East Asian world' (Deuchler 1992:27). This allowed them over the next five centuries to transform Goryeo from the top down, by both legal and ritual means, into Joseon, the most complete of Confucian societies (Map 2). Although King Sejong devised the elegant and simple Hangul system to represent the Korean language, the scholar-officials insisted on Confucian education and Chinese letters as the prerequisite for public service. Korean philosophers held their own among the Chinese. In particular, the sixteenth-century figures known as Toegye and Yulgok provoked on-going debate on the nature of Reality and in particular the relationship between the impersonal but dynamic principle (i or yi), the basis of all existence, and the material or life force (gi), which produces change by the actions and reactions of the yin and yang forces (eum and yang in Korean). In political terms, this was a struggle between those who insisted on preserving moral righteousness at all costs and others who advocated socio-political involvement (Keum Jang-tae 2000; Tao 2000:115–25).

After 1644 when the Manchus displaced the Ming dynasty in China and also invaded Korea, Koreans doubted whether these 'barbarians' could fulfil the mandate of Heaven. While they continued the tribute relationship with the new Qing dynasty, Korean scholars began an intellectual reordering of the world in which China was no longer the centre or necessary to authenticate Korean polity or culture. Joseon now saw itself as the faithful interpreter of the Confucian tradition and the last bastion of civilisation (Haboush and Deuchler 1999:3; Haboush 1999:87).

'Late Joseon' is what is generally referred to from the perspective of modernity as the 'traditional' or 'premodern' Korea in which Christianity first gained a foothold. Late Joseon society was aristocratic and bureaucratic. It was dominated by a number of kinship groups or clans that claimed their patrilineal descent from a distinguished common ancestor. They alone had access to education, public office, social status, economic privileges and political influence (Deuchler 1992:6–12, 294–99). Together these kinship groups formed a practically endogamous class or aristocracy of about 10 per cent of the population which became known as yangban. Each kinship group was also associated with a particular geographical area in which it had large landholdings, often including a Confucian academy or seowon (Haboush 1999:88–90). The yangban formed the pinnacle of a three-tier system in Korea. Below them were the yangin or sangmin, 'commoners' or peasants who lived off their own land or – more commonly in the southern half of the peninsula – worked for the yangban as tenants. At the bottom of society were the cheonmin who were bonded servants or were outcastes because of their socially unacceptable occupation, such as butcher, monk or shaman. Another social group became more prominent in late Joseon, especially in Seoul: the jungin or middle class. These were technical specialists such as translators, medical practitioners, astronomers, calligraphers and also merchants and local functionaries. The order of estates forbad the common people to improve themselves, enlarge their houses, acquire wealth or wear rich and coloured garments. On the one hand, the system of lineages and ritual purity meant that the yangban did not have close links with the rest of the population. They alone participated in the wider cosmopolitan culture of East Asian which was dominated by Chinese language and culture. On the other hand, the relative isolation, territorial integrity and centralised administration of Korea over many centuries meant that society was relatively homogeneous in terms of race, spoken language and popular culture. Confucian culture and ritual filtered down, and by the end of the dynasty it affected the behaviour of most of the population (Deuchler 1992:14, 302–3, 377–78; Walraven 1999:196–97).

Confucian culture focused on the family as the place of cultivation of right behaviour or virtue for the sake of peace in society through 'three bonds' and 'five moral rules'. The three bonds were the service of the son to his father, of officials to their king and of wife to her husband. The chief moral rule was reverence by a son to his father. The second was obedience to rulers, with associated veneration of the ruler, and of Confucius, at central shrines. The three others were subservience of wife to husband, respect for elders and loyalty in friendship. Filial piety was of central importance for inculcating the social order and maintaining family relationships, and it continued after death. It was ritualised through ancestral rites at the level of lineage and household which were performed only by the men of the family (Deuchler 1992). For neo-Confucian scholars, ancestor veneration was primarily a moral act and there was little speculation about the onto-logical or cosmological nature of departed spirits. But as its practice spread throughout society, for ordinary Koreans it became fused with traditional religious worship of ancestor spirits (Choi Ki-bok 1988; Janelli and Janelli 1982:92–99).

Confucian society was divided not only by social status but also by gender. The latter, which tended to correlate with the former, was conceptualised by two dualities: yin–yang and inner–outer (Yee Chan-sin 2003:312). The yin–yang principle was integral to Korean cosmology, and its complementary female and male forces were used to explain everything else in terms of polarities: earth–heaven, dark–light, cold–hot, old–young, weak–strong, and so on. Although they may be regarded philosophically as reciprocal and as promoting harmony, in Korea yin and yang tended to be understood as oppositional and this encouraged dichotomistic thinking. Socially, they were interpreted to justify hierarchy and domination, the higher status and authority of men over women, violence towards women, a double standard of behaviour for men and women and the separation of society into different spheres (see Yee Chan-sin 2003:313–16). The binary of inner and outer made a conceptual and functional distinction by which the public world belonged to men and the private or domestic world was the sphere of women, and there were strong sanctions against either transgressing into the world of the other (Choi Hyae-weol 2009:45–47). Some of the consequences of this in late Joseon Korea were the separate socialisation of girls and boys, the veiling of women and the confinement of upper-class women. A woman's identity was framed by the men in her life: first her father, then her husband and later her son; she was extra to the Confucian hierarchy and was hardly ever referred to by a personal name. However, married women could hold significant power in Confucian society through their control of the domestic sphere and household finances, influence over their sons and women's networks. Marriage was compulsory for both women and men to ensure the continuity of the lineage and was arranged by the parents for reasons of social status and relations; the bride left her birth family and was expected to serve her parents-in-law and to produce a son. Since the male line of descent and the father–son relation had priority over the marriage bond, even after marriage women and men led separate lives in their respective public and private spheres. If his wife died, the husband was required to remarry, but the remarriage of widows was not permitted (Deuchler 1992).

The framework of public and private is useful for conceptualising the interreligious relations of Confucian society, which were also to a large extent ethical and class distinctions (Haboush and Deuchler 1999:6–7). The Confucianism of the elite occupied the public space, and the state exercised sole authority and near-total control of society through systems of surveillance and punishment, particularly the five-household system which held a group of household heads responsible for the misdemeanours of any members of any of the families (cf. Wells 1990:26–27). Other religions could be tolerated but only if the Confucian rituals were also observed, that is, if the other religious practices remained private. In other words, the neo-Confucian government enjoyed 'ritual hegemony' (D. Baker 1999). Those who failed to fulfil their ritual obligations could be punished in a range of ways, including flogging, torture, banishment and execution (Roux 2012). Over the centuries, the public sphere of men became more

Confucianised and popular religion became the preserve of women and lower-caste men. The Confucian reformers made no accommodation to popular religion and honoured no popular deities, but they never eliminated popular religion, and perhaps they did not wish to because it served the needs of women in their family and domestic roles (Walraven 1999:197–98).

As later colonists and early Western missionaries alike never failed to point out, the Korean peninsula was rich in natural resources and its economic potential was under-realised. Economic growth was held back for several reasons. The first was ideological: Confucian teaching valued a life of scholarship above all else; most yangban despised labour and were disengaged from production. Second, Confucian morality was community based and this meant that personal profit was discouraged in favour of communal survival, stability and the standing of the lineage group (Lewis 2006:80–82). Production was mainly by cottage industries using primitive methods for domestic consumption, and trade and industry were controlled and subject to surveillance. Innovations in technology were suppressed in order to preserve the status quo. Third, owing to the tribute relationship with China, there was virtually no other foreign trade, except with Japan. In the seventeenth century, improved methods of agriculture allowed some to profit by more large-scale farming and by the eighteenth century trade across the East Sea was growing. Private merchants and markets increased, a few cottage industries broke away from state control and a money economy began to appear (Lewis 2004:49). Nevertheless, Joseon remained isolated from global trade, Sino-centric and resistant to other foreign relations until armed invasions and threats of invasion forced it open in the late nineteenth century.

CHAPTER 2

Believers, Martyrs and Missionaries, 1592–1876

It is possible that in the first millennium the Christian gospel reached the attention of Koreans travelling along the Silk Road and by sea (Min Kyoung-bae 1982:36–38; K. Baker 2006:20–30; England 1996:103–4). Two arguments are advanced for a presence of 'Nestorian' Christianity from Persia on the peninsula in the seventh to ninth centuries, but these are not conclusive. The first is from artefacts of that date discovered in Korea (Moffett 2005:461–69). The second is from doctrinal similarities between Korean popular Buddhism and Nestorian Christianity, such as a belief in heaven and hell, salvation by grace, a compassionate female figure and expectation of a future saviour. During the period when the Mongol Empire controlled the trade routes with Europe, it is likely that Koreans encountered Russian Orthodox Christians and Franciscan missionaries, at least at the Chinese court (Moffett 1988:474–75; K. Baker 2006:61).

In the mid-sixteenth century, the Korean community on the south island of Japan (Kyushu) probably had contact with the pioneer Jesuit missionary Francis Xavier, who began his East Asian work there in 1549 (the existence of Korea was reported in Lisbon in the same year), or with later Jesuit missionaries who were based in Yamaguchi. Jesuits in Japan proposed a mission to Korea as early as 1566, and from then on different Catholic missions made repeated efforts to enter but without success. Their interest in Korea was not so much for its own sake but because the Jesuit visitors in Asia especially saw its strategic importance for the evangelisation of either China or Japan (de Medina 1991:34–38).

There is only one instance before the nineteenth century in which Christians are known to have entered Korean territory. This was when the daimyō warrior Toyotomi Hideyoshi began an invasion in 1592 and pressed Kyushu Christians into his service. Between 1593 and 1595 these were accompanied by a Spanish chaplain, Gregorio de Céspedes, the superior of the Jesuit seminary in Ōsaka, and by Hankan Léon, a Japanese brother. It is not known how much contact, if any, the Korean population had with these men, but Jesuit records state that on more than one occasion Christian Japanese soldiers baptised dying Korean children to save their souls and that a twelve-year-old Korean boy, Gwon, was sent to Japan where he was baptised Vincent in 1592. Enrolled in the Jesuit seminary, he became a catechist in Nagasaki. By 1594 more than two thousand Korean prisoners of war in Japan had been baptised there under Gwon's ministry. A Korean confraternity in the city raised funds and built a church in 1610 which they dedicated to St Lawrence. The Jesuit missionaries in Japan were impressed with the devotion of the Korean Christians, and the Jesuit superior even dreamt of a seminary to train Koreans to evangelise Korea. Many Korean Christians were anxious, it seems, to spread the gospel on the peninsula and in 1612 Gwon Vincent was appointed to serve Korea, but he was unable to enter. As evidence for the strength of the Korean Christian community in Japan at least twenty-four Koreans were among the martyrs there in the period 1597–1660 (of whom nine were beatified by Pope Pius IX in 1867). They included Gwon and a second Korean who had been received into the Jesuit order. St Lawrence Church was destroyed in 1620, but missionaries believed that returning Koreans had evangelised their homeland and Catholics in Korea were included under the diocese of Funai (Nagasaki) (de Medina 1991). However, there are no Korean records of a Catholic community in Korea at this date, and, like Japan, the state was hostile to Christianity. The establishment of a church by Koreans in Japan in the early seventeenth century could be regarded as the beginning of Korean Christianity, but no historical link has been found between this Japanese-Korean church and later Catholicism in Korea (IKCH 2009:116).

JOSEON KOREAN CONTACTS WITH CATHOLICISM BEFORE 1777

China, not Japan, was the main source of influence on the kingdom of Joseon, and the introduction of Catholicism was no exception. In 1601 or 1602 the envoys in the annual Korean diplomatic mission to Beijing came into contact with the Jesuit scholar Matteo Ricci, who consequently added the Korean peninsula to the second edition of his famous world map (Moffett 2005:108–16; Kang Don-ku 1999:198–223). Information about Catholicism and its place at the Beijing court filtered back to Korea from this time on. The priests frequently asked the delegates questions about Korea, especially after 1623 when responsibility for Korea passed from the Jesuits of Japan to those in China (Shin Ik-cheol 2006:25; de Medina 1991:132–35, 166–69, 175). After the Manchu invasions, the Korean royal prince Sohyeon and his younger brother – later King Hyojong – were held in Beijing as hostages. While in China Sohyeon showed interest in European science and joined other Koreans who were taught mathematics by Johann Adam Schall von Bell. On his release in 1645, the prince took back to Korea many books and also scientific instruments given him by Schall, although he politely returned a portrait of Jesus for fear it would not be treated with appropriate respect in Korea (IKCH 2009:120–24). He requested Jesuits to accompany him to Korea but none were available, although there were Chinese Christians in the delegation that travelled home with him. However, hopes for the establishment of a Catholic community in Korea were dashed when the young prince died unexpectedly just two months later and the Christians returned to China (de Medina 1991:137–39).

Although Korea's relations with the Qing dynasty were strained, the annual delegation from Korea continued to visit Beijing and a few stayed behind each year to study under the Jesuits. Koreans in Beijing probably also encountered the Russian Christians who were permitted to establish an Orthodox church there in 1683 and a mission in 1715. A new church was consecrated in 1736 on the Russian compound, which was very near to the Korean one (K. Baker 2006:79–113). With outreach to Korea in mind, in 1711 the Jesuits established a house in Shenyang (Mukden), which was not far from the Corea Gate (Goryeomun) where the annual mission from Korea was received by Chinese officials and in an area where Chinese Christian families had settled. They recorded that there was trade across the Amnok (Yalu) River with Korea and believed that there were strong links between Catholics in Shenyang and in Korea (de Medina 1991:157–74).

By the eighteenth century, the envoys in Beijing had more freedom and regularly visited Catholic churches, where they were warmly received by the Catholic priests. Many recorded their impressions of the buildings, priests and Western art in their journals (Shin Ik-cheol 2006:14–21). The annual Korean diplomatic mission served as the chief means of transmission of Catholic literature and thought to Korea where it was disseminated among the yangban elite and became a fashionable topic of discussion. From the late sixteenth century, returned envoys brought quantities of Western and Catholic artefacts, translations of Western texts, and scientific, philosophical and explicitly religious works into Korea (IKCH 2009:140–93; de Medina 1991:131–33). Yi Su-gwang (Jibong), who travelled to Beijing several times from 1590, collected 'Western learning' (Seohak) into one great encyclopaedic work (*Jibong Yuseol* 1614) which included an outline of Catholic doctrine in the way Ricci expressed it. Heo Gyun was said to have bought and transported back four thousand books in 1614 and 1616 and even attempted to follow Catholic moral teaching (IKCH 2009:125–28).

More than sixty different tracts were among the Catholic books imported into Korea up to 1786 when the practice was forbidden. These included philosophy, catechisms, scripture portions, missals, breviaries and rituals and even portions of Thomas Aquinas (Iraola 2007:220–24; D. Baker 1999:221–24). They were widely read by those literate in Chinese, chiefly government officials and Confucian scholars. The most influential was Ricci's *The True Meaning of the Lord of Heaven* or (in Korean) *Cheonju Silui*, published in 1603. This introduced Catholic philosophy into Confucian culture and opened a dialogue which laid the groundwork for Confucian–Christian debate for several centuries, defining the theological terminology that would be used. *Cheonju Silui* 'augmented' the Confucian classics by adding a new tier of relationship to a personal creator God, membership in a global community and revealed understanding of the mysteries of the universe. But the christological doctrines of the Catholic Church are only alluded to in the last section of the book, and there is no mention of the suffering and death of Christ, a teaching to which Ricci knew Confucian scholars were particularly resistant. This 'accommodation' approach enabled the Jesuits to allow a modified version of Confucian ancestor veneration within Catholic practice but arguably misrepresented that faith (Lancashire and Hu 1985; Iraola 2007:151–73). Probably the second most influential Catholic book in Korea was *The Seven Victories* or *Chilgeuk* by the Spanish Jesuit Didace de Pantoja. This 'humanistic wisdom literature' integrated the public and private spheres of Confucian ethics, and introduced Christian morality through the idea that it is important to overcome the seven vices in order to achieve the Confucian goal of right behaviour in public (D. Baker 1979:35).

The envoys differed in their estimations of Catholic doctrine. Lee Gi-ji, who accompanied his father to Beijing in 1720, seems to have built a particularly close relationship with missionaries and was ready to help them spread Catholicism. Other envoys, especially Confucian purists, were decidedly critical, comparing Christianity to the despised Buddhism (Shin Ik-cheol 2006:26–27). In the second half of the eighteenth century, the envoys reported that they were not as warmly welcomed at the churches as before. This was partly because the priests they encountered were more likely to be Dominicans and Franciscans, who opposed the Jesuit policy of 'accommodation' (Jo Yoong-hee 2006:39–41; Choi Ki-bok 1988; Moffett 2005:120–32). Despite the suppression of the Society of Jesus in 1773, many Jesuit priests were able to continue their work in Beijing by putting themselves at the service of the bishop until it was restored, and Koreans maintained contact with them (de Medina 1991:176).

In the eighteenth century, the government was dominated by the conservative Noron, one of many factions in late Joseon. Reports that Catholicism was flourishing in China under the despised Manchus, and that Jesuits were very influential in government, were all the more reason for Koreans to reject it and maintain the purity of Confucianism (D. Baker 1999:201, 207). However, signs of strain were emerging in the social fabric of Joseon. These included, from at least the sixteenth century, prophecies by Buddhist monks which appealed particularly to the lower classes of the coming of the Mireuk (Maitreya), who would descend from heaven and rule over a new age free from suffering. Millenarian movements following individuals who declared themselves to be the Mireuk led to rebellions in 1688, 1758 and 1787 which were brutally suppressed. The more educated read the predictions in the *Record of Jeonggam* or *Jeonggamrok*, which was 'discovered' in 1785. It announced the imminent fall of the Joseon dynasty and the appearance of a deliverer, Jeong Do-ryang (Pak Ung-kyu 2005:233; Kim Chong-bum 2006:151, 158).

In this context, some scholars, especially those who were more open to the lower classes or were at least concerned about preventing social unrest, saw a need to reappraise neo-Confucian orthodoxy. They asserted their freedom to pursue truth and the priority of the life-force over the impersonal moral principle. New schools of thought emerged which may be loosely grouped under the label 'Silhak', a term that can be variously interpreted as 'true philosophy', 'practical learning' or 'relevant scholarship' (D. Baker 1981:193–201, 252). The strongest supporters of Silhak were from among the Namin (Southerners) political faction. They interacted with new schools of thought from China among which was the increasingly available Western learning, including Catholic teaching. This they read out of intellectual curiosity and because they regarded the basis of a successful state to be the right ideology. From their revised thinking, the Namin scholars proposed radical and practical reforms to land tenure, the tax system, military service, civil service exams and government organisation and a greater emphasis on wealth creation, although these were never seriously considered by the central government (see Yi Won-sun 1996:45–102; Keum Jang-tae 2000:127–46; D. Baker 1981; Palais 1975:68–69).

The philosophical response of the Silhak scholars to Western learning focused on two main areas: the creativity and personhood of the Lord of Heaven and the immortality of the soul and the other world (Keum Jang-tae 2000:147–69). Korean Confucians were inclined to agree that the Christian

God, whom Ricci described as T'ien-chu – Cheonju in Korean (the Lord of Heaven) – had much in common with the Confucian Shangdi, or Sangje in Korean (the Lord on High), and with T'ien, Cheon in Korean (Heaven), both of which were also ultimate and transcendent. However, the scholars found it difficult to accept Ricci's assertion that the heavenly being was personal (Lancashire and Hu 1985:34–35; D. Baker 1999:221–24). And since Confucians did not speculate as to the origins of the universe but focused on the processes of change in it, they did not consider Sangje as the creator of the universe. Furthermore, the doctrine of the incarnation appeared to them to be irrational and illogical. The same went for the devotional dimensions of Catholic worship of God, which were unacceptable for Confucians (D. Baker 1999:211). They were suspicious that Catholic teaching about the miraculous and mysterious was seductive and deceptive and had more in common with Buddhism than with their learning (Kang Don-ku 1999:201). However, they were generally impressed with Catholic moral teaching. The Namin scholar Yi Ik, also known as Seongho, observed that Pantoja's *Chilgeuk* could serve as a helpful aid to inculcating orthodox Confucianism but only if the references to 'God and spirits' were extracted from it (D. Baker 1979:35; Yi Ik 1999:211–13). The other fundamental area of disagreement was about the human soul and whether there was any other world. The Confucians did not regard the soul as separable from the body, or believe that it was immortal, and they had no need of a doctrine of heaven and hell. Furthermore, they regarded hell as inconsistent with a merciful and wise God. The leading Silhak scholar Shin Hu-dam thought *Cheonju Silui* was primarily concerned with the promise of eternal reward and the threat of eternal punishment; he therefore accused Catholics of trying to frighten people into believing in the same way that Buddhists did (D. Baker 1979:35–36). The Catholic concept of heaven was also problematic in that it appeared to extol self-interest in terms of expectation of reward rather than encourage virtue for its own sake. As a result, it was deemed detrimental to proper human relationships (D. Baker 1981). Despite these criticisms of the religious aspects of Catholicism, within the Seongho School, some scholars showed interest in the Catholic faith. Hong Yu-han, for example, in 1770 started keeping the seventh day and practising prayer and devotions (Yi Won-sun 1996:45–101).

WESTERN LEARNING AND THE FIRST KOREAN CATHOLIC COMMUNITY, 1777–1800

After more than a century in which Catholic teaching had been studied in Korea a decisive point was reached in 1777–1779 at a series of seminars (ganghakhoe) of scholars, some of which took place at Jueosa, a Buddhist temple in Gwangju, Gyeongi province, and at the nearby hermitage Cheonjin-am. The meetings were initiated by Gwon Cheol-sin and Jeong Yak-jeon, whose brothers-in-law Yi Byeok and Yi Seung-hun also joined, together with several other scholars. It is not clear that these seminars were explicitly to study Catholic doctrine, but, in the discussion of philosophical issues, the religious dimensions of the Western texts came to the fore (Choi Jai-keun 2006:23). At the suggestion of Yi Byeok, the scholars began to hold morning and evening prayers in which Cheonju was worshipped. They also rested every seventh day in honour of Cheonju and practised meditation and abstinence.

Those who engaged with Catholic teaching and practices through the pursuit of scholarship at Jueosa left a record of their thoughts in the two earliest writings on Catholic themes in Korean. Yi Byeok is reputed to have written the first known hymn in Hangul, 'Cheonju Gonggyeongga' (Hymn of Adoration of God; 1777). In it, faith in Cheonju both encompasses and transcends Confucian morality:

> There is an elder in the house;
> There is a king in the nation;
> There is soul in my body;
> There is Cheonju [God] in heaven
> . . .
> Let us honour parents;
> Let us commit loyally to the king,
> While keeping Samgang Oryun,[1]
> Worshipping Cheonju first.
>   (Text in Kim Yeong-su 2000:333; our translation)

In 1779, Jeong Yak-jeon and others collaborated to produce 'Sipgyemyeongga' (The Ten Commandments Hymn). As its name suggests, this proclaimed a Decalogue – although not corresponding precisely to the biblical one. It emphasised the holiness and incomparability of the name of Cheonju and included a call to follow the Catholic moral code, for example by rejecting superstition and keeping the Sabbath. The hymn stresses the importance of filial piety but also claims that 'as you honour your parents you will know how to worship God, who is Father of all' (text in Kim Yeong-su 2000:334–36; our translation). Thus it makes devotion to God 'the final tier of filial piety' (Yi Won-sun 1996:81). Although the hymns were influenced

---

[1] The Confucian teaching of the 'three bonds' and 'five moral rules' (see Introduction).

by Catholic thought, neither includes any specifically christological doctrines, and both exhibit the Riccian accommodationist approach.

An element of Catholic doctrine that particularly attracted Silhak scholars was its attempt to address human moral frailty. Neo-Confucian teaching asserted that human beings were perfectible, but the Silhak scholars struggled to square this with the obvious human failings and corruption which beset late Joseon. Nor was this just an individual problem. Although it was the role of the state to serve the development of true human potential, there was evidence against the rule of virtue in the shape of famine, epidemics and untimely death (Haboush 1999; Deuchler 1999; D. Baker 1997). Jeong Yak-yong, also known as Dasan, one of the early scholars of Catholicism and a younger brother of Jeong Yak-jeon, became convinced through his study of Confucian and Catholic texts that God must be personal because God acts with intent and intelligence and only a personal God watching over the world in judgement could instil the necessary righteous fear to produce seriousness, provoke repentance and build virtue (Keum Jang-tae 2000:181–202; D. Baker 2004; Yi Won-sun 1996:45–101). Dasan built an argument which allowed others to accept Catholicism as an alternative intellectual and ethical system compatible with Confucian thought which could bring change in Korean society. Under the influence of Catholic teaching, Dasan wrote several treatises on governance in which he criticised the evils of contemporary society and put forward an agenda to reduce the people's suffering. This included appointment to office on merit and even popular election (D. Baker 1997:129; Iraola 2007:276–77).

We cannot categorically say that those who met at Jueosa were not a Christian community; however, it is not clear that they worshipped Jesus Christ as Lord and none of them had yet been baptised (IKCH 2009:238; Choi Jai-keun 2006:23–24). But the meetings at the temple were the root of the first Catholic community. Yi Byeok particularly was drawn to the religious dimensions of Catholicism, and when he heard that Yi Seung-hun was due to accompany his father to Beijing in late 1783, he asked him to find out more about Christian teaching, to visit churches while there and to take baptism. Yi Seung-hun did as requested and went to the North Church, where he met Alexandre de Gouvea, bishop of Beijing. After being instructed, he was baptised by the French Jesuit missionary Jean Joseph de Grammont early in 1784, apparently with the consent of his father. He was given the baptismal name Peter, signifying that he was the foundation stone of the church in Korea. He returned to Korea in the spring of that year, bringing with him books, crucifixes, images and other religious items that he had been given (Iraola 2007:229–30).

After studying the books brought back by Yi Seung-hun, Yi Byeok was all the more convinced of the truth of Christianity and began to announce this faith to his friends and family and to ordinary people. He convinced his teacher Gwon Cheol-sin (Ambrose), who had initiated the study at Jueosa, and Gwon and his four brothers converted (Dallet 1874a:22). Yi Ga-hwan, head of the Namin faction, had earlier parodied Yi Byeok's hymn with a chant ('Kyeongsega') describing Catholic doctrine as nonsense because its belief in an all-powerful God of love was incompatible with hell and suffering (Kim Yeong-su 2000:337), but he was now reportedly convinced by Yi Byeok and became a Catholic, and others also conceded (Dallet 1874a:19–21). A catechism, *Seonggyo Yoji* (*Essence of the Sacred Doctrine*), in the language and style of Chinese poetry, is thought to have been written by Yi Byeok in 1785 (Yi Byeok 1986). It introduced central doctrines, detailed Jesus' life and work, warned of the wages of sin, urged believers to follow Christ in doing good and concluded with creedal affirmations and calls to worship. The catechism confesses that 'Jesus, like the ideal emperors, is a very generous king and, like Confucius, he is a scholar/sage, who taught the world' (v. 49 – our translation). Yi Byeok's work includes some specifically Korean interpretations of the biblical context: for example, the Pharisees praying in the temple are compared to corrupt officials worshipping in a Buddhist temple (v. 19), and both yangban and cheonmin are said to be invited by God to the feast (v. 13). *Seonggyo Yoji* is the first rendition of Christian doctrine by a Korean and marks the transition from a general belief in a transcendent God to a specifically Christian confession (Yi Won-sun 1996:45–101).

The first worship service of those who wished to practise the new faith took place at Yi Byeok's house at Seopogyo, on the outskirts of Seoul. As Confucians, the new believers would be interested in ritual and anxious to perform it correctly according to what Yi Seung-hun had observed in Beijing, and probably using a missal. On this occasion, or soon after, Yi Seung-hun baptised some of the other men, beginning with Yi Byeok to whom he gave the name John the Baptist, the herald of the Christ. Gwon Il-sin, the third brother of Gwon Cheol-sin, who had dedicated himself to preaching, was christened Francis Xavier after the apostle of the East (IKCH 2009:246; Choi Jai-keun 2006:28). This formation of a fraternity seems to have been very much influenced by the example of Jesuit brotherhood in Beijing and also by Ricci's tract *On Friendship*, which is often mentioned among the books brought back from China. In a society which stressed vertical lines of loyalty to a senior and the importance of blood relations, the suggestion that 'one should treat one's friend as one's self made a profound impression (Noh Yong-pil 2008:61).

The Catholic Church in Korea dates its foundation to 1784 when those who had met at Jueosa were baptised (Iraola 2007:180; Dallet 1874a:13). In recognising as the beginning of the Korean church this indigenous community, the Catholic Church proclaims it 'unique' among national churches 'by reason of the fact that it was founded entirely by lay people' and not by any foreign missionary (MEP 1924:18; IKCH 2009:255). While it is true that – unless conversion is forced – Christian movements must begin with local initiative (de Medina 1991:7–9) and that the pattern of local people calling the missionary goes back to the 'Macedonian call' in the New Testament, this should not detract from the unique standing of Korean Christianity. Not only was it founded without any foreign missionary having entered the country but, more significantly for Catholic ecclesiology, it was recognised as existing as a 'fledgling Church' before the hierarchy was even proclaimed (1831) or established (1836).[2]

Although the first Korean believers seemed convinced that Catholicism was compatible with Confucianism, the fact that from the beginning they met in secret suggests that they suspected that the authorities would not agree. For one thing, although the first Korean Catholics were yangban men, Catholicism not only offered a philosophical system but also had the dimensions of a popular religion, as the frequent comparisons with Buddhism demonstrated. It therefore soon crossed the public–private boundary of religion in Korea, which was also to a great extent a gender and class boundary. By 1790 the Christian community had diversified in both respects to include women, the jungin technicians who also studied Catholic learning and possibly other social groups as well; it seems that the Korean Christians understood that the gospel transcended social barriers. This diversity may have been why in spring 1785 the group began to meet at a clinic rather than a private house. It was run by a member of the jungin class, Kim Beom-u (Thomas), in an area now known as Myeongdong in Seoul (IKCH 2009:255–58).

In the spring of 1785 (Eulsa year[3]), barely a year after the founding of the church, lights in Kim Beom-u's clinic in the evening excited suspicions and police discovered several young men (including Yi Seung-hun, Jeong

---

[2] Mass for the Canonisation of Korean Martyrs, Homily of Pope John Paul II, Seoul, Sunday, 6 May 1984.
[3] The Korean calendar names each year, which is reckoned according to a lunar calendar and does not correspond exactly to the Western year.

Yak-jeon, Jeong Yak-yong and Kwon Il-sin and his son) on their knees in front of an image of Christ and listening to Yi Byeok preaching. The men were detained, various religious items and books were confiscated and the incident was reported to the Ministry of Justice – the first reference to Christian practice in Korea in government records (IKCH 2009:258–61). The six yangban escaped punishment, but Kim Beom-u was imprisoned. When he refused to recant even under torture, he was eventually banished and died a year or so later of his injuries, becoming the first martyr of the new church. The Noron faction took as much advantage of the situation as they could to further marginalise leading Namin families, such as that of Yi Seung-hun who burnt his books and forced him to write a recantation. Yi Seung-hun continued to associate with Catholics clandestinely, but Yi Byeok broke off contact altogether after the shame he had brought on the family led his father to attempt suicide (IKCH 2009:264).

This clamp-down was an isolated incident, but there were signs of more systematic persecution to come. In the same year (1785), Ahn Jeong-bok, a disciple of Yi Ik, produced a booklet, *Cheonhak Mundap* (*Disputation on Catholicism*), which refuted Catholic doctrine. It gained official approval and became a model for later attacks on Catholicism as a religion similar to Buddhism (D. Baker 1979–1980:9–11). In addition to Ahn's attack, several 'memorials' (representations to the throne by scholars) criticising Christianity were presented to King Jeongjo, such as one which claimed that Catholicism recognises heaven but not the king and that it seduces people with belief in heaven and hell. Informed that Yi Seung-hun and Jeong Yak-yong were teaching classes on the faith to fellow students at the National Confucian Academy, Hong Nak-eon, a Namin and the temporary recorder of the Royal Secretariat, called in 1787 for the persecution of believers in order to stop the spread of the 'disease' of Catholicism. However, King Jeongjo, advised by the leading Namin figure Chae Je-gong, expressed the opinion that the darkness of Catholicism would naturally die down in the light of true Confucian scholarship. No further action was taken against those concerned, but the king ordered the destruction of Catholic books and images and forbad their further importation. Many Catholics burnt their own books, having first memorised them; others hid them (Choi Jai-keun 2006:94–96, 112–18; IKCH 2009:266; Cho Kwang 1996a:105–6).

Meanwhile, the Christian community decided they should set up an ecclesiastical structure such as they had read about and Yi Seung-hun had seen in Beijing. Yi and ten others began to act as priests to administer the sacraments, teach and perform other clerical roles. However, after further study, some of the group, led by Yu Hang-geom, questioned this practice since church law allowed only priests ordained by a bishop to perform the sacraments. Unable to agree among themselves, in 1789 one of the believers, Yun Yu-il, was dispatched to Beijing at Yu Hang-geom's expense. He was disguised as a merchant and carried a letter of enquiry from Yi Seung-hun to Bishop de Gouvea. After receiving rebaptism, communion and confirmation in Beijing, Yun returned to Korea with the first pastoral letter to the community. In it, the bishop told them to desist in their arrangements, but he issued no reprimand since it was understood that the Koreans were doing what they thought was right. De Gouvea encouraged them to continue to administer baptism, to preach and to teach. He also told them to prepare for a properly ordained priest to be sent from Beijing and asked them to send young men to Beijing to be trained for the priesthood. No longer able to practise the ritual and receive the sacrament, the Koreans were eager to have a priest as soon as possible. The following year (1790), Yun Yu-il went again to Beijing and petitioned the bishop, reporting that a thousand people had now been baptised in Korea (IKCH 2009:277–89; MEP 1924:20; A. Finch 2008:281).

Although – following Confucian as well as Catholic custom – men assumed ritual leadership, women were also key figures in the Christian community. To avoid detection, meetings were sometimes held in the anbang or women's quarters. In addition, the spread of the faith among the yangban was mainly through women, who joined a new family when they married (Cho Kwang 1996b:119–22). Furthermore, because they were generally literate in Hangul, yangban women were able to participate in intellectual discourse with men, and some could read even the Chinese Christian literature. It is likely that it was women who first translated the Chinese texts into Korean for the benefit of other women. Women also wrote some of the earliest Christian literature. About 1795, Yuhandang Gwon (the wife of Yi Byeok) composed *Eonhaeng Sillok* (*Written Records of Words and Acts*) for her sisters in the faith, which, like other manuals that existed for Confucian ladies, taught the proper behaviour of Catholic women. These Christian virtues generally included Confucian ones, so that within marriage Catholic women were able simultaneously to satisfy both Catholic and Confucian propriety by taking care of parents, parents-in-law, husbands and other relatives while also participating in the Christian community. But *Eonhaeng Sillok* was also radical in that it prioritised the marital bond over the Confucian order of relationships. It denounced the 'subjugation of wife to husband' on the grounds that women too were made in the image of God and therefore the relationship between husband and wife was horizontal rather than vertical (Kim Ok-hy 1984:36). Catholic teaching was highly critical of the treatment of women in East Asian societies, especially concubinage, abandonment of wives, forced marriage and prohibition of remarriage for widows (Dallet 1874a:cxvi–cxxviii; Cho Kwang 1996b:120–22). However, the primary motive of yangban women in becoming Catholics was not the injustices in Confucian society but the women's inclination to asceticism and desire to live a life of faith characterised by 'virtuous acts' which would bring 'blessings from heaven'. In this way they created a new image of women in late Joseon society as they led lives centred not on the home but on the Christian community (Kim Ok-hy 1984:29–37). At a time when Korean Buddhism was promoting essentially Confucian values of the subservience of women, this new community protected women and valued them as persons of faith (Lee Young-hee 2006).

For neo-Confucians, human inequality was axiomatic, whereas in Catholic understanding the fatherhood of God over all human beings relativized social relations. Scholars were at first shocked that, for example, Christian women were permitted to sit at the same table as men and that the Pope could come from any social class and was elected by his peers. Furthermore, the first Catholics took seriously the command to love one another as themselves and on this basis they challenged the order of estates and the injustices of yangban society (Lee Ki-baik 1984:258; Cho Kwang 1996b:117–22; 2006). By 1786 commoners were included in the community. Although the Catholic Church did not forbid it, Koreans also seem to have understood that the Christian gospel precluded slave-holding. Yun Gun-myeong of Chungcheong province liberated all his bondservants after he was baptised (Dallet 1874a:271), and when Hwang Il-gwang – a butcher and therefore an outcaste – became a Christian, he was received on the same footing as other believers (Cho Kwang 1996b:118; Dallet 1874a:139–40).

While in Beijing, Yun Yu-il also enquired about the church's position on the practice of ancestor veneration. De Gouvea, who was a Franciscan, clarified that contrary to what Koreans had read in Jesuit texts, since the papal ruling on the Chinese rites, all ancestor veneration was forbidden for Catholics (Dallet 1874a:35). The yangban members of the community, for whom lineage was the basis of their social status and their promotion prospects, were the most affected by the prohibition and they were put under pressure from parents who saw their status as at risk. There was a struggle within the leadership over whether to accept the prohibition and some left the community, including Yi Seung-hun (again). In the end, the hard-line tendencies of neo-Confucianism were matched by elements in the Catholic community. Yun Ji-chung, a cousin of Dasan, had attended worship at Kim Beom-u's clinic and after two years of study and reflection he finally became a Catholic in 1787, along with his maternal cousin Gwon Sang-yeon. They were baptised Paul and James, respectively. He and Gwon challenged the authorities when after the death of his mother in 1791, Yun not only refused to make the ancestral tablets for the mourning ritual but, helped by Gwon, went even further than Bishop de Gouvea advised and burnt all the family's tablets. When this was reported to the authorities, Hong Nak-eon brought it to the attention of Chae Je-gong as a crime 'one hundred times worse than rebellion'. Failure to venerate the ancestors according to the prescribed tradition meant to Confucians that Catholicism was not merely a heterodox teaching (idan) but a perverse or evil one (sahak; D. Baker 1979–1980). Yun Ji-chung's actions provided a clear and rational motive for the opposition, who were also the rival political faction at the time, and they demanded that Yun and his cousin be executed. After the authorities began to punish the family by arresting Yun's uncle, the two turned themselves in.

Although he could have recanted and been released, under interrogation and torture Yun continued to declare that ancestor veneration was a sin against the Lord and was forbidden by the Catholic Church. He used Catholic arguments to criticise the Confucian custom as idolatrous worship of wooden tablets and even flatly contradicted Confucian doctrine by insisting that loyalty and filial piety were not absolute but were based on the law of God (IKCH 2009:306). But he also defended himself against the charge that he was disrespectful of his mother's memory, claiming that Catholicism had even more elaborate rituals than Confucianism with which to remember the dead (Choi Jai-keun 2006:100). Yun's arguments made little sense to the Confucian court for which fulfilment of social obligations was prior to any questions of right or wrong or conscience (D. Baker 1979–1980). For defying fundamental tenets of Confucianism, Yun and Gwon were beheaded near the Pungnam Gate in Jeonju (Roux 2012:78–82). A cult of the martyrs began; the gate became a place of pilgrimage associated with miracles and a towel soaked in the martyrs' blood was taken to Beijing as a relic. In accordance with Confucian practice, the family homes of the offenders were destroyed, and their relatives were banished or enslaved. The authorities rounded up church leaders and others who were deemed guilty by association. They were threatened, beaten and if necessary tortured, and then released if they apostatised. Yangban were handed back to their families for punishment or, in some cases, were offered incentives to renounce their faith (Cho Kwang 1996a:109). Gwon Il-sin and other leaders such as Gwon Cheol-sin, Jeong Yak-jeon, Jeong Yak-yong, Hong Nak-min and Yi Ga-hwan all recanted.

In this persecution in the Sinhae year (1791) the chief accusation against the Catholics was that they were anarchists: they 'knew neither parents nor king'. The accused insisted that Cheonju was both father and king to whom above all worship was owed. They maintained that Catholicism intensified filial piety by linking it to the fourth commandment and that prayer and the sacraments were a more efficacious way of venerating the dead (Song Jong-rye 2003:367; Choi Jai-keun 2006:102–3). Nevertheless, a line had been crossed by the Christian community; commitment to Catholicism was now tantamount to setting oneself against the existing order and the precedent set in the trial of Yun and Gwon spelt out the risks that it entailed. Refusing to venerate one's ancestors in the Confucian way became a profession of faith and marked out Catholicism as a form of social protest (Lee Ki-baik 1984:258). After this point the number of yangban converts to Catholicism began to decline relative to other social classes, but not all those who recanted in this and other persecutions necessarily left the faith. As the example of Yi Seung-hun, who recanted three times, shows, some – perhaps many – of them remained on the fringes of the community.

The Koreans repeatedly reminded de Gouvea of his promise to send a missionary priest. He negotiated with the Holy See and in 1791 the Propaganda Fide granted ordinary and extraordinary powers to him as bishop of Beijing to exercise pastoral ministry in Korea. But when no priest had yet appeared, in 1793 another deputation went to Beijing to speed up the process. Ultimately, Korea's first priest came not at his own initiative, nor at that of the church or a mission, but at the insistence of Koreans who realised they needed a priest to legitimise the church organisation and to serve the sacraments for a Christian community which had grown to about four thousand. De Gouvea selected a Chinese priest, James Zhou Wen-mo (Chu Mun-mo in Korean). Presumably one reason for the choice was that Zhou could escape detection more easily than a European, but Zhou was also a man well educated in the Confucian classics and a graduate of the Beijing seminary. Helped by Ji Hwang (Sabbas), a palace pharmacist, and by Yun Yu-il, Zhou was smuggled into the border town of Uiju in December 1794. Disguising him as a horse-handler, and travelling only at night, the party progressed safely to Seoul where, on Easter Sunday, 5 April 1795, Zhou celebrated the first mass of the Korean church. He then travelled around Seoul and into the countryside celebrating the sacraments. For the first time, the church had proper instruction, could celebrate mass according to canon law and had a tangible connection with the church universal (Choi Jai-keun 2006:46).

Zhou stayed first with Choi In-gil (Matthias), a jungin and Chinese translator, presumably because Choi could help him learn some Korean. But the priest's presence was betrayed to the younger brother of Yi Byeok, Yi Seok, who was vehemently anti-Catholic, and in June 1795 Zhou had to flee. During most of the rest of his six years in Korea, Zhou found safety at the home of a remarkable catechist Kang Wan-suk (Columba). Kang was a wealthy yangban woman living in Seoul but originating from Deoksan in Chungcheong province, where she had become a Catholic sometime before 1791 when she was one of those believers who were rounded up but not prosecuted. Kang soon led to faith her mother-in-law and stepson, as well as her own parents, but not her husband, who divorced her for her proselytising activities. In Seoul, Kang kept a household with several other women converts who lived celibate lives, including Jeong Bok-hye (Candida) and Kim Yeon-i (Juliana). Although rare, these 'unmarried virgins' were a noted feature of the Christian community at this stage and they were respected for demonstrating righteousness or honour (Cho Kwang et al. 2007; Song Jong-rye 2003:370).

Not only was Kang literate but she was also regarded as an expert on doctrine. Zhou put her in charge of all women in the church and gave her a key role in the propagation of the faith (Ledyard 2006:63). In a society in which the social lives of women and men were separate, the women's networks in the church soon became very strong. The 'women in the congregation' and their activities were frequently referred to in later trial records. Kang encouraged single women to evangelise and start their own congregations; they also ministered to women in need and brought them into the community. Included among the women they served were 'the poor and helpless', such as orphans and homeless old women. Jeong Jeong-hye (Elizabeth), daughter of Yu So-sa (Cecelia) and younger sister of Jeong Ha-sang (Paul), provided for others by sewing and weaving, taking food to the sick and to prisoners and collecting and distributing alms. There is evidence that some yangban women believers taught their personal servants the Christian faith and defied social barriers by sitting with them in catechism meetings (Kim Ok-hy 1984:31–36).

While the capable Kang organised the priest's schedule, probably interpreted for him at mass and contrived to keep his presence in her house a secret, Zhou focused on establishing the church as an organisation and on teaching Catholic doctrines. He set up a pastoral committee of lay people, Myeongdohoe (Society for Illumination of the Way), to maintain church activities and instruct the faithful under the difficult circumstances of the time. The whole organisation was headed by a president, the first being Jeong Yak-jong, whose baptismal name was Augustine. Under the president were individuals responsible for different areas of church life, including geographical districts, various fraternities and the women's network. Kang Wan-suk and Yun Jeom-hye (Agatha) each held the women's network portfolio in the Myeongdohoe at different times (Choi Jai-keun 2006:43–51).

As far as teaching was concerned, Zhou conducted confirmations for those who were suitably prepared and trained catechists, who then taught others in cells which met in secret in homes across Seoul and in other provinces. By 1800 the church claimed about ten thousand members in total, although some put the figure as low as two thousand (Choi Jai-keun 2006:51–52). About two-thirds of these members were women, and about one-third were uneducated commoners or cheonmin. A few yangban continued to play a leading role, and it was from among these that most of the catechists were drawn. Zhou promoted the use of a catechism written by Jeong Yak-jong, *Jugyo Yoji* (*Essentials of the Lord's Teaching*; Fig. 1). This endorsement was significant in two respects. First, the fact that this catechism was written not in Chinese like the earlier one by Yi Byeok but in the Korean language and script indicated that Catholicism was inclusive of the common people and encouraged the spread of the faith across the genders and a broader social spectrum (Iraola 2007:244). Second, Jeong's catechism was an adaptation of a Chinese catechism with the same name by Luigi Buglio, an Italian Jesuit (probably utilising some material prepared in Hangul by women leaders), which differed theologically from the Riccian approach of Yi Byeok and the reasoning of Jeong Yak-jong's brother Dasan (Noh Yong-pil 2008:80–129; Kim Ok-hy 1984:30). *Jugyo Yoji* shows little or no accommodation to Confucian thought. It follows a Scholastic form of catechism beginning with logical arguments for God's existence and the doctrine of the Trinity. Compared to Buglio's work, it gives greater emphasis to criticism of Buddhism and folk religion and to the doctrines of judgement and heaven and hell. The catechism omits the more practical matters of the Ten Commandments and instruction on baptism and confession and instead concludes with exhortations to greater devotion and faithfulness. It is intended to appeal not to the elite but to a mass audience. In its telling of the biblical stories of Creation and the Fall, and its narration of the life and work of Christ and Christology, it introduces many distinctively Korean features and local examples (D. Baker 1999:224–25). Framed in a context of confrontation between the church and the Confucian state, *Jugyo Yoji* was to be the basic catechism of the Korean Catholic Church for another century and beyond.

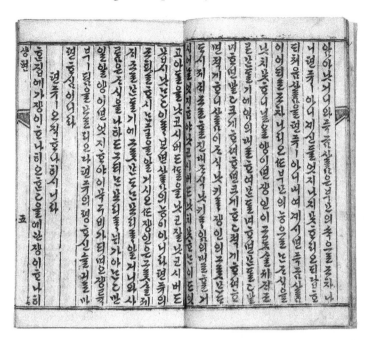

1. *Jugyo Yoji* (*Essentials of the Lord's Teaching*) by Jeong Yak-jong, 1797. The first doctrinal book written in Korean (Hangul). Korean Christian Museum at Soongsil University, Seoul.

CATHOLIC VILLAGES AND EPISODES
OF PERSECUTION, 1801–1863

The Korean Catholic Church is celebrated worldwide not only for its lay foundation but also for its martyr history. Unlike Buddhism and shamanism, Catholicism was unable or unwilling to remain in the private sphere and clashed fundamentally with Confucianism at a philosophical level, in its ritual practice – especially regarding the ancestors – and in its social outworking. Furthermore, it became caught up in the various factions of Korean politics and with the designs on Korea of more powerful nations in a way which was to have dire consequences for Christian converts. Already by the turn of the nineteenth century, twenty-one Catholics had been killed in sporadic episodes of persecution in different regions of Korea, and the real figure may be more than a hundred (Choi Jai-keun 2006:106–7; IKCH 2009:323–26). During the next seventy years, the community was subject to several systematic persecutions.

After the death in 1800 of King Jeongjo and the fall from power of his Namin advisors, the political climate for Catholics in Korea suddenly changed. Because the heir, Sunjo, was only a minor, effective power passed to his guardian, Dowager Queen Kim, whose Byeok faction was allied against the Si faction to which most of the Namin belonged. The Byeok faction decided to make a scapegoat of the Catholics. Memorials were frequently sent to the king which gave various reasons why Catholicism should be suppressed: To the accusations that Catholicism exalted God above king and parents and that belief in life after death led to the neglect of social responsibilities was now added a third charge, that class and gender inclusiveness threatened the Confucian system, and a fourth, that the encouragement of women's piety discouraged reproduction. As soon as an appropriate time had elapsed after the late king's funeral, on the tenth day of the first (lunar) month of the Sinyu year (February 1801–1802), the dowager queen formally decreed the prohibition of Catholicism. She declared a campaign against the community, stating that 'this evil teaching ... puts human beings into the position of barbarians and beasts. Ignorant people accept it and wander in the false way' (Choi Jai-keun 2006:121; Fig. 2).

The authorities targeted Catholic leaders and, according to the official figures, arrested 672, mainly yangban (IKCH 2010a:92–107). Most of these individuals were found in Seoul, but arrests also took place in other regions, indicating that Catholicism had spread across the south of the country by this time. The most severe penalties were applied. Those accused of practising Catholicism were beaten and often tortured to make them apostatise. If they did not, they were executed under the prohibition against 'making magical incantations' or, more commonly, on the basis that Catholicism was a perverse teaching (Roux 2012:82–84). Jeong Yak-jong and Yi Seung-hun were among the first of 156 to be beheaded on 8 April at the main place of execution, outside the Seosomun (Minor West Gate) (MEP 1924:21; IKCH 2010a:92–107). Unlike his brothers, Jeong Yak-jong had made no attempt to argue the compatibility of Catholicism and Confucianism or to profess loyalty to the king but defended his faith robustly as superior, and thus gave the judge little choice but to condemn him. Catholic sources claim a further 150 died in prison (IHKC 2009:90). These included Gwon Cheol-sin (Ambrose). A further 400 were exiled, including even some like Jeong Yak-yong and Jeong Yak-jeon who had renounced their faith. They were dispersed to remote places, and the five-household system and village code were enforced to monitor them and prevent their further proselytising or organising against the authorities. However, these mechanisms broke down if a group of families was

2. An official notice banning Catholicism, 1807. Korean Christian Museum at Soongsil
University, Seoul.

Christian or if the local yangban were Christians, as sometimes happened, in which case the Catholic community was protected (Choi Jai-keun 2006:140; Cho Kwang 1996a:106–12; Lee Ki-baik 1984:205–8, 252).

In social standing, most of those tried were yangban church leaders and their associates and relatives. But members of their households were also arrested and tortured, such as the bonded servant Cho Tae-seon (Peter), as were people of other classes, including the faith-healer Yi Chung-bae (Martin). In most cases the suspects' trials were carefully recorded, and some of this documentation survives. By education, yangban were equipped to debate in court; yangban women were also eloquent and there were frequent trial reports that women prisoners were evangelising in gaol (A. Finch 2009:108; Kim Ok-hy 1984:35). Until 1801 it had been highly unusual for women to be brought before the courts and prosecuted for any offence so the fact that women made up a quarter of those arrested in the Sinyu persecution demonstrates their importance to the movement (Cho Kwang 1996b:121). They included catechists such as Yun Un-hye (Lucy), widows who looked after community matters such as Kim Yeon-i and Jeong Bok-hye, unmarried virgins, commoners and outcastes.

The prosecutors were especially anxious to find Zhou, who was given a new hiding place – this time in the palace of Prince Yi In, whose wife, Maria Song, and daughter-in-law Maria Shin had been trained by Kang (Ledyard 2006:50–51). To uncover Zhou's whereabouts, Kang Wan-suk was subjected to particularly excruciating torture. She refused to recant or disclose anything and was eventually beheaded. Zhou initially tried to return to China but then turned back and gave himself up in hope of stopping the persecution. The charges against him were that he had spread a banned and heretical religion and created a subversive organisation, the Myeongdohoe. But the discovery of Zhou's contact with the court women led to allegations of treason against the Catholics and Zhou was beheaded (although since he was Chinese this caused some later embarrassment for the Korean government). The persecution intensified as Catholicism was now regarded not only as immoral but also as subversive. Fears that Catholics were seeking to undermine the state were confirmed when a plot was uncovered in which Yu Hang-geom (Augustine) and others sought to obtain missionary freedom in Korea by having the king of Portugal establish diplomatic relations with Joseon (IKCH 2010a:45–47; Choi Jai-keun 2006:127–32).

In September 1801 the president of the Myeongdohoe, Hwang Sa-yeong (Alexander), son-in-law of a prominent Namin, who was taking refuge from persecution in the village of Baeron in Chungcheong province, composed a letter to the Pope. He wrote the letter in tiny Chinese characters on silk so that it could be secreted in the clothing of a courier. However, the courier was intercepted on the way to the bishop of Beijing and Hwang Sa-yeong was arrested. The Silk Letter (Hwang Sa-yeong Baekseo) graphically described the history and situation of the Christian community in Korea and thus is one of the main sources for knowledge of this early period. Hwang asked for help: for financial support for the church, for a better system of communication with Beijing, for the Pope to put pressure on the Chinese emperor not to persecute Korean Christians, and finally, and most seriously, for Joseon to become a province of China and for battleships from the West to threaten the government. The discovery of the Silk Letter was a disaster for the Catholic community as it appeared to confirm suspicions that they were part of a foreign conspiracy. Hwang Sa-yeong was tried and convicted of 'great sedition and depravity'. He was executed by the worst form of capital punishment – death by slicing – outside the Seosomun of Seoul (Roux 2012:86–87). Up to a hundred others deemed to have collaborated with him also died (Choi Jai-keun 2006:140). Some later Catholic commentators have tried to portray Hwang Sa-yeong as one of the first nationalists, struggling against the illegitimate rule of the dowager queen to bring Korea into the modern period. They point out that the letter was written in a desperate situation of life and death, and claim Hwang Sa-yeong to be a double martyr – for the Catholic faith and for social revolution (IKCH 2010a:73–86). But although Hwang's actions may be understandable in the circumstances, it is difficult to exonerate him.

The Edict on Catholicism (Tosa Gyomun) issued by the government at the close of the Sinyu year was a defining event in the history of the Korean Catholic Church (Grayson 2002:143; Choi Jai-keun 2006:139). It proclaimed that henceforth Catholics should be treated as traitors and put to death so that they would have no descendants. Since the practice of Catholicism was now clearly deemed illegal, the church became an underground movement. Not only were the accused excluded from mainstream society but their relatives were tainted by association; whole families were deprived of their livelihoods and reduced to poverty. So, even if not actually banished, up to three-quarters of Catholics fled to isolated mountain regions mostly in the south and east of the country. There, whatever their social status, they faced great hardship in the cruelly cold Korean winters and sometimes had to move on like refugees because of threats from local communities (A. Finch 2000:577–78). These dispossessed Catholics adopted an alternative lifestyle in gyouchon or Christian villages of up to about fifty persons. Such rural villages now became a characteristic feature of Catholic life (Choi Jai-keun 2006:143; IKCH 2010a:140–46).

Other outcastes from society because of politics or low social status, who had nothing to lose and possibly a great deal to gain from conversion, joined the Catholics in the villages. The different classes lived a communal life and took corporate responsibility for children orphaned by the persecution. They survived by foraging, subsistence farming, growing tobacco, and making and peddling pottery or writing materials. Pottery especially became almost synonymous with Catholicism. Since potters were socially insignificant, the role offered Catholics anonymity and also the freedom to travel without exciting suspicion. Catholic pedlars functioned as colporteurs who sold literature and religious artefacts and at the same time spread the faith. Their travels also helped to bind the scattered Catholic community together and facilitated connections with China, from where they were able to smuggle in religious materials and later priests (D. Baker 1997).

With the death of their only priest, the leadership of the Catholic community was now in the hands of lay people again. It was no longer possible to celebrate the mass but in each village leaders nurtured the people's faith by a pattern of daily prayers to start the day, saying the rosary, and holding secret prayer meetings on Sundays and feast days. With few trained catechists remaining, the believers tended to recite the 'Ten Commandments Hymn' and *The Seven Victories* as the basis for their ethical practice (Choi Jai-keun, 2006:316). They read the scriptures and other Christian literature together, for which they used mainly Korean sources because of the changed social composition of the church and also because precious Chinese books had been destroyed during the persecution (Ledyard 2006:52; Cho Kwang 1996b:128). Myeongdohoe member Yi Gyeong-eon (Paul) and others hand copied books and produced religious art. This was not only a pragmatic response to the destruction but also a religious act, just as the copying of texts has an honoured place in Confucian tradition (Rausch 2008:54; Park Chang-won 2011:69–81). With much of the male leadership removed, the faith was passed on mainly by mothers to their children (Iraola 2007:271). Women also kept alive the memory of the martyrs and the cult of martyrdom. The younger sister of Gwon Il-sin, and wife of Yi Yun-ha, was instrumental in encouraging this when she circulated among church members the letters left for her by two of her children, Yi Gyeong-do (Charles) and Yi Sun-i (Lutgarda), who were martyred in 1801–1802 (Kim Ok-hy 1984:30–31).

It is tempting for some to see the gyouchon as enclaves of Western culture and beacons of modernisation in feudal Korea or to describe the post-1801 church as a revolutionary or liberation movement almost entirely composed of the marginalised and dispossessed. It is true that most of the church's yangban leadership had been killed or had apostatised, but their families mostly continued in the faith. Prosecutors' records from later persecutions confirm that many of the inhabitants of the gyouchon were descended from the martyrs of the yangban families. Furthermore, it appears that, at least after a time, the Korean Catholic community re-established a Confucian structure: leadership was primarily in the hands of yangban and jungin, and there was little intermarriage across classes (D. Baker 1997:137–39). Yangban and jungin family ties bound the gyouchon in the countryside to clandestine Catholics at court (Lee Ki-baik 1984:257). In their rural lands away from centres of power, Catholic yangban families who had not been identified publically were able to keep their status, and it is possible that they supported some of the gyouchon (cf. Bossy 1975:149–81).

Catholics were not the only resistance the government had to deal with in this period. In the late eighteenth and early nineteenth centuries, famines and epidemics, exploitation by corrupt officials and landlords, and ever greater local and government taxes and requirements of labour and military service led to resentment among the peasants (Palais 1975:63, 66–67; Shin Gi-wook 1996:17). As their grievances increased, they banded together for mutual assistance. These groups also became the basis for political resistance, sometimes fuelled by millenarian beliefs, and there were large-scale peasant revolts in 1804, 1811, 1813, 1817 and 1833. Moreover, Catholics scattered by persecution spread the faith, including their own millenarian beliefs, even farther than before. The Sinyu persecution somewhat backfired as the bravery with which Catholics, women as well as men, bore their sufferings in public increased curiosity about the new faith (IKCH 2010a:152–54).

Korean leaders continued in person and by letter to petition Beijing for a priest, and in 1807, on his deathbed, Bishop de Gouvea once more asked the Vatican to designate Korea a mission field. In 1811 and 1813, Gwon Gi-in (John) (nephew of Gwon Cheol-sin) and Jeong Ha-sang (son of Jeong Yak-jong) sent letters to the new bishop of Beijing suggesting that the Pope could negotiate with the king for religious freedom and permission for missionary work (IKCH 2010a:161–66). The diocese had its own problems due to persecution in China, the decline of Portuguese power and the Napoleonic Wars in Europe. However, in 1817, as a result of a personal visit by Jeong Ha-sang to Beijing, two Chinese priests were sent to Korea but they were unable to gain entry (A. Finch 2009:99). Eventually, Jeong Ha-sang and Yu Jin-gil, the senior language officer of the Bureau of Interpreters, addressed a letter to Rome which was presented to Pope Leo XII in 1827. Taking advantage of the problems of the Beijing Diocese, the

Propaganda Fide used it to persuade Leo's successor, Gregory XVI, to declare Joseon a vicariate apostolic of the Paris Foreign Mission (Société des Missions Étrangères de Paris; MEP), and in 1831 Bartholemy Bruguière was appointed its bishop. Nevertheless, the Portuguese continued to argue that Korea was their mission territory. They managed to prevent Bruguière from entering before he died in 1835, and in 1833 they sent a second Chinese priest, Liu Fang-chi Pacific. The fact that Liu was brought in with the help of Korean leaders suggests that there were differences within the church as to the wisdom of receiving French missionaries, especially in view of the sensitivity of the government to the intervention of European powers. Nevertheless, for the ordinary believers, the origin of the priest must have mattered little when they were at last, after thirty-five years, able to make their confessions and to partake of the Holy Communion.

In 1836 the Pope named as vicar apostolic another MEP missionary, Laurent Marie Joseph Imbert. Two French priests preceded him to Korea. Pierre Philibert Maubant crossed the ice on the Amnok River in January 1836 with the help of Jeong Ha-sang and became the first Western missionary to Korea, followed before the end of the year by Jacques Honorè Chastan. The young Frenchmen asserted their papal authority over the older Liu, who refused to accept it. They also accused him of using the priesthood for his own gain and keeping a concubine, and forced him out. Bishop Imbert finally arrived in December 1837 with the help of Jeong Ha-sang and Choi Shin-cheol. For the first time a church hierarchy was established in Joseon. The missionaries divided the country into three: the bishop worked in Seoul and its surrounds, Maubant in Gyeonggi and Gangwon provinces, and Chastan in Chungcheong and Gyeongsang. However, in travelling to minister to their scattered flock in an atmosphere hostile to Europeans, the priests could move only at night and even then, as a precaution, they had to be dressed as mourners, who wore huge hats like up-turned baskets that completely hid their faces (A. Finch 2008:286). Despite the difficulties, this period saw a revival of the church and the number of believers increased from six thousand to nine thousand in the three years 1836–1838. Approximately one in every thousand Koreans was now a Catholic (RFKCH 2010:55).

Until 1909 the Paris Foreign Mission was to be the sole source of foreign Catholic priests and their spirituality had a profound effect on Korean Catholicism. Like the Koreans, the French priests of the MEP were shaped by a martyr history, in their case due to the excesses of the French Revolution, and one of the first things Maubant did was to collect letters and accounts of the Korean martyrs. The priests who entered Korea were products of the faith of post-revolutionary France, with its emphasis on mystery, doctrinal orthodoxy and clerical authority together with a deep suspicion of the state and a certain contempt for the world, which to a great extent the persecuted Koreans shared. This was accompanied by a revival and eschatological spirituality that was introspective, especially in the form of contemplation on the sufferings of Jesus, through devotion to the Sacred Heart and the Eucharist, and veneration of the Virgin Mary. However, salvation of the soul depended not only on faith but also on the performance of works of mercy and charity (cf. Gibson 1989). These rituals and practices were by and large embraced by the church in Korea, which developed a ministry of caring for children and the dead. Furthermore, the self-discipline of neo-Confucianism was reinforced by the asceticism of the MEP missionaries. Their shared emphasis on soul over body and on the next world over this one enabled them to survive poverty and abuse, and encouraged self-sacrifice (A. Finch 2009:117; Yoon In-shil 2007:358).

It was the policy of the Paris Mission to ordain native priests as soon as possible but Maubant overruled Liu's plan to send two young Korean men to Beijing for seminary training; instead, he sent three men to the general seminary of the mission at Penang on the west coast of the Malay peninsula. Kim Dae-geon (Andrew) and Choi Bang-je (Francis-Xavier) were from yangban families which had already suffered greatly for the faith, and Choi Yang-eop (Thomas) was the son of a catechist (A. Finch 2008:287–88). Since no Koreans were yet ordained, the French priests dominated. Despite the church's origins as an indigenous and self-sufficient community, they tended to treat Korea as a new mission field, focusing on the conversion of souls and the building up of the institutional church. Whereas the Korean church had produced its own literature composed in the vernacular, the missionaries preferred French literature and traditions, and religious education was now mainly through translated French doctrinal books (P. Finch 2007). The priests recognised and formalised the organisation of the gyouchon, but they also gradually transformed them into their mission stations.

At the national level, the strife between yangban factions which beset the Korean administration at the turn of the century was displaced by in-law politics as the growing power of certain yangban houses – in particular the Andong Kim and the Pungyang Cho – enabled them to dominate the royal family by marrying into it. Under the Andong Kim clan, life was somewhat easier for Catholics, although there were episodes of local persecution, such as the Eulhae persecution in Gyeongsang province in 1815 and the Jeonghae persecution in Jeolla province in 1827 both of which were directed against gyouchon. However, in the Gihae year 1839 the Pungyang Cho clan, in a bid for power, sparked a persecution even more severe than that of 1801. An anti-Christian campaign in the area of Surisan (modern Anyang in Gyeonggi province) spread to Seoul, where the chief state councillor, Yi Ji-yeon, advocated the targeting and elimination of Catholic leaders (RFKCH 2010:58). The international context also fuelled anti-Catholic sentiment when the first Opium War broke out in China, and the persecution soon became national. In the fifth month Dowager Queen Cho launched an extermination policy against the church and key leaders were soon incarcerated. However, the willingness of Catholics to die for their faith caused the campaign to shift from execution to encouraging apostasy and to instilling fear by harsh penalties to prevent people from converting in the first place (Roux 2012:97–102). Altogether at least 254 Christians were arrested in this round of persecution, and of these 121 were either executed or died in prison (A. Finch 2000:562). The dead included the three missionaries, who gave themselves up in hope of saving the flock. The heads of Bishop Imbert and Fathers Maubant and Chastan were hung up for view at Saenamteo outside Seoul. Those who had brought the priests into the country – Yu Jin-gil, Choi Shin-cheol and Jeong Ha-sang – were linked by the court to the treachery of Hwang Sa-yeong in calling for foreign aid and were executed as traitors at the Seosomun. Many ordinary martyrs bore their torment with great fortitude. They ranged from Yu Dae-cheol (Peter), age thirteen, who endured fourteen sessions of torture until his skin was hanging from his body and he reportedly taunted his captors with lumps of it, to Yu So-sa (Cecelia), the wife of Jeong Yak-jong, who was seventy-nine years old yet was subjected to 230 strokes and died in prison quietly murmuring the names of Jesus and Mary. About fifty of those imprisoned recanted but anguish over apostasy could be intense and long-lasting (A. Finch 2009:100).

The Gihae persecution was even more widespread than the Sinyu persecution, covering at least the whole of the southern part of the country. Families were often arrested and perished together. This illustrates not only a strong sense of collective responsibility but also how the faith spread through families. Family allegiance was another factor that encouraged forbearance in the face of torture (A. Finch 2009:106–11). The figures demonstrate the continued leadership role of the yangban: all but two of the fourteen catechists who died were yangban, and the others were jungin (A. Finch 2009:106). However, despite the social status of the martyrs, the relative lack of political debate about the Gihae persecution indicates that the social standing of the Catholic Church had declined since 1801. Because the authorities were again selective in targeting the church leadership when making arrests, the fact that of the seventy martyrs forty-three were women shows the strength of women's leadership at the time (IKCH 2010b:72). Also indicative of this is the fact that the hierarchy discouraged the tradition of virgin women and finally, in a pastoral letter in 1857, banned the practice of celibacy for women altogether. The same letter also gave the church's blessing to the remarriage of widows – a prohibition under Confucian custom against which women had campaigned (Kim Ok-hy 1984:38). However, in the circumstances this was another way of saying that all women were expected to be wives and mothers.

Trial records for the Gihae persecution show that the motives most clearly expressed by the confessors were religious and ecclesial. They defied state authority on the grounds that God was lawgiver and judge and that the church was built on absolute foundations. As the persecution gathered pace and before his arrest, Jeong Ha-sang wrote *Sangjae Sangseo* or *Defence of the Catholic Faith*, the 'first ever Christian apologia in Korea' (RFKCH 2010:46). It established the pre-eminence of Cheonju over parents and king by arguments from the nature of the world, the existence of conscience and the testimony of the Bible. The Ten Commandments, it claimed, are superior to Confucian teaching because they govern not only practice but also the heart. Because people are weak and often sinful, they need the incentive of reward for the immortal soul and the eternal punishment of evil and so, it argued, Catholicism would do more to keep the well-being of the country and spread peace in the world than Confucianism could (D. Baker 1999:225–28).

After King Hyojong came of age, a decree (Cheoksa Yuneum) ended the persecution while simultaneously justifying it and attacking the arguments in Jeong's *Defence*. It began by asserting the superiority of the Confucian way of praising heaven over the Catholic one. Second, it claimed that the fact that Jesus was executed as a criminal obviously proved the evilness of Christianity. Third, citing the faith's popularity with women and commoners, it described Catholicism as a kind of fanaticism. Fourth, it argued that the incarnation was nonsensical and unbelievable. And fifth, it denounced celibacy as a threat to filial piety and the mixing of men and women in the church as immoral (Jeong Ha-sang 1999; Choi Jai-keun 2006:187–88). Despite such condemnation, for the time being the persecution was stopped.

The three trainee priests who were studying abroad were spared the persecution but Choi Bang-je died of fever in 1837 in Penang. Kim Dae-geon and Choi Yang-eop moved on to train for the priesthood in Manila and then at the Jesuit Seminary in Shanghai, where Kim was ordained deacon in 1844. He was sent immediately to Korea to investigate the situation there and find sea-routes for smuggling in the newly appointed vicar apostolic, Jean Joseph Ferréol. Kim returned to Shanghai in 1845, where he was ordained priest and then went back to Korea by sea, escorting the bishop and a priest, Marie-Antoine-Nicholas Daveluy. After several months ministering in Seoul and Yongin, Kim was arrested in the islands between China and the west coast of Korea. Although at first he tried to persuade the authorities he was Chinese, he was discovered to have Korean-language Christian texts as well as images of the Sacred Heart of Jesus and the Virgin and Child. His arrest occasioned the so-called Byeong-o perse-cution of 1846. The perceived threat of Catholicism was heightened during the trial of Kim and others by the appearance of three French warships off the coast with a message condemning the execution of the three missionaries in 1839. The foreign missionaries were spared on this occasion, but more Korean Catholics were killed, including Kim, who was executed.

Until he reached the canonical age for ordination to the priesthood in 1849, Choi Yang-eop continued in China. When he re-entered Korea, along with the MEP priest Joseph Ambroise Maistre, Choi identified 127 Catholic villages in five provinces, many of which he visited as part of his pastoral ministry. He is remembered as a dedicated priest who laboured among his people until he collapsed and died in 1861 – giving him the status of a 'white martyr' (A. Finch 2008:286). Choi encouraged popular devotion by distributing French crucifixes, rosaries, religious pictures and histories of the saints, but he also made the meaning of these symbols intelligible to ordinary Koreans and composed many of the best Cheonju Gasa – hymns written in a popular Korean style. These became an effective means of teaching doctrine and of proclaiming the faith and were handed down through the generations. The following extract from a hymn by Choi is typical of the comfort he offered to a suffering people:

> Let's go, let's go, let's go to Heaven!
> Where is Heaven?
> It's where there are ten thousand blessings.
> Heaven is high in the sky.
> The glory of God appears there.
> The Trinity is shining there, and the grace of the Holy Spirit is bestowed.
>
> (Kim Yeong-su 2000:417; our translation)

Without any government recognition, the priests in Korea could not establish a parish structure. Instead they continued to travel around the regions they served and to complete the pastoral work done by the laity by investigating the validity of marriages, training native clergy, hearing confessions and celebrating mass. Access to a priest was such a rarity that the faithful were prepared to walk long distances to receive ministry. It was reported that nursing mothers, the elderly and young girls would travel for up to a week in icy winter weather to make their confessions. The people enthusiastically spread the faith to their neighbours and friends and baptised the sick, especially dying children. The prevalence and use of books in the records presupposes a continued high level of literacy in the community, at least in the Korean script. Access to literature was increased after about 1860 when a Hangul printing press was set up in Seoul managed by Choi Hyeong (Peter), brother of the deceased trainee priest (A. Finch 2000:571–75). There were many other church activities, including strong women's and men's networks. Choi Yang-eop promoted various devotional fraternities among the laity, following the example of Bishop Ferréol and Father Daveluy, who had established the association of the Arch-confraternity of the Immaculate Heart of the Virgin Mary in 1846. In 1854 Father Maistre formalised some of the provision for orphans by founding the first of many charitable groups; it became part of the Society of the Holy Childhood in 1864 (Iraola 2007:271–72; Dallet 1874b:386–87).

There was a small school in Seoul for the laity run by a layman, Peter Deok-bo, which taught secular and religious subjects, but most Catholic education was entrusted to parents (Rausch 2008:59). In 1855 a theological college was started in Baeron, where Hwang Sa-yeong had written his famous letter. Three trainees for the priesthood returned from Penang to study, along with several others who were beginning to learn Latin. The instruction also included philosophy, geography, mathematics, history and some science according to the interests of the priests, although 'St Joseph's College' consisted of only two rooms and living conditions were cramped and unhealthy (A. Finch 2008:286–87; Rausch 2008:58–59). Several students died, and none had actually satisfied the criteria for ordination by 1866. The requirement of celibacy for priests was a major stumbling block in Confucian society, but not an insurmountable one since Buddhist monks were celibate (cf. A. Finch 2008:289–90). Threat of persecution, together with the low social status of the community, may have affected the calibre of those coming forward for the priesthood but another explanation for the shortage of native priests is the relative ease with which French missionaries were now able to enter the country as France became the major colonial power in the region. Bishop Ferréol died in 1853 and was replaced as vicar apostolic by Siméon-Françoise Berneux who arrived in 1856. By then there were five French priests, and by 1866 there were twelve clergy. With this level of foreign personnel, the prospect of real leadership in the church for Koreans must have appeared remote.

THE FORCED OPENING OF KOREA AND THE GREAT PERSECUTION, 1863–1876

As the West continued its expansion in East Asia, news reached Korea of the Taiping rebellion and the Anglo-French invasion of north-east China in 1858, as well as of the looting of parts of Beijing in 1860 and the imposition of the Convention of Peking, which ceded more territory and further opened China to Western trade. The sight of refugees fleeing south from the Chinese border and the report by the returning tribute mission in 1861 that Korea should expect imminent invasion combined to produce a state of near panic. Some people reportedly tried to get hold of Catholic books or ornaments to gain favour in case of future attack from Western nations (Dallet 1874b:318–19). Threats from outside combined with the unjust and unbearable living conditions and virtual bonded labour to which many were reduced by debt contributed to the rise of millenarian movements and widespread social unrest in Korea in the years 1862–1864. The most serious episode was the Imsul Farmers' Revolt (1862–1863), which broke out in Jinju, Gyeongsang province, and triggered other uprisings, especially in the south-west, against landlords and merchants (Palais 1975:63, 66–67; Lee Ki-baik 1984:201–55). This unrest had a religious dimension in the Donghak movement, whose founder, Choi Je-u, was suspected of Catholicism, arrested in 1863 and eventually executed. Choi, a scholar from Kyeongju, strenuously denied the charge. But although he had developed Donghak – literally, 'Eastern learning' – as an alternative or even antidote to 'Western learning', which he regarded as a threat to Asia (Bierne 2009), it also resembled the latter in being monotheistic and eschatologically oriented. Choi understood the universe to be in a process of evolution towards a new society of peace and social equality brought about by the Great Spirit of Korean religion, for which he used the name the Lord of Heaven (Cheonju and Sangje) like the Catholics (cf. Grayson 2002:198–202). Donghak hymns also referred to this God as Haneunim/Hananim, the God of Dangun.[4] If derived from 'haneul', meaning 'sky' or 'heaven', this would be the Korean equivalent of 'Lord of Heaven' – either Sangje or

---

[4] The Donghak hymns used an earlier spelling system in which the modern difference in vowel sound between Hananim and Haneunim was not recognised. Hence we use the two terms together in this period.

Cheonju (D. Baker 2002). Like the Catholics, Choi taught that there was no further need for ancestor veneration and he incorporated many of the ideas of rights and liberty that were being mediated from the West (Ahn Sang-jin 2001:49–71; Kim Sung-hae 2008).

At this critical juncture in Korean history, in 1863 King Cheoljong died. The previous two decades had been relatively peaceful and the king had protected Catholics in the so-called Gyeongsin persecution of 1859–1860. On the king's death, Grand Prince Heungseon (Heungseon Daewongun), father of the heir Gojong, who was still a minor, used the influence of his in-laws, the Yeo-heung Min clan, to seize power. The grand prince tried to address the country's multiple problems, particularly peasant unrest, by a series of conservative reforms. Among these was the closure of many of the powerful Confucian academies and the destruction of many shrines. Heungseon was not initially unfriendly to Catholics; indeed, his wife was a sympathiser, his son's wet nurse, Martha Park, was a baptised believer and there were Catholics at court. He also seems to have had wide contacts with Namin hereditary Catholics who had fallen from power (Palais 1975:178). Nor were the grand prince and his government entirely averse to contacts with foreigners such as trade, but they were aware of foreign territorial ambitions and fearful that Western ideas would spread (Chang Dong-ha, Lee Ki-baek and Choe Ching-young 1972).

From 1866 onwards Korea faced a series of foreign incursions which encouraged further isolationism. Russia, pursuing its southward policy, was a signatory to the 1860 Convention of Peking, by which it took over territories in Manchuria from where it threatened full-scale attack. At the suggestion of the Cho clan, the grand prince turned to known Catholics at court – Nam Jong-sam (John) and Hong Bong-ju (Thomas) – to mediate with the French missionaries with a view to arranging an alliance with France to protect against the Russians. News of a proposed meeting between Grand Prince Heungseon and Bishop Berneux leaked to the Catholic community, who became excited that they might at last gain religious freedom. But this drew attention to the embarrassing presence of French priests in the country, and even more seriously to Catholic willing-ness to encourage French intervention. In 1866, Byeong-in year, when Bishop Berneux finally agreed to meet the grand prince, the Kim clan managed to turn the tables and, as the threat from Russia had abated, the grand prince instead followed the example of China at the time and moved against the Catholics (Chang Dong-ha et al. 1972; Roux 2012:90–91).

The persecution at first followed earlier patterns as the authorities arrested ninety-one representative Catholic figures, many of them from the Nam clan. Bishop Berneux and eight French missionaries were executed but three other priests in the country at the time – Félix Clair Ridel, Stanislas Féron and Alphonse Nicolas Calais – evaded arrest and fled to mobilise foreign support. In the name of Dowager Queen Cho, a nationwide order was issued to burn all Catholic books, to report Catholics through the five-household system and to guard the west coast. It was not long before other foreign aggressors were sighted. In August 1866 an armoured US merchant ship, the *General Sherman*, penetrated inland to Pyongyang laden with goods to trade. As the ship headed illegally up the Daedong River towards Pyongyang, Korean Catholics fleeing the persecution tried to board. Forbidden to trade, some of the crew tried to force entry to the city, took a hostage and fired on local people, but the vessel became stranded on a sandbank. The Koreans eventually set fire to the ship and all those on board perished.

Once the persecution had begun, each incident provoked further xenophobia and increased the severity of the persecution, which extended through several phases until 1871. In September 1866 a squadron of French warships led by Rear Admiral Pierre-Gustave Roze appeared on a punitive mission after the beheading of French missionaries. The MEP priest Ridel, who had raised the alarm, was on board one of the ships together with three Korean Catholics – Choi Seon-il, Choi In-seo (John) and Shim Seon-ye – who were supporting the mission as translators and navigators. Apart from wishing to save his two fellow priests who were still in Korea, Ridel believed that the best way to achieve freedom for the Catholic religion in Korea was for the country to be defeated by the Anglo-French alliance as China had been (Piacentini 1890:102–25). However, in a letter to Admiral Roze, the Korean government defended its opposition to Catholic mission, also on grounds of freedom of religion: 'You are attempting to preach your religion in Korea which is an evil act. . . . We follow our religion and you yours. . . . Why are you imposing your ways and calling on us to abandon ours?' (Choi Seok-u 1991:332–33; our translation). Korean troops battled French forces for a month at the mouth of the Han River on which Seoul is situated and on nearby Ganghwa Island. As the French left, they destroyed and looted royal treasures. The actions of the French missionaries made them and Korean Catholics complicit in the violence and cemented the connection in Korean minds between Catholicism and the Western 'barbarians'. Efforts to root out Catholics and execute them escalated, and Catholics were charged not only with disobedience to the king and associating with foreigners but also with actively encouraging foreign intervention. The grand prince decided that

3. Martyrs' Memorial, erected in 2000, below Jeoldusan (Beheading Mountain) Martyrs' Shrine, Yanghwajin. Photograph by Kim Dong-hwan.

the place of execution of Catholics should be the point on the Han River to which the French ships had penetrated: Yanghwajin (Fig. 3).

In 1867 evidence emerged that the Japanese were conspiring with the West against Korea and even preparing for a conquest of the peninsula. Following the Meiji Restoration of 1866, the Japanese government had terminated the traditional relations which recognised Korean superiority and began to relate to Korea diplomatically along Western lines and as a weaker neighbour. To make matters worse, in 1868 a German adventurer, Ernst Oppert, landed at Deoksan in Chungcheong province and raided the tomb of the grand prince's father, in what was seen in Korea as both the ultimate affront to the grand prince and the lowest of crimes. When it transpired that Oppert had plotted with Féron and received help from Korean Catholics, the Catholics became the scapegoats for all foreign aggression (Kang Woong-jo 2005:16–18). Following 1868 (Mujin year), the number of Catholics arrested declined but the numbers being martyred continued to increase as the general populace took out their anger on them, bypassing the judicial system and official records. The final phase of persecution was in 1871 (Sinmi year) on the occasion of the US retaliation for the destruction of the *General Sherman*. Ridel had informed the Americans of its fate, and he and some Korean Catholics now accompanied

US warships as they reconnoitred and engaged the batteries on Ganghwa Island before withdrawing. It was reported that Catholic believers treacherously made contact with them at night. In response to this the grand prince erected the Stele Rejecting Conciliation (Cheokhwabi) throughout the land, with the inscription: 'If you do not fight when Western barbarians attack, in effect you are colluding with them. If you call for conciliation with them, you are betraying your country' (IKCH 2010b:277–78; our translation). He then redoubled his persecution of Catholics, although they were now so widely scattered that most evaded capture.

Before this period being a Catholic had not in itself led to martyrdom, but this 'Great Persecution' was wholesale and indiscriminate (A. Finch 2009). Terrified Catholics were among the many thousands who fled across the porous border into Russian-controlled Manchuria and the Maritime Provinces of Siberia (Foley 2003:7; Griffis 1894:179–80). The missionary estimate of eight thousand Catholics killed in the Byeong-in persecution (1866–1871) was more than half the Christian community (IKCH 2010b:279–83; Roux 2012:89). Of these, the church records 877 as officially executed, but many others were killed by the authorities or by neighbours who took advantage of the general atmosphere to settle old scores, or they were ostracised and starved to death in the mountains. Out of the thousands killed, only twenty-four people were accepted by the church as martyrs. Of the 1,935 arrested, 507 were women – a significantly lower proportion than in the Gihae persecution and an indication of how women's leadership had been undermined by the French missionaries (IKCH 2010b:280). There were few martyrs who can be clearly identified as yangban. The church leadership seems to have been mainly jungin. However, the vast majority of those killed were cheonmin and those tried were ordinary believers. Overwhelmingly poor and uneducated, they were unable to defend themselves in court and showed a poor grasp of Christian doctrine. Rather than being intellectually persuaded, most of the martyrs of 1866 onwards were motivated by a hope of heaven and fear of hell. Their religious practice consisted mainly in secretly attending the mass and in popular practices such as praying the rosary or repeating the names of Jesus and Mary, much as the Buddhists called on the Amitabh Buddha (Choi Jai-keun 2006:317–22).

The role of Catholicism at this crucial period in Korean history is the matter of much debate. Korean Catholics definitely wished to open up Korea to foreign influence. But the church's association with foreigners encouraged Korean isolationism rather than international relations, and therefore Catholicism could be accused of holding Korea back at a time when it needed to modernise to preserve its sovereignty against Japanese aggression (Lee Ki-baik 1984:263). On the other hand, the persecution faced by Catholics, who had introduced Western learning in Korea, could be blamed for marginalising the faith at a time when it was being encouraged in Japan, with considerable benefits for modernisation (Nahm 1989:142). The offer to the grand prince to bring in the French military to respond to the threat from Russia was ill-judged and a few Catholics were guilty of actively supporting foreign invasion in the hope of religious freedom. However, to argue that the Catholics intended revolution, or that they were consciously betraying the nation to an imperial power, is going too far (IKCH 2010a:73–86). Unlike the missionaries, Korean Catholics struggled against the government not only for religious reasons but also for the sake of the survival of their descendants and for the future of their country. Their struggle took place at a time when there were many other reform movements and revolts. The latter involved much regional conflict with government forces, whereas the Catholics were largely passive victims of persecution. Ordinary Korean Catholics had to pay a heavy price for the actions of outsiders, either the church hierarchy or imperial military forces, and for the actions of a few who encouraged them.

By 1873 the grand prince's policy was no longer sustainable, since his government was now resisting on all sides, and he was forced from power by King Gojong, supported by the Yeo-heung Min clan, who ended the persecution. The new government was compelled to give in to the increasingly aggressive demands of foreign nations for trade. The first in line was Japan, which imposed a treaty on Korea in 1876. Although the treaty recognised Korean sovereignty, it also rejected China's claim to tribute which had effectively allowed Korea's autonomy, and it gave to Japan the same kind of privileges in Korea that the unequal treaties of the Western powers had demanded of China.

THE CHURCH OF THE MARTYRS

Whatever the reasons for the persecutions, the legacy of the first turbulent century of Catholic history in Korea was to have a profound effect on the church well into the twentieth century. Comparison of the trial records from 1801 and 1866 shows that under persecution the nature of the Catholic community gradually metamorphosed. From a clandestine association of yangban male urban elite, but open to other classes and to women's leadership, Catholicism became a marginal movement spread across the country, led by yangban and jungin men but made up mainly of the lower classes and women (Choi Jai-keun 2006:275–323). The faith had changed from an intellectual quest motivated by social concern and using Confucian models to a more mystical and other-worldly religion akin to popular Buddhism in its form and influenced by contemporary French devotional life. Whereas the church had started as a Korean experiment that was later helped by Chinese priests, it was now linked into the global hierarchy of the Roman Catholic Church through European clergy (cf. D. Baker 1997:134–35).

The martyrs were not typical members of the Korean Catholic community but a 'religious elite' of 'the more fervent or committed', and a further process of selection took place as some apostatised (A. Finch 2000:564). Their lives revolved around prayer, contemplation, abstinence, receiving sacraments, exhortations to the indifferent and evangelisation, together with saintly activities such as the baptism of infants in mortal danger, the retrieval and burial of corpses, and other works of charity. For women, choosing martyrdom was an expression of autonomy, equality and dignity, which they maintained even in the face of execution, for example, when they insisted on not being stripped. For a few, martyrdom was a consequence of the self-sacrificial and righteous life of chastity, but several well-known married Catholic women died because they loyally refused to reveal their husbands' whereabouts or they followed their parents-in-law when they were arrested (Song Jong-rye 2003:368, 369–74). When the thought-world of the martrys is analysed, based on the interrogation documents and church records, several characteristics emerge. First, martyrs were conscious of emulating other martyrs, who were often members of their own family killed in earlier persecutions, or European martyrs, or biblical figures and ultimately Jesus Christ himself. Second, they saw themselves as indebted to God as to a king or father and to Christ for his love of them as sinners. By martyrdom they were repaying some of that debt, expiating sin and accruing spiritual benefits. Third, they considered life in this transient and fallen world to be of little worth compared to the glories of heaven. They set their suffering within a wider conflict between good and evil and had a strong awareness of temptation and the burden of accumulated sins. In their struggle to detach and purify themselves, some adopted celibacy, although, despite the rewards promised and some exaggerated stories, celibate martyrs were rare (A. Finch 2000). The martyrs' values were not exclusively, or even mainly, French but were found in contemporary Korean Confucianism and Buddhism. The Analects of Confucius included examples of scholars who died out of loyalty to conscience and a desire to cultivate Confucian virtues. Mahayana Buddhism enjoined the compassionate giving of one's life to aid others and had a tradition of religious suicides. Popular Buddhism especially believed in a corrupting world and also had a strong teaching about the hope of heaven and the threat of hell. So the martyrs were being faithful not only to their Catholic confession but also to their formation as Koreans and it is difficult to separate the two (Song Jong-rye 2003:365–66; A. Finch 2009).

Although the martyrs were individuals, they were encouraged by other Christians in prison and by the wider Christian community with prayer and practical support. Their families and dependents also became the responsibility of the church. Often, the martyrs gave their testimony and were sacrificed in the presence of other Catholics and their heroic examples were disseminated to the rest of the Christian community. Efforts were made to retrieve the bodies of executed Christians to bury them decently; furthermore, the martyrs' personal effects became relics and their family homes or places of execution became shrines. The martyr cult that developed helped to root Catholicism in the Korean context and thus contributed to its later expansion (A. Finch 2009:112–18). Commemoration of the martyrs, encouraged by Confucian as well as Christian tradition, was already strong before the arrival of the Paris Mission (Song Jong-rye 2003:370–71); the French missionaries further strengthened it and presented it according to the norms of post-revolutionary France. Daveluy collected historical material on the martyrs, and in Paris, Charles Dallet presented it as part of a campaign for the martyrs' canonisation. On the one hand, this martyr history helped to form the unique identity and reputation of the Korean Catholic Church. On the other hand, the enthusiastic reception of these heroic stories by Europeans suggests that Koreans not only kept the faith but also added to the Catholic martyr tradition from their own heritage.

The historian's dependence on the records of the martyrs should not be allowed to distort the picture of the nineteenth-century church (A. Finch 2000:561–62). Persecution was sporadic, whereas prayer meetings, distribution of charity and eucharistic devotion made up the day-to-day life of the Christian community. Although the Catholic Church in Korea was poor and deprived compared to its origins among the elite, the laity continued to play the major role in its day-to-day running, especially when priests were unavailable, killed or in hiding. Despite the fact that the priests were from France, Korean Christians also maintained links with Beijing and northern China. However, the books on which the community continued to place great emphasis, and which were important in its spread, were now more often in Hangul than in Chinese, reflecting the emphasis on literacy, the process of indigenisation and the lower social status of the membership. The prevailing theological pessimism and dualism was not only due to persecution. Like all Koreans, Catholics were experiencing the social dislocation and economic insecurity of contemporary Korea, including a series of disastrous crop failures that occurred between 1869 and 1875 in northern Korea (the Gisa famine). Their thought reflected the general millenarianism of the period as well as their particular circumstances (A. Finch 2000:575–80). In other words, the Catholic Church in Korea was shaped not only by persecution and the martyr cult but also by the circumstances of its original lay foundation and by the wider Korean context.

Many scholars explain the severity of the reaction to Catholicism primarily in terms of the culture-clash theory that ideological difference made conflict inevitable (e.g. D. Baker 1999:228–30). Others tend to see the Catholics' troubles as largely the result of power struggles among Korean political factions (e.g. Choi Jai-keun 2006). And a third group stresses the problems caused for Catholics by their links to foreign, non-Chinese powers and to foreign interference in Korean affairs in the nineteenth century (e.g. Lee Ki-baik 1984). It seems wise to include all these factors, which were relatively more or less significant at different times and in different periods of persecution – as we have shown.

Catholicism posed a powerful challenge to Joseon Korean society and contributed to social disruption and the eventual demise of the Yi dynasty and Confucian hegemony. Catholic theology offered more convincing explanations of the human condition, and its virtuous life was attractive. Furthermore, it was useful in suggesting alternative models for Korean society, as well as having the foreign links that could help bring this about. Its appearance accelerated the formation of both modern society and modern culture which was already in process in Korea (Cho Kwang 1996b). Catholic teaching and practice encouraged social equality; it promoted the personhood of women; and it also stressed the dignity of children, enjoining parents to consult their sons and daughters about decisions which affected them, especially betrothal and marriage. Catholics facilitated the formation of modern culture particularly by encouraging the use of Hangul. By promoting the Korean language and script it contributed to the education of women, mass education and the rise of Korean popular culture. Additionally, Catholicism provided an alternative polity and even, by the model of election to papal office, could be said to have implanted the idea of democracy in Korea. It challenged political and legal structures by asserting that the laws of the state did not necessarily reflect the law of heaven or divine law, and that every person had a duty to the 'law of conscience', which could override human laws. And by maintaining that truth was universal, Catholics promoted the opening up of Korea to an encounter with and exploration of the wider world. So it can be argued that Catholicism contributed to changes in human relations, family ethics and social ethics in Korea (cf. Cho Kwang 2006:29–37). Two other modernising effects also deserve mention: first, the gyouchon introduced a novel approach to religion in the notion that communities of believers form discrete family or village communities practising distinct religious traditions and beliefs (D. Baker 1997:137–39). Second, the Catholic Church could be regarded as the first non-governmental organisation (NGO) in Korea: it was a worldwide institution which sought the right to operate in the country without arbitrary government intervention. Catholicism was therefore at the vanguard of the formation of civil society (Ledyard 2006:63).

Not only did it presage social change, but Catholicism was a multifaceted religion which had something to offer to both 'the intellectual quest for a monotheistic deity to provide a moral compass and the popular desire for a saviour figure to ward off a rising tide of evil and suffering' (Finch 2009:98). Catholicism in its various forms could inspire and cater to Confucianists and devotees of popular Buddhism and Korean traditional religion, to the elite and the masses, to men and women, to the public and the private of Korean society. In this respect, it was a potentially unifying force in Korea, and this gave added reason for its suppression.

Most commentators observe, quoting Tertullian, that in Korea 'the blood of martyrs' does indeed appear to have been 'the seed of the church'. However, the immediate effect of the persecutions was the weakening and marginalisation of the Catholics. Although from the 1880s there was no further attempt to destroy the whole community, the persecutions had created a 'ghetto', or at least counter-cultural, mentality which was still detectable in the 1970s (Biernatzki, Im and Min 1975:5, 8). The community was poor, disadvantaged and damaged in the public eye by its treasonous association with hostile European powers.

CHAPTER 3

Evangelism, Patriotism and Revivalism,
1876–1910

In the 1860s and 1870s French gunboats, Russian infiltration, American business and Japanese designs threatened Korea from all sides, and internally there was much suffering and unrest. It was clear that 'Korea was not the arbiter of its own destiny but that its fate would be decided by outside powers motivated by their particular selfish interests' (Lee Ki-baik 1984:281). By the 1870s many Koreans had heard of Christianity. Owing to Catholic resistance to oppression, it was well known that Jesus Christ had been crucified, although Christian doctrines had been distorted by Catholicism's political opponents and by Donghak teaching (D. Chung 2001:68). Catholicism was known to be inclusive of the poor and outcaste and, like popular Buddhism, to have a compassionate female figure in Mary, the mother of Jesus. Catholicism had opened up Korea to outside influences and in many respects paved the way for modernity and for other forms of Christianity. But in the late nineteenth century Korea was strongly anti-Western and Cheonjugyo, the Teaching of the Heavenly Lord (Catholicism), was distrusted by many who associated it with treason and collusion with foreign powers.

Meanwhile, Protestant Christianity was spreading in East Asia, especially by the translation and distribution of the Bible and other literature and by literacy work (Neill 1990:209). The first Bible in Chinese was published in 1823, and the production of other Protestant literature in Chinese was booming. By 1870 there were about eight hundred different tracts and books, in addition to scriptures, commentaries and hymnals. Among the most popular were William Burns's translation of *The Pilgrim's Progress* and William A. P. Martin's *Evidences of Christianity* (Dixon 2012; Oak Sung-deuk 2006). These were distributed by Chinese colporteurs in the employ of the missions and were certainly being smuggled into Korea by the 1870s. So, as had occurred with Catholicism, it was through Chinese literature that Koreans first encountered Protestant Christianity. These works were to have an ongoing influence on the formation of Korean Christianity through the terminology they introduced (Oak Sung-deuk 2013:308–10).

Since Korea was somewhat removed from the shipping lanes used by Western merchants en route to China or Japan and had a smaller population than its neighbours, it was not considered a priority for mission work. Furthermore, hearing of its isolationism and persecution of Catholics, missionary societies generally did not encourage interest in Korea until it had concluded treaties with Western powers: the United States and Germany in 1882, Britain in 1882–1883, Italy and Russia in 1884 and France in 1886. In addition to the risk, the strict controls that the Korean state exercised over communication with foreigners prevented the entry of would-be missionaries before these treaties, with two notable exceptions. In the first, Karl A. F. Gützlaff, a German Lutheran with the London Missionary Society, travelled as an interpreter for the East India Company down the west coast of the peninsula in 1832 and distributed Christian literature whenever he had contact with Koreans (Gützlaff 1834; Heo Ho-ik 2009a:47–80). Korean Catholics who visited his ship expecting to meet a priest were surprised by Gützlaff's style. Some recognised a copy of the Lord's Prayer in Chinese but indicated that they might be beheaded and refused to give Gützlaff any information about Korean Christianity (Paik Lak-geoon 1970:45). In the second instance, Robert Jermain Thomas, a Welsh clergyman with the London Missionary Society, met two refugees from Korea in Chefoo (Yantai), China, at the office of the United Presbyterian Church of Scotland and the National Bible Society of Scotland. They proved they were Catholics by the rosaries and medallions concealed on their persons, but they seemed to know nothing of the Bible. So, with the Korean Catholics as his guide, Thomas spent two-and-a-half months at the end of 1865 distributing Bible portions and tracts along the coast of Hwanghae province. The following year he travelled to Korea again on board the ill-fated armoured US merchant ship *General Sherman*. When the ship became stranded below Pyongyang, Thomas managed to toss some copies of Chinese New Testaments ashore. As the ship was set alight and he was forced to leap ashore, he was said to have prayed before his killer and to have offered him a Bible. Opinion is divided on whether Thomas should be considered to be the first martyr of the Protestant Church in Korea or an intruder. Critics point out that he was the interpreter on an armed vessel that was trespassing in Korean waters and moreover, according to Korean records, he was carrying a dagger and a pistol (Goh Moo-song 2001:186–206, 241–60; IKCHS 1989:137–41).

BIBLE TRANSLATION AND THE FIRST PROTESTANT
CHURCHES, 1876–1884

A few of the Protestant missionaries stationed in north-eastern China took interest in Korea and sometimes visited Corea Gate. They included John Ross, a missionary of the United Presbyterian Church (Scotland), who sold books at the gate from 1873 (Ross 1903:17). From his encounters with Koreans, Ross learned that there were some twelve thousand Catholics but no Protestants in a population of about 10.5 million in Korea. Ross was inclined towards the 'Three-self' mission method. According to this strategy for church planting, new churches should as early as possible become self-propagating, self-supporting and self-governing. He therefore stressed the importance of reaching the people with native evangelists rather than foreign missionaries, whose role should instead be that of resourcing, training and guiding (Ross 1903:97–101). Observing that Koreans enthusiastically bought his books, Ross was determined to translate the Bible and distribute it in Korea by means of colporteurs. However, mindful of the grand prince's warning to anyone associating with foreigners, Koreans were reluctant to help Ross learn their language for this project. Eventually a merchant who had fallen on hard times, Yi Eung-chan, agreed to teach him Hangul in secret. In 1877, from his mission station at Mukden (Shenyang), Ross published the first Korean-language primer in English and in 1879 the first English-language history of Korea (Ross 1877; 1891). Together with fellow missionary John MacIntyre, he gathered a team of Koreans, who worked on translating the scriptures by referring to the Delegates Version of the Chinese Bible as well as Greek and English texts. The gospels of John and Luke were published in 1882 with funds from the National Bible Society of Scotland (NBSS) and circulated throughout the Korean community in Manchuria. From then on, the British and Foreign Bible Society undertook to support the translation of the whole New Testament into Korean and its publication. Before the first Protestant missionaries arrived, hundreds of scripture portions were smuggled into the Korean peninsula from the north by Ross's co-workers; some copies of their gospel of Luke were shipped to Japan and from there to the treaty port of Busan, where the NBSS organised their distribution from the south of the peninsula.

Meanwhile, another literature initiative was underway in Japan. Following its treaty with Japan in 1876, Korea embarked on a modernisation programme. Elite young Koreans sent to Japan to study under this policy made contact with Protestant Christians and foreign missionaries. Progressives regarded

Protestant Christianity in the same way that Silhak scholars saw Catholicism: as an ideological aid to Korea's development. Dissatisfied with the pace of progress at home and hearing of the power of the Western nations, especially the United States, which Japan was successfully emulating, some progressives among the elite reasoned that the adoption of Protestant Christianity would be a first step on the road to modernisation. That Americans were predominantly Protestant and not Catholic was a significant factor in this reasoning because Koreans had heard of the separation of church and state in the United States and this suggested they would not interfere in politics (Oak Sung-deuk 2013:20–21). One progressive, Yi Su-jeong, was baptised in Japan in 1883 after studying the Bible. He gave his testimony at a Christian meeting in Japan, and it was later published in Chinese – the earliest extant Protestant writing by a Korean. Yi understood that salvation, or forgiveness of sin and the promise of heaven, is not a matter of attaining enlightenment – as it is in Buddhism – but a gift of God's grace evidenced by a conviction of the truth of the Triune God and total commitment to him (Rhie and Cho 1997:21–24). Yi was involved in the establishment of the first Korean Protestant community in Japan in 1883. But he died shortly after he returned home in 1886 – possibly murdered for his political views. At the request of the American Bible Society, Yi transliterated tracts from Chinese into Hangul, which made it easier for Koreans to understand them. Employing the same method, he completed a collection of New Testament books (Matthew, Mark, Acts), the first of which (Mark) was published in Yokohama in 1884. His versions were not used for later translations. Ross – for one – was critical, arguing that Yi's work did not help the untutored, but the first Protestant missionaries to Korea carried copies with them. Protestant literature was reported to be widely available in Korea by 1884, although it was another decade until it became legal (Oak Sung-deuk 2006:73–74).

In translating the scriptures, both Ross's team and Yi had to make crucial decisions about the way Christianity related to existing Korean beliefs and in particular how to translate the divine name. Yi used Sin, the Korean version of the generic Chinese name (shen) for God or gods and spirits, which was also preferred in Japan (where it is pronounced kami). However, Ross claimed that he had identified a distinctive and almost universal Korean name for God – Haneunim/Hananim. He used it in his Bible and understood it to be the vernacular version of the Chinese term preferred by Protestants: Sangje (Ross 1891:355; Oak Sung-deuk 2013:49–55). There is little literary evidence for the use of Haneunim/Hananim before the 1880s aside from in Donghak hymns, and it has even been suggested that it was a missionary fabrication because, although the early Catholics had used a number of different names for God, they had not chosen to use that one, even when they were writing in Hangul (D. Baker 2002:123). But there is no reason why Ross and his team should have invented the Korean word for God. It was not in their interest to do so if they wanted the gospel to spread, and it is reasonable to suppose that they 'followed the public demand' (D. Chung 2001:178). Haneunim/Hananim had the advantage of being a native term and was also regarded as useful in distinguishing Protestantism from Catholicism. Significantly, it was this Korean name for the Divine, possibly arising from indigenous Korean religion, but certainly associated with the Donghak movement, that became identified with Protestant Christianity.

By 1879 at least four of the Korean men working on Bible translation with Ross and MacIntyre had taken baptism – the first known Korean Protestants: Yi Eung-chan (who died of cholera in 1883 after six years of translation work), Baek Hong-jun, and two others possibly identified as Yi Seung-ha and Kim Jin-gi (IKCHS 1989:142–46; Yi Mahn-yol 1998:60–69). They probably worshipped with the Manchurian Chinese congregation at Ross's church in Mukden. These and other associates of Ross were to become the first Protestant apostles to Korea. By 1884, associates of Ross had founded several Korean congregations. These followed a Manchurian style of worship which was Bible centred and led by the laity and included elements of Chinese religious practice (Kim Kyeong-jin 2012:69–71). Probably the first Korean Protestant Church in China was in the 'Korean valleys' of West Gando in Manchuria (Liaoning province in contemporary China). It was founded by Kim Cheong-song, a medicine seller from the area who had sought aid at the mission house in Mukden and took baptism in 1882. He returned to the valleys the same year with copies of Luke's gospel and soon reported that there were many in the region who wanted to be baptised. Eventually, in the winter of 1884, Ross visited; he baptised eighty-five heads of families and placed many more on a waiting list. Among them were political progressives who had recently arrived as refugees from Korea following a coup (Ross 1890:241–48). When they returned to Korea, they took the Christian message with them.

It is likely that the first Korean church to be established in Korean territory was at Uiju, just inside the northern border. As early as 1879, Baek Hong-jun travelled there for evangelistic purposes and by 1882 he was joined by Yi Seung-ha. They smuggled gospels across the river and established a meeting there which had eighteen members in 1885. The town became a centre of Christianity in the far north and a connecting point between the Korean Christians in Korea and those in Manchuria. However, the best-supported claimant to be the first Korean church is Sorae, a village on the coast of Hwanghae province. It was founded by the brothers Suh Sang-ryun and Suh Sang-u, also known as Kyeong-jo. Suh Sang-ryun, the elder of the two, had been found on the verge of death by MacIntyre and nursed back to health. Ross baptised him and he became a colporteur with a reputation for indefatigable evangelising zeal and courage (Yi Mahn-yol 1991:64–66). By 1884 his brother was settled in Sorae and pastoring a group of believers while Sang-ryun continued his itinerant activities (Fig. 4). Sorae is widely accepted as the 'cradle of Protestant Christianity in Korea' (Paik Lak-geoon 1970:139, 204; Min Kyoung-bae 1982:171–72; IKCHS 1989:152–56). It also became a symbol of the self-supporting Korean church lauded by later missionaries and source of many of the Christian leaders of the first few generations (A. Clark 1971:459–61). As in the case of Catholicism, it is the boast of Korean Protestants that baptised Koreans established Protestant communities – even (from a Free Church point of view) churches – before any foreign missionaries had been admitted to the country.

4. Suh Sang-ryun, founder of the church at Sorae, and his family, circa 1897. Moffett Korea Collection, Princeton Theological Seminary Library.

REVIVED CATHOLIC CHURCH, 1876–1884

For another decade following the outbreak of persecution in 1866, Korean Catholics had been left to organise themselves without any priests – foreign or Korean – as they had done for most of their hundred-year history. This was an opportunity for the Catholic teaching they had received to become further integrated with their own culture and with their recent experience of persecution. They were still an outlawed movement with strongholds in isolated villages and little overt presence in urban centres or in the north where Protestantism was soon to establish itself.

Félix Ridel had been named as Bishop Berneux's successor in 1867 but he was called to the First Vatican Council and finally returned as bishop only in 1877, along with two more French priests. Because of the role he had played in bringing French warships to Korea, Ridel was soon arrested pending deportation but he was released owing to pressure from the French legation and Japanese advice. The priests who returned in 1877 came with a new resolve to build up the indigenous church by communicating more in the Korean language, training locally elected lay leaders through a catechist system and establishing a Korean priesthood. During their ten years of exile in China, with the help of three Koreans – Francis Kim, Choi Ji-hyeok (John) and Gwon Chi-mun (Thaddeus) – the priests had compiled a grammar and a Korean-French dictionary as a step towards implementing this plan, and Ridel had these printed in Yokohama in 1880 and 1881, respectively. Soon the same press was moved from Nagasaki to Seoul and began to produce affordable popular religious literature (IKCH 2010b:221–25). Among these was the prayer book *Seonggyo Gonggwa*, first published in 1886 and used for the better part of the next century. It consisted mostly of translated European material, reflecting the orthodoxies of Vatican I as received in France (D. Baker 1997:135).

Catholic believers were still arrested from time to time – in 1879 a priest was deported and as late as 1888 a believer was martyred – but the government had ceased to harass believers and the church began to grow again. After the treaty with France in 1886, the Catholic community was relieved of fear of state-sponsored persecution and the priests began to go around openly in clerical dress. The extraterritorial powers France negotiated for its citizens included greater freedom of movement for their missionaries than for those of other nations, and French priests travelled far outside the treaty ports on horseback to visit the Catholic villages. The treaty also included a clause allowing them to 'teach' Joseon people, which was taken as permission for proselytising activities

(Ryu Dae-young 2003:183). In 1882 there were reported to be 12,500 believers (RFKCH 2010:79). By 1885 there were eleven French missionaries in the country but these were still too few to meet the pastoral needs of the flock. Between 1881 and 1884 twenty-three Korean men were sent to Nagasaki and then to Penang to begin training for the priesthood, but seven of them died overseas. So from 1885 candidates for the priesthood were educated at a new St Joseph's Seminary at Baeron to replace the earlier one that had closed during the persecution. In 1887 this seminary was relocated to Yongsan, Seoul, near the place of execution of martyrs and a two-story building was erected in 1891.

Being an underground movement, mostly without priests, until this point, the church had never implemented the parish structure mandated by the Council of Trent for administration of the sacraments. But in 1882 the very first parish was established in Myeong-dong in Seoul, which had been the site of Kim Beom-u's home and clinic, and land was purchased there for church buildings. With the formation of parishes came the possibility to collect church dues and keep church records, but the church remained poor. Even in 1905 two-thirds of the church budget came from the Paris Mission (Rausch 2008:61). The normalisation of Catholic life in Korea continued with the creation of institutions. The Sisters of St Paul de Chartres were invited to take over the running of an orphanage started in Daegu as an extension of the tradition in the gyouchon of Catholic families caring for orphaned and abandoned children. This first religious order arrived in 1888 in the shape of four sisters, two French and two Chinese, who were soon joined by Koreans – all of them descendants of martyrs (J. Kim and Chung 1964:703–5). The first ever old people's home in Korea was founded around 1885. In 1882 the first Christian school in Korea was established (Inhyeon School) in the first parish. It welcomed pupils from the wider community and offered an alternative to the Confucian academies or seodang. As new parishes were set up, mostly in the cities, these also started parish schools. In 1900 twenty-one schools were reported, but most were for Catholic children only. They were small and locally financed, making them short-lived (Rausch 2008:66–67). In 1899 the Sisters of St Paul opened a non-parochial school for girls in Incheon (Jemulpo); several other parishes followed suit, and by 1910 there were ten of these schools nationally (RFKCH 2010:92). The number of Catholic schools was soon outstripped by the number of Protestant ones, and then by government provision. Despite their longer presence in the peninsula, because of their very limited resources, Catholics did not gain a reputation for institutions of any sort until after the Korean War.

On June 8, 1888, Bishop Blanc fulfilled a dream of his predecessor Bishop Ridel by consecrating the vicariate apostolic of Korea to the Sacred Heart of Jesus and in 1890 he declared that it was under the patronage of Mary, Mother of God (RFKCH 2010:98–99).

THE GAPSIN COUP (1884) AND PRESBYTERIAN AND METHODIST MISSIONS

Korean progressives were frustrated by the gradual pace of modernisation under the guidance of China. With treaties in place and with the encouragement of Queen Min, the wife of King Gojong, some of them, such as Yi Su-jeong in 1884, requested missionary help from Western nations to modernise Korea. Despite these requests, the mission boards of the leading US churches were reluctant to get involved. For one thing, the treaties did not permit overt evangelistic activities and, for another, foreigners were only welcome insofar as they contributed to modernisation. However, in 1883 the first Korean delegation to the United States, which included Min Yeong-ik, nephew of Queen Min (also Hong Yeong-sik, Seo Kwang-beom and others), encountered an influential Methodist, John F. Goucher, who was moved to pledge funds for work in Korea, and the following year Robert S. Maclay of the (Northern) Methodist Episcopal Church mission board came to Korea on an exploratory visit. Guided by Kim Ok-kyun, whom he had known in Japan, Maclay secured permission to do medical and educational work, for which he arranged for land to be bought. Meanwhile in 1884 the Presbyterian Church in the United States of America (PCUSA) sent to Korea Dr Horace Newton Allen, who became the first Protestant missionary to work in the country, although as far as the secular authorities were concerned he was a medical doctor attached to the American legation (A. Clark 1971:72–78).

The Gapsin Coup d'état (Gapsin Jeongbyeon), staged by the Korean Reform Party (Gaehwadang) with Japanese support, took place three months after Allen's 1884 arrival. The leaders, and others linked to the plot, were among those who had had contact with Western missionaries, including Kim Ok-kyun, Park Yeong-hyo, Seo Jae-pil and Yun Chi-ho. The coup failed and further put back modernisation by strengthening the pro-China conservatives who were pre-eminent for the next decade while the plotters and other progressives fled the country (Chandra 1988:48–49). Despite its association with the Gapsin plotters, the Protestant mission survived in Korea, largely because on the night of the coup Allen had had the good fortune to be on hand to save the life of Min Yeong-ik, who had been attacked as a progressive. This naturally conferred favour on him in the eyes of King Gojong. Allen and other early US missionaries became close to the king and the royal family, and this relationship both protected them and facilitated their activities. An additional reason the mission survived was the key diplomatic role of the US missionaries since the Korean government saw friendship with the United States as a useful counterbalance to French (represented by Catholic), Russian and British interests but the United States sent few official envoys (Hunt 1980:79–83). Allen went on to work as the US consul, in which capacity he greatly aided the mission work. Over the years, the missionaries persuaded the king and other high-ranking Koreans that the United States was far enough away not to be a threat to Korean territory and could be counted on as a friendly nation that could offer help, in spite of indications that US policy was becoming pro-Japanese (Park Chung-shin 2003:25).

Despite the uneasy political situation, two Protestant clergy were appointed to Korea. Horace Grant Underwood and Henry Gerhard Appenzeller, who were to lead the respective Presbyterian and Methodist missions, travelled together by steamship from Japan and landed in Incheon on Easter Sunday 1885. Proselytising was still proscribed, but both men intended to plant churches nevertheless. More medical and also educational missionaries followed (A. Clark 1971:88–123). Although they were from different denominations, the Protestant missionaries who came to Korea up to 1910 were mostly college graduates from the United States and Canada recruited through the Student Volunteer Movement (SVM) or its precursor, or through the Young Men's Christian Association (YMCA), which was closely related to the SVM. By and large they shared the common 'holiness' tradition of the D. L. Moody revivals and the annual Northfield Conference of the 1870s. In addition to the evangelical emphases on the Bible, the Cross, conversion and activism, they stressed the perfecting work of the Holy Spirit in the believer and the rescue of souls who were perishing. A tendency to premillennialism motivated the evangelisation of Korea within the shortest possible time (Ryu Dae-young 2008:390–91). Like the progressive Koreans who had invited them, and their fellow missionaries in Japan, they regarded the dependence of Korea on China as the main reason for its 'backwardness' and aimed to liberate Korea from sadae with respect to China (Hunt 1980:90–92). Although they were for the most part from the conservative end of the evangelical spectrum (Ryu Dae-young 2008:376–78), it is anachronistic and misleading to cast these early missionaries as 'fundamentalists' or apply later allegations that they were more concerned with rescuing people for the next world than with reforming society (notably, A. Brown 1919:539–42). While they regarded conversion to Christianity as a prerequisite for all other progress, most followed the basic SVM mission strategy which combined individual salvation with social uplift, institutional reform and technological advancement (Grayson 2002:157; Ryu Dae-young 2008:392; Hutchison 1987:91). Moreover, they did not disregard Korean religions but looked at them for 'points of contact' with Christianity (Oak Sung-deuk 2009:30). Several missionaries became experts on the Korean language and produced some of the earliest studies in English of Korean history and culture (e.g. Hulbert 1905, 1906; Gale 1924). However, they concluded that there was little in Korean religion that would inspire the people and give them resources in their encounter with modernity (Gale 1909:67; Hulbert 1906:403–4; H. Underwood 1908:77–91; cf. Oak Sung-deuk 2013:12–20).

From the start there was a sense of competition between the two Protestant missions which was encouraged by their respective mission boards in New York; initiatives by one were generally replicated by the other (Hunt 1980:42–45). However, the leading missionaries also formed the Mission Council, which was ecumenical. Among the aims they shared was a desire to demonstrate the superiority of Protestantism to Catholicism. They admired the sacrifices Catholics had made for their faith and took advantage of Catholic knowledge of the country, such as maps, dictionaries and primers. In addition, Underwood secured as his language teacher Song Deok-jo, a Catholic who had taught French missionaries. Nevertheless, the Protestants deliberately distinguished themselves from the Catholics not only for doctrinal reasons but also to reassure the king and to avoid persecution of their flock, and there was little contact between the two kinds of Christian missionary (Oak, Sung-deuk 2013:20–25; e.g. Appenzeller – see Poitras 1994:178, 180 n.8). Apart from ecclesiastical differences, they spoke different languages: the Protestants were English speaking and the Catholics mainly Francophone. There were cultural differences too between the entrepreneurial Americans, who tended to look on non-English-speaking Europeans as 'old-fashioned and undemocratic', and the conservative French priests, who distrusted democrats and revolutionaries (cf. D. Baker 2006b:289). The missionaries also had different lifestyles and income levels. For instance, the Protestants were mostly teetotal. Whereas Protestants were accompanied by their families and built American-style homes to live in, the celibate Catholic priests lived in mission stations constructed in traditional Korean fashion, and Catholic missionaries estimated that even a bishop had only half as much to live on as an unmarried Protestant missionary (Rausch 2008:61; cf. D. Clark 2003:137–38). To Koreans, the

Catholic priests known as sinbu ('spiritual father'), who used native Korean or clerical dress, appeared quite different from the Protestant moksa (pastor; literally, 'shepherd-teacher'), who was likely to be wearing a Western suit. The two forms of Christianity used differing vocabularies and symbols and appeared as two different religions: Cheonjugyo (Catholicism) and Gidokgyo (Protestantism – a Chinese name derived from *Christos*[1]). Catholic worship centred on the Latin mass had little in common with Protestant congregational services in the vernacular that were mostly derived from Reformed and Wesleyan practices. Furthermore, Protestants soon established themselves as representatives of modernity, whereas the Catholic Church was in retreat from modernism and many aspects of the modern world (D. Baker 2006b:290–91; Paik Lak-geoon 1970:207, 257; Yun Kyeong-no 1996).

Medical work provided the initial opening for Protestant mission work in Korea. Allen's qualifications and favoured status with the royal family enabled him in 1885 to open the first Western-style hospital. This government hospital fell victim to corruption, but it was later refounded and reformed as a Presbyterian institution by a Canadian missionary doctor, Oliver R. Avison, with funds donated by Louis Severance, who gave it his name. Allen began by working with the elite, but those missionaries who came after him were more concerned about treating the common people, including women and girls. The first Methodist physician, Dr William B. Scranton, began by setting up mobile clinics for the poor and was soon busy dealing with an outbreak of cholera. The Methodists founded a hospital for poor women in 1887 and a network of dispensaries as far as Jemulpo. Underwood and Dr Lillias Horton, who became his wife, opened a clinic in an area where the sick were abandoned outside Seodaemun (Great West Gate), as well as other facilities (A. Clark 1971:112–14). However, the two approaches came together when the medical training offered at Allen's hospital developed into Korea's first medical school, which became Severance Hospital Medical School in 1904 and supplied the first Korean doctors. The Methodists opened the country's first nursing school in 1903 (Lim Hee-kuk 2013:40–46).

Christian medical work led to improvements in the health of the people and demonstrated Christian love for the sick and poor but it tended to be used by the missions as a means to the higher goal of conversions. From the point of view of the mission leadership, the greater effectiveness of Western medicine compared to the Chinese-style clinics of apothecaries, the healing

---

[1] Protestantism in Korea is also called Gaesingyo – Reformed Teaching.

practices of the monks at the Buddhist monasteries or the rituals of the shamans enhanced the attraction of Protestantism and greatly facilitated their evangelistic work (D. Baker 1994; H. Underwood 1908:100–102). So even when it was no longer needed as a pretext for evangelism, medicine remained an integral part of Korean missionary activity and from 1902 the Mission Council stipulated that no new mission station could be opened without a doctor on the staff (C. Clark 1937:115).

Although Underwood and Appenzeller were hindered from preaching and outreach by political conditions and their language limitations, they soon found Koreans coming to them for baptism anyway. The first was Noh Chun-kyeung (Noh Dosa), who had been Allen's language teacher and had read the gospels of Mark and Luke in Chinese (H. Underwood 1908:105–6). Underwood, assisted by Appenzeller, baptised him in July 1886. More requests followed, mostly from Koreans who had been reached by the literature work begun by Ross in Manchuria. Unable to enter Korea to baptise the believers at Sorae, Ross gave Suh Sang-ryun a letter of introduction to Underwood to whom he presented himself in Seoul in late 1886 (Ross 1890:241–48). The following January, several believers from Sorae were baptised by Underwood, assisted by Appenzeller. Underwood found that three of them were able to understand the faith and had been practising for some years (A. Clark 1971:99). By the end of 1887 he had baptised ten believers from Sorae and twenty-four unsolicited Koreans in total who had been led to faith by Suh, Baek Hong-jun and other Koreans (IKCHS 1989:242–44; T. S. Lee 2010:10–12).

In September 1887, Ross was able to travel by sea to Seoul. While Ross was visiting, Underwood founded what was to become Saemoonan (Saemunan) Presbyterian Church, the first church in Korea led by an ordained minister. Fourteen Korean members, thirteen of them disciples of Suh and Paek from Sorae, met in his house. The translation work of Ross and his team and the evangelistic efforts of Suh, Baek and others were now brought under the mission of the Presbyterian Church in the United States of America, which authenticated their work and connected it to transnational Presbyterianism. The following week, Underwood ordained two Koreans as elders, and in 1888 he baptised the first four Korean women in that denomination (Paik Lak-geoon 1970:140–41). Ross understood that there were three hundred more believers in Seoul (Ross 1890:241–48); if so, it is not surprising that within a decade Saemoonan Church had already planted several daughter churches. Appenzeller did not have such a head start with baptisms as Underwood, but through Maclay's Japanese network in Korea, on 24 July 1887 he baptised Park Jung-sang, who had first learned about Christianity in Japan, as the first Korean Methodist, and in October Appenzeller baptised the first Korean Protestant woman (Ryu Dong-sik 2005a:73–80). Chungdong (Jeongdong) Methodist Church was founded by Appenzeller as Bethel Chapel in October 1887 and a decade later the first Western-style Protestant building was erected on the site (Ryu Dong-sik 2005a:73). However, its first member was also a product of the Presbyterian mission in Manchuria, having received a Ross New Testament in Uiju (A. Clark 1971:87). In 1888 an indigenous Methodist ministry was begun when two men – Jang Jeom-hwa and Yu Chi-gyeom – were licensed as local preachers (Ryu Dong-sik 2005a:88). In 1893, Scranton opened a second Methodist church in Seoul, Sangdong Church, which gained a reputation for serving the poor. Jeon Deok-gi, who was initially a servant of Scranton, became a leading evangelist (jeondosa) there (Ryu Dong-sik 2005a:95–105, 210–24).

In the first few years, when no public meetings were possible, Korean 'helpers' facilitated the entrance of male missionaries to sarangbang or the outer quarters of a traditional Korean house to engage the elite in discussion of religion. As well as visiting Korean homes, the missionaries created their own sarangbang in which they explained Christian teaching and also taught English (Paik Lak-geoon 1970:160–61; H. Underwood 1908:104–5). Soon women missionaries gained access to anbang, the women's quarters of a house. They could not have operated in this way without the help of a 'Bible woman' who admitted them, interpreted for them as necessary and evangelised other women. The Bible woman model was adapted in Korea from China; indeed, one Methodist missionary brought a Chinese Bible woman with her when she relocated. In Korea the practice was begun by Mary F. Scranton, a widowed educator and the mother of William, who was appointed by the Methodist Woman's Foreign Missionary Society; she was employing eight women by 1898. Methodists continued to make greater use of Bible women than other denominations did, and close relationships often formed between the Bible women and the women missionaries (Chou 1995:30–31).

The new churches followed North American rather than Manchurian patterns of Christian worship. For example, Korean Christians were used to singing Chinese hymns in Korean pronunciation but the missionaries introduced Western four-part harmonies and translated English hymns. The first hymnbook was published by the Methodists in 1888. A Presbyterian hymnal produced in the 1890s included several hymns written in Korean (Lim Hee-kuk 2013:88–94). In Seoul, where houses were crowded together and doors were made only of paper, it was not easy to hide activities such as hymn singing from neighbours and, in the absence of active government opposition, church services soon became semi-public. However, social norms made it difficult for male clergy to minister to women, or indeed for women to attend church at all. At the request of converted Korean men, in 1888 Mary Scranton began a class for their wives on Sunday evenings which soon attracted more than thirty students (A. Clark 1971:100–101). It was she who suggested hanging a curtain down the length of the first churches to separate men from women and yet allow women full participation. The clergyman would then avert his eyes from the women's half of the room (Huntley 1984:17, 78).

Gradually the political situation eased, and as their language improved, foreign missionaries were able to interact with people who, out of curiosity, gathered around them on the street. Although it was illegal, beginning in April 1887 Protestant missionaries began to venture into the rest of the country with the blessing of the king (Hunt 1980:70, 76). Underwood made several trips north along the tribute route, stopping by the already-existing Christian communities along it, which had mostly been started by Ross's disciples. In 1889 he reached Uiju where, of a hundred men prepared by Baek and Yi, he baptised thirty-three in the Amnok River – but from the Manchurian side to avoid trouble with the Korean authorities (Paik Lak-geoon 1970:209–10). In the same year, Appenzeller and George Heber Jones travelled southwards through Wonju to Daegu and Busan, encouraging the growth of the Methodist church on the way. In 1891 the missionaries Samuel Moffett and James Scarth Gale travelled all the way through to Manchuria, visiting the 'Korean valleys' and meeting Ross in Mukden (A. Clark 1971:106).

The Protestant missionaries also founded schools. In 1886, following her conviction that the education of women and girls would produce 'the most speedy advancement of the country', Scranton founded Korea's first school for girls (Huntley 1984:82). The king supported the educational initiative and named the school Ewha (Ihwa; Pear Blossoms). At the time, educating women was ridiculed and girls were kept at home; nevertheless, the school started with one pupil whose parents could not support her and gradually its enrolment grew to 120 in 1901. Ewha students engaged in education, evangelism, medicine and social work as part of their training, and missionaries and graduates went on to found similar day schools for women all over the country (Kim Chong-bum 2008:15–17). Since women could not become pastors, the tertiary-level courses that Ewha offered from 1909 turned out Korea's first women professionals (Chun Chae-ok 2009). The Presbyterians began a girls' school in 1887 – Jeongdong Yeohakdang

(Chungshin Girls' School) – and the Southern Methodists opened another institute for poor girls in 1893. That same year the Mission Council endorsed Mary Scranton's policy by making the conversion of women a strategic priority. Appenzeller started a school for boys in 1886, for which there were plenty of takers, and in 1887 it was given royal approval and a name: Paichai (Baejae) Hakdang (School for Cultivating Talent) (Lim Hee-kuk 2013:16–23). Also in 1886, Underwood opened a boarding school and orphanage for boys. The mission schools were intended to bring about conversions to Christianity, while also introducing Western knowledge and training church leaders. In addition, Underwood insisted that each local church should have a school, paid for by the congregation, to make sure that Christian children were not sent to 'heathen schools' (H. Underwood 1908:111–14). Korean Christians saw wider benefits in this idea and responded enthusiastically, beginning with the church in Sorae. It became the norm that if a village had a Protestant church there was also a local church elementary school, and these became feeder schools for the secondary and tertiary institutions run by the missionaries, leading to the development of a network of Christian schools and the rise of educated Christians.

Literature ministry and Bible translation were also priorities for the leading Protestant missionaries. Literature in Chinese was much appreciated by Confucians, and Underwood distributed three thousand tracts at the last Confucian civil service exam in 1894. The Korean Religious Tract Society, later renamed the Christian Literature Society of Korea, founded ecumenically in 1890, translated many of the Chinese texts into Hangul and produced new ones for the Korean market, thereby reaching a much wider readership. In 1891 the Methodists founded the Trilingual Press (Sammunsa), which was operated mainly by students of Paichai school. It turned out tens of thousands of copies of works in Chinese, Korean and English, including school textbooks and works of general interest. By 1894 there was sufficient variety available to open a bookstore. The press also founded the Christian media by producing the first Christian newspapers and magazines, beginning with *The Independent* (*Dongnip Sinmun*) in 1896, followed by the *Korean Christian Advocate*, and later the *Christian News* (IKCHS 1989:290; H. Underwood 1908:120–223).

The use of Hangul suited both missionary aims: to reach the masses and to liberate Korea from China (Kim In-soo 1996:67–76). The missionaries saw the 'Sinification' of Korea as obscuring the plain truth which they wished, through the medium of straightforward Hangul rather than archaic Chinese characters, to make accessible to all. Similarly, the failure to use the vernacular and the obfuscation of truth were among the chief criticisms that evangelicals levelled against Catholics. Despite the Catholic record of opposition to Confucian patriarchy and struggle for religious freedom, Protestant missionaries tended to dismiss Catholicism through post-Enlightenment European eyes as another form of tradition that would hold Korea back from progress. The production and dissemination of the Korean Bible was thus central to their mission. Underwood, however, was critical of the Ross gospels for using the dialect of the Pyeongan region, which reflected the origins of most of the translators. Ross endeavoured to correct this before publishing the complete New Testament in 1887, of which five thousand copies were printed and distributed. Nevertheless, Underwood determined that there should be a new translation, for which he also gained the combined support of the Scottish, British and US Bible Societies (Paik Lak-geoon 1970:254–55, 346). Despite the full-time labour of Koreans and some missionaries, the complete New Testament was not published until 1906, followed by the whole Bible in 1911. Therefore in the formative period until 1906, the Ross version was the only complete Korean New Testament, and its importance in the history of the Korean church 'cannot be overstated' (Grayson 1999:169; cf. IKCHS 1989:142–48; Paik Lak-geoon 1970:148–53; Min Kyoung-bae 1982:147–48; Yi Mahn-yol 2001:175–211; 1998:60–94).

THE EXPANSION OF CHURCHES IN THE 1890S AND BIBLE WOMEN

In 1891, Gustave-Charles-Marie Mutel arrived in Korea as bishop of the Catholic Church, and he was to remain in charge until 1933. The growing confidence of the church was shown in the building of impressive mission churches which were designed by priests in the French Gothic style. The first to be consecrated, in 1893, was Yakhyeon Church, which was built in red brick on a hill above the site outside the Seosomun where martyrs had been executed. However, plans to build a cathedral on the land purchased in Myeongdong were opposed by the government because of the prominence of the site, which dominated both the palace and the city. Catholic persistence with the support of the French legation caused a backlash of anti-Western feelings. These ran particularly high in 1888 when they were fuelled also by anti-Christian literature from China, including stories of atrocities by foreigners, especially against children. The subsequent riots interrupted Protestant mission work as well (A. Clark 1971:105–6; Huntley 1984:52). But the French insisted, the government backed down and the work went ahead, despite further protests. The result was the most impressive

Western building so far in Korea, and the first to use stained glass (which was imported from France). The brick edifice was consecrated and dedicated in 1898 to the Virgin Mary of the Immaculate Conception at a ceremony attended by thousands of Catholics from all over the country, as well as by government ministers and representatives of foreign powers. By 1894 the number of Catholics in Korea had reached twenty thousand (RFKCH 2010:79), and in 1896 three students who had studied in Penang were ordained – the first Korean priests since Father Choi Yang-eop (Thomas) died in 1861.

Their alliance with Russia from 1892 and their part in the European success in putting down the Boxer Rebellion in China further increased the power of the French in Korea and the acceptability of Catholicism in public and at court (Hanson 1980:21). The king's mother, the wife of the grand prince, was secretly baptised Mary by Bishop Mutel (J. Kim and Chung 1964:317–18). The grand prince himself was said to be filled with remorse at the memory of those who had died in the persecution and had Buddhist sacrifices made for them (MEP 1924:63–64). In 1895 the government pardoned a few of the martyrs and King Gojong met Mutel who heard the king's regret for the persecution of 1866 (RFKCH 2010:87). Freedom for missionary work steadily increased. After 1890 priests began to make permanent bases in different cities, setting them up in homes nominally owned by Koreans to evade the restrictions on foreigners owning property. Eventually churches were built in the countryside as well and after 1904 these were constructed in a European style. Catholic communities grew alongside Protestant ones in the north-west and the Catholic Church was established on Jeju Island (Quelpart) to the south. Catholicism was spread among Koreans across the Duman (Tumen) River in North Gando in Manchuria (Jilin province in contemporary China) by a Korean who sought out missionaries in Wonsan in 1896 to find out more about the faith. The following year, a Catholic priest went to Gando to baptise a hundred more, and from 1909 on priests were resident in the region (MEP 1924:64–66).

By 1890 so many Catholic missionaries were openly engaged in mission work in the interior – not to mention Japanese traders illegally resident there – that the Protestant missions considered themselves free to ignore both Korean and consular restrictions and to expand to other cities, 'occupying' or 'taking charge' of the new 'territory' and establishing national churches (Ryu Dae-young 2003:196–97). In fact they generally set up churches in places where believers had already pioneered. Church members would deliberately move into non-Christian villages on the pretext of family or trade, gather an interested group, acquire property and then send for a foreign missionary or Korean mission worker to instruct, baptise and eventually constitute the group as a church (C. Clark 1937:104, 114–15). Both Presbyterians and Methodists opened up mission work in the important city of Pyongyang. The Methodists expanded from Incheon west to Ganghwa Island, clashing with Anglicans already working there. The Presbyterians set up a base in Busan in 1893, and later at Daegu. In 1893–1894 both Presbyterians and Methodists established missions in Wonsan (Paik Lak-geoon 1970:206–9, 285–86; A. Clark 1971:107). Once the Korean field was opened up by these Presbyterians and Methodists from the northern United States, other missions also entered. In 1891 Rev. James Mackay, his wife and three unmarried women missionaries established the Australian Presbyterian mission in Busan, which was distinctive in that the missionaries lived among Koreans (Brown 2009:268–69, 274). In 1892, seven missionaries of the Presbyterian Church in the United States (the Southern Presbyterian Church) began work, focusing mainly in the south-west of the country (Paik Lak-geoon 1970:214, 287–88). In 1896, the Methodist Episcopal Church South sent experienced missionaries from China into Korea as a result of the encouragement and financial support of Yun Chi-ho (A. Clark 1971:147–48), a progressive nobleman who had undergone a personal conversion experience at the Southern Methodist Anglo-Chinese School in Shanghai while in exile after the Gapsin Coup. Following the sudden death of Rev. William J. McKenzie, a Presbyterian with a Canadian student mission who worked in Sorae, and a request from the Koreans there, the Presbyterian Church in Canada sent in missionaries beginning in 1898 (Paik Lak-geoon 1970:192–94, 204–5, 278–79).

To avoid clashes and confusion as their work overlapped, in 1892 the various Presbyterian missions established a comity system, and by 1908 this system had been extended to include the two Methodist churches as well. For the most part, territory was apportioned according to where the missions were already established, although all six churches worked in Seoul and Pyongyang (Grayson 2002:159). While the comity agreement made life easier for the missions, it divided the Korean church according to imported divisions from the West. It also encouraged regional differences, some of which were already present in Korean society, and it exacerbated the factionalism to which yangban society had been prone. Moreover, since the whole country was covered by this agreement, new missions or indigenous churches were not welcome anywhere (cf. Rhie Deok-joo 2001:39–41). Nevertheless, new missions continued to be started in Korea during this period.

Anglican work in Korea began piecemeal from 1880 (A. Clark 1971:327–34). Eventually, in 1889, the Society for the Propagation of the Gospel (SPG), representing the Anglo-Catholic wing of the Church of England, sponsored the consecration by the archbishop of Canterbury of Charles John Corfe as missionary bishop to Korea. Like the Presbyterian and Methodist missionaries, Corfe started with medical work. He founded St Luke's Hospital in Incheon, which was helped by the arrival of the Sisters of the Community of St Peter (Kilburn) in 1892. The work moved into Seoul in 1891, where a compound and the Church of the Advent were established next to the British embassy. The Anglican Church retained its links with the coast and did not expand to other provinces, preferring a focused work to what they regarded as the shallow efforts of the Americans (Corfe 1905). It was not until 1897 that the first Korean believers, Kim Hui-jun (Mark) and Kim Gun-myeong (John), were considered ready to receive baptism. The former developed a strong community in his home area of Ganghwa Island, where St Peter and St Paul's Church was consecrated in 1900 (Lee Jae-jeong 1990:28–44). It was deliberately built in traditional Korean style and made unusual use of Confucian and Buddhist symbols to express the dominant theology of the mission, which regarded Christianity as the fulfilment of other religions (O'Connor et al. 2000:109–10). The Anglican missionaries tended to be highly educated, and the mission invested a great deal of time in learning the Korean culture and language in order to be able to represent faithfully the 'fundamental truths of religion' to both the educated and the poor. From 1891 to 1904 they ran a press which produced their literature, including the English journal *Morning Calm*. By 1910 there were more than five hundred baptised, mostly on Ganghwa Island, but as yet no indigenous ministry (Paik Lak-geoon 1970:87–90; Trollope 1915:26–82; Rutt 1979). Coming from the 'high' church, the Anglican missionaries had little in common with the evangelical missionaries, and they did not join the Mission Council (Gale 1909:238).

In 1891 the Presbyterian missions officially adopted the Three-self (samja) method of church planting as practised by John Ross and formulated for China by John L. Nevius (Nevius 1899; C. Clark 1937:86–96; Grayson 1999). Eventually it was espoused by the six main missions in Korea (see A. Clark 1971:112–21) to varying degrees: the Methodists were less committed to it and the Presbyterians in Pyongyang were the most enthusiastic. It aimed to establish a strong, independent native church which was missionary in its own right and not dependent on the foreign mission. Small congregations would be organised in believers' houses with two or three of the most able in charge. These leaders would be trained under systems of instruction and discipline run by the missionaries and adapted from the Methodist system of Bible classes (Nevius 1899:26–29, 84–86). After several groups of believers were established within walking distance of each other, an individual would be selected as 'superintendent' to exercise pastoral responsibility over this 'circuit' of churches (C. Clark 1937:116–18). These churches would raise all or most of his salary. However, the superintendent was identified as a 'helper' to the missionaries and was responsible to them and not to the churches that paid his salary. The missions therefore continued to exercise strong overall control of the churches in this period and were legally the governing bodies (H. Underwood 1908:110–11). From the missionaries' point of view, the Nevius method saved them money and also relieved them of direct evangelistic and pastoral work (cf. Paik Lak-geoon 1970:219–20, 227, 291–99). Missionaries made annual or biannual visits to the churches to examine candidates brought for baptism and to administer the sacraments but otherwise stayed in their mission compounds where they held Bible schools and training classes and administered mission institutions (Shearer 1965:464–65). From the point of view of Korean Christians, the Nevius method put a heavy financial strain on church members, especially as the Presbyterian mission expected the churches to erect their own buildings, following the example of Sorae Church in 1890 (H. Underwood 1908:108–9; Hunt 1980:77). However, the association of Protestantism with self-reliance was to be a key feature which linked it to later independence and nationalist movements.

The Nevius method also enjoined discipline, and the foreign missionaries had the status to impose on Korean believers high religio-ethical standards (C. Clark 1937:27–28). By the 1890s rigorous conditions for church membership were in place in both Presbyterian and Methodist missions. Probationers had to graduate from the catechumen class and be approved by the missionary before being publically enrolled and instructed for at least a further at least six months. Finally, they were re-examined and then baptised as members of the local congregation (Ryu Dae-young 2008:373–78, 382–85; Paik Lak-geoon 1970:224–25). On examination, candidates were expected to demonstrate that they knew the Bible and basic doctrines, which was also usually a test of literacy; that they had engaged in evangelistic works, for example, by bringing others to church; and that they were regularly observing the Sabbath. They were also expected to show that they had adopted a Christian lifestyle, chiefly defined in the negative and with respect to male predilections: no laziness, no gambling, no involvement with alcohol or drugs and generally no tobacco (T. S. Lee 2010:26–27). Penalties for misbehaviour included admonishment, reprimand, suspension and ultimately excommunication. The insistence on ethical standards strengthened the tendency before the revivals of 1903–1907 to understand Protestantism as a code of ethics, similar to Confucianism, rather than as personal devotion to God (Ryu Dae-young 2008:390).

Church discipline was all the more strongly enforced after an influx of enquirers from the mid-1890s. The missionaries were critical of many practices of Confucian society, particularly ancestor veneration and keeping concubines or, as they referred to it, 'polygamy'. In the first case, in common with general missionary policy in the Far East – Protestant and Catholic – in this period, they viewed ancestor veneration as idolatry, and from the beginning they forbad it for Christians and encouraged them to burn their ancestor tablets. Although this prohibition was certainly a barrier to conversion to Christianity, it was much less so in the late nineteenth century than in the eighteenth because by this time Koreans themselves were critical of Confucianism and seemed to agree that discontinuing ancestor veneration was the only possible position based on the New Testament, even though families could still punish and ostracise converts (Paik Lak-geoon 1970:157–58, 220–26; Kim Myung-hyuk 1988). To address the issues of the divisions this caused in families and the guilt incurred by converts, a Christian substitute for ancestor veneration, commonly known as chudoyebae, emerged among Korean Protestants sometime before 1897 which proved acceptable to the missionaries (Grayson 2007). The second case – concubinage – was not quite as straightforward, especially because international missionary opinion was divided. The Methodists were the first to decide to exclude 'polygamists' in 1895 and other churches followed suit (Ryu Dae-young 2008:387). The missionaries also condemned the superstitious and traditional practices they lumped together as 'shamanism'. Foreign missionaries were less likely to encounter Korean beliefs and practices regarding the spirit world, but it was common practice for Korean evangelists to perform exorcisms on those believed to be possessed by demons based on what they had learnt from the New Testament (Huntley 1984:123–25; C. Clark 1937:112). Over time, however, long-term missionaries also became involved in destroying fetishes, praying over the possessed and condoning the destruction of shrines by Christians; they even began to give credence to Korean beliefs while also insisting that the Holy Spirit was more powerful than any other spirit (Oak Sung-deuk 2010a).

As with Catholicism, Protestantism altered traditional gender relations to raise the status of women. Western missionaries tended to portray Korean women as powerless, nameless and captive, and they campaigned against the injustices done against them (e.g. Baird 1909). However, although single female missionaries offered models of women in public life, most women missionaries – whether single or married – emphasised 'women's work for women' in a way that fitted closely the existing public–private divide of Confucian society (Choi Hyae-weol 2009:25, 177–79). Nevertheless, Korean women who became Christians testified to the social change that conversion wrought (see Huntley 1984:73–80). For a start, in baptism women were given a name and therefore an independent identity. They had a place to go outside the house, and if they were mistreated at home, they had a reason why it was unacceptable and a support network to help them deal with it. Moreover, they were expected to learn to read the Bible, and having become literate, they could read newspapers as well and be introduced to the public world of men (Chou 1995:35–38). Women's education was one of the factors undermining the Confucian order as the women questioned patriarchal patterns and double standards of sexual morality (Choi Hyae-weol 2009:179–82). Protestant Christianity brought women into a new and more powerful network in the church. They took action by campaigning for literacy, starting a temperance movement and demonstrating against the keeping of concubines (Lee Yeon-ok 2011:42–54).

The division between men's and women's worlds allowed the gospel to spread among women unhindered by considerations of public life. Women were the leaders of the local prayer meetings or 'family services' (gajeong yebae) that took place in their homes. Converts testified to other women and brought them into the church. One of the first three women baptised as Protestants, Chun Sam-deok, was reputed to have led six hundred persons to Christ. In addition to helping women missionaries, Korean women began to be employed by the missions as colporteurs (gwonseo) to sell Bibles and Christian literature and as itinerant evangelists (jeondo buin). In this capacity they were educators who read the Bible aloud, taught literacy and travelled considerable distances at great personal risk (Chang Sung-jin 2005). Kim Gang (Dorcas), who became a Methodist Bible woman in 1900 at the age of fifty-two, was given a circuit of 1,450 miles of often mountainous territory. On the road, she was verbally attacked, refused food by local people and once imprisoned (Huntley 1984:126–27). As early as 1898, Presbyterian women of the First Church in Pyongyang organised the first Home Missionary Society and sponsored Bible women to evangelise distant villages (Choi Hyae-weol 2009:71). They were expected to settle in the villages, reach out to local women and draw them into prayer and Bible study groups. In time their husbands would become interested and an institutional church could be founded (Lee Yeon-ok 2011:344–67).

Eventually Bible women were supporting native church leaders, and later pastors, by spearheading educational and community initiatives or even by organising churches that existed without a permanent pastor (Chou 1995:34).

Most Bible women were widows; others were unmarried women over twenty or cast-off wives (Chang Sung-jin 2005:165–70). They had 'considerable power but no acknowledged authority' and no official role (Chou 1995:30–35). In leading others, they drew on the traditional patterns of leadership in Korean society, as well as on what they learnt from their reading of the Bible and from the missionaries' example. In many respects, they occupied the role of shamans in advising, healing and dealing with troublesome spirits (Strawn 2012:126–29). The prayer meetings led by the Bible women were functional substitutes for shamanic ritual, and to those who feared the spirit-world they offered a greater power, the Holy Spirit, to address problems (Huntley 1984:123–25). Like shamans, early Bible women often took on their role after prolonged suffering or 'disease of the spirit' (sinbyeong) (Harvey 1979). The apparent similarity of their trajectory and activity to that of the shamans may also account for some of the abuse that they suffered (Strawn 2012:132–37). After baptismal instruction, Bible women would attend the special Bible schools run by missionaries (Chang Sung-jin 2005:170–76). Then they would become teachers of other women, organising their own courses and schools across the country. Arguably it was Bible women who laid the foundations of women's education in Korea (Chou 1995:37–42).

Before the 1890s Catholic missionaries had generally assisted the Protestant missionaries in Korea, and in 1889 they invited the Protestants to work together in coordinating famine relief in the southern provinces. But there was a growing rivalry between Protestants and Catholics, and there were reports of clashes between the two communities in Seoul. For example, in 1889 a group of Catholics attacked the office of the *Hwangseong Daily*, a Seoul newspaper edited by a Protestant, over what they saw as a story biased against Catholics. In 1894 Catholics complained that Protestants wielding weapons had trespassed on the building site of the cathedral in Myeongdong (Yun Kyeong-no 1996:9–12). In the increasingly unstable political situation of the late nineteenth century, Christians of all kinds were threatened. While the anti-Western Boxer Rebellion in China was underway, Protestant Christians and missionaries were beaten and some churches and mission properties were set on fire (Lim Hee-kuk 2013:61–63). The disenfranchised Catholic gyouchon communities were particularly vulnerable. Catholic priests made use of their extraterritorial powers to protect the poor against local officials and landowners and to help them reclaim rights and property they had lost during persecutions. At least some of the growth of baptisms in this period seems to have been due to a desire to have church support in such disputes or its protection from reprisals (RFKCH 2010:102–5). For Protestants, the Nevius policy included missionary 'non-interference in law suits', which lessened – but did not eradicate – similar abuse of extraterritorial powers (Ryu Dae-young 2003:193–94). From the Catholic point of view, attacks on their community constituted another persecution (MEP 1924:67–68), and they tended to appeal to the French legation for protection. But this expectation of help from a foreign power appeared to the rest of the population to be arrogance and confirmed earlier suspicions about Catholic loyalty. In some places serious clashes over land, extortion and corruption broke out between Catholics and other groups: supporters of Donghak, pro-Japanese groups and sometimes Protestants. Between 1886 and 1905 there were scores of such local disturbances, known as gyoan, across the country (RFKCH 2010:153–68). The most serious incident involving Catholics was in 1901 on Jeju Island, where a small Catholic community and two priests had formed a separate enclave that seemed to consider itself under the protection of France and therefore not accountable to local authority. Catholic condemnation of superstition alienated powerful mudangs on the island, and clashes arose with a local movement against taxation after some of the Catholics took up employment as tax collectors. When several hundred Catholics were killed, two French ships were diverted to the island and afterwards the whole population was required to pay reparations for damages to the Catholic Church, which further heightened resentment against Catholics (IKCH 2011:208–20; Walraven 2009).

Other serious disturbances took place between 1900 and 1903 in Hwanghae province, where Protestantism was well established at Sorae and several other centres, and where in 1896 the MEP priest Joseph Wilhelm had started a very successful work around the Cheonggye area of Sincheon district. The conflict, portrayed in the press as Catholic versus Protestant, was eventually settled by French and US diplomacy but not before whole villages had been attacked and looted (IKCH 2011:221–35; Yun Kyeong-no 1996:12–21). To deal with the gyoan, the government made the Treaty with Catholic Believers (1899), guaranteeing freedom to Catholics to practise their faith, and in 1904 the Missionary Treaty officially permitted Catholic missionaries to travel, buy land and erect churches (IKCH 2011:243–55). When the Protestant Revival started to take hold in Korea from 1905, the conflict with Catholics became doctrinal. Both sides published pamphlets against the other using Reformation rhetoric which can only have come from missionary sources (Yun Kyeong-no 1996:21–33). Catholics especially saw Korea as their mission territory, which they had won by much suffering, and resented the Protestant incursion and their rivals' apparently unlimited funds for evangelism. They complained that Protestants boasted of the power of the United States and misled Koreans into believing that Catholicism was an outmoded religion unknown in America and that all Americans were Protestants (MEP 1924:70). The antagonism and lack of trust between the two forms of Christianity was set to continue as Protestantism became dominant in Korea and increasingly conservative.

THE SINO-JAPANESE WAR (1895) AND THE GROWTH OF CHRISTIANITY

'Peasant activism' was another important factor in the complex situation in Korea in the 1890s (Shin Gi-wook 1996:3). In 1894 agitation by farmers against deteriorating socio-economic conditions and for a government that would 'sustain the nation and provide for the people' erupted into armed rebellion, mainly in Jeolla province (Eckert et al. 1990:218; Robinson 1988:23). Under the influence of Choi Je-u's ideology the movement took on messianic overtones. The Donghak Peasant Revolution precipitated the Sino-Japanese War, which was fought on Korean soil and ended with total Japanese victory in 1895 and the relinquishment by China of any claim to Korea. The Japanese took over the Korean administration and imposed the modernising measures known as the Gabo reforms (Gabo gyeungjang). Among others, these ended the Confucian school and examination system for public office in favour of modern education using Hangul, outlawed some traditional punishments, abolished the social class system, prohibited early marriage, allowed remarriage of widows, deregulated clothing and decreed that men's topknots should be cut off. Many Korean Christians and foreign missionaries applauded the ending of the Confucian system and welcomed the social reforms, which incorporated many changes for which they had been campaigning. Furthermore, they saw the defeat of China as providing an opportunity to advance civilisation in Korea (Yang Hyeon-hye 2009:46–48). But Donghak supporters and many others were outraged by the Japanese intervention. Villagers across the country took it upon themselves to form resistance armies (literally, 'righteous armies'; uibyeong) to protect themselves from the troops and wage guerrilla warfare against them from mountainous regions and remote islands.

To fend off Japan, Queen Min and the government controversially courted the Russians. In 1895, in the midst of a power struggle and with the endorsement of the grand prince and other Korean officials, the queen was assassinated by Japanese agents. While the nation was in a state of shock, at the request of the US ambassador, the missionaries Underwood, Avison and Homer Hulbert stayed with the king to protect his person and smuggled him into the Russian legation. This may have saved his life, and it certainly further enhanced the reputation of the missionaries (Paik Lak-geoon 1970:244–45). The king remained within the legation until a balance of power was agreed on between Russia and Japan; he then re-emerged to proclaim himself emperor of the Great Han Empire, asserting the parity of Korea with the empires of China and Japan. Gojong welcomed back to Korea progressives who had fled into exile after the failed coup of 1884. Many of them had travelled to the West with the help of Protestant missionaries and had become Christians (Wells 1990:47). They included Suh Jae-pil (Philip Jaisohn), the first Korean to gain an MD, and Yun Chi-ho, both of whom had become Methodists. Although their conversions were expressed in personal religious terms, yangban converts understood the Christian message to be one of social transformation and a 'quasi-political doctrine' to rebuild Korea now that its dependence on China and Confucian tradition had been ended (Kim Yong-bock 1981a:113–16; Yi Mahn-yol 2004:43). Progressives tackled Korea's general dependence on foreign powers by espousing 'independence' in the sense of self-reliance as their main aim, and Protestant leaders now saw the desirability, and possibility, of bringing about a modern nation-state without recourse to violence by 'awakening' the people through free speech and educating them about Western values and social responsibility through church, school and press. This Protestant or 'self-reconstruction nationalism' was largely the vision of Yun Chi-ho, who had become convinced that Korea's problems lay primarily with the internal weakness of Korea itself (Wells 1990:viii, 15, 47). He saw Christianity as offering a transcendent power to overcome evil and to inculcate an innate morality, rather than the elite, self-cultivated virtue of Confucianism, which lacked public-spiritedness and failed to recognise the human propensity for evil. Politically, in place of the filial piety of Confucianism Yun advocated the civic morality or public responsibility he saw in Protestant Christianity in the United States. Economically, he promoted capitalism as an extension of the Christian public spirit by investment in industry and public enterprise (Wells 1990:47–70).

Yun organised a highly influential debating society (Hyeopseonghoe) at Paichai school which also attracted government officials, and in 1896 Suh

Jae-pil formed the Independence Club (Dongnip Hyeophoe), the first modern nationalist organisation in Korea, of which Yun became president. The club was organised democratically and soon had branches around the country which were closely connected with Protestant churches (Park Chung-shin 2003:127), especially Methodist ones. At the centre of its activities was *The Independent* (*Dongnip Sinmun*), the first newspaper to be published entirely in 'pure' Hangul, that is, without any Chinese characters, although it was simultaneously published in English with the help of the Trilingual Press. From 1898, Yun took over the editorship. He made the paper, which had a circulation of about three thousand copies, into a daily and gave it a distinctly Christian tone (Wells 1990:57; Yi Mahn-yol 2004:52–61). Some club members, like Rhee Syng-man (Syngman Rhee), later the leader of the Korean Provisional Government in Shanghai and the first president of South Korea, called for political confrontation, but Yun and Suh resisted this.

The Independence Club advocated limited economic and political reforms, some of which the king implemented at first, and members were given government posts. Ironically considering their rejection of sadae, club members favoured US companies for concessions and encouraged Protestant missionaries to found more schools, hospitals and other initiatives. The government eventually suppressed the club in 1898 with the arrest of most of its leaders. Several of these who were not already Protestants converted while they were in gaol, where they were visited by missionaries (Gale 1924:182–84). These converts included Rhee Syng-man, who had already been in contact with Christianity as a student at Paichai school. From prison he produced several publications arguing that Confucianism, which is limited to the ways of humans, is superseded by Christianity, which is God's way, exemplified by Christ, the symbol of love and author of peace. Rhee advanced the theory that the nation should be founded on Christianity, which would ensure freedom and equality (Rhee Syng-man 1993). Rhee's death sentence was commuted and in 1905 he was released. With church sponsorship, he went to the United States, where he earned a doctorate from Princeton University.

The crisis of Korean identity caused by the 'de-centring' of China and dismantling of Confucian structures (Schmid 2002:55–100) attracted many more to Christianity, especially to Protestantism. The Protestant Jesus appeared to be more activist than Buddha (cf. D. Yoo 2010:54), more progressive than Confucius, more powerful than the spirits of traditional religion and more modern than the Catholic Lord of Heaven. On the one hand, elites joined the churches in the hope of bringing about social reform.

On the other hand, as the political circumstances help to explain, ordinary Koreans turned in significant numbers to the Protestant churches between 1894 and 1910, so that by about 1907 these churches had overtaken the Catholic Church in membership (D. Baker 2006b:292). Desperate, fearful and disaffected people were attracted by the preaching about the kingdom of God. As well as practical help, protection and new values, Christianity offered access to power: religious power in the form of the strength to cope in troublesome times, and also the power of knowledge, legal power and the possibility of political power (cf. Paik Lak-geoon 1970:260–62, 356–58). The victory of modernised Japan over Confucian society and over Donghak increased the Korean people's belief that the best future for their nation lay in the Western education offered by Protestant institutions and in adopting the Western values exemplified in the churches (Grayson 2002:158; Paik Lak-geoon 1970:234). Considering the extraterritorial powers of the missionaries and their influential connections, becoming a Christian – of any kind – was an attractive option for those seeking legal help or physical protection. During the Donghak Revolution, McKenzie in Sorae had hoisted the red cross of St George above the church to distinguish it from other places of worship. This quickly became an identifying feature of Protestant churches which indicated divine and missionary protection and also took on associations of millennialism, modernity and nationalism (Oak Sung-deuk 2010b). Furthermore, as events gradually revealed Japan to be the enemy, and not the West, the religion of the Americans became not only less objectionable but even politically attractive. The churches now began to be seen by nationalists as allies and as a means of saving the nation by raising awareness and organising against the Japanese.

Whatever their social class, converts understood the Christian message to be one of social as well as individual transformation, and Protestantism can be said to have contributed to modernisation in a number of ways. First, Protestantism especially emphasised conversion, individual conscience and personal responsibility; Christians were reborn in their personal lives and encouraged to do good and make progress rather than accept the status in life determined by their birth. Furthermore, Presbyterian polity laid foundations for Korean democracy (Wells 1990:85–86). Second, the missionaries challenged the strict hierarchies of Korean society and absolute obedience to a monarch (Wells 1990:85). Christian medical facilities treated both rich and poor. Like the Catholics earlier, Protestants also attempted to liberate butchers before their outcaste status was revoked by the reforms of 1895 (Huntley 1984:66–73; D. Clark 2003:17–18). Third, establishment of schools and promotion of Hangul allowed the illiterate and previously uneducated, including women, to know their culture, history and script, which contributed not only to education but also national pride. In this way, Protestantism 'exerted a tremendous influence on political and educational activities' (Eckert et al. 1990:249). Fourth, the wider education provided by churches, Christian institutions and newspapers imparted Western scientific and technical knowledge, historical consciousness and morality (Yi Mahn-yol 2004:46; Paik Lak-geoon 1970:161–62); encouraged open-ended enquiry rather than the refutation of falsehood which dominated the Confucian academies (Ryu Dae-young 2008:384); led to the breaking down of superstitions and questioning of traditional ceremonies; and developed ideas of human freedom and social justice which led to the growth of a social conscience and movements for the betterment of society (Paik Lak-geoon 1970:161–62; Min Kyoung-bae 1982:241–42).

Since Protestantism now presented itself as a contender for the place in public life left open by the disempowering of Confucianism, in 1894 Korean men began converting in significant numbers and this meant the conversion of entire households. In the village setting, conversion could easily lead to clashes between the convert and traditionalists (T. S. Lee 2010:30–31). Because a man who converted could be persecuted and forced out of the village he had an incentive to gain wider support by interesting others in Christianity. The conversion of an influential man could lead to the conversion of the whole village (Paik Lak-geoon 1970:296–97; Huntley 1984:125). As was true in their practice of other religions, once they converted to Christianity, Koreans demonstrated tremendous loyalty and aimed at mastery of the new religion, becoming in many cases 'ethical-spiritual overachievers' (Ryu Dae-young 2008:385).

Pyeongan province in the north-west and centred on Pyongyang proved especially receptive to the Protestant message, despite the fact that the chains of the unfortunate vessel the *General Sherman* adorned the city's main gate. Presbyterian Christianity grew rapidly in the region in the 1890s, and it was to become the heartland of Korean Protestantism. It is estimated that by 1898 nearly 80 per cent of Korean Presbyterians lived in this province (IKCHS 1989:258). Pyongyang came to be referred to as 'the Jerusalem of the East' because of the number of its churches. Several reasons are advanced for this growth. The first is the example of the Protestant missionaries Rev. Samuel A. Moffett (Presbyterian), his wife, Alice, who was a physician and Dr W. J. Hall (Methodist). They demonstrated their power when they took up residence in the region in 1891 in defiance of the governor and showed Christian compassion during the Sino-Japanese War in tending the injured and dying despite heavy fighting in the area

(Ryu Dae-young 2003:197–98; Paik Lak-geoon 1970:211–12, 255–57; Huntley 1984:117–18). Another explanation is that Pyeongan province was better prepared for such growth because it had had contact with Protestantism longer than anywhere else. Robert Thomas had been killed in Pyongyang, and some of the new converts claimed to have witnessed his martyrdom and showed literature which he had distributed. Places along the old tribute route, which passed through the province, had churches planted by Ross's disciples (A. Clark 1971:61–64; Moffett 2005:545–46). More deep-seated reasons lie in the marginal position the province had held in Joseon Korea. Economically, it lacked arable land compared to the south and so was relatively free of large landowners. Fewer yangban meant poor representation in government, but it also implied that Confucian tradition was relatively weak and that greater religious and social freedom was therefore possible. In Confucianism's place, traditional religion was dominant, giving the region a reputation as backward, immoral and uncouth (Paik Lak-geoon 1970:272). The residents were mostly independent farmers, traders with China and producers of handicrafts (Park Chung-shin 2003:27). These more self-sufficient people enthusiastically embraced the Nevius method which Moffett enforced more rigorously than anyone else. They had the independence to make their own decisions, freedom to travel, economic power to support the church and the kind of entrepreneurship the Nevius method required (Shearer 1965:462–70; Huntley 1984:121–30). For similar reasons, the people of Pyeongan province were well placed to take advantage of the new opportunities brought by industry when, following the Sino-Japanese War, the region became the centre of Japanese industrial development (Wells 1990:139). Missionaries encouraged enterprise in the area as a way of helping Koreans find employment, and nationalist Christians like Yi Seung-hun and Cho Man-sik, looking for ways to strengthen the Korean economy and improve the conditions of the poor, also began commercial enterprises (Moffett 2005:535–36; Wells 1990:138, 148). In this context, the churches functioned as a catalyst in the transition to modernity by introducing modern lifestyles and forms of discipline, systems of organisation and accounting and methods of debating. The growth of Protestant churches also meant a growth in schools, and soon Pyongyang led the way in Western education. Churches formed an element of a new civil society and schools fostered the formation of a new elite who were also networked together. Their education, business interests and political awareness meant that many independence leaders and future national leaders were from Pyeongan province (M. Shin 2011).

The foremost early Presbyterian leader, Gil Seon-ju, was an elder (jangno) of Jangdaehyeon Church in Pyongyang and also the founder of the local branch of the Independence Club. He had been a committed Buddhist of a Taoism-influenced ascetic tradition but after personal tragedy, the loss of most of his sight, and shock at the defeat of China on the Pyongyang battlefield he had turned to Christianity in 1897. A tall, energetic and physically strong figure, Gil carried over into his new religion the holistic, rigorous spirituality he had been used to in the old, and combined it with 'Bible-centred' preaching and the Three-self method to produce a self-reliant, indigenous faith. He had become a Christian after reading *The Pilgrim's Progress* and in 1904 he published his own version of this book, which he called *Haetaron* or *Overcoming Laziness* (Heo Ho-ik 2009b:152–58; Choo 1998:36–41; Wells 1990:173–74). Laziness was a key Japanese and missionary accusation against Koreans, which Gil refuted by exercising daily and by starting the dawn prayer meetings (saebyeok gido) which by 1905 became the established pattern of Korean Protestantism (Heo Ho-ik 2009b:5–13, 135–43). Gil also organised all-night prayer meetings, prayers on the mountains and prayers with fasting, and he campaigned against smoking, drinking and vice as harmful to the nation. Gil preached a strong ethic of sacrificial love and encouraged service and giving. In 1905 he initiated the practice of donating a day for labour in the church (nalyeonbo), which soon became a popular method of giving in a rural economy where cash was hard to come by (Kim In-soo 1997:265–66). He also encouraged the existing practice of women giving to the church by saving a handful of rice daily (ssalyeonbo). Gil argued for the equality of women and men and promoted women's education; he also urged the women's group that met in his church, led by Mrs Lee Sin-haeng, to organise formally in 1898. Soon each local church had its own women's group, and the denominational networks these groups formed became national women's movements (Heo Ho-ik 2009b:102–8).

Although it had dismantled the Confucian education system, the Korean government was slow to implement a replacement to cope with the nation-wide rush for Western education in this period. Instead, missions and churches largely took over the educating role which had been the foundation of Confucian power (Lee Sung-jeon 2009:131; Wells 1990:30, 32). The Bible was the new classical text; Christian theology and Western thinking, which Koreans did not yet distinguish, provided the new philosophy; and the church was the new moral institution. In 1897, the Presbyterians had between twenty and thirty church schools and one boys' secondary school in Seoul run by missionaries. A few years later, in 1902, the Methodist mission reported eleven day-schools for boys and fifteen for girls, and the Paichai secondary school (A. Clark 1971:141). But there was an on-going debate among the missionaries in Korea and elsewhere as to the purpose of mission investment in education. The policy of the Presbyterian missionaries in Korea was not to support general education but to educate Christians as church leaders and as the next generation of teachers. However, there was pressure from mission boards for a more liberal academic approach and generally it was modern curricula that made the schools popular (Huntley 1984:87–96; Sunquist 2009:1–14). The missionaries' main concern was that a Western education too far in advance of their compatriots would lead to Christians becoming foreigners in their own country (Paik Lak-geoon 1970:216). Furthermore, students might be tempted to use their education for their own ends or might acquire knowledge that would challenge the truth of the gospel. Consequently, the missionaries focused the curriculum on the Bible and resisted using critical methods. Similar considerations affected mission decisions about the languages to be used and taught in schools. At first the use of English was necessitated by a shortage of qualified Korean teachers and a lack of Korean text-books but in the longer term the missionaries opted for the vernacular. The use of Hangul made the language of the masses respectable, and so it is credited with contributing to the development of indigenous culture and nationalism; but students at the Presbyterian secondary school complained that they were being held back by not learning English (Robinson 1988:28; Paik Lak-geoon 1970:233–37). The dissatisfaction gave the mission the opportunity to close the school (Huntley 1984:90–91) and instead, in 1897, open Soongsil School in Pyongyang, which was evangelistically focused and where church growth meant there were more students to attend (C. Clark 1937:113–14). The closure left the Methodist institution Paichai as the only Christian secondary school in the capital. In 1902 it too focused the curriculum more on educating future Christian leaders, cancelling its contract to receive government students, despite student protests and a fall in enrolment (Paik Lak-geoon 1970:309–12).

Despite the narrowly based curriculum, the Christian schools did help to meet the demand for education. Even as late as 1907, there were more than twice as many students in church and mission schools than in government institutions. Moreover, the missionaries introduced higher education to Korea, beginning with the medical college and theological seminaries (Huntley 1984:93; Suh Kwang-sun 1986). Since Nevius stressed that church leaders should be educated in the context of their ministry and discouraged them from going abroad for training, Soongsil School eventually developed a strong academic base to rival what was available in Japan. In contrast to the Confucian academies, in which physical work was despised, the curriculum also included industrial skills, physical exercise and student labour to keep the fees down. In 1905 the school and college had 367 students. In 1906 it added tertiary courses, awarding Korea's first degrees in 1908 (Lee Sung-jeon 2009). Eventually, in 1915, the Presbyterians in Seoul, whose approach was not as narrow as those in Pyongyang, opened Joseon Christian College, which offered modern subjects and admitted non-Christian students, in order to reach the elite of the capital (D. Clark 2003:130–33).

The education offered by the Protestants was not only in schools and colleges for young people; they also introduced mass adult education in the form of Bible classes. Thus Protestant churches became centres of literacy. Such was the hunger for education in Korea that, contrary to the Nevius method, the Presbyterian missionaries invited the whole church – not just the leaders – to its special Bible classes, which were modelled on Keswick or Northfield conventions or Chautauqua adult education. Such classes were held for men and women in a district for a period of one to two weeks during the quiet times of the agricultural calendar. The classes were generally attended by hundreds, and sometimes by thousands, of Koreans, some of whom walked more than a hundred miles to get to them (C. Clark 1937:109–12). People came at their own expense and catered for themselves. Meetings took place in the church sanctuaries where, clothed in the white dress of the peasants and leaving their shoes outside, people would sit on the floor in traditional style (C. Clark 1937:149). In addition to prayer meetings and Bible study, classes included discussion of church problems, training in hygiene, instruction in singing hymns and practical exercises such as house-to-house evangelism (Ryu Dae-young 2008:392–93). Besides the general residential Bible classes, there were local classes held in individual churches or homes and special sessions for Bible women and church workers instructing them in pastoral ministry and in how to lead a simplified form of worship. The (male) church workers' courses eventually developed into specialist theological instruction and training for ordination, as the brightest students were identified to become the first clergy (H. Underwood 1908:110–11). Classes started by Moffett in Pyongyang in 1901 had become by 1903 part of a five-year practical curriculum that was approved for ministerial training by the Presbyterian Council in 1905 and named Union Theological Seminary because initially the Methodists were also partners (Paik Lak-geoon 1970:303–8).

The tradition of Bible study and the Bible-examining meetings (sagyeong-hoe) became so much the hallmark of early Korean Protestantism that it was described as 'bible Christianity' (BFBS *Report* 1907:70). Once Korean Christians accepted the Bible as their sacred text, it was reverenced as the authority above others. Students read it in the Confucian manner: aloud, memorising texts and reciting them, and then following its teaching literally in daily ethics, moral conduct and matters of socio-political principle. People accepted the texts as authoritative, without critical evaluation or consideration of their validity in the context of Korea, and such an uncritical reading was encouraged by the conservative missionaries who dominated in Pyongyang and were resistant to critical methods of interpretation. Once they had adopted this biblicist approach, Koreans continued it because they wished to maintain their initial commitment. Any new interpretation had to be measured by the original interpretation as given by the first missionaries, who were treated as apostles (S. C. H. Kim 2008a:130–34; C. Clark 1930:85).

THE STRUGGLE FOR THE NATION AND THE JAPANESE PROTECTORATE (1905)

After the suppression of the Independence Club with its pro-American tendencies, further concessions were given to Japanese and Russian companies. During Russia's pre-eminence, some Korean emigrants to Siberia and Manchuria returned and an Orthodox mission to Korea was authorised by the church in 1897. Missions were established on the Russian side of the Korean border and there were conversions, mainly in Hamgyeong region, but only one priest, Nicolai Alexeyev, was able to enter Korea. In 1900 an Orthodox mission in Seoul was consolidated by the arrival of Archimandrite Chrysanthos Shetkofsky, who celebrated the first official liturgy in a makeshift chapel in the Russian consulate. A permanent church dedicated to St Nicholas was completed in Seoul in 1903 (K. Baker 2006:167–68).

After 1898 Russia's interest in Korea lessened and the power of Japan over the government and people increased. Life for ordinary Koreans became harder as a result of banditry, cholera epidemics, famine in 1900–1902 and Japanese migrants who were in a better position to take advantage of business opportunities. More millenarian movements arose, notably one following Gang Il-sun, also known as Jeungsan (Kim Sung-hae 2008). Some turned to Protestantism because they believed it fulfilled prophesies of *Jeonggamrok*, and they identified Jesus with the deliverer Jeong Do-ryang (Kim Chong-bum 2006:159). Priests helped to ameliorate Catholic poverty by offering education in ceramics, raising silkworms and tending vineyards (Rausch 2008:68). But many desperate Korean families, unable to make a living in Korea, moved abroad temporarily. Some trekked across the mountainous northern border to Manchuria and Siberia, where they braved extreme living conditions and Chinese warlords and eventually transformed a wilderness into productive farmland (Foley 2003:6–10). Among them were Christians and, hearing their need, Canadian Presbyterian missionaries started work in North Gando in 1898. In 1903, with the diplomatic help of Horace Allen, 120 Korean Methodists departed for Hawaii, where George Heber Jones had discovered through the global missionary network that plantation work was available. The new arrivals endured back-breaking labour and basic conditions; however, by 1905, when further migration was forbidden, and with the help of two workers from their church in Korea, the Methodists had established a network across the islands of nine churches accompanied by schools (D. Yoo 2010:8, 35–45; D. Oh 2011:184–85).

When tensions between Japan and Russia escalated into full-scale war in 1904–1905, the Japanese won and ousted the Russians from Korea. In November 1905, Korea was declared a 'protectorate' of Japan, which then occupied it. The Japanese resident-general, Marquis Itō, exercised almost total power over Korean affairs and Western legations were withdrawn. Christian missionaries were among the few Westerners who observed the military crackdown as the country was made an extension of Japan. They reported the seizure of land, looting and abuse but the US government turned a blind eye, having reached an understanding that Japan could colonise Korea – the so-called Taft-Katsura Agreement (Hulbert 1906:213–19; Huntley 1984:147–55). When it was clear that Korea was humiliated, a wave of nationalist fervour was unleashed. However, in Pyongyang, Gil Seon-ju called for repentance of personal sin as the first step towards national recovery. He likened Korea to Israel and, like the Old Testament prophets, preached that the country's sufferings were the result of its own sin and disobedience against God, and he called for prayer meetings for the nation. In Seoul, Jeon Deok-gi led thousands of Christians at Sangdong Church in a week of prayer. A 'Prayer for the Nation' (Wiguk Gidomun), which was to be prayed between 2:00 PM and 4:00 PM each day, was published in the *Daehan Daily*. It called on God as 'King of kings!' to 'Have mercy on Korea and save the nation' and establish it as an independent country by making the people repent and become 'people of the kingdom of heaven' (Rhie and Cho 1997:122; IKCHS 1989:294–95). Many elite Koreans protested the annexation by resigning their government posts, and some committed suicide, including the prominent Christians Cheong Jae-hong, Hong Tae-sun and Yi Gyu-eng. Thousands more flocked to join resistance armies and fight for independence.

Tens of thousands emigrated in this period because they did not wish to live under Japanese rule; most of these emigrants went to Manchuria and Siberia (IKCHS 1989:353). Church communities moved en masse and founded Christian villages as a witness to what a Christian society should be (Wells 1990:82). Yi Sang-seol established Yongjeong, North Gando, in 1906, which became a centre of Korean nationalism; the Presbyterian elders Yi Jong-sik and Yi Gwon-ho established a new Christian town, Gusechon (Salvation Village), in the same year (Kang Wi-jo 1990); and Kim Yak-yeon re-founded Myeongdong Church in North Gando to be a model Christian community (D. Oh 2011:186).

The Catholic Church, under Bishop Mutel and a French-dominated hierarchy, had opposed the growing power of Japan in Korea and in 1904 there was a large Catholic gathering outside the cathedral in Myeongdong to protest Japan's 'cultivate the wasteland' approach to Korean development and to pray for Korean sovereignty (RFKCH 2010:108). But the defeat of Russia destroyed the political basis (the Franco-Russian Alliance) on which the Catholics had asserted themselves and left the church vulnerable. By 1906 Bishop Mutel was supporting the Protectorate as the inevitable result of global politics (MEP 1924:69). That year the church established its first newspaper, the *Kyunghyang Shinmun*, which, until it was shut down in 1910, published in Hangul regular news and information from a Catholic perspective (RFKCH 2010:108–10). It made clear to the Catholic masses that it considered the Japanese government as the lawful and God-ordained authority in Korea. It condemned the resistance armies and argued that Japanese rule would be a civilising influence (D. Baker 1997:142–43). The definitive position taken by the Catholic Church to support the Japanese Protectorate in 1906 ran counter to popular sentiment at the time and this is partly reflected in the church's lower growth rate in 1905–1909 (Rausch 2008:79).

The Protestant missionaries generally refrained from commenting as a body on the political situation and eschewed any involvement. In 1901 the Joint Mission Council of the Presbyterian missions had adopted principles explicitly intended to avoid church entanglement with the state and politics (Rhie Deok-joo 2001:46) and the General Council of Evangelical Missions, formed in 1905, focused instead on the opportunities in Korea for mission work (e.g. L. Underwood 1918:234–36) and cooperation with the Japanese (Wells 1990:35–36; Hutchison 1987:72). Missionaries and Korean church leaders were fearful for the future of the church if it became a vehicle for political insurrection (Paik Lak-geoon 1970:369, 416; Yi Mahn-yol 2004:64). They disciplined anyone found to be involved in nationalism, and the Methodist youth group, the Epworth League, was disbanded in 1905 because of fear that it was being used as a resistance organisation (T. S. Lee 2010:34; Huntley 1984:155–56). Another reason the General Council avoided taking a clear stance regarding the Protectorate was that the missionaries themselves were divided about it. A few hard-liners blamed Koreans for bringing this calamity on themselves (e.g. Gale 1909:34), but most were sympathetic to Koreans. However, they were convinced that Korea was not yet ready to govern itself and, since the West was not prepared to take responsibility for it, they saw a Japanese empire in the East as the next best hope for peace, for a just administration and for modern development, and certainly as preferable to Russian rule (e.g. WMC 1910:51; cf. Ryu Dae-young 2008:396–97). The mission boards gave strategic priority to Christianising Japan hoping that its empire would then become a vehicle of evangelisation (A. Brown 1919:660; WMC 1910:66–67).

Nevertheless, despite their avowed neutrality in politics and refusal to support armed insurrection, Protestant churches and schools were perceived as pro-nationalist and implicitly encouraged Korean nationalism in several ways (Min Kyoung-bae 1996:122). First, they used the Korean vernacular and encouraged self-reliance. Second, they symbolised an alternative modernisation as represented in the Western-style hymns they sang and in their choice of a hybrid Korean-Western or simple Gothic architectural style for their churches and institutions as opposed to the classical or modernist style of Japanese public buildings (Lim Hee-kuk 2013:73–84). Third, their Three-self policy and educational work stimulated a 'patriotic and pro-independence attitude', and the missions' non-elitist approach mobilised the whole church (Yi Mahn-yol 2004:52; Kim In-soo 1996:49–52). Fourth, the General Council brought the churches together and became a national forum and soon a lobbying group on behalf of Koreans in their dealings with the Japanese. Fifth, Protestant churches, schools and Bible classes were also 'training agencies for activists' and offered leadership skills for the 'new intellectual class' (Park Chung-shin 2003:123–26; Suh Kwang-sun 1986:15). Finally, sixth, the political elite were attracted to Christianity. Although the missionaries targeted the masses, they saw the importance of the conversion of national leaders and also reached out to young leaders, so that most nationalist leaders had some form of Christian background (cf. Park Chung-shin 2003:128). Many Koreans saw the Protestant churches as part of the struggle for self-reliance, modernisation and Korean language and culture, and this is one of the main reasons for the rapid Protestant growth in this period (Suh Kwang-sun 1986). Now even the more traditional of Korean officials were prepared to join, seeking reform and Western education and even using church networks to coordinate political activism or to protest US policy (T. S. Lee 2010:32–33; Choi Young-keun 2010:138).

Although missionaries on the ground in Korea were troubled by the instances of arrogance and mistreatment they witnessed by Japanese towards Koreans, they tended to put them down to undesirable elements among the Japanese rather than to government policy. On such occasions, they generally took the side of the Korean people and appealed on their behalf to the administration, believing that it at least was just (Rhie Deok-joo 2001:48; H. Underwood 1908:35–36). But some Protestant missionaries became close to the nationalists (Min Kyoung-bae 1996:122; cf. D. Baker 2006b:294–95). For example, President Theodore Roosevelt replaced Allen in 1905 because he was too anti-Japanese (A. Brown 1919:501). A handful of missionaries actively supported the patriots against the Japanese. The most active and vocal was Homer Hulbert, who documented instances of Japanese abuse towards Koreans, siding with the latter and, although not free from colonial attitudes himself, began to see the Koreans rather than the Japanese as the hope for the region (Hulbert 1906:7–8, 213–19; Schmid 2010:7–23). Hulbert had been in Korea since 1886 and was known especially for editing the *Korean Repository* and the *Korea Review*, which disseminated information about Korea in English. He was close to the emperor Gojong at whose request Hulbert undertook a secret mission – together with Yi Jun, a keen Methodist, and two others – to the peace conference at The Hague in 1907 which ended the Russo-Japanese War. But since Japan was a participant, they were denied admission and all they could do was make speeches outside the conference hall.

The Japanese administration behaved with caution towards the missionaries, tried to appease and reassure them and even succeeded in persuading some that the Japanese and the West shared a common 'spiritual' goal of the 'uplift' and 'redemption' of Koreans (Kang Man-gil 2005:157; Rhie Deok-joo 2001:44–45; Schmid 2010:7–23). This was not only because the United States and Japan were now allies or because Japan was sensitive to international opinion, but it was also because the missionaries wielded power in Korea, especially in view of their control of most higher education in the nation and their extraterritorial rights (Lee Sung-jeon 2009; Wells 1990:32–33). The Japanese feared that Protestant institutions were a front for patriotic activity and in 1905 were already criticising them as nationalistic (Min Kyoung-bae 1996:122; Yi Mahn-yol 2004:67–69; D. Clark 2007; Kang Wi-jo 2006:97).

THE REVIVAL (1903–1907) AND THE RESISTANCE

The famous Korean Revival of 1903–1907 was part of a global phenomenon of revivals in the late nineteenth and early twentieth centuries arising from the Holiness movement and spread through missionary networks, which are also seen today as giving rise to Pentecostalism and charismatic forms of Christianity (Anderson 2004a:136–39). Most of the missionaries were products of a revivalistic faith and emotional conversions, and they prayed and encouraged Koreans towards the same experiences (Ryu Dae-young 2008:393; Huntley 1984:131). Some were affected by the new wave of revivals which focused on 'fullness of the Spirit' or 'baptism in the Spirit', and a few months before the Pyongyang revival, Christians in Korea were told about the revivals in Wales in 1904 and in the Khasi Hills in India in 1905 (T. S. Lee 2010:14–18, 24–27). But although belonging to a global movement, the Korean Revival should also be understood as a response to the national crisis of the early twentieth century. In this context, Western missionaries and Korean church leaders tried to direct church members' attention to 'spiritual matters' rather than to a political struggle which they foresaw would inevitably end in Japan's favour (Min Kyoung-bae 2008:44–62). This was partly to protect the church against becoming embroiled in politics and to make it clear that the church was a religious and not a nationalist organisation (Choi Young-keun 2010:139). It was also because some saw revival as a 'golden opportunity' to turn Christians' attention 'from the national situation to their own personal relation with the Master' and to encourage them to repent, even of their hatred of the Japanese (Blair and Hunt 1977:67; Paik Lak-geoon 1970:369, 416). The analogy between Korea and ancient Israel was used to encourage Christians to believe that God would rescue them in his own time and that they could overcome the Japanese by religious means. Missionaries even pointed out that the very name 'Joseon' (especially in the Japanese romanisation Chōsen) was similar to the English word 'chosen', confirming that Koreans were elected for a special salvific purpose (Pak Ung-kyu 2005:157–59).

The early part of the revival centred on the treaty port of Wonsan and the Methodist churches in the triangle from there to Songdo and Seoul. The catalyst was the confession of Dr R. A. Hardie, a medical missionary of the Southern Methodist Mission (Paik Lak-geoon 1970:283–84). This sparked a series of daily meetings for prayer at which Koreans confessed their sins in unison, while kneeling and bowing to the floor. Praying aloud simultaneously (tongseong gido), a type of prayer also reported from the revivals in

Wales and India, was characteristic of these events from 1903 (L. Underwood 1918:224; T. S. Lee 2010:14; C. Clark 1937:149). In the next year, Hardie and Korean Christians from Wonsan, including Jeon Gye-eun and Jeong Chun-su, spoke at meetings arranged in other parts of the country, including Songdo, Seoul, Incheon, Pyongyang, Hamheung and Mokpo (IKCHS 1989:269). Participants prayed for baptism of the Holy Spirit and fire. On some of these occasions there were outbreaks of emotional or ecstatic behaviour (Ryu Dong-sik 2005a:257–61; Huntley 1984:131–32; T. S. Lee 2010:15). In late 1905, in the aftermath of the Japanese annexation, the General Council issued a nationwide call for 'a Special Effort' to bring about revival. In Pyongyang in particular, from the latter part of 1906, Gil Seon-ju led his congregation at Jangdaehyeon Church in early-morning prayer about the crisis in the country and for revival. They expressed the hope that a revival would break out during the two weeks of the Bible study classes scheduled for the winter in Pyongyang when leaders from all over the country would attend (Kim In-Soo 1997: 246–47).

In January 1907, one thousand five hundred mainly white-clad Korean men filled with great expectation arrived in Pyongyang for their annual Bible classes. Jangdaehyeon Church was so full that the women had to meet elsewhere. Morning prayers, daytime classes and evening meetings were led by Gil and by missionaries, mainly William Blair and Graham Lee, who called on everyone to confess their sins. On one evening, men broke down, wept and threw themselves on the floor, beating it with their fists. Some followed this demonstration by making restitution to their neighbours, and both missionaries and Koreans confessed their sins against one another. In language clearly influenced by the biblical Pentecost account, the Pyongyang Synod record states that in January 1907: 'When the Holy Spirit came, one person started crying aloud and confessing his sins and others joined in. In the evening as missionary Graham Lee was leading the service, there was the presence of a strong wind and then eventually the Holy Spirit descended. All people in the hall cried aloud and confessed their sins. The sound of confession could not be distinguished from the sound of crying' (Rhie Deok-joo 2001:110–11, our translation; cf. Blair and Hunt 1977:71–75).

At Pyongyang's Union Theological College, Methodist students joined in the revival which had erupted among the Presbyterians and it spread from there to the Methodist churches in the city that had initially been antagonistic to such events. After the meetings ended, students and visitors returning to their home villages began to hold prayer meetings and women's meetings and schools also experienced revivals. From February to June of

1907 revival leaders travelled around the country facilitating a nationwide confession of sin and experience of the fullness of the Spirit (Paik Lak-geoon 1970:372; Huntley 1984:136–37; Rhie Deok-joo 2001:116–33). It did not stop at the borders of Korea. In May, Christians in Manchuria heard of it and sent a delegation to Pyongyang to investigate. After they returned in 1908, revival spread to Manchuria and other parts of China (Ryu Dae-young 2008:371–98; Gale 1909:201–23, 245) (Fig. 5).

For Koreans, the revival became a cathartic opportunity to pour out their distress and panic at what had befallen their country but it also had a wider significance for four main reasons. First, because of it the church became distinctively Korean. This was 'the Korean Pentecost' which in many respects formed the Korean church and its devotional practices (Blair and Hunt 1977; cf. Paik Lak-geoon 1970:374–75). The Korean Revival was the confluence of the missionary evangelical tradition with the Korean hope for the salvation of the nation which moulded the Korean church into a national religion (Choi Young-keun 2010:145; Ryu Dae-young 2008). Second, the revival captured something of the spirit of the times and connected with Korean culture in a way other religions and Catholicism at that time could not; this gave Protestantism a popular appeal. Through the revival, Protestantism was revealed not only as an intellectual and social reform movement but also as a religious one (Min Kyoung-bae 1996:130; Paik Lak-geoon 1970:367–78; Ryu Dong-sik 2000:416; Wells 1990:44–45). The language of the Old Testament and gospels appealed to Korean villagers, and Protestant use of the vernacular facilitated continuity with popular belief. Furthermore, the spirituality of the revival connected with traditional cultural forms such as communal singing, daily patterns of prayer, ecstatic prayer and asceticism (Paik Lak-geoon 1970:367–78, 420–21; Grayson 2002:158). The nationalist Christian writer Choi Nam-seon later argued that it was natural for Koreans to embrace Protestant Christianity, and from this time onwards, revival meetings became a regular feature (Park Chung-shin 2003:14). Third, the revival brought Koreans from different backgrounds together. Heart-felt religion for personal salvation did not exist among the Confucian elite, but the revivals enabled a 'crossover' with Koreans from backgrounds in Buddhism, traditional religion and new religious movements (Wells 1990:25–26, 35–37). Those who were worried about emotionalism were reassured, especially by the statistic that there was a hundredfold increase in colporteurs' Bible and book sales compared to 1905 (C. Clark 1937:149; Paik Lak-geoon 1970: 374–77). In this respect, Christianity was a unifying force for the nation, embracing within one movement what had previously been separated into different

5. Gil Seon-ju and church members in front of Jangdaehyeon Church in Pyongyang during the 1907 revival. The Institute of Korean Christian History.

religions and philosophies in Korea (Min Kyoung-bae 1996:130). The revival dispelled any perception that religion somehow differed for Westerners and Asians, and it contributed to the confidence of the missionaries in Korean leadership and to the building of genuinely reciprocal relations (Huntley 1984:132–38; Paik Lak-geoon 1970:376; Ryu Dae-young 2008:393–95). Fourth, even if spirituality and confession were 'ostensibly limited to immoral acts', personal repentance and righteousness were connected theologically to national calamity and the struggle for justice (Suh Kwang-sun 1986:11). The revival encouraged a hope in heaven that was natural in the circumstances. However, for Koreans, heaven was the restoration of the nation within the coming of the kingdom of God (Wells 1990:38–39). Although it depoliticised the church as institution, the Korean Revival linked it with nationalism because it 'sanctified the nation' even more than it brought about the 'nationalization of Christianity' (Choi Young-keun 2010:131–32, 140–45; T. S. Lee 2010:36; Wells 1990:21).

Lack of institutional support from the churches had not deterred Christians from leading patriotic activities. The YMCA, founded in Seoul in 1903 by the Christian leaders Yi Sang-jae, Rhee Syng-man and Namgung

Eok together with missionaries (Nahm 1989:211), was also a centre of political activism and soon became a rallying point for nationalist sentiment. Protestants got up a petition against the Protectorate, refused to pay taxes, and held demonstrations in Seoul and other cities at which they distributed memorials to the people and delivered patriotic addresses. Ahn Chang-ho (Dosan) and other former members of the Independence Club who had become Christians in exile returned to the crisis in Korea in 1907 and revived the 'Korean Enlightenment' through 'self-cultivation' or 'self-strengthening' (suyang) and other self-help and self-improvement organisations, many calling for conversion to Christianity. In many cases, the returnees brought with them the encouragement and financial support of overseas Korean churches.

Although the Korean Revival had a certain unifying effect in holding together spiritual, ethical and cultural forms of nationalism, its rejection of violence was not shared by all nationalist Christians. Ahn Chang-ho had moved to the United States in 1902 in search of education; there he founded the San Francisco Korean Methodist Church and also several societies to develop, and to speak for the interests of, the small immigrant community (D. Oh 2011:184–85). The United Korean Association formed by Ahn in 1905 produced a newspaper – *Sinhan Minbo* – which circulated widely and had a much larger readership in Korea, where the Korean press was censored, than it did locally (Schmid 2002:248). Like other patriotic Christians, Ahn called for national repentance and the building of a Christian civilisation. He emphasised self-reform by a combination of discipline and the inspiration of divine love, which for him was self-denying love rather than the altruism of Yun Chi-ho. Although he took a long-term view and emphasised the building up of education and expertise, Ahn was also a revolutionary who refused to compromise with the Japanese and did not renounce armed struggle (J. Pak 2006; 122; Wells 1990:90–92, 121–26). He actually assaulted Samuel Moffett and Graham Lee in the street in Pyongyang for distracting believers from the nation's political woes (T. S. Lee 2010:166). In the same year as the revival, Ahn founded the Sinminhoe (New People's Association), a secret revolutionary body that linked together patriotic leaders in Korea, mostly Christians, with those in the United States (J. Pak 2006:133). It aimed to 'reconstruct a strong nation' by mobilising people to resist Japan, although members were divided over whether this was to be by education or by arms (Wells 1990:83; IKCHS 1989:295–302). It was based in Sangdong Methodist Church in Seoul, where Jeon Deok-gi was sympathetic (Park Chung-shin 2003:130–31).

Six months after the revival, in July 1907, there was further national humiliation when Emperor Gojong was forced to abdicate in favour of his son Sunjong. The resistance armies were strengthened after the regular Korean army was forcibly disbanded, and there was widespread insurrection for two or three years which was only ended by brutal suppression. The fact that Japanese action included crucifixions of Korean rebels indicated that they saw significant Christian involvement in the armies. Korean church leaders struggled to keep patriotic Christians from taking up arms. Gil Seon-ju resisted on the one hand any accommodation with Japan and on the other a request from King Gojong to mobilise Christians to resist the aggression (Kim In-soo 1996:115–16). He called for restraint on both sides, and he and other pastors in the north-west negotiated with the resistance armies to get them to lay down their arms (Wells 1990:36, 43). Gil was credited in missionary reports in 1908 with preventing the level of violence experienced in the south and even with avoiding revolution in Korea (A. Brown 1919:559; Wells 1990:42–43). But he and other Korean leaders were also threatened as 'traitors'. Many patriots left the church in protest, and there was a danger of Christians becoming the enemies of the resistance (Blair and Hunt 1977:61–65).

Although the mission-led churches eschewed any official involvement with patriotic causes and also rejected violence as a solution to Korea's problems, they did encourage other forms of patriotic activity. After the Protectorate was declared, there was another surge in the desire for Western education as a means of patriotic nationalist resistance (Eckert et al. 1990:247, 249). As a result of public pressure, Bishop Mutel encouraged general education in Catholic schools from 1905. By involving lay Catholics as well, the schools rapidly expanded from just 739 students in 1906 to 3,048 students in 1910; these included ten schools for girls (Rausch 2008:78–79; RFKCH 2010:92). Both Catholic and Protestant schools were inundated, and returning patriots founded private schools, often with funding from overseas Christians, as a way to continue their aims when open political activity had become almost impossible (Paik Lak-geoon 1970:391; Lee Ki-baik 1984:331). Yun Chi-ho had been vice-minister for foreign affairs at the time when Korea was forced to sign the Protectorate Treaty. After this he resigned and turned to educational work. In 1906 he founded an industrial college (Hanyeong Seowon in Songdo – now Kaeseong), a type of educational institution that was emulated by many others. He also began to develop a vision of a Christian settlement, somewhat like a mission station, with good quality housing and model farms attached. In 1907 the Sinminhoe founded a private secondary school, Daeseong in Pyongyang, with Yun Chi-ho as principal. Yi Dong-hwi founded about a hundred schools, beginning on Ganghwa Island, and Yi Seung-hun, a Presbyterian businessman, started Osan School in 1910 (IKCHS 1989:292–302).

Another initiative was to collect money to pay off the Korean national debt, which was mostly payable to Japan, hoping in this way to gain financial independence. This mainly Christian campaign was started in early 1907 by Kim Gwang-je, the president of a printing company, and his vice-president, Suh Sang-don (Augustine), a Catholic. The campaign was promoted by the Catholic *Kyunghyang Shinmun* and also by the *Daehan Daily*, edited by a Protestant, Yang Gi-tak. Much of the fund-raising activity was led by church women. Both Protestant and Catholic women's groups organised rice collections, and they enjoined men to refrain from smoking and drinking for three months and donate the money saved (IKCHS 1989:349–50; RFKCH 2010:108–10).

In a further expression of patriotism, individual Christians were associated with high-profile assassinations and attempted assassinations in this period. In 1908, Durham White Stevens, a pro-Japanese US advisor on foreign affairs to the Korean government, was killed in San Francisco as a result of actions by Jang In-hwan, a Protestant, and Jeon Myeong-un, a Catholic. The men were members of two different Korean-American church-related independence groups in the Bay Area. The details are confused, but it seems they both acted independently to kill Stevens. Jeon, who had been baptised in Korea before moving to the United States, was acquitted and remained a firm Catholic and patriot (D. Baker 1997:145). But the Protestant churches were heavily involved in responding to the fall-out from the event and supported the trial of Jang (D. Yoo 2010:94).

In the most well-known assassination case in 1909, Ahn Jung-geun (Thomas), a Catholic, killed the former Japanese resident-general Itō Hirobumi at the railway station in Harbin (then in Russia). Ahn had been baptised at the age of eighteen by Father Wilhelm in Hwanghae province and was a convinced Catholic active in evangelisation and educational work (IKCHS 1989:340; Rausch 2008:78–79). But when he suggested that Catholic scholars be brought from France to found a university, Bishop Mutel, for whom universities were associated with modernism, refused. Ahn's shock and anger at this response seems to have contributed to his decision to fight the Japanese (Rausch 2008:69–76). He joined a resistance army in North Gando and there met Woo Yeon-jun, a Protestant, who plotted with him. The Catholic Church in the area rejected Ahn's request for help with his plan, but the Protestant Myeongdong Church provided him with space for gun practice. Ahn continued to make confession and

6. Ahn Jung-geun giving his last words to his two younger brothers and Father Joseph Wilhelm while Japanese officials look on, 1910. Ahn Jung-geun Memorial Hall.

receive communion up to his arrest. During his imprisonment and trial, he expressed his firm belief that the assassination was the will of God because, he said, to do nothing when someone is plundering your house is also a sin (IKCHS 1989:338). Among others, Korean Methodists in Hawaii gave money for his defence (Murabayashi 2004) (Fig. 6). But as Ahn awaited execution in 1910, Mutel denied that he was a Christian and refused him the last rites; he punished Father Wilhelm when he administered them anyway (D. Baker 1997:144).

THE INDIGENISATION OF PROTESTANTISM

The Protestant movement encouraged self-cultivation or self-strengthening forms of nationalism by its Three-self approach and also contributed to ethnic nationalism by the choice of Haneunim/Hananim as the name for God. While Catholics continued to pray to Cheonju, ordinary Protestants – following Ross's translation of the Bible – called God by the indigenous term. The translation committee of missionaries, which represented all the Protestant missions and also the Anglicans, agonised with their Korean colleagues about these and other possible terms for God for more than a decade (Paik Lak-geoon 1970:254–55, 346; D. Baker 2002:118–19). They were eventually persuaded to use Haneunim/Hananim – except the Anglican representative, who continued to prefer Cheonju for reasons of relations with the Catholics. They made this decision not only because Haneunim/Hananim was a popular and indigenous term and equivalent to the Chinese Protestant term Sangje but also because they were persuaded by an argument that it was actually derived from 'hana' and 'nim' – 'One Lord' – and therefore represented a primitive Korean monotheism. Furthermore, they believed this made Korea 'unique' among nations in that God had revealed himself to the ancient Koreans, as he had done to the people of Israel (H. Underwood 1910:246; Oak Sung-deuk 2001). This discovery or 'invention' of indigenous Korean belief in one God allowed foreign missionaries and Korean Christians to take an affirmative approach to Korean tradition and to see Christianity as its fulfilment (D. Baker 2002:105; Oak Sung-deuk 2009). The leading example of this was Choi Byeung-hyeun (Taksa), who was the first successor to Appenzeller as minister of Chungdong Methodist Church and a professor at the Methodist theological seminary. He recounted a discourse between a Christian young person and a Confucian scholar, a Buddhist monk and a Taoist leader which supposedly took place over three days in a mountain-side pavilion. Its result was that all three non-Christians came to believe in Christ (Ryu Dong-sik 2000:64–67).

This theological development was paralleled in nationalist thought. In 1908 the nationalist and historian Shin Chae-ho offered a new reading of Korean history which defined the nation not in terms of the ruler or the territory but as the people (minjok) who were the descendants of the progenitor Dangun (Shin Gi-wook 2006:4–8, 41–42; Schmid 2002:175–88). Shin's genealogy of the nation functioned to bind together the people, including the growing Korean diaspora communities, and during the colonial period nationalism founded on Dangun became a great bulwark of national identity (Shin Gi-wook 2006:1–4). Although Shin and others advanced the Dangun myth as a historical theory, the record that Dangun was descended from heaven and the spiritual definition of the nation also added religious dimensions to belief in Dangun. In 1909, Na Cheol established a new religion, Daejonggyo, which worshipped Dangun and 'Haneulnim' and was supported by Korean intellectuals, including Shin (Schmid 2002:192–97). In this context, the fact that Protestants were also worshipping Haneunim/Hananim made Protestantism appear to be a revival of traditional Korean religion as well as a route to modernisation.

The Nevius method envisaged self-government for mission churches at the earliest opportunity. The Presbyterians ordained Korean elders from 1900 who took charge of churches under a missionary. In 1901 the Joint Presbyterian Council began to admit Korean members, who gradually began to enact more measures under the supervision of the missionaries, and from 1903 missionaries began training Korean clergy with a view to setting up an independent Korean church in 1907. In 1901 the Methodists ordained two deacons – Kim Chang-sik and Kim Gi-beom – who could fulfil most of the tasks of a minister except for presiding at communion (Paik Lak-geoon 1970:306; Moffett 2005:540). Kim Chang-sik played a key role in the opening up of Pyongyang, where he was imprisoned and almost killed, and is credited with founding 125 churches before he retired in 1924 (Lim Hee-kuk 2013:132–35). From 1905 the General Council of Evangelical Missions considered an ambitious plan to establish 'one Protestant Christian Church' in Korea which would include both Presbyterian and Methodist churches. In this spirit they transferred members between churches as part of regularising the comity plan. But such ecumenism was resisted by the home mission boards and some missionaries (Rhie Deok-joo 2001:41–42; Ryu Dae-young 2008:376; Kim In-soo 1996:80).

Another difficulty in forming one national church was that while Protestantism was chiefly represented in public life by the Presbyterians and Methodists, a number of other Protestant churches entered Korea at around the turn of the century. The Baptist churches in Korea were founded by missions from North America. Malcolm C. Fenwick arrived from Canada in 1889 and first worked in Sorae. As a result of support he raised in the United States, two couples and two single women arrived in 1895 and worked independently in Chungcheong province until 1900. After that Fenwick, who was by then based in Wonsan, assumed oversight of all the Baptist churches (cf. A. Clark 1971:288–89). The Korean Seventh Day Adventist Church was founded when in 1904 a Korean emigrant en route to Hawaii through Japan, Son Heung-jo, met Adventists there, aborted his journey and became a member. He returned to Korea as an evangelist in Jinnanpo and Yonggang, where he was joined by a Japanese evangelist and a US missionary in 1905. Two Koreans in Japan, Jeong Bin and Kim Sang-jun, who had graduated from the Tokyo Bible Institute of the Oriental Missionary Society (OMS), returned to Seoul in 1907 to bring to the existing churches the 'full' or 'pure' gospel (sunbogeom) according to the fourfold doctrine of the Holiness movement. They founded Gyeungseong Mission Hall in Seoul, and other graduates founded Jinnampo OMS church in 1908 and Kaesong church in 1909. The OMS sent John Thomas from Britain as bishop in 1910 and established their own Bible training school in 1911. The first Korean pastors were ordained in 1914 and the church expanded rapidly. In 1921 the work became the Korean OMS-Holiness Church (Choi Mee-saeng 2008). Salvation Army missionaries arrived in Seoul in 1908 and immediately began their military-style worship on the street, causing some to think they were another armed group against the Japanese and attracting large numbers of converts (Paik Lak-geoon 1970:409–10). None of these groups was party to the comity agreement made by the Presbyterians and Methodists, and this was a source of friction at times.

Since no agreement could be reached on a united church, the National Presbyterian Church of Korea was established on 17 September 1907 in Pyongyang in the presence of thirty-eight missionaries and forty Korean elders. The Confession adopted for the new church was based on that of the Presbyterian Church of India and this, together with the Westminster Confession, defined its doctrines. A Korean synod was formed, although Underwood was retained as its moderator. The ceremony was followed by the ordination of the first seven pastors (moksa). These were Gil Seon-ju, Suh Kyeong-jo, Han Seok-jin, Song In-seo, Yang Jeon-baik, Pang Ki-chang and Yi Gi-pung. The new church was centred not on Seoul but on Pyongyang, where most of the Protestants were concentrated (A. Clark 1971:138–40, 172–73). Gil became senior pastor of Jangdaehyeon Church, the largest in Korea, with a congregation of two thousand five hundred. As well as pastors and elders, others held non-ordained positions as jipsa (deacon) and jeondosa (evangelist or trainee pastor). In 1908, Gil baptised 201 people in the first baptism ceremony ever led by a Korean pastor; he also encouraged a truly national church as reflected in the use of Korean music, drama, art and architecture. In this way the nation, although stateless, was at least partially realised in the Presbyterian Church (Kim In-soo 1996:116–24). However, the other Korean pastors served under Western missionaries and were able to exercise less leadership. The Methodists were not able to form a nationally organised church at this point, but in 1908 churches founded by the Methodist Episcopal Church (North) established their own annual conference, giving them a measure of self-government. When the National Presbyterian Church was formed, the Methodists pulled out of Union Theological Seminary and re-opened their own seminary, Hyupsung (Hyeopseong), in Seodaemun, Seoul, which graduated its first students, including Jeon Deok-gi, in 1911 (Ryu Dong-sik 2005a:232, 292–94).

Korean church growth, the Korean Revival and the establishment of an indigenous Presbyterian Church raised a distinctive profile for Korean

Protestantism among other churches worldwide. News of the revival, as well as of political events, was spread by foreign correspondents and mission executives, and the attention of the Christian world was briefly fixed on Korea (cf. Paik Lak-geoon 1970:269, 364–66). Events brought world mission leaders to see for themselves, including John R. Mott, secretary of the Student Volunteer Movement, in 1907. In his extensive travels around the world preparing for the World Missionary Conference in Edinburgh in 1910, Mott held up Korea as an example of the transforming power of Christianity socially as well as spiritually (Mott 1910:5–7). He stressed Korean Christians' commitment to Bible study, prayer, giving, evangelism and missions, and reckoned that the midweek prayer meeting in Pyongyang was 'possibly the largest meeting for united intercession . . . anywhere in the world' (Mott 1910:88). At the Edinburgh conference, the rapid Christianisation of Korea was described as 'one of the marvels of modern history' (WMC 1910:71). It was thought that Korea might best exemplify the Student Volunteer Movement watchword and achieve 'the complete evangelisation of the nation within this present generation' (WMC 1910:80). This view was confirmed by Yun Chi-ho, who attended the conference as one of the small number of invited representatives of the 'native churches' (WMC 1910:36–37).

The recognition of the new Korean church as a member of the world church motivated Koreans to become involved not only in evangelising Korea but also in pastoring the Korean diaspora and in world evangelisation (C. Clark 1937:146). The first meeting of the Korean Presbyterian Church established the Board of Foreign Missions and commissioned Reverend Yi Gi-pung to go to Jeju Island, where no Presbyterian missionary work had yet been established and which, though a part of Korea, could be considered 'overseas'. The first unmarried woman missionary, Yi Seon-kwang, was similarly sent to work on Jeju Island (in 1908) by the Presbyterian women of Pyongyang (Lee Yeon-ok 2011:43–47). She was the first of 164 Bible women sent abroad in the period up to 1945 (Choi Hyae-weol 2009:72). The first recorded church worker to the diaspora was the evangelist Ju Sang-do from the Pyongyang Committee on Missions, who was sent to Manchuria in 1901. Methodists sent evangelists with the migrants to Hawaii from 1903, and when in 1908 a group of Koreans migrated to the Yucatán peninsula in Mexico, missionaries were sent there too (C. Clark 1937:154–55). In 1909, Choi Kwan-heul, a Presbyterian pastor, was selected to begin work among the Koreans near Vladivostok. Another pastor, Han Seok-jin, was sent by the Presbyterian Church to work with the Joseon YMCA in Tokyo, which had been founded in 1906. He established a joint

Presbyterian-Methodist church which led to the formation of the Korean Christian Church in Japan (Park Heon-wook 1995:48–49; Yang Hyeon-hye 2009:224–40). In 1911, Son Jeong-do became the first Methodist pastor sent to Manchuria, where he established a work in Harbin (Ryu Dong-sik 2005a:383–84).

Not only did the newly independent Presbyterian Church send workers to support diaspora communities, but wishing to demonstrate that it was mature like the Western churches, it also determined to send missionaries to non-Korean peoples. In 1913 a cross-cultural mission was begun by commissioning Park Tae-ro, Sa Byeong-sun and Kim Yeong-hun to work in Shandong province in China. There, although serving under the Chinese presbytery, the Koreans steadfastly applied Korean methods, and so successful were they in growing the church that the Chinese presbytery turned further territory over to them. The mission included medical work with Korean doctors, as well as well-attended Bible classes and revival meetings attracting thousands. The first official woman Presbyterian missionary, Kim Sun-ho, was sent to join the Shandong mission in 1931 (Lee Yeon-ok 2011:67–69), by which time, despite the disruption caused by the Communist insurgency, there were more than a thousand baptised and the churches were largely self-supporting and self-propagating (C. Clark 1937:229–36; Choi Young-woong 2002).

By 1910 Protestant numbers stood at about one per cent of the Korean population, a figure that was much larger than that in China or Japan in the same period and about the same as in India, which had a much longer Christian history (Latourette 1944:428–30). A number of different explanations have been advanced for this statistic. Some literature gives most of the credit to the missionaries, especially the pioneers (Ryu Dae-young 2008:377; Shearer 1965:462–70, 468). Certainly, the Protestant missionaries attained a high stature in late nineteenth-century Korea and were invested with authority. This was partly due to their wealth and the extraterritorial powers they enjoyed together with other foreigners plus their special social status as associates of the royal family (Kim In-soo 1996:54–58). But it was also partly because they presented themselves as teachers and scholars, they represented Christianity as a teaching (gyo) and they stressed the importance of the Bible and other literature. This accorded them the respect that Koreans afforded to scholars and scholarship, especially when there were ancient texts involved. In practice their status gave them wider latitude to disseminate their principles and more power to impose them than was usual in other mission fields (Ryu Dae-young 2008).

Some emphasise the importance of the establishment of mission institutions, especially medical and educational ones, and missionary campaigns on social issues. These engendered the good will of the people and gained the support of the authorities in an otherwise hostile environment (e.g. Paik Lak-geoon 1970). But compared to other fields, such as in China, there was relatively little investment in Korea in institutions or staff (Park Chung-shin 2003:14–15). Others give more credit to early missionary policies, such as the decisions to prioritise the evangelisation of the common people and to use the medium of Hangul, without which Christianity could not have become a popular movement (Suh Kwang-sun 1986:10). The adoption by Ross of Haneunim/Hananim and its eventual ratification by the American missionaries were also significant for the rapid inculturation of Christianity, and other affinities between the Protestant gospel and Korean religions have also been pointed out which may explain the speed with which Koreans adopted Protestant Christianity (Palmer 1967; D. Chung 2001). Church-growth theorists have argued that the application of the Nevius method was from the beginning the main reason for the numerical growth of the church and particularly for the superior growth of the Presbyterians in Pyongyang who, led by Moffett, adopted it most rigorously (C. Clark 1937:73, 84; Moffett 2005:536, 539, 551). But attributing success to institutions, inculturation and the Three-self method is another way of saying that Koreans themselves grew the Korean church. Its spread owed most to the witness of faithful believers, courageous leadership and the labours of colporteurs and Bible women, and to the efforts of believers who multiplied churches, schools and hospitals around the country (Paik Lak-geoon 1970:420–44; Grayson 2002:158). Moreover, the rapid growth for which the Korean Protestant churches are famed began only after 1894 (Moffett 2005:536–37; Park Chung-shin 2003:23; IKCHS 1989:254). This suggests that the receptiveness to change produced by the rapidly evolving social and political situation of the 1890s and early 1900s was a more significant factor in pushing or pulling people towards Protestant churches. In the final analysis, neither missionary policies nor religio-cultural affinities nor socio-political circumstances can fully explain the growth of Christianity. Koreans must have wanted it. They 'found it fundamentally fitting to their morality and temperament and reshaped it with their own aspirations' (Ryu Dae-young 2008:398).

CHAPTER 4

Oppression, Resistance and Millennial
Hope, 1910–1945

The Japanese occupation of Korea, which began de facto in 1905 with the Protectorate, was formalised in 1910 by the annexation which brought the formal end of Korean sovereignty and of the Yi dynasty. The country became an 'outer territory' or extension of Japan. By this time the resistance armies had been driven into Manchuria and the Russian Maritime Provinces, and such was the Japanese stranglehold within Korea that military resistance was impossible. The size and powers of the Japanese military police had been increased, and these police now subjected Korea to 'a reign of terror' (Nahm 1989:219; cf. Kang Man-gil 2005:149, 158). Koreans felt humiliated and were also mystified by how Japan, whose earlier development had come from Korea, could now have such power over them (Ham Sok-hon 1985). During its occupation of Korea, which lasted until 1945, Japanese policy evolved and changed, and it had a significant influence on church life (Kang Wi-jo 2006).

Despite the dire political situation, the General Council of Evangelical Missions in Korea decided in 1910 to follow up the revival, which was intended to deepen faith, with an organised nationwide campaign targeting non-Christians. It aimed to reach 'A Million Souls for Christ This Year' and openly took advantage of this moment of 'supreme national hopelessness' to proselytise (T. S. Lee 2010:23–24; Paik Lak-geoon 1970:385; A. Clark 1971:185). The Bible Societies printed a million copies of the gospel of Mark, and revivalists from the United States were pressed into service. Christian adherents, who were estimated at only two hundred thousand believers, gave approximately one hundred thousand days of work to the campaign. Meetings were widely advertised, tracts were distributed systematically and house-to-house visits were made (A. Brown 1919:545). This movement inaugurated the pattern of revivalism that was to become characteristic of the Korean church (Paik Lak-geoon 1970:385–87, 413). But, not surprisingly, these activities antagonised the Japanese authorities, who were suspicious that this was some kind of revolutionary movement, and they intimidated those involved. Uniformed military police, along with spies, attended the special church services, and pastors were required to report to the police the names of converts, who were sometimes then threatened and harassed. The infiltrators found plenty of reasons to read revolutionary motives into revival preaching from the hymns such as 'Onward, Christian Soldiers!' and the sermons on topics such as the liberation of Israel in Egypt, little David's besting of the huge, armoured Goliath and the captivity of God's people by the Babylonian Empire. Above all, the topics of the kingdom of Heaven and the expectation of the Messiah were construed as threatening to the Japanese empire (cf. A. Brown 1919:569–71; Park Chung-shin 2003:61–65, 131–32). Given these conditions, it was not surprising that the Million movement did not match the hopes for it, even if the figure of a million was an aspirational rather than a realistic target.

CHURCHES AND SCHOOLS UNDER JAPANESE OPPRESSION, 1910–1919

The Japanese governor-general had almost complete power over Korea, which, like a 'prison camp', was guarded by military police. Even the Japanese public servants and teachers wore swords (Cynn 1920:114–17). The Japanese authorities penetrated deeply into Korean society through a highly centralised system of bureaucracy which carried surveillance to village level (Cumings 2005:152–53). Economically, they increased their exploitation of the commercial potential of their new territory and made Korea a granary for Japan. The Land Survey (1912) dispossessed many Korean peasants and further concentrated ownership in the hands of large landowners, both Japanese and Korean (Kang Man-gil 2005:98–100). The Japanese proclaimed a policy of 'assimilation' on the grounds of what they regarded as close ethnic and cultural affinities, but since at the same time they instituted racist policies in employment and education, the policy amounted to 'replacement' of the Korean elite by their modern Japanese counterparts (Wells 1990:72–81). There was an active campaign to suppress the Korean language, discredit Korea's cultural heritage and insert Korean history into a Japanese version of events to justify Japan's right to rule Korea. Freedom of expression for Koreans was almost eliminated as all Korean newspapers, magazines and journals were banned and a system of censorship was introduced (Eckert et al. 1990:262).

During the first decade of colonial rule, the government-general prohibited all social and political organisations except for the religions, which they intended to use to support colonial policy if possible (Kang Man-gil

2005:155–58). The supremacy of Confucianism was already ended but the Japanese valued its moral influence so they pursued a conciliatory and protective policy towards it. Because of its shared history, Buddhism was seen as useful for the process of assimilation and as a counter to the influence of Protestantism (Grayson 2002:184). As part of the Gabo reforms, Buddhist monks had been readmitted to Seoul, and in 1915 a temple was established in the city (A. Brown 1919:334–35). But Korean Buddhism was simultaneously pressured to conform to Japanese practices, and in 1935 it was forced to unify under Japanese control (Mitchell 2008:264–66). The Japanese looked down on shamanic practices but shamanism was so pervasive that they tolerated it. However, they regarded indigenous Korean religions as fronts for nationalism. They immediately suppressed Daejonggyo and other smaller sects dedicated to Dangun, but Cheondogyo (Chondogyo) – the religious successor to the Donghak movement – survived because it had adopted a modernising stance in this period and briefly formed an alliance with the Japanese (Kang Wi-jo 1987:45–80). Christianity had a contentious history in Japan (Mullins 1995:70–73), and its links with Japan's rivals for control in Korea probably made political persecution of the churches inevitable. From the 1880s and 1890s, Japanese scholars had exploited the tensions between Western philosophy and Christian theology. This enabled them to criticise Christianity and thus oppose the West – whether Russian, British or American – but without rejecting the sociological and technological systems of Western imperialism (Paramore 2009:109).

For all the churches linked to foreign governments, an immediate effect of the Japanese annexation was that foreign missionaries lost the extraterritorial rights they had previously enjoyed. Protestantism and Catholicism were classified together as one in a general category of religions (A. Brown 1919:629–31). Otherwise, the churches fared differently. The Catholic Church, which depended on France, had already declined in power since the defeat of its ally Russia. Its foreign leadership preferred not to confront the administration but to seek peace for the freedom and flourishing of the church, and Catholic activities did not appear as threatening as Protestant ones or attract the same attention from the police (Kim Nyung 1993:217; D. Clark 1986:11–12). The Anglican Church in Korea, which was officially constituted in 1910 and held its first synod in 1916, benefited until the early 1920s from the Anglo-Japanese alliance. The fine Romanesque-style Cathedral Church of St Mary the Virgin and St Nicholas was dedicated in 1926. Bishop Mark Napier Trollope, who served from 1911 to 1930, was an oriental scholar of note and oversaw the completion of a polished Korean liturgy (Whelan 1960:160). St Michael's College for training catechists and clergy was started on Ganghwa Island in 1914 (Trollope 1915:90). In 1915, Kim Hui-jun (Mark), the first convert, was ordained as the first Korean priest and the Korean priesthood gradually expanded into the 1930s. In 1925 a convent of the Society of the Holy Cross with Korean as well as English sisters was founded to work among the disadvantaged (IMC 1932:30). The Orthodox Church was supported after 1910 by the church in Japan, while the Russian Church, under pressure from Communists at home, formally relinquished its jurisdiction over Korea in 1921. By 1914 the Orthodox Church had grown to three thousand five hundred converts in nine mission stations. Kang Han-tak (John) and Kim Hui-jun (Luke) were ordained deacon respectively in 1911 and 1913 and priest in 1922 and 1924 (K. Baker 2006:167–68, 189; Latourette 1944:428; Pozdnyaev 2012:209–348).

The mission boards of the leading Presbyterian and Methodist denominations, whose government recognised Japanese authority in the region, officially welcomed the annexation. The newly independent Presbyterian Church of Korea deliberated until 1912 before opting for 'loyal recognition' of Japanese rule and voting to exclude from responsible positions in the church those who did not share that view (Kang Wi-jo 1987:15; Rhie Deok-joo 2001:38; T. S. Lee 2010:34). But despite its diminished political power, mainstream Protestant Christianity (Presbyterian and Methodist) continued to pose a threat to the Japanese project in Korea for several reasons: first, because most Christians resisted Japanisation. The churches were active in promoting an alternative development agenda for the nation through self-reconstruction, nationalism and expansionist policies of evangelisation (cf. Wells 1990:71–77, 85). Second, the churches represented a different source of authority, and in the Pyongyang region particularly, they amounted almost to an alternative state (Lee Sung-jeon 2009; Wells 1990:32–33). The Presbyterian mission station was an extensive Western enclave – probably 'the most conspicuous ... on the peninsula' – which included a college (Soongsil), several schools and workshops, a seminary, Bible institutes, a hospital and a church, as well as spacious missionary houses (D. Clark 2003:121–25). Through their schools, Christians were promoting – with foreign mission help – a Western-oriented ideology which the Japanese regarded as incompatible with their rule. Third, the churches constituted the largest organised Korean community, or communities. Although no militarists were now being reported in church congregations, Protestant churches and their associated institutions provided a safe place for patriots to carry out their activities and potentially mobilise against the Japanese (Wells 1990:84; Park Chung-shin 2003:132; Kang Wi-jo 1987:15). Fourth, the churches continued to invite foreign missionaries who, even though they accepted the annexation, had links with the world church and influence with foreign governments (cf. Suh Kwang-sun 1986:14). Although the Protestant churches were dangerous for the colonial government because of their public and international profile, it hesitated to move against them but instead created difficulties for their operations (Park Chung-shin 2003:129–34). Korean Christians and foreigners were subjected to harassment, such as being required to take down their red cross flag, and bureaucracy (cf. D. Clark 2003:43–44). The smaller and less well-connected Protestant churches – Salvation Army, OMS-Holiness and Baptist – tended to be harassed the most, because they had less influential foreign connections and they were more likely to engage in unauthorised public preaching and singing with anti-authoritarian and millennial messages (A. Clark 1971:238–39).

The government-general was careful at this stage not to express disrespect for Christianity as a religion but tried to win over missionaries and Korean church leaders and at the same time to drive a wedge between them (cf. F. Brown 1916:619). So while he entertained the missionaries, gave gifts to Christian work and praised the missionaries' efforts to 'uplift' Koreans, to Koreans (and to pro-Japanese missionaries) the governor-general suggested that the problem with Christianity was the power that conservative missionaries held over Korean churches and the anti-Japanese attitudes of some US missionaries (A. Brown 1919:559, 629–31). The Japanese also blamed the missionaries for the disunity of the Korean church and urged Koreans to unite and preach their own 'oriental Christianity' (Welch 1922:358). Christian churches in Japan generally supported the effort to claim Korea. Towards Koreans they adopted the same rhetoric as their government about Japan bringing 'spiritual salvation' to Korea. The Japanese authorities encouraged them to expand into the peninsula and to assimilate Korean denominations into theirs (Wells 1990:74–75). The largest Protestant church in Japan, the Japanese Congregational Church, sent missionaries to Korea from 1903. As early as 1911, through the Japanese YMCA, selected Korean Protestant pastors were invited to visit Japan and its churches and were pressured to bring their own churches under the Japanese denomination. By 1917 the Japanese church had twelve thousand Korean members in 143 congregations, mostly led by Korean ministers who had separated from the mainline churches (Yang Hyeon-hye 2009:52–54; Wells 1990:74–75). In 1905 the Japanese Methodist Church was established in Seoul with the encouragement of Merriman Colbert Harris, who was bishop in both nations and strongly pro-Japanese. However, the Japan Presbyterian Church kept its distance and was even critical of colonial policies (Park Heon-wook 1995:53).

In addition to winning over Christians, the Japanese regime also tried to discredit them in the public eye. In late 1911 several hundred men, mostly Christians, were detained across the country, including leaders of the Sinminhoe, which was the main target of the operation. The authorities announced that they had uncovered a plot to assassinate Governor-General Terauchi by Ahn Myeong-geun, a cousin of Itō's assassin (Wells 1990:75–78; Kang Wi-jo 2006:98–101). Ahn, also a devoted Catholic, had been raising money for resistance activities in China. He was arrested in January 1911 following information passed by Bishop Mutel (Choi Seok-u 1996:153; IKCHS 1989:352–53). One hundred and twenty-three men were remanded for trial, and in February 1912 Yun Chi-ho, who had refused to join the Japanese government-general, was charged with masterminding the plot. At their trial in 1912, which was known in Korean as the 105-man Incident and in English as the Conspiracy Case or Trial, almost all of the indicted men complained of torture; three had already died. The charges against them were obviously fabricated, and their eventual confessions were plainly ridiculous. There was no jury and no evidence was given by witnesses. On the strength of signed confessions, one hundred and five were convicted of treason and sentenced to between five and ten years in gaol. Of these, ninety-two were Protestants, mostly Presbyterians. They included Gil Seon-ju's eldest son Gil Jin-hyeong, and Jeon Dok-gi, the pastor of Sangdong Methodist Church. Two others were Catholics: Yi Gi-dang and Ahn Seong-je (IKCHS 1989:308–23). Although none was arrested or charged, Western missionaries were accused of encouraging the plotters, which united them in protest against the trial to the Japanese government and also caused an international reaction (A. Clark 1971:188). Under pressure from the United States and other nations, appeals were heard in 1913. The convictions were not over-turned, but the sentences of the main figures were reduced and the remaining ninety-nine were freed. The Conspiracy Trial was a disaster for Japanese public relations and revealed to even the more naïve among Western Christians the injustice of the Japanese occupation of Korea. Rather than discrediting Christianity, the inclusion of missionaries among the accused also contributed towards restoring their relationships with Christian nation-alists and to the development of Christian nationalism.

In prison, Yun Chi-ho became more convinced that only religious renewal and practical education could help Korean independence. In a speech to the YMCA in Seoul on his release in 1915, he encouraged the nation to reject violence and pursue self-cultivation and perseverance. But Yun's self-development nationalist discourse was now becoming problematic; its pre-mise that Korea needed development was easily co-opted by the Japanese to support their colonial project since, after the annexation, the development of Korea could only benefit Japan (Schmid 2002:101–3; Robinson 1988:36). In the search for national identity, a religious alternative to self-reconstruction nationalism began to emerge as Christians read their Bibles in the context of Japanese rule. The leading Presbyterian, Gil Seon-ju, preached especially in this period on the story of the Exodus from Egypt and frequently compared the Korean people to Israel suffering under the pharaoh and expecting their delivery (Kim In-soo 1996:113, 116). These parallels naturally led to messianism and the expectation that God would deliver the Korean people into the promised land not metaphorically but literally in history (Wells 1990:89, 95–97, 170; Suh Kwang-sun 1981:22). So despite the dire political situation, Christians continued to hold out hope of national salvation (Min Kyoung-bae 1996:134).

After the initial excitement of the first revival and the fearful period of the annexation and the Conspiracy Trial, Protestant church life settled down to regular patterns of worship, prayer meetings, Bible study and revival meetings. Although the baptised population of the two main Protestant denominations continued to increase from 1910 to 1919, the number attending church actually declined (Wells 1990:82, 87–88; T. S. Lee 2010:32) in what was described as a 'consolidation' of Korean Christianity (Welch 1922:351). The drop in congregations was largely seen as the result of a loss in the attractiveness of Christianity to those who were politically motivated. Other factors suggested included emigration, the greater pressure of business on people's time and a greater critical ability among Koreans which challenged the authority of the church (A. Brown 1919:545–47), although these did not seem to affect the Catholic Church. Nevertheless, despite the lower growth rate, by 1920 the Protestant population had doubled to nearly 2 per cent of the population. There were twenty-eight mission hospitals, seven hundred to eight hundred primary schools and three thousand three hundred Sunday schools for children and youth. Although the standard of these schools and the level of education of their teachers were often low, it was estimated that about nine-tenths of the Protestant community could read and write. The leaders of the two main missions observed that Korean Christians exhibited huge self-development in comparison to other sections of Korean society and by the standards expected by Western missionaries of the time, which were 'cleanliness, health, intelligence, alertness, progressiveness' and morality (Welch 1922:356–58). They described high levels of religious devotion: church attendance, Sabbath observance, Bible study, giving, prayer and work for the church. Foreign support for the missions was increasing but the amount of money contributed by the Korean churches was growing faster. In the Presbyterian churches especially, levels of giving by Korean Christians outstripped global comparisons and amazed observers, as did the fact that, owing to the Nevius method, hardly any Koreans were employed by the missions. It was said that no other Christians in the world knew their Bibles better. The churches had a vibrant prayer life which encompassed personal prayer, dawn and midweek prayer meetings, weeks of corporate prayer and impromptu prayer meetings held in inns, in prisons, at the roadside and on mountains. Worship was stirring, with lusty congregational singing. Christians were highly committed to the evangelisation of Korea and even to overseas mission. Korea was likened to a 'modern Holy Land', and the success of the Protestant churches may be judged by reports that Buddhists were imitating Christian evangelistic methods, organisations and institutions (Welch 1922:357–59; A. Brown 1919:330–32, 525–36; F. Brown 1916:621). This imitation included recording the numbers of their adherents. Most Koreans, however, were not members of any organized religion, although they probably engaged in indigenous and Confucian religious practices.

Another distinctive feature of the Korean mission field was the level of cooperation between the Presbyterian and Methodist churches and, as the Japanese grip tightened, with other Protestants as well. The two denominations jointly operated Severance Hospital and Medical College, cooperated to run the YMCA and worked together in Bible translation and evangelism (A. Clark 1971:112–14). Furthermore, the Korean Revival had encouraged new initiatives such as the joint publication of Sunday school literature, a union hymnbook (1908) and a journal, the *Korea Mission Field* (Paik Lak-geoon 1970:378–82; Welch 1922:355–58; A. Brown 1919:539–52). In 1912 the General Council of Missions was replaced by the Federal Council of Protestant Missions, which included the YMCA, the Bible Societies and other ecumenical organisations, after the pattern established by the International Missionary Council (IMC). From 1918 the Korean Church Federal Council brought together the Korean leaders of the two churches especially for its dealings with the regime. In 1924 both the mission and church bodies joined in forming the Korean National Christian Council, which became the Korea National Church Council in 1931; it was dissolved in 1937.

Sunday schools were growing rapidly, especially among adults who could not get an education any other way and among children whose elementary schools closed because of Japanese regulations. The ecumenical Korean Sunday School Association was established in 1912. In 1916 the membership was more than 177,000 (F. Brown 1916). The Christian Literature Society published the weekly Sunday school lessons and the hymnbook, and its publications increased tenfold in the period. The complete Bible prepared by the translation committee with the support of the Bible Societies was published in 1911 and immediately sold out. In 1915 sales of the Korean Bible reached 825,000, the highest for a single field in the whole history of the British and Foreign Bible Society, higher even than in much larger fields such as India and China (Welch 1922:354–55). This suggests that the Bible was reaching and was valued by a much larger population than those who attended church. At the same time, the Bible Christianity of Korea was also the main area of concern to some commentators who were worried that believers took the Bible too 'literally' and interpreted it 'simplistically', resulting in a theology that was 'primitive', 'black and white', 'legalistic' and 'inherently conservative' (Paik Lak-geoon 1970:425–27; D. Chung 2001:78). New mission ventures in this decade included the first community in Korea for sufferers from Hansen's disease (leprosy), which was founded in 1910 by the Australian Presbyterian missionary Rev. James Noble Mackenzie on Ulreung Island near Busan, and the first of many Salvation Army homes for boys in 1918 (A. Clark 1971:279–80, 286–87; Brown 2009:310–12). Such charitable initiatives were lauded by the Japanese as what they considered appropriate for missionary work.

Catholic growth continued steadily. In 1909 the Benedictines of St Ottilien in Bavaria established a community in Seoul, which became an abbey in 1913. These were the first priests in Korea who lived a religious life in community, and they offered a new model of spirituality. The Benedictine mission also started a school for training in various trades and set up a press which published books on catechesis, liturgy and theology (Rausch 2008:68–69). In 1911 a second vicariate apostolic with a second seminary was created at Daegu, where the Sisters of St Paul de Chartres had been working (RFKCH 2010:108–10, 116). However, Japanese policies began to cause problems for the established patterns of church life, first because they often required labour on Sundays (A. Brown 1919:578). In 1915 the regime put legal and other obstacles in the way of evangelism through an ordinance under which permission was needed to open a new church or employ paid workers (A. Brown 1919:580). As the decade wore on, through 'espionage upon church services, the multiplication of required reports', 'delays and annoyances by local officials' and more blatant discrimination against Christians, the Japanese occupiers' bias against Christianity and relative favour towards Buddhism and Shintoism became more apparent. So did criticism by Japanese officials of Christians' ignorance and stress on church growth (Welch 1922:343).

Education had a central place in the project of Japanese nationalism, so it is not surprising that this was the field in which the Japanese most vigorously pursued their policy of making Korea a permanent colony and that it became the focus of conflict between Christians and the Japanese authorities (Kang Man-gil 2005:150). In Japan, the Imperial Rescript on Education was also the basis of public morality and was itself invested with a spiritual power. The government and Shinto priests insisted on the veneration of the scroll in schools and in public ceremonies (Hardacre 1989:108–9). The refusal of a Christian teacher, Uchimura Kanzō, to pay homage to it had led to a huge controversy in Japan that was framed as a conflict between religion and education and resulted in the subjection of religious organisations to the ideology of the state (Paramore 2009:107–44; Vanderbilt 2009:61–66). This background explains why in Korea as early as 1906 the Japanese established government control of textbooks and the curriculum in public schools and from 1908 required all private schools to obtain a license and to provide an annual report (Kang Man-gil 2005:10). After the annexation, the Japanese began to build hundreds of their own schools in Korea with public funds (Wells 1990:82). Initially, these schools, although finely appointed and without fees, were much less popular than the Christian ones which offered a curriculum in Korean (Paik Lak-geoon 1970:407; A. Brown 1919:587). But the Japanese soon set about undermining the Christian schools. In 1911 the colonial government announced its intention to use education to create 'loyal and good subjects' of the emperor. This was to be done in the Japanese language medium but to a lower academic level than Japanese students received (Eckert et al. 1990:262–63). As a result, tertiary-level courses at Soongsil and Ewha Colleges were abolished and requests to establish new colleges, including a Benedictine teacher-training college, were denied (Kang Man-gil 2005:151–52; Rausch 2008:68–69).

The Japanese continued to be concerned about Christian schools' association with nationalism and promotion of Korean culture. In particular, Yun Chi-ho's (Methodist) Hanyeong College and Yi Seung-hun's (Presbyterian) Osan College were attracting large numbers of motivated students (Park Jae-soon 2000:140). Under its principal Cho Man-sik, a Presbyterian and a follower of Gandhi, Osan educated many future national leaders within an ethos of self-reliance and mental, moral and physical training. In 1915 the authorities claimed to have discovered links between several Christian schools, including Osan, and military training camps in Manchuria and North America. Known Christian nationalist leaders were arrested again. However, Christian educational institutions continued to be strongholds of nationalism. In 1917 a branch of the Korean National Association

(Daehan Gukminhoe), which had been formed by Ahn Chang-ho, Rhee Syng-man and others overseas, was established in Korea. It emphasised military strength to realise 'Korea for the Koreans' and drew students mainly from Pyongyang Presbyterian Seminary, Soongsil College and Yeonhui Special School in Seoul (Wells 1990:78, 82–83).

In 1915 a further measure was proposed to de-register all private schools not following the curriculum laid down by the government and require all teachers to use only Japanese within the classroom. Another major consequence of this ordinance for Christian schools was that religious instruction would be excluded from the curriculum (Kang Wi-jo 2006:101–2). The missionary community was divided about how to respond (A. Clark 1971:191–94; Wells 1990:80). A ten-year transition period was negotiated on the basis of which most mission institutions made concessions and were re-registered (Lee Sung-jeon 2009). However, the majority of Christian schools were not run by the missions but were elementary schools maintained by local village churches. For these schools the problems of compliance were much greater, especially since Japanese-speaking teachers were expensive to employ. The crisis for the Christian schools was compounded by the demand in the same year that they follow the prescribed ceremonies on days when the emperor offered sacrifices at Shinto shrines. These involved bowing to a portrait of the emperor, which the Protestants regarded as an idolatrous act. They accused the government of breaking its own rules about religious observance in schools. But Christians had little choice but to go along with these practices (Wells 1990:81; A. Brown 1919:555, 601–2).

The peak years of emigration were 1910–1919, mostly northwards to Manchuria and Siberia but also to Japan and China. Nationalists were worried that Koreans in diaspora (Hanin) would lose their national identity in foreign lands, but with the help of church workers sent out from Korea, these communities set up Korean schools, newspapers, cultural activities and political organisations which supported the homeland (Schmid 2002:224–40; Kang Man-gil 2005:162–65). In particular, church services and church schools taught the next generation the Korean language and nurtured the culture; the church notices became important means of sharing information about global political developments and events in Korea; and the collection expressed the reciprocal relations of the diaspora and the mother church. Nationalist fears proved unfounded because Christians abroad tended to see themselves as exiles, like the Israelites in Babylon, and envisaged a return to Korea when independence was achieved. This parallel also provided the conceptual link between the diaspora community and the nation (Wells 1990:89, 94–96; David K.Yoo 2012:104). Before long, as the Japanese policy of assimilation took hold at home, Koreans abroad began to claim that, far from losing their identity, it was they who preserved true Korean-ness. Theologically they portrayed themselves as the true nation, the faithful remnant untainted by collaboration and compromise that would one day return and 'restore the kingdom'. Nationalist leaders were in exile in several different countries and the political response to the Japanese was now being worked out in exile as much as at home, although there were pronounced differences among exiles over the means to independence (Schmid 2002:20, 240–52; Wells 1990:89, 97).

By 1910 there were more than one hundred thousand Koreans in Manchuria, and about half that number was also settled in the Maritime Provinces of Siberia. Many thousands more were to join them, and in 1921 a Korean presbytery independent of the Chinese churches was established in northeast China. After the annexation, migrants were more likely to be politically motivated and many went deliberately to join the resistance armies which had now been pushed north out of the peninsula. These included many Christians, including Catholics such as Kim Sang-tae who had fought in the area of Gyeongsang province (Foley 2003:9–14; IKCHS 1989: 353–56; Wells 1990:89–90; RFKCH 2010:108). Church communities gave them shelter, some Western missionaries in China protected them from the Japanese authorities and the networks of Christian colporteurs enabled underground communication. Christians and nationalists were inseparable, and the Japanese suppression of Korean nationalists often destroyed Christian villages (Kang Wi-jo 1990). Not all migrants went north. Japan continued to be a place of exile and further study for the better off when conditions in Korea became too difficult. Several Korean Protestant churches in Japan were led by exiled nationalists at different times. The YMCA in Tokyo received newly arrived students and urged them to 'build a new Korea' by cultivating self-reliance, real strength and civic responsibility, and many were also influenced this way by the Japanese democratisation movement that began in 1915 (Wells 1990:89–94). Christians in Hawaii and the United States raised financial support for nationalists and worked through church agencies and diplomatically to support Korean independence. For much of this period, Rhee Syng-man was resident in Hawaii and organised nationalist activities there but he returned to Korea in 1910 as dean of the academic arm of the YMCA. With the help of missionaries, he avoided capture in the 1912 Conspiracy Case but fled to the United States and claimed asylum there, where he wrote *The Persecution of the Korean Church* (1913). In 1915, Rhee and his supporters left the Korean Methodist Church in Hawaii and started an independent church with a strongly nationalist agenda (D. Yoo 2010:58–82).

CHRISTIAN NATIONALISM AND THE MARCH 1ST INDEPENDENCE MOVEMENT, 1919

After more than a decade of Japanese rule beginning with the Protectorate, Koreans had built up many grievances. In addition to their loss of sovereignty, they faced ill-treatment at the hands of the Japanese police, discrimination in education and the workplace, restriction of religious and other freedoms, exploitation of their resources and persons, and dispossession of their property or tenancy. This pent-up oppression was soon to erupt in the most significant and widespread protest during the thirty-five years of annexation. The March 1st Independence Movement (Samil Undong) was mainly organised by students, educators and religious leaders in Korea encouraged by nationalists abroad, and Christians were among the main instigators.

The movement erupted in the period of global social change generated by the Bolshevik Revolution in Russia and the restructuring of Europe after the Great War. It was also inspired by Mahatma Gandhi's satyagraha (non-violent resistance) campaigns in India and influenced by what became the May 4th movement in China. The most immediate cause was US President Woodrow Wilson's 'Fourteen Points' speech in January 1918, which promised the right of self-determination to colonised peoples (Park Heon-wook 1995:53; Cynn 1920:16; Choi Anne-soon 2008). With the Korean press in Japanese hands, these developments were mediated to Korea mainly through the growing émigré network. Nationalists in China, in the United States and in Korea itself tried to send representatives to Paris to make the case for Korean independence at the Peace Conference which concluded the First World War. Kim Gyu-sik, an elder of Saemoonan Church who was sent by nationalists in Shanghai, actually arrived in Paris but was not allowed to present the Korean case. The expatriate nationalists also sent agents into Korea to raise support and to encourage a simultaneous demonstration to show that Koreans were dissatisfied with Japanese rule and wanted independence. Gil Seon-ju, Yi Seung-hun, and other church leaders agreed to arrange a peaceful event based in Pyongyang (Kim In-soo 1996:161). Church leaders in Seoul also joined in, and Park Hui-do, the YMCA youth secretary, began to mobilise Christian youth. But while these preparations were underway, activists of Cheondogyo approached Christian leaders asking them to participate in a nationwide demonstration they had been planning (Min Kyoung-bae 1996:126–27). Among the Christians approached, Yun Chi-ho declined to participate in a popular uprising and Park Hui-do was reluctant to cooperate with another religion, but Yi Seung-hun and others offered to gather Christian support for cooperation and Gil Seon-ju endorsed the plan provided it was non-violent (Wells 1990:107; Yi Mahn-yol 2007:37–86; Ra Dong-kwang 1987:74–78; Kim In-soo 1996:161–62). A further motivation to protest arose when the former emperor Gojong died on 21 January 1919, and it was suspected that he had been poisoned by the authorities (Kang Wi-jo 1987:77). In other developments, on 1 February 1919, assistant Presbyterian pastor Yeo Un-hyeong and other activists declared Korean independence in China, and on 8 February Korean students in Tokyo demonstrated outside the YMCA building where they read a declaration drafted by Yi Kwang-su (Kang Man-gil 2005:26–27). These events excited an intensely nationalistic atmosphere in Korea, and large crowds were expected in Seoul for several days around Gojong's funeral, which was planned for early March (IKCHS 1990:26).

The writer Choi Nam-seon drafted the Declaration of Independence (Doknip Seoneonseo) for the occasion. It declared the identity and right to self-determination of the Korean people, referring to five thousand years of Korean history (since Dangun) but otherwise using modern secular language of human equality. It was signed by thirty-three religious leaders: sixteen Protestants (including eleven ordained pastors), fifteen from Cheondogyo and two Buddhists. Although Gil was the leading Christian figure, nine of the sixteen Protestants were Methodists. Cheondogyo printed the declaration and passed it to Protestants who used their international connections to send it to the US president, the delegates to the Peace Conference and the Japanese government. A demonstration was set for the 1st of March at 2:00 PM, but instead of going to Pagoda Park for a public announcement, the signatories chose to read the declaration to the Japanese officials in a restaurant (Taehwagwan). They were inevitably arrested. When they did not arrive at the park, where a crowd of young people was waiting, Jeong Jae-yong, a Methodist student, read the declaration out to the crowds, who responded with cheers of 'Long live Korean independence!' (Daehan doknip manse!). Similar scenes were repeated across Seoul and in other cities (cf. Lee Ki-baik 1984:338–44). Taken by surprise, the Japanese did not know how to react and the first day passed off largely peacefully, except in Pyongyang. There, although Christians took the lead in peaceful demonstrations following memorial services in the two largest churches in honour of the emperor Gojong, the day ended with numerous protestors being gunned down by police (Cynn 1920:29–31). The next day being Sunday, Christian leaders insisted there should be no demonstrations and the Japanese forbad the holding of church services. Instead many met in the mountains or in homes, while the Japanese began their arrests (Kim In-soo 1996:162–69).

The independence movement gathered overwhelming support from all sections of the community. Youth, students, teachers, urban workers and merchants continued demonstrating for several weeks and those returning to their homes after the funeral soon spread the movement from urban to rural areas and made it truly nationwide (Cynn 1920:62). National Christian networks played an important part in its spread (Kang Man-gil 2005:157). Although churches were not institutionally involved, Protestant church property was frequently used for demonstrations (Kang Wi-jo 2006). Altogether it has been estimated that two million people, roughly a tenth of the population, were involved in the demonstrations (Kang Man-gil 2005:28–29). Foreign observers were unanimous in noting that these demonstrations were orderly and non-violent but were met with brutal force and gratuitous violence. The Japanese police cut down demonstrators with their swords and soldiers opened fire on them; when some Koreans retaliated, the demonstrations turned into riots. Thousands were arrested in Seoul alone, and on several occasions police raided Severance Hospital and took away injured men. Once arrested, prisoners were held without trial, without counsel and often without any contact with relatives or friends for as long as it suited the authorities. They were then subjected to ill treatment, repeated torture, rape and flogging (McKenzie 1920:2–5). The Japanese recorded 553 dead and 1,409 injured; nationalist figures are about fifteen times as large (Shin Gi-wook 2006:44).

One of the most striking aspects of the independence movement was the leading role played by women and girls. In particular, Protestant women made up 60 per cent of the 471 women arrested, and the most prominent women in the movement – Maria Kim, Esther Hwang, Yu Gwan-sun, Cho Hwa-bok, Gwon Ai-ra and Oh Yun-hui – were all Protestants. Although the missionary principal had attempted to prevent them from leaving school, Ewha students marched at the front of the procession in Seoul and several were killed, wounded or imprisoned (T. S. Lee 2010:43; Huntley 1984:163–64) (Fig. 7). However, perhaps the even more counter-cultural aspect of the uprising, and the most significant for Korean nationalism, was the leadership shown by young people – many only in primary school – and the initiative of the student protest in Tokyo (cf. Wells 1989:5–21).

The Protestant missionary community was largely taken unawares by events (D. Clark 2003:46–47), and when they heard of the independence movement many foreign missionaries actively dissuaded Korean Christians from joining in. The missionaries did so not only because they feared for the safety of the Korean Christians but also because most regarded such political action as futile and thought that Christian participation would put the

7. Yu Gwan-sun, a student at Ewha school and member of Chungdong Church, Seoul, leading a demonstration in Byeongcheon, Chungcheong province, during the March 1st Independence Movement. Photograph of the bronze relief at Tapgol Park, Seoul, by Kim Dong-hwan.

churches and Christian missionary activity at risk. However, the severity of the Japanese reaction was such that missionaries were soon drawn in, initially giving medical treatment to victims and then defending Koreans. The Japanese government-general did not officially blame the missionaries but the Japanese-controlled press openly accused them of having instigated the violence and harassed them. Probably only one missionary knew of the actual plans beforehand: a Canadian veterinary doctor, Frank W. Schofield, who was co-opted to send a copy of the declaration to the White House and to take photographs, which he then smuggled out (Huntley 1984:169–70). Another missionary was later charged with sheltering in his house five Korean students wanted by the police; one of them was Gil Jin-kyeong, second son of Gil Seon-ju (Kim In-soo 1996:167). With only one exception (Frank Herron Smith), who had a reputation as an apologist for Japan, the foreign missionaries who saw the violence of the Japanese response – even those who had hitherto urged Koreans to focus on church growth and comply with Japanese rule – now supported and defended the Koreans and argued that there could be 'no neutrality for brutality' (T. S. Lee 2010:41; D. Clark 2003:47–59). Schofield, together with others including H. H. Underwood, son of the pioneer missionary, formed an investigation committee to document and verify incidents. Other missionaries used their contacts to get the matter raised in the US Senate (Huntley 1984:179). They issued several statements on the situation, calling for religious freedom and political rights, condemning Japanese brutality and urging the Japanese to use persuasion rather than force (e.g. Cynn 1920:191–219). But US churches were slow to respond because their greater mission concentration was in Japan and their mission boards feared for their work there and for the Japanese in the United States (e.g. Welch 1922:344). The eventual committee report suggested only that Americans should offer 'moral support' to those Japanese working for the overthrow of militarism (CCA 1919:4, 7) and saw independence for Korea only as the 'ultimate' end of Japan's gradual reforms (CCA 1920:26). Diaspora churches in the United States attempted to mobilise wider support. Ahn Chang-ho published an open letter to the Christian churches of America, Suh Jae-pil assembled a liberty congress in Philadelphia and Shin Heung-u (Hugh Heung-woo Cynn) publicised events in a book (Cynn 1920). The Korean Christian Association in North America was formed with Min Chan-ho as chairperson. It painted Japan as an evil force in the world and argued that it was a 'holy duty' to further the cause of Korean independence (D. Yoo 2010:99–100). Although neither the missionaries nor the exiles succeeded in mobilising the international church bodies to effective action for Korean independence, the Korean situation was brought to the attention of the Western powers sufficiently to shame the Japanese in international circles and contribute to a change in colonial policy.

The March 1st movement was jointly organised by Cheondogyo and Protestants. At the time, Cheondogyo adherents were estimated to be almost ten times as many as members of Protestant churches. However, numerically, Christian participation in the movement was disproportionately strong, both at the leadership level and on the streets. Of the forty-eight people involved in the planning, half were Christians, and of those imprisoned, 22 per cent were Christians (Yi Mahn-yol 1991:335–55; IKCHS 1990:38–39; Kang Wi-jo 1997:351–52). In terms of the character of the event too, the pacifist Christian leaders such as Gil Seon-ju and Cho Man-sik played a major role. There were no Catholic signatories to the declaration, and only 0.3 per cent of those detained were Catholic (D. Baker 2006b:294). Bishop Mutel condemned the March 1st movement, directed Catholics not to participate and expressed pride that Catholics had, by and large, showed loyalty to the Japanese government (Kim Nyung 1993:219). However, students from the Catholic seminaries in Seoul and Daegu did take part and as a result some were expelled and the ordination ceremony scheduled for 1919 was cancelled. In Ganghwa and Gwangju, Catholics led the movements, and in Anseong, Father Antonio Gombert protected in his church villagers who were pursued by the Japanese police for their part in the movement (Choi Seok-u 1996:153; RFKCH 2010:108–10).

The March 1st movement was very important for Korean Protestantism because it further re-established the link between the churches and nationalism, which had earlier been called into question by the church's opposition to armed resistance and the willingness of missionaries especially to work with the Japanese (Yi Mahn-yol 2004; Wells 1990; Cynn 1920). Now even the foreign missionaries and the 'Christian' nations they represented, especially the United States, were seen to be on the side of the Koreans. Although it may also have had to do with the regime's subsequent change of policy, the fact that church membership figures, which had been declining, rose again after 1919 was a sign that Protestantism's place in society was restored. So is the fact that the Japanese Congregational Church in Korea declined after 1919 (Kang Wi-jo 1987:31; T. S. Lee 2000:141). The link between Protestantism and nationalism was made not only by Korean observers but also, and especially, by the Japanese. That the authorities regarded Christians as the main instigators was shown by the way they deliberately targeted Christians for arrest: of the 489 clergy arrested, half were Protestant ministers. Virtually every pastor in Seoul and Pyongyang was imprisoned, and so were many other church workers (Cynn 1920:178–80). In some areas of the provinces it was reported that people were stopped, beaten and rounded up simply because they were Christians. Forty-seven churches and two schools were burned or otherwise destroyed (Kang Man-gil 2005:29). There were many records of atrocities. One of the worst instances was at the village of Jeamni (near Suwon) in which some thirty village men lost their lives when the Methodist church they had been herded into was torched (Kim In-soo 1997:408–11).

Christians, especially Protestants, undoubtedly played a major part in the March 1st movement but such was the dominance of reporting by Western observers and missionaries that this has perhaps been overplayed and the leading role of Cheondogyo has been neglected. Because it was inter-religious and political, not all Christians were committed to the movement and those who did take part were criticised from within the Christian community. The fact that of four signatories to the Declaration of Independence who did not attend the event, all were Christians, and that Gil Son-ju arrived late, is indicative of this (Min Kyoung-bae 1982:315–16; Yi Mahn-yol 1991:335–55; Heo Ho-ik 2009b:282–90). Further evidence is that Cheondogyo delivered ten thousand copies of the declaration but Christians only three thousand

(Ra Dong-kwang 2003:180). Moreover, closer scrutiny of the Jeamni reports shows that the men killed in the church were not only Christian; some were Cheondogyo, and only the few village men who did not belong to an organised religion were spared (CCA 1919:68–81; D. Clark 2003:51–53). The initiative for the nationwide March 1st movement was with Cheondogyo, which also lent it considerable support, but Christians and their local and international networks greatly facilitated the movement.

The March 1st movement was a watershed event in Korean history, and a considerable achievement for the churches and others. The spirit generated by it continued into 1920 as Christians collected funds for those in prison and other victims. The movement has been portrayed as mainly a continuation of the Protestant nationalism of the Independence Club, with its ethos of self-reconstruction, its gradualist approach and its republican aims. But the failure of the supposedly Christian West to support Korean claims to independence called into question whether Korea could ever achieve it by self-cultivation, non-violent resistance and diplomacy. Beyond the demonstration of a Korean desire for independence, it seems that the religious leaders who planned the March 1st event had no long-term strategy (Wells 1990:100). Young people were frustrated that the movement had not gone further to challenge Japanese rule, especially when it had received such overwhelming support from the populace. In their view, the declaration and demonstration by Korean students in Tokyo had been more forward looking (Kang Man-gil 2005:26–29). However, the refusal of Yun Chi-ho to join the protest and proper consideration of Cheondogyo's involvement suggest that March 1st did represent a development of Protestant thinking, and that this was toward ethnic nationalism. The central symbol of self-reconstruction nationalists – the identification of Korea with Israel – was problematic for bringing about national unity because, although powerful for Christians, it was not shared by other groups within the nation (Wells 1990:98). However, the 1919 declaration, which drew on the myth of Dangun, used a new basis for nationalism: an ethnic Korean identity.

Christians who wanted to work for independence for Korea were now faced with the following options: to work with the Japanese to develop the people in the hope of Korea's being granted independence in the distant future, to pursue a diplomatic approach of persuading church leaders and world powers to recognise Korea, to preach the gospel and pray for divine intervention, to espouse a military solution to take back the nation by force or to adopt some form of Socialism and put their hope in International Communism to rescue Korea. During the next decade all five of these were tried. In the immediate aftermath of March 1st, there was little that those inside Korea could do to forward independence since international assistance was not forthcoming and the massive Japanese military presence precluded a coordinated armed resistance movement. In frustration, a few individual Protestants took matters into their own hands by attempting to assassinate the new governor-general, Admiral Saitō Makoto, and attacking police and government buildings (Kang Man-gil 2005:29; Wells 1990:105). There was further migration to Manchuria and the Maritime Provinces of Siberia by Koreans who sought a military solution. In the early 1920s the family of Kim Il-sung, the future leader of North Korea, who were Presbyterians from the Pyongyang area, went into exile in Manchuria but whether primarily for nationalist or economic reasons is unclear (Cumings 2004:108).

As a direct result of the March 1st movement, nationalists in exile set up the Provisional Government, which was based in Shanghai. Three of the leading figures – Rhee Syng-man, Ahn Chang-ho and Yi Dong-hwi – had all at one time converted to Protestant Christianity. The fact that Rhee Syng-man, a Protestant committed to democracy, republican government and a diplomatic approach to gaining independence, was selected as the Provisional Government's president emphasised its continuity with Protestant nationalism (Wells 1990:101; cf. Kang Man-gil 2005:29). So does the fact that it adopted as its anthem a patriotic song from the 1908 union hymnbook with words attributed to Yun Chi-ho (although authorship is also claimed for Choi Byeong-heon and Ahn Chang-ho), including the line 'Long live our nation under the protection of God!', and set to the music of 'Auld Lang Syne'. However, the Provisional Government by its nature was a departure from self-reconstruction nationalism and one of its first acts was to try to coordinate the different resistance forces in Manchuria. The Provisional Government's existence made it easier theologically to support the cause of independence, and it gained widespread support from the Protestant churches. Furthermore, the fact that the resistance groups were now counted as the army of the Provisional Government legitimised them in the eyes of Christians who refrained from violence but were prepared to countenance 'just war'. Overseas Koreans raised funds to support resistance activities. In Pyongyang, Presbyterians associated with the theological seminary reorganised the Korean National Association in August 1919 to support the Provisional Government. Several similar groups were started in Seoul, including the Women's Patriotic Society, which had been founded in April 1919 by some Protestant women to collect funds for the families of those imprisoned, but by the end of the year the leaders of all the groups were in prison (Wells 1990:104–5). There were Catholics involved in the Provisional Government as well – including Ahn Jeong-geun and Ahn Geong-geun (younger brothers of Ahn Jung-geun) and Gwak Yeon-seong (Joseph) – and also in the resistance groups. One of the most influential was the Uimindan (People's Justice Corps), a Catholic group led by Bang U-ryong in North Gando. They were helped by a priest, Father Youn Ye-won (Thomas) of Eunyul. Another priest, Ahn Hak-man (Luke), actually joined a resistance group in Manchuria (RFKCH 2010:108–10; Choi Seok-u 1996:154).

The consensus represented by the Provisional Government did not last for long, and its factions showed how the unity of Christian nationalism was crumbling. Yi Dong-hwi, who had formed the first Korean Socialist party, Hanin Sahoedang, in 1918, supported the Russian Revolution and received funds from Lenin for recruiting and training guerrillas. While Rhee stayed in exile in the United States to continue diplomatic activities, Yi began to advocate armed action, and he refused to accept Rhee's proposal of a League of Nations mandate for Korea (Wells 1990:102). Ahn Chang-ho tried to reconcile the factions, but eventually Yi, Ahn, Yeo Un-hyeong and Kim Gyu-sik all resigned from Rhee's government. From the mid-1920s onwards, nationalists struggled to find common ground on which to present a united front and the Provisional Government became largely dysfunctional.

CHURCHES AND SOCIALISM UNDER THE CULTURAL POLICY, 1920–1931

Japan had emerged from the First World War in a much stronger position and made no secret of its plans to extend its empire in the East or of its designs on Manchuria and China (cf. A. Brown 1919:406–7, 425–26, 465). However, after the independence movement Japanese colonial policy in Korea was overhauled. Governor-General Saitō introduced the new, more internationally acceptable 'cultural policy' (munhwa jeongchi) which allowed cultural freedoms, including Korean-language newspapers, and reduced the military appearance of the regime, for example, by having teachers and officials remove their swords and the police change their uniforms (Wells 1990:103). But the objective of assimilation remained the same, and the policy was effective in its aim to divide the people by fostering the growth of pro-Japanese elements (Kang Man-gil 2005:149).

Saitō, who spoke fluent English, took care soon after his arrival to hear the grievances of the Federal Council of Missions. At his request they submitted a list of policy suggestions, some of which were implemented. For example, churches were now permitted to form legal organisations to hold property, official authorisation was no longer needed to establish new churches or other facilities, and fewer reports were now required (Cynn

1920:Appendix A; Welch 1922:346–47). Changes were made in 1920 in education policy which made the only required subjects morality and Japanese language. From 1922 to 1923 the Korean language could be taught and spoken in schools, and from 1923 'designated' schools could teach religious education as part of the curriculum (Lee Sung-jeon 2009; Kang Wi-jo 2006; 1987:30–31). Missionaries were also pleased to see that religious matters were given a more central place in the administration and that Japanese Christians were appointed to the new Department of Religion. The Seoul Diocese of the Catholic Church was the first to agree to work with this new body (D. Baker 1997:147). However, arguably, control of churches was actually increased under the new regime. Spying on Christian activities continued, and the government reserved the right to close church buildings if they were believed to be used for anti-government activities (Kang Wi-jo 1987:31). The Japanese authorities, while purporting to support the same mission of 'uplifting the Koreans and promoting their happiness', threatened the missionaries and continually raised questions about their loyalty to Japan. Local officials were encouraged to work with them and, under the guise of respect and friendship, to pressure them to support the regime (Welch 1922:346–49).

The relative cultural freedom allowed by the post-1919 Japanese policy enabled the limited development of national identity through newspapers, art, novels, language and the new medium of film, and also made it easier to found social organisations. Yi Kwang-su, with Choi Nam-seon and others, pursued non-political 'cultural nationalism' as a way of developing the nation separate from the state until such time as independence (Robinson 1988:14, 39). Although he did not identify as a Christian, Yi integrated many Christian themes into his novels, often argued from the Bible, and regarded Christianity as the source of freedom and therefore, by his definition, the highest form of civilisation (Wells 1990:107–14). Ahn Chang-ho's more political form of Protestant nationalism continued in the 1920s as 'self-strengthening' societies (suyanghoe) proliferated and reached even rural districts. In the 1920s and 1930s, under the leadership of Cheong In-gwa, Sunday schools were strongly linked with this movement (Choi Young-keun 2012:21–22). Cheondogyo and Buddhist leaders also continued to support it (Wells 1990:127). The new Korean-language newspapers were a forum for debate between cultural and Protestant nationalists, and specifically Christian literature also flowered in this period, with many new Christian periodicals issued in the 1920s. In 1921 the Society for the Promotion of Korean Christian Literature was established. Under its auspices Methodist seminary professors published the magazine *Sinsaengmyeong* (New

Life) between 1923 and 1925, which took a theologically progressive and nationalist stance as far as censorship allowed.

A side-effect of the expansion of Japanese government schools was that relatively fewer students were in Christian schools. By 1926 private schools, almost all Christian, taught less than 5 per cent of the student population. But the relaxation of some of the restrictions on Christian education encouraged a new generation of schools founded by Christian nationalists: Jang Deok-su in Hwanghae province, Song Jin-u and Kim Seong-su in Seoul and Cho Man-sik in Cheongju (northern Pyeongan province). Christian nationalists also continually tried to improve the educational prospects for Koreans, for example, by seeking to raise Osan School and Yeonhui and Boseong technical colleges to university status. Upon their release from gaol in 1922, Yi Sang-jae and other Protestant signatories of the March 1st declaration formed a committee to establish a national university, to which Yun Chi-ho also lent his support. But fund-raising, although impressive, was hampered by floods and drought, and then in 1924 the Japanese undercut the movement by announcing the founding of Keijo Imperial University, which would admit some Korean students (Kang Man-gil 2005:153; Wells 1990:110–12, 115–20).

For most Koreans, any new cultural freedom meant little while general hardship increased because of the global economic depression and the fact that the Japanese colonial economy was designed to exploit the peninsula. Unusually for a church founded in a colonised country, the membership of the Protestant church in Korea was not predominantly urban but lived mainly in some of Korea's twenty-six thousand villages. In 1927 the rural membership of the church matched that of the general population: 73 per cent (Brunner 1928:114–16, 141, 167); in other words, the Korean church really was an indigenous phenomenon. Consequently, rural conditions and developments were of great importance to church life. Korean villages were quite isolated and self-contained; most had more than one religion present, and shamanic practices were widespread, but few had more than one institutionalised expression of religion – a church, temple, ancestral hall or meeting house. In Protestant villages, all but the very newest church buildings were built in Korean style in the shape of a square or were, like traditional rural Catholic churches, in the shape of an L. The congregation sat on the floor, and men and women were segregated by the L arrangement or by a curtain. There were invariably fewer men than women in membership. Church buildings were lit – if at all – by oil lamps, and musical accompaniment was by a reed organ. Average membership was between eight hundred and one thousand three hundred and between 13 to 35 per cent of the population of the village would be in church on Sundays. The church programme was a mixture of preaching and prayer services, Sunday schools and vacation Bible schools. Some churches offered leadership or teacher training and ran kindergartens and night schools. Most churches had active women's and men's groups, usually oriented to evangelism. Villages with churches tended to be more developed in that they usually had their own Christian schools and more social and cooperative organisations than did villages without churches. Under the influence of the temperance movement, which was begun by the Methodist Church in 1912 and supported by the interdenominational Korean Women's Christian Temperance Union (WCTU), Christian villages prohibited drunkenness and refused to license undesirable premises such as the opium dens and brothels that the Japanese encouraged (Brunner 1928:155–74).

Despite Japanese government-general programmes for rural health, to which mission clinics contributed, village life was in decline in Korea and there were many signs of increasing economic pressure on the people, such as a reduction in rice consumption per capita and a drop in school enrolment, together with high levels of emigration. The incomes of Christian households were further stretched by a family's contributions to the church and its subsidiary organisations, as well as by the cost of the higher standard of living the church advocated, such as when it urged educating girls as well as boys, and resting on the Sabbath (Sunday) and Christian festivals. To add to the pressures on rural life, Japanese control reached far into the countryside through the ubiquitous police. Churches and missions attempted to address the rural problems of Korea under the influence of contemporary social Christianity. The YMCA, led by its secretary, Shin Heung-u (Hugh Cynn), set up a village programme in 1923 which paralleled some of the government initiatives but included a 'spiritual' dimension (Brunner 1928:134–36, 159, 163–64, 176–77). By 1930 the YMCA was involved with 209 villages, and its work was supported by foreign workers sent through the International Committee of the YMCA (Chai Soo-il 2003:539). After the Jerusalem Conference of the International Missionary Council in 1928, which Korean delegates attended and at which a survey of Korean conditions was presented (Brunner 1928), the Korean National Christian Council began to support rural mission. Inspired by a visit to Denmark, Kim Hwal-ran (Helen Kim) and Hong Byeong-seon set up a project to develop self-supporting rural towns in Korea. These communities would have their own spiritual, educational and medical institutions and other union and cooperative organisations. The Presbyterian General Assembly also set up a rural committee, and it published a widely read agricultural magazine. However, the rural movements had weaknesses. First, they were focused on improving productivity and on rural morality but they did not, and could not, address the question of the distribution of land, although it was recognised to be the root cause of rural problems, and one for which the Socialists claimed to have a clear answer. Furthermore, their attempts to develop Korea increasingly appeared to suit the agenda of the Japanese. Second, the new organisations for social reform mostly had only tenuous links with the life of the churches because pastors and missionaries tended to criticise Christians who were interested in political or social affairs as insufficiently committed. Samuel Moffett and others who were dedicated to the Nevius method and Bible teaching were particularly opposed to what they saw as a Christian version of Socialism (Park Keun-won 1985:54; Park Chung-shin 2003:146–48).

The Catholic Church, which had been firmly established in villages since the persecutions of the early to mid-nineteenth century, was only now, with the help of foreign missions, beginning to establish a nationwide ecclesial structure. During the First World War many of the missionaries of the Paris Mission were mobilised on the home front so Bishop Mutel handed over much of their work to other missions. In 1920 a third vicariate was erected which was centred at Wonsan and entrusted to the Benedictines. They established a large abbey at Yeongil in Deokwon region to cover an extensive mission area not only in north-east Korea but also in North Gando. In 1925 they were joined by the Missionary Benedictine Sisters of Tutzing, who built a convent at Wonsan and specialised in medicine and education. In 1923 the Catholic Foreign Missionary Society of America, known as the Maryknoll Fathers, entered the Korean field under the leadership of Father Patrick J. Byrne. They took over the work in Pyeongan province, which became a prefecture in 1927 with Byrne as prefect apostolic. The fathers set up a chain of stations from Pyongyang to the Yalu River and established various social projects, including schools, kindergartens and homes for the disabled and the elderly (RFKCH 2010:112–16; D. Clark 2003:133–40). In 1925 a group of Maryknoll Sisters opened a new station at Uiju. Among them was a Korean, Jang Jeong-eon (Mary Agneta Chang, sister of Chang Myon who was later prime minister of South Korea), who had been professed in the United States (D. Clark 2006:181–82).

Under the pressures of life during the Japanese occupation, Catholics turned increasingly to the cult of the martyrs. This was further encouraged by the beatification on 5 July 1925 of seventy-nine of the martyrs by Pope Pius XI in Rome, following a campaign by the Paris Mission of nearly a century (Launay 1925). In 1938 a committee was established to campaign for their canonisation. It is probably not incidental that it was also in the 1920s that Protestants identified a martyr in Robert Thomas, who had travelled with the ship *General Sherman* up to Pyongyang. O Mun-hwan portrayed Thomas as a pioneer of Christian mission, founder of the Protestant Church and the first Protestant martyr, and he established the Thomas Memorial Association (1926) which built the Thomas Memorial Church in Pyongyang in 1932 (A. Clark 1971:64; O Mun-hwan 1928).

By the late 1920s the failure of the March 1st movement to rid the country of the Japanese and their anti-Christian policies, the complicity of Christians with cultural nationalism and the rise of Socialism were among the factors contributing to a slowing in Protestant church growth, disaffection with the church by young people and a 'definite anti-Christian movement' (Brunner 1928:173–74, 179). For the first time in three decades the Protestant churches found themselves on the defensive. The earliest public criticism was voiced by Yi Kwang-su in 1917, and by the 1920s, his arguments had become commonplace (IMC 1932:30). The first complaint was directed at the Korean leadership for setting pastors and elders above lay people, making a sharp distinction between believers and unbelievers, exhibiting a conservative fear of scientific education and tending to despise all but religious occupations. Furthermore, the first generation of church workers, who were selected on the basis of faith rather than intellect and education, were said to be ill-equipped to lead the modern church and out of touch with young leaders who had the benefit of high school as well as seminary education. The second area of criticism was of missionary dominance. The Western missionaries were accused of teaching a 'superstitious' or simplistic form of the faith to Koreans, whereas to the Japanese, they preached a rational and scientific version (Kim In-soo 1997:390–92). Certainly, the second generation of missionaries were more influenced by theories of racial superiority than the first had been, and they were also more distant from Koreans by virtue of being part of a larger expatriate community and fulfilling more of a management role rather than engaging in primary evangelism. In addition, at this time the fundamentalist–liberal controversy was at its height, and most of the missionaries in Korea focused on Bible teaching and church planting and eschewed modern, critical views (Brunner 1928:180; Adams 2012:35–54).

Efforts were made in the mid-1920s to achieve a better understanding between Korean leaders and missionaries, notably at a meeting on the occasion of the visit of John Mott, as secretary of the YMCA International Committee, to Seoul in 1925. But Rev. Han Seok-jin challenged veteran missionaries at the meeting, including Moffett explicitly, to put their Three-self theory into practice and withdraw (IKCHS 1990:173–75). In 1920, in the cultural nationalist newspaper *Dong-a Ilbo*, missionaries were accused of banning ancestor veneration because they misunderstood and even despised Korean culture (Park Chang-won 2011:150–56). In addition to such allegations, the reputation of the foreign missionaries was badly damaged by an incident in 1925 when C. A. Haysmeir, a Canadian Seventh Day Adventist in charge of a mission hospital, deliberately disfigured a twelve-year-old boy (Min Kyoung-bae 1982:345–47). Tension with Western missionaries was experienced in most denominations. In 1930 the resentment by Korean pastors in the Holiness Church reached such a pitch that the pastors declared themselves independent and held their own general assembly. This resulted in the 1936 formation of a separate Korean-led denomination, the Church of God (Min Kyoung-bae 1982:378–80). Rather than try to wrest control of their existing churches, a number of Koreans simply set up independent churches. Some of these emphasised cultural freedom in theology and worship in keeping with the new government policy. In the late 1920s, Kim Gyo-sin, a Holiness preacher influenced by Uchimura's Non-church Movement in Japan, founded a journal, *Seongseo Joseon* (*Bible Joseon*), and a movement which aimed to combine the Korean spirit with scripture. Kim's 'Korean Christianity' distanced itself from the existing churches and struggled against both Japanese and Western dominance (Choo Chai-yong 1998:140–46). Other new churches tried to overcome imported divisions, such as Joseon Christian Church, established by Byeon Seong-ok in Manchuria in 1935, which Korean immigrants joined from a wide variety of denominational backgrounds.

A major reason for anti-Christian feeling in the 1920s was the rise of Communism, which was inherently critical of religion. Socialist ideas spread through Korean students in Tokyo and among Koreans in Manchuria and Siberia, where the first conflicts between Korean Socialists and Christians took place (Kang In-cheol 2006:59). Initially patriots were attracted to Communism for nationalist rather than ideological reasons: International Socialism appeared as the best hope for freeing Korea (Wells 1990:111; Robinson 1988:107–36). So, for example, after the Western nations refused to hear the Korean case in Versailles, Kim Gyu-sik also attended the Congress of Far Eastern Nations in Moscow in 1922 along with Yeo Un-hyeong. Socialism tended to push the self-cultivation Protestant nationalists towards the cultural nationalists. Both rejected violence and took a gradual approach to independence, which made them ultimately indistinguishable from one another and from the Japanese cultural agenda (Kang Man-gil 2005:150). Moreover, it was suspected that Korean church leaders favoured culturalism for reasons of self or class interest since as they were among the best-educated members of society, they had gained status and respect and become secure religious professionals (Robinson 1988:127–29; Park Chung-shin 2003:36–37).

The Catholic Church also warned against the dangers of Socialism (Chérel-Riquier 2013:70). However, it was an attractive option for Koreans suffering under exploitative landlords and for the growing numbers of industrial workers whose wages were 40 per cent lower than those of Japanese workers even though they worked longer hours (Kang Man-gil 2005:40; Wells 1990:128–32). Socialism also drew in Korean youth, particularly those already exposed to the social gospel and Christian Socialist movements through the YMCA, of which a Pyongyang branch was founded in 1921. Under the auspices of the Seoul YMCA, many other Christian youth organisations for education, industry and ethical development came together in the first all-Korea youth organisation in 1920 (Joseon Cheongnyeon Yeonhaphoe) (Wells 1990:106–7). The YMCA facilitated a dialogue between Christians and such Socialists as Yi Dae-wi, a YMCA worker. Other intellectuals introduced Socialist ideas in the main YMCA journal (*Cheongnyeon*) and described the Jesus movement as a kind of Socialism (Park Chung-shin 2003:144). In 1922 the national youth association split as one of its leaders, Kim Myeong-sik, left to publish the moderately leftist journal *Sin Saenghwal* (*New Life*), also under the auspices of the YMCA, with Park Hui-do, Yi Dae-wi and others (Park Chung-shin 2003:143–44). Alarmed at the rapid spread of Marxist-Leninist ideas, the Japanese banned *Sin Saenghwal* in 1923 – thereby further increasing the popularity of Socialism among young people (Robinson 1988:115–17).

Socialism was strongest in the heavily Christianised, more educated and more industrialised Pyongyang area, where it was strongly opposed equally by the conservative Protestant church leaders and by the US Presbyterian missionaries, who also objected to the social gospel theology of the YMCA (Wells 1999:207; D. Yoo 2010:121–26; Kang In-cheol 2006:59). The Catholic Church was also against Socialism, which it held violated human dignity by its materialism and collectivism. In China the church was supporting the Kuomintang against the Communists (Hanson 1980:51), and Korean Catholics who joined the latter were treated harshly. Apart from the disapproval of their leaders, the most obvious barrier to Christians joining the Communists was the Communists' denunciation of Christians for collaborating with imperialists, suppressing the will of the people and believing in superstitions (Park Chung-shin 2003:145–46). They alleged that Christians and missionaries were hypocritically preaching an exclusive, other-worldly salvation while leaving others to suffer. Young Socialists criticised the

teaching of religion in Christian schools, complained about a lack of attention to science, demanded a more democratic approach and encouraged
students to strike (Paik Lak-geoon 1970:398). In 1925 Socialists rallied against
the Sunday School Convention in Seoul, and revival meetings – especially by
Gil Seon-ju and Kim Ik-du – were disrupted (T. S. Lee 2010:62).

Protestant leaders responded in one of four ways to Socialism. Some, like
Yi Gap-seong, Hyeon Sin-deok and Pyeon Seong-ok who organised the
Sisa (Contemporary Affairs) Club, reasserted Christian truth and called
Christians to spiritual renewal, criticising the Socialists for materialism,
atheism and a mechanistic world-view. Others went further, including Gil
Seon-ju and Yi Myeong-jik in the 1930s, in condemning Communism as a
symptom of the last days and of Satan (Kang In-cheol 2006:68). Another
group adopted the social gospel, emphasising the need for deeds to match
words and for faith to be worked out in practice, and committed themselves
to serve the rural movement. A third group developed Christian Socialism,
stressing the importance of social structures and portraying Jesus as a social
revolutionary and the church as the prototype of the new society. Yi Dae-wi,
for example, advocated a society that promoted the welfare of the minjung
or masses as an alternative to both capitalism and Marxism. Before long,
however, doctrinaire Socialists began to attack Christian Socialists so that
the latter gradually became 'apologists for Christianity' (Park Chung-shin
2003:145–46). A fourth group, including nationalist Protestants Yi Dong-hwi
and Yeo Un-hyeong, became Communists.

Cho Man-sik claimed the term 'Christian Socialist' to describe his economic activities in Pyongyang. Cho identified failure to develop the Korean
economy as the reason for its capitulation to Japan and argued for economic
self-sufficiency. Cho became known as the 'Gandhi of Korea'; he adopted a
simple traditional lifestyle and offered a version of Gandhi's swadeshi (self-
sufficiency) movement, the Korean Products Promotion Society (KPPS),
which he inaugurated in 1920 and based in the Pyongyang YMCA. It
encouraged industrialists to avoid collaboration with the Japanese and yet
build up Korea's industry and economy by organising large cooperatives to
manufacture home-produced goods (Wells 1990:148–49). The KPPS gained
the support of the Youth Association and of leading Christians such as
Yun Chi-ho, the Presbyterian Yi Gap-seong and the Methodist minister
Oh Hwa-yeong, and the Korean press got behind it. By 1923 the movement
had spread to the villages and across political and religious divides. But its
popularity provoked the authorities to disrupt lectures, arrest campaigners
and severely restrict the fairs needed to sell the goods. By 1924, however,
there was also strong criticism from the left, who complained that the real

beneficiaries were the company owners, and there were strikes at the textile plant owned by Kim Seong-su in 1925, 1928 and 1931 (Robinson 1988:133–35). Although the initial enthusiasm somewhat died down, the movement retained a lot of its support, and even as late as 1931 new cooperatives were being formed (Wells 1990:141–47).

By the mid-1920s, the Socialists had more adherants than the churches and Socialism had taken hold of the Youth Association. In the late 1920s student strikes spread throughout the country. They culminated in the Gwangju Student Independence Movement of 1929 during which the city in Jeolla province erupted and demonstrations against discrimination, oppression and imperialism, encouraged by Socialist leaders, spread nation-wide (Lee Ki-baik 1984:363–64; Kang Man-gil 2005:47–50). In 1927 nation-alistic Socialists and cultural nationalists managed to come together and form a legal organisation, the Singanhoe (New Shoot Society), led by Yi Sang-jae, now the publisher of the daily newspaper *Chosun Ilbo* (Wells 1990:112–13). It attracted thirty thousand members, including 255 Protestant pastors and evangelists – or 17 per cent of all pastors and evangelists (Cumings 2005:156). A parallel women's organisation, the Geunuhoe, was also founded mainly by Protestants and members of the Young Women's Christian Association (YWCA) and the Temperance Union. However, Socialists soon got the upper hand in both organisations and they were dissolved by the government-general in 1931 (Wells 1999:205–17; Shin Gi-wook 2006:58–68; Kang Man-gil 2005:55–62).

The 1920s saw significant changes in gender relations in Korea and the emergence of the 'new woman'. Some reforms were pioneered in the Protestant churches in Pyongyang. Segregated seating began to be abolished after 1913 when Gil Seon-ju, setting a precedent, removed the curtain dividing the men's and women's halves at his church (A. Clark 1971:119). The Presbyterian Church also began to regulate gender relations: they began issuing marriage certificates in 1911, and in 1914 the General Assembly forbad child marriages and set the age for marriage at seventeen for men and fifteen for women. They also permitted the remarriage of widows. Protestant church women's groups were powerful because of both the strength of women's networks and the responsibility women traditionally had for managing domestic finances. Furthermore, because they increasingly had paid employment, women contributed significant funds as well as labour to the running of church activities. The local Methodist Women Missionaries Associations and Presbyterian Women Evangelists Associations were now led by Koreans. The groups were pietistic and focused on evangelism and at the same time part of the Protestant nationalist movement (cf. Yi Hyo-jae

1985:97; Kim Chong-bum 2008:21). Tertiary levels of education were introduced at some government-registered institutions for women – for example, at the Martha Wilson Memorial Bible Institute at Wonsan (Presbyterian) and the Hyupsung Woman's Bible Institute in Seoul (Methodist) – to meet the higher educational standards now expected of church leaders generally (Chang Sung-jin 2005:226–27). At the same time, there was an expansion in the number of women's Bible schools, which as religious institutions were now allowed to operate outside of the regulations for general education and to teach in Korean. These small institutions training Bible women provided access to education for mainly poor women over marriageable age who could not be admitted to normal schools, although the qualifications gained by the women at the Bible schools were not widely recognised (Chou Fan-lan 1995:40–41). Despite the greater opportunities for training, the numbers of Bible women employed by the churches declined steeply in the 1920s now that there were more male leaders who had qualified from seminary. Nevertheless, many other women worked in different ministries and were often paid out of funds raised by women. Since the Bible women were usually trained in hygiene, they also worked both formally and informally for women's health. Many served in a way similar to hospital chaplains and counsellors, ministering to patients and their families and also following up on discharged patients at home. Educated women were employed as teachers in mission and village girls' schools and also worked in hospitals or clinics. Moreover, some Korean women, for example, Cha Mirisa and Yeo Mae-rae, founded nationalistic girls' schools (Chang Sung-jin 2005:271–79).

The growing self-confidence and knowledge of Korean Protestant women led them to challenge the dominance of men in the church. In 1922 the Bible women of the Southern Methodist Church demanded equal rights with male pastors, who were paid three to five times more than a woman's stipend and were also entitled to a clergy house (Chou Fan-lan 1995:35). Efforts to improve the conditions of Bible women continued through the 1920s and 1930s, but the women had limited bargaining power (Choi Hyae-weol 2009:76–77). In 1933 the Women Evangelists Associations petitioned the Presbyterian Church to ordain women as elders, but this request was rejected. Prevented from joining the men, the Women's Associations of both the Presbyterian and Methodist churches began to work more autonomously. For example, they despatched their own overseas missionaries instead of going through the denominations as previously. Methodists sent women missionaries to Manchuria in 1925, and in the 1930s to India and Japan (Yi Hyo-jae 1985:97–98), and the Presbyterians sent their first woman cross-cultural missionary (Kim Seon-ho) to China in 1931. Their mission activity was not only an indication of the transformation of women's lives, it also signified their new status in two respects: that women, like men, were called and equipped by God, and that women were the equal of the Western missionaries who had come to Korea (Choi Hyae-weol 2009:72–75, 181).

The foundation of the Korean YWCA in 1922 opened doors for many women. Following their attendance at the World Student Christian Fellowship conference in Beijing in 1922, Kim Hwal-ran, a Methodist, and Kim Pil-rye, a Presbyterian, founded an independent Korean branch themselves with no missionary help. This enabled the new body to avoid being included under the Japanese branch (Choi Hyae-weol 2009:149–51). The YWCA reached beyond the church membership in order to proselytise and also to share a social gospel. It gave women a taste of democracy and was a modernising force. In keeping with the organisation's international activities (Robert 2002:8), the YWCA supported women's higher education, but most of its work was at a grassroots level in many projects across the country, including running kindergartens, teaching women English and Hangul in night schools, raising pigs to support Bible women, organising a vocal anti-vice campaign and supporting factory workers (A. Clark 1971:366–69; see also Kim Chong-bum 2008:21).

The ideal of the New Woman (Sinyeoseong) was introduced in the 1920s through Western, Japanese and possibly Chinese sources and was associated with female students and intellectuals who challenged Confucian gender norms and advocated gender equality in both their writing and their lifestyles. Uniquely in Korea, the New Woman movement had a significant connection with Protestant Christianity (Choi Hyae-weol 2009:146–47, 161, 237). The leading figures were mostly graduates of Christian schools; many were from Christian homes, and some worked in Christian organisations, especially the YWCA. Kim Hwal-ran was one of the best-known Christian women and possibly the most widely respected female leader in the late 1920s (Wells 1999:209–16). In 1931 she became the first Korean woman to receive a PhD, and she became president of Ewha College in 1939. She later held government and ambassador positions and won many awards for her public service (A. Clark 1971:416–23). She was dedicated to public life and blazed a trail by remaining single, cutting her hair short and refusing to wear restrictive clothing (Kim Chong-bum 2008:27).

Women's groups took advantage of the relaxation of rules about Korean publications to launch journals in the 1920s. The most well known was the *New Woman* (*Sinyeoseong*), founded in 1920 by Ewha College graduate Kim Weon-ju (penname Kim Il-yeop). Even in its first issues *New Woman* went well beyond the domesticity model for women to directly assert the equality of women with men and attack men for their alleged oppression of women (Wells 1999:209–10). Kim formed the Cheongtaphoe (Bluestocking Society), which also included Park In-deok and Na Hye-seok – all three graduated from Protestant schools and each challenged church and Confucian norms in a different way by, respectively, rebelling against parental authority, divorcing her husband for infidelity and questioning the equation between women and motherhood (Kim Chong-bum 2008:26; Choi Hyae-weol 2009:161–69, 179). The backlash against the New Woman from the church leadership, which in the context of the fundamentalist–modernist controversy tended to treat women's assertion of their rights as being opposed to the agenda of evangelism, was compounded by the colonial disempowerment of men (cf. Wells 1999:194). Another difficulty for both the Christian women's movement and the Socialist one was that women's interests and the feminist agenda were treated as secondary to nationalist goals.

PROTESTANT REVIVALISM, GIBOK SINANG
AND MILLENNIALISM IN THE 1920S

After the independence movement of 1919 the Japanese tightened their control and surveillance in Korea. Further organised political action was impossible, and Korean Protestants became divided between those who took various practical approaches to solving the problems of Korea – either by military or diplomatic methods in exile, or by cultural, social service or Christian Socialist means within Korea – and those who pursued a more purely religious path. Oppression under Japan helped to consolidate two incipient features of Korean Protestant religiosity: 'ethical-theological conservatism' on the one hand, especially in reaction to the social gospel, and 'revivalistic-evangelistic practices' on the other (Ryu Dae-young 2008:396). The first was most associated with the characteristic Bible Christianity, and the second was known as gibok sinang or 'faith seeking blessings'. The latter expected – despite adversity – God's blessing for those who had faith and believed that God would intervene directly to solve their problems (S. C. H. Kim 2007). Activists at the time criticised both spiritualities for fundamentalist theology and other-worldliness, and it is true that there were those in the churches who criticised earlier activism, but a religious approach was not necessarily apolitical or escapist (Park Chung-shin 2003:66–67). More specifically, religious activities could also threaten Japanese power and even ordinary church life challenged Japanese hegemony. Merely attending

Bible study and prayer and revival meetings was a sign of resistance, and attendees could be blacklisted by the authorities who recognised this (Park Jong-chun 1998:61, 64–72; Suh Kwang-sun 1991:56; Yi Mahn-yol 2004:66).

Since 1907, periodic revival meetings (buheunghoe) had become a regular feature of Korean church life and increasingly they cultivated the popular religiosity of gibok sinang. Yi Myeong-jik led a popular series of revival meetings in 1921 in the Holiness Bible School in Seoul with the support of his students, who fasted and prayed for fifteen days and held early-morning prayer meetings. Yi emphasised repentance and healing in a moderate movement which set a pattern for future revivals. But increasingly in this period, interest shifted away from the repentance associated with the 1907 revival and towards healing. Stories of healing and exorcism were commonly encountered in the churches as well, especially in the Holiness churches and among women (e.g. Welch 1922:356–57). The constitution of the Presbyterian Church of Korea asserted that supernatural healing was limited to apostolic times, and Presbyterian and Methodist church leaders ridiculed Holiness healers and women exorcists for their claims, denouncing such practices as superstitious or shamanistic. Nevertheless, from late 1919 a respected minister and sometime moderator of the Presbyterian Church, Kim Ik-du, led a popular ministry of healing and exorcism which was reported seriously in the press at the time and verified by a committee that included at least one well-known doctor. Up to ten thousand people flocked to a single meeting in 1920 – the largest Christian gathering yet recorded. But people soon became sceptical about the claims of healing, especially under the influence of Socialists and pro-Japanese individuals who accused Kim of being a 'high-class shaman' and of fostering ignorance and blind belief. Despite Kim's popularity and their concerns that he might be diverting offerings to resistance movements, the authorities did not prevent his rallies, presumably because it suited them for people's energy to be directed away from explicitly political activities (T. S. Lee 2010:74–78; Lee Young-hoon 2009:43–48; A. Clark 1971:435–42).

Kim Ik-du's popularity with the lower classes may also have been because he preached judgement on riches and power. His healings were taken as signs of the end and supported his premillennialist message in which the Japanese government was the Antichrist. Other revivalists also had a millennialist message. Kim Sang-jun, another popular Holiness preacher, drew on the biblical apocalyptic and on *The Pilgrim's Progress* to remind people to expect Christ's return and the millennial kingdom (in that order) (Pak Ung-kyu 2005:140–43, 169, 206). As we have noted, millenarianism was already strong among indigenous Korean religions and forms of premillennialism and eschatological speculation were encouraged by some missionaries, notably James Gale. The high view of scripture and rejection of a historical approach by Korean Protestants inclined them to see contemporary events as signs of the times, and by the 1920s millennialist views had come to dominate the Korean Protestant church. Perhaps this was because the hope this engendered helped to resolve the contradiction between the dire circumstances of Korea and the belief that Koreans were the special people of Dangun (Pak Ung-kyu 2005:163–70, 199–200).

Between 1928 and 1933 a young Methodist called Yi Yong-do introduced a mystical style of revivalism which drew even stronger criticism, and especially comparisons with the despised shamanism (Ryu Geum-ju 2005). Yi's experience of imprisonment and torture for his independence activities in 1919 led him to give up political struggle as fruitless and seek a purely religious solution to Korea's problems. After he was healed from illness in a miraculous way, he turned from politics to a life of prayer and fasting in the mountains. Following a vision, Yi led mass meetings across the country in which he encouraged crying and other emotional outpouring (Park Jong-chun 1998:61, 64–65). He preached that by identifying with Jesus' sufferings believers would experience Christ's unlimited love, exchanging the sin and materialism of earth for the life and holiness of heaven. Yi also advocated engagement in a spiritual struggle against the devil, calling upon the name of Jesus in order to overcome evil (Ryu Dong-sik 2000:155–65; Choo Chai-yong 1998:140; Park Jong-chun 1998:61, 64–72). He was highly critical of church leaders, whom he felt were constrained by the conservative theology inherited from the missionaries and whom he believed were guilty of hypocrisy, and he was against the West, believing it to represent materialism, whereas the East was essentially spiritual (Pak Ung-kyu 2005:147–48). These attitudes, together with his syncretism and association with cults denounced by the churches, led eventually in 1933 to Yi's investigation by the Presbyterian Church, his condemnation as a heretic on the grounds that he maintained that the scriptures were not sufficient for salvation without an ecstatic experience of the Spirit and his suspension from ministry by the Methodist Conference as well (T. S. Lee 2010:82).

Some of the strongest millennialist messages came from Gil Seon-ju after he was released from a two-and-a-half-year prison sentence for his part in the March 1st movement. During this imprisonment he was said to have read the book of Revelation several thousand times. He was now convinced that nothing further could be achieved by political action and that all that Koreans could do was to trust in God and wait for God's intervention on behalf of the weak. In 1927, Gil resigned his pastorate and became a full-time revivalist until his death in 1935. His apocalypticism became even more intense as he was harassed again by the Japanese, who imprisoned him for his preaching of an end to their empire; by Socialists, who disrupted his meetings and church services; and by more theologically liberal members of his own church, who objected to his literalistic approach to the Bible. Although technically premillennialist, Gil's unorthodox millennial doctrine made special provision for the virtuous from Confucianism and Buddhism and it is difficult to accuse Gil of the escapism and pessimism about the present world that is usually associated with that position (Kim Chong-bum 2006:152–57; Pak Ung-kyu 2005:134–39; Kim In-soo 1996:123–24; Park Chung-shin 2003:62–63). Gil was a 'transitional figure' who bridged several eras and held together gibok sinang and Bible Christianity and also two forms of revival or 'Holy Spirit movement'. The latter have been described in a yin–yang analogy: as a 'maternal' movement of popular religious revivalism, which Yi's movement exemplified, and a 'paternal' movement of national revitalisation and social reform. The maternal revival tended to be associated with women and lower-class men and the paternal movement with elite males. In terms of worship expression, these corresponded roughly to popular shamanic and charismatic religion on the one hand and the elite Confucian and text-based form of Korean religion on the other. These two faces became characteristic of Korean Protestantism (Ryu Dong-sik 2000:414–26; K. Kim 2006; cf. Chou 1995:42–43).

A new form of 'maternal' revivalism entered Korea in the late 1920s: Pentecostalism. Although their missionaries had been in the region since 1907, the Pentecostal denominations did not send directly to Korea. The first Western Pentecostal missionaries to enter were independent women – as many as a dozen in the late 1920s and the 1930s. Pre-eminent among them was Mary Rumsey, a product of the Azusa Street Revival (Anderson 2004a:38–44) who arrived in 1928 and founded Joseon Pentecostal Church. It is likely that Rumsey met R. A. Hardie at the Methodist hospital where the headquarters of the Joseon Pentecostal Church was later housed, and so she would likely have heard of the 1903–1907 Korean Revival (Lee Young-hoon 2009:66–69). Although there is no record of glossolalia or speaking in tongues at that time, she and other Pentecostal missionaries claimed a direct connection between the worldwide Pentecostal movement and the Holy Spirit movement in Korea. It was Rumsey who arranged for the ordination of the first three Korean Pentecostal pastors in 1938: Heoh Hong, Park Seong-san and Bae Bu-geun. These men founded several congregations on the outskirts of Seoul where the new movement thrived among the dis-possessed (Kim Ig-jin 2003:56–62). The Pentecostals were not popular with the existing churches, especially because they did not follow Confucian-Presbyterian decorum – they sang with drums, danced in the street and held baptisms in the Han River. But much Pentecostal teaching on healing and eschatology was familiar from the already established Holiness movement and the revivals of Kim Ik-du and Yi Yong-do.

NATIONAL CHURCHES, ETHNIC NATIONALISM
AND INTERNAL TENSIONS IN THE 1930S

During the creation of Manchukuo (1931–1932), the puppet state the Japanese set up in Manchuria, and afterwards, the militarists dominant in Japan used Korea as an industrial and logistics base in their wars against China and the Allies. Christians and other Koreans – nearly 700,000 in total – who had moved to Manchuria to escape Japanese rule were now subjected to it. Poor Koreans from the agricultural south moved to the new towns and cities that were being rapidly created (Foley 2003:18–19). Meanwhile, the resistance armies relocated into China and Siberia where they also had Korean community support (Kang Man-gil 2005:90). Korean church workers had been sent to Manchuria since 1901, and the Protestant missions already had a comity arrangement for these territories (IKCHS 1990:114–33). The Catholic prefecture apostolic of Yenki had been established in 1928 and entrusted to the Benedictines of Deokwon (RFKCH 2010:113). Despite opposition from Communists, the churches had grown. By 1932 there were estimated to be 16,000–18,000 Korean Protestants in Manchuria (D. Oh 2011:186), and in 1937, when Stalin forcibly deported the 170,000 Koreans living in the Russian Far East to Uzbekistan and Kazakhstan, a presbytery of fifty-five congregations and many other Christians were among them (Cumings 2004:109, 114–15; Foley 2003:20–21; C. Clark 1934:201).

Church activities continued for the most part without regard for the politics which impinged on them, although the increasing financial plight and displacement of the people imposed limitations. In 1931 the Catholic Church celebrated the centenary of its becoming a vicariate apostolic. Regional synods were held, and a Korean directory of canon law and catechism was produced (RFKCH 2010:120–21, 128). In 1934 both the Presbyterian and Methodist missions celebrated fifty years of mission work in Korea, and both presented glowing reports of numerical growth, dedicated missionary service, native leadership and social transformation, and especially in the case of the Presbyterians, of self-support and gospel preaching (PCUSA 1934; BFMMEC 2001:835–51). There was still significant cooperation between the Protestant churches in 1934. Presbyterians and Methodists shared a single church newspaper, the *Christian Messenger*, the same hymnbook and the same translation of the Bible, a further revision of which was completed in 1937. But despite their spectacular growth, Protestant missionaries were not entirely comfortable with their progress because the Catholic Church was now growing faster. Catholics made up 40 per cent of Korean Christians in 1934, and Protestants were concerned that Korea might yet become a Catholic country (PCUSA 1934:140–41).

Protestants, especially Presbyterians, were overwhelmingly concentrated in the Pyongyang area, and by 1940, 90 per cent of Protestants, 82 per cent of their churches, and 83 per cent of their clergy were in the north-west (IHCK 1996:343–44). This was partly because Korean migrant workers in the growing factories there were attracted to the church communities, who also reached out to them. The Anglicans, under Bishop Cecil Cooper, also saw the potential in the industrial north and began an urban ministry there which resulted in the opening of eight new chapels in one year – 1936 (IMC 1937:14; Lee Jae-jeong 1990:187–97). As with the Protestants, the Catholic population was also increasing in the north-west, and a fourth vicariate was created in Pyongyang in 1939. The Maryknoll Fathers, who were responsible for the region, took much of the credit for this growth. With a strong support base in the United States, they began Catholic Action in 1933 to encourage lay commitment, and this was held to be the reason that up to 1941 the prefecture produced eight priests, thirty-nine nuns and an increase in believers of eighteen thousand. But the main concentration of Catholic laity remained in Seoul, while 57 per cent of the priests were in the north-east because of the location of Deokwon Abbey there (IHCK 1996:116–19, 343–44).

Across the churches, leadership was gradually being handed over to Koreans. This was not entirely due to recognition of the churches' maturity; it was also because association with Westerners brought more difficulties than benefits to the Korean churches, especially after 1933 when Japan pulled out of the League of Nations, and because the Japanese pressured the churches to distance themselves from foreigners. Numbers of Korean Catholic priests were steadily increasing and, at more than seventy by 1936, were approaching the missionary total of a little over one hundred. Two Koreans had now attained the status of vicar forane: Kim Myeong-je Peter in Hwanghae-do (1928) and Kim Yang-hong (Stephen) (1931) in the newly erected vicariate of Jeolla province. In 1937, Kim Yang-hong was appointed to the new prefecture apostolic of Jeonju (North Jeolla province), which was now exclusively composed of Korean clergy (RFKCH 2010:112–13, 128). However, Catholic missionary numbers continued to increase. In 1933 the Paris Mission, German Benedictines and American Maryknollers were joined by ten Irish priests of the Missionary Society of Saint Columban (Maynooth Mission). The Irish, who shared with Koreans recent experience of colonialism, began their work in remote parts of the south-west and in Jeju Island and established a new vicariate and seminary in Gwangju, South Jeolla province (D. Clark 1986:11–12). In 1938 the Columbans were also assigned to a separate mission in a rural area of Gangwon-do. As in most cases of missionary expansion in Korea, Catholics were already there, descended from a gyoucheon community. In 1940 the Chuncheon region was added to the responsibilities of the Columbans. Other missions also arrived in the 1930s: the Order of Friars Minor from Canada in 1937, and in 1940 Discalced Carmelites from France, who opened a convent. In 1932 the Maryknoll Sisters established the first Korean women's religious order, the Sisters of Our Lady of Perpetual Help, which worked in parishes, schools and social welfare. Two more communities of Korean women were begun: in 1935 what later became the Handmaids of the Sacred Heart of Jesus and in 1943 the Little Servants of the Holy Father. The religious orders took over and formalised much of the work previously done by lay women catechists, wives of catechists, widows and young women (Kim and Chung 1964:703–20).

The Methodists in Korea from both missions came together in 1930 to form one national church, the Joseon Christian Methodist Church (Ryu Dong-sik 2005a:511–21). As a result of the close cooperation of the two denominations in Korea, the new Korean Methodist Church adopted aspects of Presbyterian polity, including elders, bishops appointed for a fixed term and ministers called by local churches rather than appointed by the bishop (Grayson 2007:435–36). But although the two main Protestant denominations were largely self-supporting by the 1930s, the Korea National Church Council, which was mainly concerned with cooperative mission work for overseas Koreans, evangelistic work in Korea and some literature activities, was still largely foreign subsidised (PCUSA 1934:97). So were most of the mission institutions in which foreign missionaries were still heavily involved. The proportion of Presbyterian mission funds going to education almost trebled between 1915–1916 and 1931–1932, mostly at the expense of funds for evangelism, owing to the government requirements for 'designated' status and the impoverishment of Koreans which reduced fee revenue (Wheeler 1950:321). With regard to medical work, now that epidemics were largely controlled, the missions were contributing in other ways: they had three hospitals for leprosy to the government's one, and the Methodists also ran a sanatorium for tuberculosis sufferers. The rural schools for vocational or agricultural training were operating successfully, while in the cities, missionaries, women's organisations and Korean evangelists were trying to minister to the country girls who were brought in increasing numbers by middlemen to work in the factories and mills (IMC 1932:28–29).

Because of its strategic position, Korea's passivity was now of the utmost importance to Japan and the limited freedoms of the 'cultural policy' were terminated. The programme of assimilation was stepped up, and the Japanese authorities tried to eradicate the Korean language and script and Korean personal and place names. After 1938 Protestant mission schools, which were popular because they offered a Korean alternative outside the state system (IMC 1932:28), lost this advantage when, if they wished to remain registered, all schools were required to exclude the Korean language and literature from the curriculum (Wells 1990:132, 153–54). Moreover, from 1937 people were required to recite the new 'oath of imperial subjects' at all school and organisation meetings. Increasingly, Japanese policy amounted to 'thought control' or 'domination over the soul' of the Koreans (Lee Chul-woo 1999:42–49). Under the Peace Preservation Law any acts, and later, thoughts or even potential thoughts, which were regarded as contrary to the Japanese spirit could lead to imprisonment and re-education. Socialism was the chief target of this policy, but any other creed originating from Western civilisation which was thought to put individual or sectional interests above the interests of unity was also targeted, so Christians suffered too (Kang Man-gil 2005:17–20, 149; Blair and Hunt 1977:91–92).

Between 1928 and 1933, when it was suppressed, the main Protestant nationalist organisation, the Alliance for Self-cultivation (Suyang Donguhoe), grew within the wider unity created by the Singanhoe. It was joined by some ethical Socialists and moved towards the left and a conscious focus on independence. A new interdenominational nationalist group, Gukmin Hyeopseonghoe (National Society for Cooperation and Success), led by Shin Heung-u in 1933–1935, which was anti-Socialist and supportive of Rhee Syng-man, was opposed by the Donguhoe and the YMCA and denounced by both mainline churches. The Presbyterians found its opposition to the conservative missionaries, its liberal theology of natural revelation and its campaign for human rights and gender equality unacceptable, and the Methodists were worried about its political agenda. The Protestant political figure who commanded broadest support, Ahn Chang-ho, was arrested in 1932. On his release in 1936, he tried to bring the Protestant nationalists together around proposals for a central organisation created by Cho Man-sik, who had the advantage of not being formally affiliated with any of the main nationalist bodies. Cho tried to revive self-reconstruction nationalism and to bring about national revival through proclaiming the gospel and large-scale evangelisation (Wells 1990:132–35). But instead, in the 1930s the predominant Korean nationalism shifted to an ethnic form.

Japanese colonial racism and ethnic nationalism, and their investigations of Korean customs and traditions intended to provide a 'scientific basis' for assimilation, had the side-effect of encouraging Koreans to insist on their own unique racial origins and to focus on bloodline, character and folk traditions as definitive of the nation. Nationalist academics revived the Dangun myth, stories of Korean heroes and the belief in the Korean spirit of three decades before. This encouraged resistance to imperialism and internationalism (Shin Gi-wook 2006:44–53; Kang Man-gil 2005:162–72). Shared beliefs and values, not race, had been the basis of Protestant nationalism (Wells 1990:175), but the frequent comparisons with Israel suggested that common race was a given in Protestant preaching, and in the climate of Japanese racism, ethnic nationalism became a greater part of Christian rhetoric too.

At an academic level, a group of Christians at the Methodist Theological College in Seoul (the result of a union of men's and women's colleges in 1925) devoted themselves to Korean studies, and Paik Lak-geoon advocated the development of an indigenous theology which expressed the Korean spirit to replace the imported confessions and literature (Min Kyoung-bae 1982:408–9). Methodist theologians enjoyed more theological freedom than their Presbyterian counterparts, first, because their tradition generally set less store by faith confessions, and second, because most were educated in more liberal institutions influenced by cultural theology (cf. Adams 2012:35–37). So, for example, Jeong Gyeong-ok could argue for a liberal theological approach (Kim Yeong-myeong 2008). The first theological journal, *Sinhak Weolbo*, was published between 1900 and 1910 by George Heber Jones and included contributions from Koreans, including Kim Chang-sik, Jeon Deok-gi and Choi Byeong-heon. A second journal, *Sinhak Segye*, was founded by Hardie at the Methodist seminary in 1916; the first Korean contribution was by Yang Ju-sam in 1917 (Ryu Dong-sik 2000:103–22; Choo Chai-yong 1998:101–7). While *Sinhak Segye* raised cultural issues, the journal of the Presbyterian seminary, *Sinhak Jinam*, launched by C. A. Clark in 1918, was more conservative and had mostly missionary contributors. Discussion of gospel and culture naturally focused on the question of ancestor veneration. In 1920, Yi Sang-jae, then general secretary of the YMCA, argued that, if it did not involve superstitious practices, then it was a legitimate form of filial piety (Park Chang-won 2011:150–56), and the Christian writer and later politician Pyun Young-tai argued systematically that it was not what the Bible condemned as idolatry (Pyun Young-tai 1988; Adams 2012:55–58).

In addition to the external pressures of Japanese oppression, economic difficulties and the atheistic threats of Socialism, Korean Protestant churches also faced internal problems of church politics: fighting over positions, interests and regions; questions of authority; and, as the missionaries were forced to withdraw, squabbling over the control of church institutions (Park Chung-shin 2003:153–54). It is against this background that the criticisms of the church by Yi Yong-do and others should be understood (Kim Ig-Jin 2003:56). These many stresses also contributed to three major theological controversies which erupted in the Presbyterian Church and the seminary in Pyongyang in 1934–1935. The 'Bible Christianity' and adherence to the Westminster Confession brought by the first generation of missionaries had become the dominant theological tradition in Korean Presbyterianism (Ryu Dae-young 2008:385). So whereas the Methodist Byun Hong-gyu, influenced by Barthian neo-orthodoxy, could advocate holiness as the key to understanding the God of the Hebrew Bible (Ryu Dong-sik 2000:198–205; Choo Chai-yong 1998:112–17), in Presbyterian circles any other hermeneutic provoked a strong reaction both from the church leadership and in theological circles. A few Korean theologians engaged with the new ideas, for example, Namgung Hyeok, professor at Pyongyang Seminary, who responded to biblical criticism in his commentaries on the Pauline epistles. However, theology taught at the seminary was not innovative but deeply conservative and considered new trends only to refute or contain them (Adams 2012:35–54).

The controversies focused on questions of biblical interpretation which were the key issue over which J. Gresham Machen and other conservatives had recently (1929) left Princeton Seminary in the United States, where several Korean leaders had been studying. The first controversy was raised by Kim Chun-bae, who suggested at the 1934 Presbyterian General Assembly, on behalf of women activists, that the church should allow women to be ordained as elders. The assembly denounced the view, citing prohibitions in the letters of the Apostle Paul, and Kim was forced to retract. The second offender, in the same year, was Kim Yong-ju, who cast doubt on whether Moses was the author of the Pentateuch. This view was declared to violate the commitment of the church to biblical inerrancy. The third incident was caused by the publication by Methodists in 1935 of the Korean translation of the Abingdon Bible Commentary, to which some young Presbyterian pastors had contributed, although it made use of biblical criticism and inclined toward liberal theology unacceptable to Presbyterian church leaders (Choo

Chai-yong 1998:152–73). The young men involved included Han Kyung-chik, who had graduated from Princeton in the year Machen left, and Kim Jae-jun. Both were forced to apologise. The Presbyterians decided to sponsor instead the translation of the Standard Bible Commentary, the chief editor of which was Park Hyeong-ryong, who emerged as the leader of Korean fundamentalism. As a student at Princeton he had sided with Machen and the fundamentalist wing, and he completed his studies at the Southern Baptist Theological Seminary (Adams 2012:82–87). Park held to 'plenary inspiration' and insisted that doing theology in the Korean church meant not creating something new but continuing to uphold the 'apostolic' traditions. This conservative and evangelical approach to the text was also reflected by many leading theologians, such as Park Yun-sun and Rhee Jong-sung (Choo Chai-yong 1998:152–73).

In each of these controversies, the conservative position prevailed. But Presbyterians supported by the Canadian missionaries in Hamgyeong province had been exposed to a less conservative theology and were also influenced by the leftist politics of the region, and they formed a progressive group (D. Clark 1997:180–82). Central to this effort was Kim Jae-jun, who believed that the work of Karl Barth offered a middle way between liberalism and fundamentalism (Ryu Dong-sik 2000:231–62; Choo Chai-yong 1998:183–201). Not wishing to compromise the gospel they had received, the conservative Presbyterians experienced increasing difficulties working ecumenically with the Methodists. The Doctrinal Declaration adopted by the new Joseon Christian Methodist Church in 1930 was more accepting of biblical criticism and more liberal theologically than the position of the Presbyterian Church. In 1935 the Presbyterian General Assembly withdrew its support for the jointly published *Christian Messenger* (T. S. Lee 2010:53). And in 1936 the church left the National Church Council, which was then suspended (IMC 1937:13).

The rejection of a critical approach to the text by Presbyterian leaders was not a mere imitation of the squabbles at Princeton. Korean accommodation to culture and openness to the spirit of the times in the colonial period could only mean affirming Japanese culture and spirit. The fundamentalists were resisting the cultural theology which some Japanese theologians shared with theologians of the 'German Christian' movement and which allowed them to be co-opted to support the militarist regime (Parratt 2011:195–210). Furthermore, whereas leading Japanese theologians, in common with their German colleagues, were highly critical of the Old Testament and drew a sharp distinction between the church and the people of Israel, the Pyongyang revival and Korean theology were built largely on identification with Israel's story. Like the Confucians at the fall of the Ming dynasty, Pak Hyeong-ryong and others were determined that whatever happened to the churches in the West or in Japan, the Korean church would remain true to 'the faith', that is, to the conservative, biblical theology which they had received. However, Pyongyang Seminary was closed by the Japanese in 1938 (A. Clark 1971:275). Frustrated with what they described as the ideological constraints of American missionaries and with the hard-line approach of Korean leaders, and taking their opportunity, in 1940 Kim Jae-jun and his colleagues founded a new Presbyterian theological school, Joseon Seminary, in Seoul, asserting that 'the time of missionary control is ended' (see D. Clark 1997:173). However, the General Assembly refused to recognise the new seminary and conservatives reopened Pyongyang Seminary in a borrowed building. But war intervened and the problem was deferred.

WAR, SHINTO CEREMONIES AND THE SUPPRESSION OF CHRISTIANITY, 1935–1945

In the late 1930s, the whole Korean population was mobilised for the war effort and kept in a high state of stress (Kang Man-gil 2005:19). Owing to economic necessity, forced labour programmes and the draft, the last decade of colonial rule saw migration on a scale rarely matched anywhere (Cumings 2005:175–76). Notwithstanding all the suffering involved, such a mixing and scattering of people presented Christians with new opportunities for witness and must have further spread knowledge of the Christian gospel among Koreans. However, regular church activities were severely disrupted. Sunday observance became very difficult, young people were discouraged by police and their teachers from attending church and many congregation members were sent away as forced labour. On top of this there was growing pressure to participate in Shinto ceremonies.

Although the first Shinto shrine had been established in Seoul in 1915, it was not until 1925 that officials and students began to be compelled to participate in Shinto ceremonies (Park Chang-won 2011:156). Shrines, which were directly controlled by the Japanese military, proliferated in the 1930s. The governor assured the people that the rites were dedicated to the ancestors, and therefore were patriotic and not religious in character, but Korean Christians, having abandoned the worship of their own ancestors as idolatrous, were not easily convinced of this (Kang Wi-jo 1987:35). Nor were they persuaded by the arguments developed by Christians in Japan for observance of State Shinto, such as that serving the emperor was equivalent to serving God, that the Japanese empire was bringing the kingdom of God and that the Japanese were the chosen race to spread peace and prosperity across Asia (Vanderbilt 2009:63–66). Many individual Christians faced agonising choices because refusal to participate could cost them their jobs or qualifications (Blair and Hunt 1977:89). Christian schools in particular faced a dilemma when they were required to take students to the shrines. Church decision-making bodies understandably hesitated to take a firm stance on the issue so each school authority had to make up its own mind and most complied out of practical necessity. If individual pupils did not conform, pressure was put on their parents (Kim Yang-sun 2004:93–100; A. Clark 1971:221–26). A crisis came when in autumn 1935 two Presbyterian missionary educators in Pyongyang publically refused to participate in the shrine worship and were stripped of their licenses to teach in Korea. Opinion was divided among both missionaries and pastors, but some of the latter, notably Park Hyeong-ryong and Ju Gi-cheol, pastor of Sanjeonghyeon Presbyterian Church in Pyongyang, strongly advised that there should be no compromise. A committee of Japanese church leaders was sent to Korea to persuade them otherwise (A. Clark 1971:224–228). After petitions and further negotiations with the government-general by leading figures such as Yun Chi-ho and Yang Ju-sam produced no workable compromise (IMC 1938:3–10), US Presbyterian missionaries reluctantly closed their mission-run Christian schools. Many parents objected strongly to the loss of their children's education, and in a few instances the missions transferred their schools to them (Kim Yang-sun 2004:99–103; Lee Sung-jeon 2009; Brown 2009:390–91).

In 1937 the authorities ordered the churches themselves to conduct Shinto rites and visit shrines as part of their activities. The Methodists, under pressure from the mission, decided to comply. Their cultural theology allowed them to justify accepting the Japanese authorities' insistence that the ceremonies were civil and not 'purely' religious acts (Ryu Dong-sik 2005b: 641–54). Catholics also complied because in May 1936 the Sacred Congregation for the Propagation of the Faith had signed a concordat with the Japanese government which declared the rites to be civil acts only. They reminded the faithful that the Propaganda Fide had from the beginning accommodated all customs that were not in contradiction to faith and morals. This was a reversal of the previous position which prohibited participation in ceremonies on the grounds that they were religious. The apostolic prefect of Pyongyang, John E. Morris, a Maryknoll father, was forced to resign when he objected to this new ruling. Other clergy and women religious resigned in protest, and some institutions had to close (RFKCH 2010:124–26). Ironically, the same magisterial logic also resulted in Catholics being allowed to practise Confucian-style ancestor veneration, which they had resisted at such cost in the nineteenth century. In 1939, Pope Pius XII declared ancestor ceremonies to be merely a civil rite, and from 1940 the Korean Catholic Church allowed certain practices, including bowing before ancestor tablets, burning incense in front of a corpse or picture, offering food and wine before the memorial to the ancestor, giving prayers for the dead, and also paying respects at the graves of ancestors, as other Koreans did on the death days and memorial days (Park Chang-won 2011:158–59; Kim Myung-hyuk 1988:25–26; Rausch and Baker 2007:383–91).

Meanwhile, some Presbyterians were engaged in a battle against the Japanese regime similar to that fought by the early Catholics against Confucian hegemony. The fact that the Catholics and Methodists had complied with demands for participation in Shinto ceremonies only increased the conservatives' determination not to compromise. When the influential North Pyeongan Synod passed a resolution in February 1938 admitting that Shintoism was civic and not religious, Pyongyang Seminary students protested. They started a movement to censure those responsible and to put pressure on the other synods not to comply. Nevertheless, within a few months seventeen of the twenty-three synods had followed suit (A. Clark 1971:226; Kim Yang-sun 2004:103–4). Furthermore, the government-general told the leaders of the General Assembly that at their meeting in September 1938 they would have to agree to the following motion: 'We understand that Shintoism is not a religion nor is it against the doctrines of Christianity, and we acknowledge that attending the Shinto shrine is a patriotic national ceremony' (Rhie and Cho 1997:149; our translation). On 9 September 1938 when, with a heavy police presence, delegates from all the synods met in Seomunbak Church in Pyongyang, each representative was under threat of arrest if he did not approve the motion, and some of their fellows like Ju Gi-cheol were already in gaol. When the motion was put to the meeting by the moderator, Hong Taek-gi, several delegates who had been ordered to do so spoke in support. Hard-line missionaries who attempted to speak against the motion were shouted down by police or roughly removed from the room. The vote for the motion was weakly voiced, and no opportunity to vote against it was given. Afterwards most of the delegates paid obeisance at the main Shinto shrine (A. Clark 1971:228–29; Kim In-soo 1997:505–10).

Although the General Assembly had approved participation in Shinto rites, Presbyterian resistance continued and the Alliance of Women Evangelists Associations managed to postpone their decision beyond 1940 (Chang Sung-jin 2005:290–91; Yi Hyo-jae 1985:98). The main areas of dissent were the Pyongyang region, the south-east and Manchuria, and the leading dissenter was Ju Gi-cheol. He cited the example of the prophets who proclaimed the word of God fearlessly and prepared himself for martyrdom, and his church stood out against the authorities until it was closed down. In a sermon in February 1939, Ju was heard to declare: 'O Pyongyang, the Jerusalem of the East, the glory has departed from you!' (J. Kim 1992:345–46). Ju and others – notably Rev. Han Sang-dong in South Kyeongsang province and the evangelist Yi Ju-won in South Pyeongan province – tried systematically to create a national movement and a re-unified 'true' church. Some conservative missionaries also lent their support, including Australian missionaries in the Busan area and, in Manchuria, Bruce F. Hunt, a friend of Machen and a founding member of the Orthodox Presbyterian Church which had split from the Presbyterian Church in the United States. The Koreans covenanted together that children should be home-schooled rather than attend schools where Shinto ceremonies were practised and that resisting believers should undermine the existing churches and create a new church body. The numbers in the official churches dropped significantly in the parts of the country targeted by the plan, but the level of surveillance – through a strengthened Japanese version of the five-household system – was such that in most cases it was impossible to coordinate the Korean believers. In July 1940 the police uncovered the network and made multiple arrests in the different regions (Kim Yang-sun 2004:112–16; Park Chung-shin 2003:155–56). Many other ordinary Christians took their own measures to avoid submitting to shrine worship. Uncounted numbers of Christians abandoned the visible church as apostate; in order to maintain their faith they emigrated, escaped to mountains or worshipped in private, hoping for the Second Coming and Judgement Day (Pak Ung-kyu 2005:191–98; Blair and Hunt 1977:94–95). These included some Catholics and Methodists as well (Kim Yang-sun 2004:100; Choi Seok-u 1996:154).

If the mainline Protestant churches were under attack, the smaller denominations were even more so. The Salvation Army had already had its name changed in 1940 to the less threatening Salvation Society. Two years later it was forcibly disbanded. The Holiness churches were targeted because of their millennial message, which was reinforced in the late 1930s in commentaries on the books of Revelation and Daniel by Yi Myeong-jik, in the journal *Hwalcheon*, in the revised hymnbook produced in 1937 (*Buheung Seongga*) and in the preaching of the most well-known Holiness evangelist, Lee Seong-bong, who made a nationwide impact in 1938 in the style of Kim Ik-du (Pak Ung-kyu 2005:143–45, 167). In 1941 the denomination was closed down; so also were the Seventh-day Adventists, the East Asia Christian Church (the Korean Baptists) and several Pentecostal congregations. Many members of these churches joined the resisting Presbyterians (Kim Ig-jin 2003:56–62, 71–76).

The Presbyterians were the only national group to mount serious opposition to the requirements for Shinto worship. In addition to the argument of religious freedom, they gave three religious reasons for resistance and drew on corresponding religious resources: first, Shinto rites were worship of another god, or gods, and therefore against the first and second commandments (Kang Wi-jo 2006:108). Second, they expected the end and impending judgement of unjust empires (Pak Ung-kyu 2005:191, 198). The more tyrannical the Japanese regime and the greater the suffering around them, the more convinced they were that these were the last days. The third reason was the biblical logic of suffering, which led from the suffering messiah to the coming of the messianic kingdom; this encouraged Christians to believe that they suffered on behalf of the whole Korean people (Kim Yong-bock 1981a). Their resistance was motivated 'not for the sake of the national independence movement per se but rather to maintain their [own] monotheistic beliefs' (Jang Suk-man 2004:137), but because Shinto was the chief civic symbol of imperial power neither the resisting Christians nor the Japanese could separate religion and patriotism in this matter (D. Clark 1997:172; Park Chang-won 2011:156). Resistance may have been expressed in religious terms but those who resisted Shinto ceremonies regarded them as an affront to their national pride and their resistance as part of the struggle for the nation. It is estimated that between 1938 and 1945 seventy Protestants were imprisoned for their resistance to Shinto rites and two hundred Protestant churches were closed down. Before the war ended, fifty Christians were to be martyred (Kim Yang-sun 1956:44–45; 2004:87–92, 103–16; Suh Kwang-sun 1991:55).

To better control Korean Christians, the Japanese government wished, first, to eliminate their foreign connections and, second, to bring the remaining Korean churches under one umbrella and into closer contact with Japanese churches. In May 1937 the Japanese claimed to have uncovered a treasonable plot and moved against personnel from the YMCA, Donguhoe and Heungeop Gurakbu (a Protestant self-reconstruction group identified with Yun Chi-ho and Shin Heung-u). Ahn Chang-ho died under guard in 1938, and Yun Chi-ho, Shin Heung-u and several staff members of Christian colleges were forced to resign (Wells 1990:160–61). The Korean Bible Society, Christian Literature Society, Sunday School Association and other organisations were required to cut their links with their global bodies and their properties were seized. Western missionaries were the next to be targeted. In 1939 when the archbishop of

Canterbury criticised Japan's war in China, several Anglican missionaries in Korea were temporarily imprisoned. As tensions rose, in November 1940 many US missionaries were in any case evacuated; most remaining North Americans, British and Australians had left on the advice of their respective governments before the attack on Pearl Harbor in 1941. Following that event, most of the remaining missionaries in Korea were interned. They included sixty-seven Roman Catholics, mostly from the Columbans and the Paris Mission. At great personal risk, Korean believers brought the imprisoned missionaries food and other necessities for several years. Only the German Benedictines were able to continue their work. The only benefit was that there were now for the first time more Korean priests than foreign clergy (D. Clark 1986:12; Choi Seok-u 1996:154; IMC 1942:10–11).

From 1942 the Protestant churches were forbidden to use their denominational names and were pressured into discussions aimed at an organic union of all Christian denominations (A. Clark 1971:231). This took place at an administrative level only, but it hindered future ecumenical relationships among Korean churches by raising questions about the motives for church unity. On a day-to-day level the institutional churches were now effectively under the control of the regime and were unable even to hold meetings and services without police permission and presence (Kang Wi-jo 1987:39–41). Now every church building had to install a Shinto shrine, and every service or meeting had to open with a Shinto ceremony and a pledge to the emperor. Larger gatherings and Christian education were forbidden, seminaries were closed and publications were shut down. The Sunday holiday and other religious holidays were abolished, so there were few opportunities for Christians to meet. The Japanese now expected churches to pray and raise funds for the war effort, which they described as a 'Holy War'. Some church employees collaborated under pressure by encouraging Christians to give their possessions to the war effort and send their sons to fight and their daughters to work for the Japanese. Among the most prominent named as collaborators after the Liberation were Yun Chi-ho, Kim Hwal-ran and the educator Paik Lak-geoon (Park Chung-shin 2003:156; Wells 1990:115–16; Choi Hyae-weol 2009:151–55). Pastors, priests and other church workers were either conscripted or pressed into factory work, and most of the social projects of the churches had to be discontinued. The Japanese commandeered churches and stripped them of their bells to melt down for ammunition. Catholics were required to offer masses for the war dead, and the Catholic press published propaganda linking martyrdom with sacrifice for Japan – a strike at the heart of the Church of the Martyrs (RFKCH 2010:124). Christians were no longer allowed to make any claim for the supremacy or transcendence of God over earthly rulers. Portions of the Bible dealing with judgement and the Second Coming were not to be read or preached on. Any reference in hymns or prayers to the kingdom of God or the lordship of Christ had to be excised. All that the churches could boast of was that they continued to use Korean for their activities, which no other public body did (Kim Kwan-sik 1947:127–28, 132–35).

Structurally, in the Catholic Church, Japanese aims were achieved by forcibly replacing Western bishops (with the exception of one German) with Japanese and Korean ones in an attempt to 'purify' the church. In 1942 for the first time a Korean, Noh Ki-nam (Paul), was ordained bishop and appointed acting vicar apostolic for Seoul, Pyongyang and Chuncheon, but he had little autonomy (Choi Seok-u 1996:154). On 1 August 1945 – just days before the end of the war – the remaining Korean Protestant churches became simply a Korean division, Joseon Gyodan, under the United Church of Christ in Japan (Kim Yang-sun 1956:43). But the obliteration of the Korean church's independence did not mean the end of Korean Christianity. The Catholics had a long history as an underground organisation, and the lay community could continue to meet for prayer. Protestants also had their tradition of self-support, and their practice of 'family worship' or local prayer meetings was a form of on-going resistance in the colonial period. In this way, Christian communities held out until the Liberation.

CHAPTER 5

Liberation, Service and Divisions, 1945–1961

Protestant and Catholic leaders in Korea welcomed their liberation from Japan on 15 August 1945 wholeheartedly and saw it as the opportunity they had been waiting for to shape a Christian future for the nation. Christian leaders urged that the Japanese be allowed to leave peacefully with no reprisals, while, ironically, popular wrath was directed at Korean collaborators instead (Foley 2003:25). The unexpected defeat of Japan was greeted more with relief than with ecstasy because, although the resistance armies had fought the Japanese occupiers for decades, Koreans were not the ultimate victors over them, and the circumstances of Korea's freedom only served to underline the country's dependence on foreign powers (Park Chung-shin 2003:158). The Japanese left behind a country with little national capital or technological capability and woefully unprepared – politically, economically, educationally, socially or culturally – for independence (Eckert et al. 1990:263; Kang Man-gil 2005:22, 98–100). Nevertheless, Koreans were 'determined to construct a strong state as an answer to foreign domination, military weakness and economic "backwardness"' (Armstrong 2007a:5). However, Korea was soon faced with even greater problems: another trusteeship leading to the division of the peninsula into two parts by occupying forces with a growing rivalry and the deepening of ideological divisions.

LIBERATION AND CHRISTIAN LEADERSHIP, 1945

In 1945 Christians were perhaps only 2–3 per cent of the population but they comprised a high proportion of educated Koreans and so they naturally presented themselves as leadership candidates as the retreating Japanese hastily looked to transfer power. The man who accepted the invitation was Yeo Un-hyeong, who had studied at Pyongyang Theological Seminary and worked as an assistant pastor. He called for unity and restraint from the people and set up the Committee for the Preparation of Korean

Independence (CPKI), which brought together leading nationalists of different persuasions, including many Christian figures such as the intellectual Yi Dong-hwa, the 1919 signatory Kim Chang-jun and the well-known Methodist minister Yi Gyu-gap. Koreans mobilised themselves at the local level in 'people's committees', of which most local chairpersons were Protestant ministers or lay Christian leaders (Armstrong 2004:119–20). On 6 September 1945, Yeo announced the formation of the Korean People's Republic (KPR) and a schedule for elections. The new government announced moderate leftist reforms and denounced several hundred accused of collaboration as 'national traitors' (Eckert et al. 1990:331–32).

Now all the churches had martyrs and liberated Christians were remembering the dead as well as trying to survive in this uncertain period. At the same time they were attending to the needs of many others who were left 'homeless, hungry and restless' by oppression and war (Kim Kwang-ok 1997:219). Protestant churches across the country were reopened and celebrated not only political freedom but also religious freedom through what they saw as the unexpected grace of God. Many who had continued their activities during the war in unregistered groups flocked to churches to give thanks, and gratitude for their liberation motivated them to spread the good news even more and plan further evangelistic campaigns. For the approximately one hundred and ten thousand baptised Catholics in 1945, the fact that Liberation fell on the feast of the Assumption further cemented the church's devotion to Mary, Mother of God (RFKCH 2010:132). Because the German missionaries had been able to operate throughout the war, Catholic practice had been continuous, especially in the north-east where the missionaries were based, and after Liberation it emerged very strongly. Pyongyang Diocese was ten times bigger than before the war, and 80 per cent of Sunday attendees were new members, although the total Catholic population was less than 1 per cent of the whole (IHCK 1996:373–74). Church members helped the repatriation of foreign priests – both those who had been interned and the Japanese ones – and, before any new missionaries arrived, institutions were reopened, popular devotional practices reappeared and work was resumed on building churches.

The arrival of foreign troops was greeted with the suspicion that this was yet another foreign occupation. In the north, many Christians were fearful of Communist control, even if only temporary, because of its anti-religious attitude and the stories from Christians fleeing Soviet-occupied Manchuria of looting and attacks on Christians and churches and about the killing of priests of Deokwon Abbey (Kang Wi-jo 1990; J. Kim and Chung 1964:341). The Russians stopped at the 38th parallel (of latitude) as agreed, and US forces moved into the south where Protestant Christians at least had high expectations of this 'Christian' nation. The announcement in December 1945 by the victorious powers of a five-year Soviet-American trusteeship over Korea was greeted with deep dismay and anger reminiscent of the reaction to the Japanese Protectorate imposed in 1905. It called forth more nationalist fervour for independence and Korean identity, and diaspora Christians in Hawaii and on the US mainland did their best to lobby against it (D. Yoo 2010:150).

Although the ideological context was different, both halves of the peninsula faced the same enormous challenges of the post-colonial period which were further exacerbated by the division into two isolated zones – north and south. For the churches as institutions there were two main issues to be addressed after the departure of the Japanese: administrative restructuring and dealing with collaborators. Restructuring was needed because of the logistical difficulties of having churches split between US and Soviet administrations. Because its centre was in Seoul rather than in the north, the administration of the Catholic Church was not so much affected. The vicariate of Yeonbyeon in Manchuria was formally placed under the church in China, and the two provinces in the north became de facto separated from the rest of the Catholic Church. The loss of Pyeongan province, which, after Gyeonggi province, had had the second highest concentration of Catholics in Korea in 1941, was a great blow and meant that an estimated twenty-five thousand Catholics in the north were split off from the rest of the church (D. Baker 1997:148).

The mainline Protestant churches were in a more complicated situation administratively. The Presbyterians were particularly badly affected because northern Korea, the north-west especially, was their stronghold. In 1945 there were approximately two hundred thousand Protestant Christians in the north in about one thousand five hundred churches (Heo Myung-sup 2009:80). On the one hand, they had been divided north and south, but on the other hand, the Protestant churches had been forcibly united by the Japanese into the Joseon Gyodan. On 8 September 1945, the day of arrival of the first US troops, the Gyodan met in Seoul as a southern synod only. Although it was an imposed colonial construction in the last months of the war, its leaders argued that the Gyodan should continue because a single church was an expression of church unity; moreover, it would give the church a clear voice in the political turmoil of the time and offer better support to the leaders of the interim government. They formally changed its name to Joseon Gidokgyodan to indicate its independence of Japan. They also agreed to start a weekly Christian newspaper and to hold a special memorial service for war martyrs (IHCK 2009:15–18). Meanwhile in Pyongyang both Presbyterians and Methodists held rival meetings in which they publically repented of Shinto worship (IHCK 1996:354, 361). Although many Presbyterian church leaders in Seoul wished the Gyodan to continue, many Methodists followed Yi Gyu-gap in protesting its leadership by collaborators and left, so the Gyodan could no longer function as a united church. Methodists held a general conference in January 1946 which re-established the church and agreed to set up a new seminary to replace the one closed by the Japanese (A. Clark 1971:238; IHCK 1996:362). However, in 1948 the church in the south split over the collaboration issue and there were two rival bishops until 1949 when they came together under the leadership of Kim Yu-sun (Ryu Dong-sik 2005b:702–8).

Dealing with Christian collaborators was not only an internal church matter because among those who were being publically identified were leading Protestant nationalists. It was also a complex issue because there were different levels of collaboration, from those who had actively pursued the aims of the colonial government and held posts in the administration to others who had done the minimum to comply with the Shinto worship imposed on the churches. The issue of collaboration within the Presbyterian Church was particularly intense because of the strong stand taken by some against Shinto shrine rites. Already in August 1945 one millenarian group, the Empire of Mount Sion Movement led by Park Dong-gi in the Gyeongju area declared independence from the rest of the Presbyterian Church, which they accused of idolatry (Grayson 2011). The Presbyterian ministers in the north had imposed on themselves a one-month suspension for penance in which they would not preach or take part in public activities. However, for many of those pastors just released from prison – chulok seongdo or 'released believers' – this was not enough. Twenty pastors and church leaders met on 20 September in Sanjeonghyeon Church in Pyongyang, where Ju Gi-cheol, who had died in prison for his opposition to shrine worship, had been the pastor. They declared that all pastors should take a two-month suspension and confess their sins of collaboration publically before resuming their ministry. Furthermore, they denounced the church as sinful and fallen for not having held firm in the face of the Japanese temptation and called for 'restoration' of the churches, which implied both restructuring and purification (Kim Yang-sun 1956:45–46; IHCK 1996:353–55).

On 14 November 1945, under worsening circumstances for Christians in the north, approximately two hundred representatives of the presbyteries of Pyeongan and Hamgyeong provinces plus some Methodist and Holiness church leaders met and Park Hyeong-ryong presented the case of the 'released believers'. It provoked heated debate. Hong Taek-gi, who had been the moderator in 1938 when the church had submitted to shrine worship, argued, first, that the more urgent problem was dealing with tensions and conflicts with Communists and, second, that he and other leaders who had not been imprisoned had nevertheless suffered to maintain the church in a difficult time. Others urged that sins were a personal matter best left to individual conscience, and the released believers' proposal was firmly rejected (Kim Yang-sun 1956:46). By accusing everyone else of being collaborators, the released believers had alienated most of the church leaders (IHCK 1996:356). In April 1946 they established a separate Restoration Church (Jaegeon Gyohoe) with seventy-one members and led by Lee Gi-seon. Under the slogan, 'Let us ... cut ourselves off from all injustice and hypocrisy', they gathered about thirty congregations and formed a separate presbytery (Rhie and Cho 1997:167; our translation). Their radically counter-cultural views led to constant tension with the Communist government, and many were killed or escaped southwards.

The northerners made contact with the Presbyterian Church in the south, and to address the problem of the division of the country it was agreed that, until unification, they would form two separate administrations (A. Clark 1971:234–36). The northern church met in December and agreed to use the constitution in its pre-Gyodan form. It was decided that the entire church would confess their sins of collaboration and that church officers would do two months' penance, as proposed by the released believers, but this was later commuted to probation because the radical conservatives and the active collaborators had already left (IHCK 1996:356–58). At the same time, the synod called the church back to what was seen as its core business by instigating a nationwide evangelistic campaign to mark the Liberation (Park Chung-shin 2003:163–64). The meeting also endorsed the reopening of Pyongyang Seminary in October under the local presbytery. Without any alternative seminary, in 1946 the General Assembly in the south approved Kim Jae-jun's Joseon Seminary, although there continued to be misgivings about its doctrine (A. Clark 1971:274–77). In early 1947 it was reported to have 306 students, 80 per cent of whom were high school graduates. There were also sixty women 'in attendance'. Some of the students were preparing hopefully for ministry in the north when the border reopened (Kim Kwan-sik 1947:134).

THE SUPPRESSION OF CHRISTIANITY IN THE NORTH, 1945–1950

In the northern zone of occupation, the Soviets initially needed the cooperation of the religions, including the approximately three hundred thousand Christians – about 18 per cent of the population (Heo Myung-sup 2009:98). They declared freedom of religion and invited religious people to work with them. Although also tainted by collaboration, Cho Man-sik became the leader of the interim government in the north (Armstrong 2004:55). In that capacity in October 1945 he presented the thirty-three-year-old freedom fighter and Communist Kim Il-sung to the people in a ceremony which included a Christian service. Kim, born in Mangyeondae near Pyongyang, had himself originated from the 'Christian, upwardly mobile, budding middle class' of the colonial period (Cumings 2004:108). His father had attended Soongsil Middle School. His maternal grandfather was a Presbyterian elder in Chilgol Church in South Pyeongan province, where his mother, Kang Ban-seok, to whom he seems to have been close, was also an active member. Kim attended the youth activities there before the family's move to Manchuria (cf. Cumings 2005:417–24).

Discussion at the northern synod in Pyongyang in December 1945 was not just about internal matters but also about the stance that the church should take vis-à-vis the new regime. Although many Christians were sympathetic to the social aims of Communism, the familiar taunts of the 1920s and 1930s were now repeated. Christians were accused of being the enemies of Socialism, first because they were religious, second because they were associated with Americans, third because most of them had received a rightist education and fourth because many were included in the rising middle class, which had collaborated with the Japanese. Most Christian leaders therefore strongly resisted the prospect of a Communist government. They argued that religious freedom should be their priority and that therefore the church must get involved politically to defeat materialism and replace it with a spiritual foundation for the nation based on Christianity (Heo Myung-sup 2009:58–71). Protestant leaders reasoned that the Americans intended to establish 'Christendom' in the US-occupied areas accompanied by human rights, freedom of speech and other values which they believed were founded on Christian teaching and a form of democracy superior to Communism. Furthermore, since the leaders of the interim government in the south – Rhee Syng-man, Kim Gu and Kim Gyu-sik – were all Protestants, they thought that Christians could unite the nation under one religion. With this vision of founding a unified Christian nation, and the prospect of elections, Protestants formed Christian political parties inspired by those arising in European countries after the end of the war as alternatives to the Communist Party (Han Kyung-chik 2010b:419).

Han Kyung-chik, who as a young man had been reprimanded for his role in the Abingdon Bible Commentary controversy, emerged as a key leader in this period. As pastor of the Second Presbyterian Church in Sinuiju, he urged his congregation to exercise the democratic leverage they now had to bring about 'freedom and equality supportive of human development' (Han Kyung-chik 2010b; Lee Won-sul, Lee and Han 2005). Han co-founded one of the first parties, the Christian Socialist Democratic Party, in Sinuiju in September 1945. District branches were organised with local churches as the headquarters. But with Christians calling for liberal democracy and effectively expressing their preference for the regime in the south, co-operation with the Communists could not continue (Kim Heung-soo and Ryu 2002:67; Heo Myung-sup 2009:98). Despite dropping the word 'Christian' from its name, the new party was targeted, and in October Han fled south. Outright conflict broke out in Sinuiju in November, when local metalworkers were mobilised to attack a party meeting and one elder was beaten to death. When a week later, in protest, about five thousand Christian students from Sinuiju and other towns marched on the Workers' Party headquarters in Sinuiju, at least twenty were shot dead. Protestant leaders were beaten and arrested, including the Christian thinker Ham Sok-hon (Ham Seok-heon), who was at that time a member of the provincial people's committee, and the party was dissolved. The largest of the other Christian-led parties was Cho Man-sik's Joseon Democratic Party (Joseon Minjudang). It attracted the propertied and professionals in the north, especially Christians, and also Socialists who opposed the trusteeship arrangement which the Korean Workers' Party, led by Kim Il-sung, under pressure from the Soviets, now backed. By early 1946 the Democratic Party had half a million members, whereas all the Communist groups together had only about four thousand five hundred (IHCK 1996:385). But Kim Il-sung and his party were determined to seize power and unscrupulous in their means, and they pushed through their plans to create a Communist society in the north (Nahm 1989:378–420). Cho Man-sik disappeared from public view in January 1946 and is presumed to have been killed while in custody (A. Clark 1971:239–47; Kim Heung-soo and Ryu 2002:65–66).

The next main clash between Protestants and Communists was over the anniversary celebration of the March 1st movement in 1946. Christians planned special services, but the Communists insisted that they should attend a People's Assembly instead that day, saying that the anniversary belonged to the proletariat not the Christians and accusing them of sectarianism. Christians went ahead with their services, which were also protest meetings against Socialist policies and the arrest of Cho Man-sik, and in support of freedom of religion, but they were disrupted by Communists (IHCK 1996:394–95). In Uiju, Communists led a mob into the church, wrecked the pulpit and dragged the pastor around the city in an ox-cart while he wore insulting placards round his neck. The following week it was reported that even more Christians met in the desecrated church; however, even this freedom was soon to be denied them (D. Clark 1997:173–76; A. Clark 1971:241–42; Kim Kwan-sik 1947:129).

In March 1946, after suppressing the opposition, the Communist Party moved rapidly to establish Socialism through radical land reform and de-Japanisation, which were hugely popular measures (Armstrong 2004:56; IHCK 1996:376; Cumings 2004:130–32). Peasants and workers were delighted to gain rights to a property and smallholding, which must have appeared to poor Christians to be the fulfilment of 'good news to the poor'. But many landowners who were deprived of their holdings and offered instead a similar plot of land in a different region preferred to take the opportunity to move to the south; these included many leading Christians (IHCK 1996:377, 385, 396). In August 1946, all Japanese- or collaborator-owned properties were confiscated. Again Christians, who formed much of the business class, were adversely and disproportionately affected and even more chose to leave. After this confiscation of land, the largest landowners remaining were the organised religions: Buddhism and Christianity. Protestant churches owned most properties in total, but Deokwon Abbey in particular had vast tenanted holdings (Kim Heung-soo and Ryu 2002:70–73). So, although Kim's anti-religious policies may not have been ideological given his Protestant background and the fact that his party included Christians, Kim and his Russian backers had little choice politically but to move against the churches (Park Chung-shin 2003:161; Cumings 2005:232).

Even though many of the elite had left for the south, church attendance seems to have increased in the north in the first few years after 1945. But there was no longer any social benefit attached to being a Christian, and Christians were subjected to discriminatory treatment varying 'from imprisonment, restraint and ridicule to intimidation and annoyance' (Kim Kwan-sik 1947:129; D. Clark 1997:178). After 1946 the regime operated a totalitarian state. Christian publications were closed down, Christians were called out for public work or information meetings on Sundays and pressured to self-criticise and anti-Communists were re-educated (Cumings 2005:231–32). Communist youth propaganda teams constantly discredited the church as 'unscientific, unproductive and opiate', and rural churches especially suffered 'constant ridicule, intimidation and persuasive propaganda' (Kim Kwan-sik 1947:129–30). Refugees escaping south complained that the north was worse for Christians now than under the Japanese (Wheeler 1950:328). Religious education was prohibited in the expanded state schools, and young people were under strong pressure to join the Communist Youth League, although by 1948 still only 38 per cent of Christian youth had joined (IHCK 1996:382; Armstrong 2004:100–101). Even if the youth were not turned against Christianity, membership made it difficult, if not impossible, for them to participate in church activities. From June 1946 even pre-teens were organised into the Young Pioneers. In July 1946 equality of the sexes was proclaimed in law and centuries-old patterns of male preference were overturned (IHCK 1996:378; Cumings 2004:130–32). This called into question some of the gender practices of the churches, but such questions were largely irrelevant now because all women between thirty and fifty years of age were required to work to support the revolution and the middle-aged women who had been the backbone of the churches now had little time to spare for the Christian community (Nahm 1989:338–40).

Elections were scheduled for 3 November 1946, but the churches were marginal to the political process. To better control them, and to get out the Christian vote, the Communists set up an alternative Christian association, the Chosŏn[1] Christian Federation (CCF; Joseon Gidokgyo Yeonmaeng), which resembled the Japanese Gyodan. It was chaired by former Presbyterian pastor Kang Yang-uk, a high-ranking official and a relative of Kim Il-sung's mother. Several prominent Christians joined, including Park Sang-soon, a former missionary to China, and the revivalist Kim Ik-du (D. Clark 1997:177–78). The elections were widely boycotted by Protestants who were not members of the CCF: first, because only Communist candidates were allowed to stand, and second, because the elections were held on a Sunday. The northern synod insisted, as they had done under the Japanese, that Sunday observance was 'a life and death matter'. The Catholics also strongly reacted to the election date and for theological reasons prohibited the baptised from joining the Communist Party (Kim Heung-soo and Ryu 2002:76–81). The churches also insisted that they would not yield to pressure to open their premises for campaign events. The CCF countered by declaring their support for Kim Il-sung's

---

[1] This is the preferred North Korean transliteration of Joseon.

government and their opposition to the regime in the south, and by arguing that the church should set an example to the people by actively participating in the elections (IHCK 1996:398–39; A. Clark 1971:242). Kim Il-sung called the resisting Christian leaders and displayed his familiarity with Christianity by asking them what was wrong with doing good on the Sabbath – implicitly comparing them to Pharisees. He also pointed out that in the Protestant churches the election of officers is on Sunday (see Kim Heung-soo and Ryu 2002:82–83). The elections went ahead. A few Christians who stood for the Communists were among the successful candidates, but others remained in their churches all day, singing, praying and preaching, so that they could not be forced to vote (D. Clark 1997:176–79; T. S. Lee 2010:64–65).

In 1947 the CCF was organised at the local, provincial and national level and a third of Protestant pastors joined. Its establishment dismantled the roots of the Protestant community by closing many local congregations and ending the old denominational structures, but much ordinary church life continued under its umbrella (D. Clark 1997:178). In April 1947 the number of Protestant churches in Pyongyang had actually grown since the war, along with Pyongyang's population. United dawn prayer meetings were held to celebrate the anniversary of the Pyongyang revival, and on one occasion fifteen thousand to twenty thousand people gathered for an outdoor united service. Even the Presbyterian seminary was functioning, although the chair of the faculty, Kim In-jun, was in prison along with five pastors. Elsewhere on the mission compound, Russians and Korean elite were living in the former missionary houses and the mission hospital was being run by the party (Wheeler 1950:325–26; IHCK 1996:359). But when a delegation from the Presbyterian Church in the United States of America (PCUSA) was refused permission to visit Pyongyang, it was clear that the northern churches were cut off not only from the south but also from the Western Christian world (Wheeler 1950:328; Kim Kwan-sik 1947:129–30).

The Catholic Church was also pressured to support the government; priests and believers were pressured to join the CCF, but the bishop of Pyongyang, Hong Yong-ho, ordered Catholic believers to refuse. From 1947 the authorities began closing churches and insisted that monks and nuns take up employment (Chérel-Riquier 2013:75–76). In May 1947 the authorities moved to take over the land attached to the abbey at Deokwon, ostensibly because anti-election leaflets had been printed at its facilities (Kim Heung-soo and Ryu 2002:80–82). The regime put the remaining Catholic missionaries and all believers under strict surveillance. Arbitrary arrests of Christian leaders, attacks by thugs and unexplained disappearances increased (Choi Seok-u 1984:11; Park Chung-shin 2003:165).

After the establishment of two separate republics in 1948, the Communists quashed the remaining independent church activities. Leaders of the old denominations were taken into custody, and membership in the CCF was forced on all church officers; congregations which did not join were closed. Redundant churches were taken over for government information activities ('enlightenment'), and Christian hymns were replaced by revolutionary songs, which used the same musical style as congregational singing (Hoare and Pares 2005:95–107; Pratt 2006:279–303). The Presbyterian and Methodist seminaries in Pyongyang kept operating independently until 1949 when the CCF insisted that only staff and students who pledged loyalty to the party could teach and study, and that Communist doctrine also had to be taught (IHCK 1996:397; D. Clark 1997:177–78). By 1949 all Protestant schools had been national-ised, and by 1950 all church workers not in the CCF were in prison (D. Clark 1997:178; A. Clark 1971:243–44). In May 1949 the Benedictines of Deokwon were imprisoned together with the local priests and nuns and the seminary was turned into Wonsan Agricultural College. The Wonsan Convent was taken over for use as a hospital, and Haeseong School became an institute for the children of Russian soldiers. Thirty-six of the Deokwon community were later martyred, including the abbot, Bishop Boniface Sauer, and a Korean priest, Kim Chi-ho (Benedict) (J. Kim and Chung 1964:433–72). Bishop Hong of Pyongyang wrote a letter of protest at the arrests to Kim Il-sung, whereupon he was also detained, together with other priests in the Pyongyang vicariate. With only a handful of priests left, most churches were closed. Lay Catholics were also arrested and their houses and property confiscated (D. Baker 1997:148; J. Kim and Chung 1964:341–42).

In a speech in October 1949, Kim Il-sung made clear his position: 'Even though Christians continue to believe in God, they should not believe in the God of other nations but in the God of Joseon' (Kim Heung-soo and Ryu 2002:83; our translation). Although nominally tolerated, faced with this imperative, 'meaningful organized religion, whether Buddhist, Confucian or Christian', had 'ceased to exist' in North Korea even before the Korean War (Buzo 2002:110.). In 1950, as part of their preparation for invasion of the south, Communists rounded up the remaining leaders of all the churches. These included Kim Yi-han (Alexey), who had served as priest for the Russian Orthodox Mission to Korea since 1947 (K. Baker 2006:205). Church buildings were designated enemy property because of their mission history, and during the war they were taken over for use as offices on the understanding that Western forces would not bomb them. When the US military learned of this, they deliberately targeted churches, ironically helping to finally destroy any public form of Christianity in the north (D. Clark 1997:178).

Meanwhile, to the US forces arriving in the south in September 1945 under General Douglas MacArthur, the Korean People's Republic with its people's committees looked like a Soviet-orchestrated attempt to institute Communism (Eckert et al. 1990:337). General John R. Hodge, the new military governor, forcibly disbanded the committees and instead re-established much of the colonial administration, largely staffed with the same personnel who were loathed as collaborators. Landowners and industrialists, including collaborators, were allowed to keep their property, and the Americans acted like conquerors (D. Clark 2003:288–91). Naturally there was great resentment expressed in strikes, civil disobedience, guerrilla activity and popular uprisings. In addition to political instability, the colonial economy had collapsed, and soon there was rampant inflation so that the country was almost completely dependent on a massive US relief programme. A further complication was large-scale immigration. In the period 1945–1949 more than two million mostly destitute refugees were repatriated to southern Korea from the former Japanese empire, not to mention those who had been internally displaced by the Japanese (Foley 2003:23).

For Protestants in the south, the fact that liberation from Japan had come from the 'Christian' nation of the United States confirmed the superior power of their faith. Missionaries had long assured Koreans of American good intentions and that, unlike other foreigners, they came to give instead of take. Now for many Koreans, the Americans appeared as 'angels of salvation' and 'God's army' to rescue them from tyranny (Heo Myung-sup 2009:58–60). Catholics also took comfort from the fact that among those accompanying General Hodge to witness the Japanese surrender was Francis Cardinal Spellman, the influential archbishop of New York and former aide to Pope Pius XII, who was equally outspoken in his condemnation of Communism (Hanson 1980:9, 44). The Christian nature of the US administration was confirmed in Korean eyes when one of the first acts of the US military government was to declare freedom of religion. Other actions also suggested that Christianity was the preferred religion of the occupiers: Sunday was made a day of rest and Christmas a public holiday; Shinto shrines were destroyed and most of the properties were allocated to

Christian groups; some former Protestant missionaries, and in some cases their children, were employed by the US military government as advisors and interpreters; and troops and members of the US administration actively assisted the churches in their rebuilding (Heo Myung-sup 2009:126–42).

The American regime was sympathetic to Christians because both Protestant and Catholic leaders shared its anti-Communism, because the churches presented organised networks for the distribution of aid and because Christians were most likely to have some English and awareness of Western culture. Christians were best placed to take advantage of opportunities to work with the regime as interpreters, aid workers, advisors, and so on. So being a Christian was soon perceived as advantageous in the new order (D. Clark 2007:174–75). The US regime appointed many Christians to prominent positions. In 1946–1947 seven out of thirteen administrative advisors were Protestants who had studied in the United States and thirty-five out of the fifty highest positions in the US administration were held by Protestants (Park Chung-shin 2003:106, 167–75; T. S. Lee 2010:66; cf. Kim Kwan-sik 1947:131). Also prominent among the advisors was the Catholic educator Chang Myon (John; Jang Myeon), a descendant of nineteenth-century martyrs, who had the backing of the Catholic hierarchy. However, despite the boost that the US occupation gave to Christianity, the regime's favouritism towards Christians should not be overemphasised. The military regime cooperated first with the Japanese and the pro-Japanese and then with well-to-do Koreans. It was guided primarily by pragmatic considerations intended more to protect Japan than Korea, first by preventing the Soviet advance and second by establishing Western-style liberal democracy in the south (Heo Myung-sup 2009:110–25).

In this context, churches faced not only structural issues and the legacy of collaboration but also the question of how to build a new nation (Heo Myung-sup 2009:58–60). Anticipating democratic elections and with an agenda to make Korea a Christian nation, Protestants formed Christian political parties not just as private individuals but also as church communities, contrary to the earlier missionary insistence on the separation of the church from politics (Heo Myung-sup 2009:76–83). Most tended to the political right, but the Joseon Christian National Youth Association supported Kim Gu and Kim Gyu-sik, who had been leaders of the CPKI, which was denounced as Communist by conservative Protestants (IHCK 2009:38–40; Heo Myung-sup 2009:79–80). In selecting their political allies, the Americans rejected all the explicitly Christian parties and identified the right-wing Korean Democratic Party (KDP), founded by a group of landlords and businessmen (including the Christian businessman

Kim Seong-su), as the group they could work with. The KDP persuaded returned anti-Japanese exiles to lend it legitimacy, notably the seventy-year-old Rhee Syng-man, who had patriotic credentials and was close to the Americans (Eckert et al. 1990:341–42).

After so many years in exile, Rhee did not have strong support in Korea itself, but he could call on Protestant networks and particularly Methodist support. He also had access to the leadership of the Catholic Church. Cardinal Spellman had supported him and his Austrian Catholic wife, Francesca Donner, who worked as his secretary; Rhee kept in close touch with Father, now Monsignor, Byrne, who became apostolic visitor to Korea, and later with John J. Muccio, the US envoy, 1948–1952, and also a Catholic (Cumings 2005:346–47). During his years in the United States and Europe, Rhee had come to identify Western culture and its political system with Christianity and to link ideology with religious conviction, so he encouraged the nexus between faith and politics. Although in November 1945, the three most prominent political leaders, Kim Gu, Kim Gyu-sik and Rhee Syng-man, shared a platform at Chungdong Church and urged that Korea be built on the basis of the Bible and on 'Christ, the Rock', Rhee soon accused the other two of appeasement towards Communism (IHCK 2009:44). Christians who had fled from the north tended to back Rhee because they saw him as most strongly anti-Communist, and church leaders under attack for collaboration found Rhee's party much more welcoming than the others. So, despite there being fewer Christian leaders initially among the KDP than among the CPKI, in time more gravitated towards Rhee's party (Park Chung-shin 2003:175).

The Protestant churches in the south were robbed of three-fifths of their membership and many of their ablest leaders were in the north; nevertheless soon after the Liberation evangelistic campaigns were held in Seoul and Daegu. They used the pre-war methods of dawn prayer meetings, Bible study classes, personal evangelism and mass revival meetings, and the results were impressive. Christian schools and colleges, medical work, social welfare projects and theological education were also reopened. The churches were denominationally divided once more, but the Gyodan remained in existence as the ecumenical organisation of the churches, particularly in relating to foreign agencies, until October 1946 when the Christian Council of Korea (later the National Council of Churches in Korea) was organised. The council now included the Presbyterian, Methodist and Holiness churches; the Church of Christ (a mission started in 1927 in Hamgyeong province by Dong Seok-gi, who had converted in the United States); the Salvation Army; the YMCA and YWCA; the Christian Union of Korea; the

Christian New People's Society; the Korean Bible Society; and six Western missionary bodies (Kim Kwan-sik 1947:125–29).

Churches which had been closed completely by the Japanese were reopening and connecting with international networks. The well-known revivalist Lee Seong-bong was invited to lead the re-establishment of the Holiness churches, supported by the Oriental Missionary Society. The Salvation Army and the Seventh Day Adventists re-established their head-quarters, training institutions and activities. In 1949 the churches which had been associated with Fenwick came together to appeal to the Southern Baptists for support, and the US denomination sent a missionary couple (Kim Seung-jin 2000). The Korea Baptist Convention was founded in 1950 and a seminary in 1954. By 1959 there were 221 Baptist churches and preaching points, and Baptists were running a hospital in Busan, a theological seminary in Daejeon, orphanages in Incheon and a high school, Zion Baptist (cf. A. Clark 1971:238–39, 288–91). The Church of the Nazarene was 'officially organised' in 1948 as a result of an appeal from a native Korean Nazarene missionary, Jeong Nam-soo (Robert), who had gathered a handful of churches. The Pentecostals were constituted as a denomination only after the Korean War, but despite their lack of institutional recognition, they were very active.

In the Catholic Church, Japanese bishops and priests were replaced with Koreans or other foreigners. Two new Korean mission territories were added by the Holy See: the vicariate of Daejeon was assigned to the Paris Mission, and the Prefecture of Chuncheon was assigned to the Columban Fathers. In the three years to 1948 twelve thousand converts were received into the church (Considine 1949:168). On 6 October 1945, Father Peter Yang Gi-seop started a daily newspaper with the same name as the one suspended in 1906: *Kyunghyang Shinmun*. It took a firmly anti-Communist stance, as did other Catholic papers, and this is why the US military government was confident it could entrust the press it confiscated from the Communist Party in 1946 to the church (Chérel-Riquier 2013:70–71). Priests who fled from Manchuria and the north reported that clergy had been arrested, property confiscated and Christians discriminated against there, and this fanned anti-Communism in the south (Chérel-Riquier 2013:72–73). The Martyrs Committee was re-established in 1946, and the following year, as a statement that patriotism and Catholicism went together, the assassin Ahn Jung-geun was exonerated as a 'patriotic martyr' and given a high mass. Since the church's prohibition had been lifted, Catholics now venerated not only the martyrs but also the ancestors so that much of their devotional life was centred on remembrance of the dead.

At General Hodge's invitation, Western missionaries started to return to Korea in earnest beginning in the summer of 1946. They met regularly with the administration and with Hodge every Friday morning (Chérel-Riquier 2003:4). The re-entry of missionaries was particularly significant for the Catholic Church, which was still classified as under the missions. Many young Irish priests arrived to replace the older Columbans who had gone back home to recuperate after being interned. Once investigations, led by Monsignor Byrne, had shown that the government in the south was committed to democracy and against Communism, the Maryknoll Fathers returned to play a key role in the development of the church (J. Kim and Chung 1964:338). The apostolic delegate, Byrne, denounced the Communist persecution in the north and stressed the importance of growing Catholic youth movements to counteract it (Chérel-Riquier 2013:76–77). The monthly youth magazine was restarted in 1947, for the first time since 1936. With the Paris Mission eclipsed and the German Benedictines trapped in the north, English became the main language of the Catholic missions. Mainly with US support, welfare agencies – hospitals, clinics, orphanages, old peoples' homes and a leprosy colony – were re-established and expanded (RFKCH 2010: 132–34).

North American Protestant mission organisations and Korean leaders also identified written works as a priority, especially because the Communists were well armed with their own literature, and they organised large shipments of New Testaments and Christian tracts and books (Kim Kwan-sik 1947:135–40). A union committee of Presbyterians, Methodists and Holiness members was formed which produced a new union hymnal of 586 hymns, and J. Merle Davis prepared a special edition of his booklet *The Christian Answer to Communism* which was widely distributed (A. Clark 1971:266). The Protestant churches had governed themselves since the 1930s, but most foreign mission organisations seemed to expect that they would need their direction as well as financial support for some time to come. Whereas Koreans were starting afresh in a post-colonial context, returning missionaries tended to be more concerned with rebuilding what had been lost and had difficulty adapting to the new situation. There were clashes over mission property, appropriation of funds and support for theological education (IMC 1949:9; D. Clark 1986:17–18).

Until the establishment of two separate Korean states in 1948, Christians and others dissatisfied with the regime in the north were allowed to leave. A disproportionate number of Christians did so, both because they feared arrest or attack and because they were adversely affected by the social and economic reforms. Christians were also among the intellectuals who disliked the lack of freedom of thought, the students who went to Seoul for education and the young men who left to avoid being drafted into the Communist army. Most still could not imagine that the division would last so they left their families behind, with the result that later they became permanently separated (Foley 2003:30–35, 43; Kim Kwan-sik 1947:126). Refugees from the north were outsiders in the south, and Christians from the north showed a high degree of solidarity with each other. Instead of joining southern churches, they founded new ones, mostly in the larger cities, and attracted other Koreans from the north to them. One of the early arrivals after the events in Sinuiju was Han Kyung-chik, who in December 1945 founded Bethany Evangelistic Church in Seoul with twenty-seven other Sinuiju refugees (Youngnak Church 1998:64–68). Already by spring 1946 it had five hundred members. Han and Kim Jae-jun persuaded the US authorities to hand over to them about forty Tenrikyō (a Shinto sect) properties in Seoul. They used these to build churches and institutions. The congregation of Bethany Church was allocated the site of the main Tenrikyō shrine, which was not far from the Catholic cathedral, and its national headquarters became the new site of Joseon Seminary (Heo Myung-sup 2009:126–38; Kang In-cheol 2004:158–60).

By 1947 the site of Bethany Church, now renamed Youngnak Church, was full of activity in tents equipped with loudspeakers. Many of the members had already established themselves in business and were supporting the church. Other refugees got any work they could but were homeless, so they came to the church after work for the evening service, were fed from a communal kitchen supplied by a women's rice collection, and then slept there (Wheeler 1950:328; Lee Won-sul et al. 2005:128–31). The church supported an orphanage and student hostels and mobilised the young people to preach and offer practical help in refugee camps, slums and rural areas. Since it was clear that there was no immediate prospect of return to the north, the congregation began work on a permanent building using mainly funds raised by the refugees themselves. The congregation eventually constructed with their own labour a 2,500-seat stone building in Gothic Revivalist style. The sanctuary was filled at the morning service, so to cope with demand Youngnak became the first church to hold more than one service on a Sunday morning. Han Kyung-chik prayed that the church should be 'a centre for evangelisation of the Korean people', 'a stronghold of liberal democracy' and 'a source of social renewal' (Han Kyung-chik 2010b:377), and it became the prototype of later Korean 'megachurches' (Fig. 8).

8. Youngnak Church building opened in early 1950. Originally founded by refugees from the north in 1945 as Bethany Church, it became the first Korean megachurch. Photograph by Kim Dong-hwan.

The Christian migration from the north, where churches had been strongest, was to have a lasting impact on Christianity in the south. Many refugees were destitute but a significant proportion of them were from the north-west elite who had relatively high levels of education and knowledge of English, business acumen and, if they were landlords or industrialists, sometimes capital in the south. They shared a strident anti-Communism, and they told stories of ill-treatment by the Communists to the Christians in the south who were sheltering them. The Protestant northerners, comparing themselves to Israel entering the promised land, exuded an 'air of martyrdom' and a 'spirituality of resistance', and they soon challenged the leadership of the churches in the south to adopt their own conservative evangelicalism (D. Clark 1986:18). They also had a clear agenda to build up the church and evangelise the nation to ward off Communism. By 1950 northerners, especially Presbyterians, had used their relative wealth to establish 90 per cent of the two thousand or so new Protestant churches in the south (T. S. Lee 2010:65; Heo Myung-sup 2009:104; Kang In-cheol 2004:167).

The refugees from the north organised regional associations based on the churches, notably the North Korean Refugees Presbyterian Commissioners

(NKRPC; Ibuk Sindo Daepyohoe), which aimed to provide religious guidance, education and support for refugees from Pyeongan and Hwanghae provinces and to cooperate in restoring the church in the north (Kang In-cheol 2004:161). There was a similar but less powerful organisation of Presbyterian refugees from the north-east. Han Kyung-chik persuaded the Board of Foreign Missions of the PCUSA to loan the NKRPC one hundred and fifty thousand US dollars it had allocated for missionary work in the north on the understanding that the money could be reallocated as soon as conditions for missionary work there become feasible. The support network that these funds enabled the churches in the south to provide was so good that refugees, whether religious or not, joined the churches in order to benefit from the material relief they offered and to meet fellow refugees (Park Chung-shin 2003:43–44). The NKRPC established itself as a formidable pressure group on the churches in the south which were not as strong in numbers or social influence and were overwhelmed by the influx of refugees. At first, refugee churches founded by northerners existed outside the structures of the church in the south and therefore were without a voice in the denomination, but in 1947, with the churches in the north now firmly under Communist control, the southern General Assembly decided that it should be considered the 33rd General Assembly of the whole Korean Presbyterian Church. It also agreed that refugee pastors and church workers from the north could join a presbytery and serve churches in the denomination if they were vouched for by three other ministers. In November 1947, Youngnak Church joined its local synod – Gyeonggi – and other churches followed suit. Before long the northerners were integrated into the church in the south and began to take over its leadership (Kang In-cheol 2004; Kang In-cheol 2006:433–54).

As a result of migration movements, the old comity system established and maintained by the missionaries had now broken down completely but the churches that had resulted from it bore unmistakable regional characteristics and theological differences. Now that northerners were far from home, and intermingling with people from other regions, such allegiances called forth great loyalty, and regional rivalry fuelled division in the church. In particular, the northern Presbyterian churches were divided into the Jesus Group (Yejang), which had its origins in the north-west and was theologically conservative, and the Christ Group (Kijang) from the north-east, which had a more progressive agenda and was prepared to engage with biblical criticism. Disputes came to a head around the one Presbyterian theological seminary in the south, Joseon Seminary, where worries persisted among the north-westerners especially that the principal, Kim Jae-jun (originally from the north-east), was teaching and encouraging 'new theology', 'higher criticism', 'pragmatism' and 'liberal theology'. Claiming that they were 'shocked' and had had their faith in the Bible 'turned upside down', conservative students complained to the General Assembly, and also campaigned within Gyeonggi Presbytery, where both the seminary and Youngnak Church were situated (Rhie and Cho 1997:182–83). Kim admitted that he was liberal in theology but insisted he was orthodox in faith and accused foreign missionaries of stirring up the students in order to 'restore their pre-War authority' (Rhie and Cho 1997:195; cf. Adams 2012:87–92). Eventually, the north-westerners got their way in the General Assembly; in 1949 it also recognised the Presbyterian Theological Seminary, which had been re-founded in Seoul in June 1948. The arch-conservative Park Hyeong-ryong, a member of the NKRPC, was appointed as its first principal, and the seminary had the backing of the majority of US missionaries. Han Kyung-chik persuaded the mission board of the PCUSA to grant the NKRPC further funds to support it (Kang In-cheol 2004:160–64; D. Clark 1986:23–24).

Meanwhile, many of the Restoration (Jaegeon) congregations founded in the north by the released believers had also fled south. In February 1948 they declared their intention to 'trash the evil buildings', 'renounce all injustice and hypocrisy' and 'destroy all the idols' in the rest of the church (Rhie and Cho 1997:168). One of the released believers, Ju Nam-seon, had returned to his home near Busan where he became head of Gyeongnam Synod. Concerned, along with others in that region who had resisted shrine worship, about the liberalism of Joseon Seminary, in September 1946 he started a new institution, Goryo Theological Seminary, with Park Yun-sun as principal and support from the Orthodox Presbyterian Church. This action split the Gyeongnam Synod, which eventually sent two representatives to the General Assembly in 1949 (Lim Hee-kuk 2013:221–25). When it rejected the representative of the new seminary group, the Goryo party was isolated. By 1950 there were sixty-seven of these militantly conservative and separatist churches (IHCK 1996:360; Jang Suk-man 2004:136–38; D. Clark 1997:174; Kim Kwan-sik 1947:133–34).

On the one hand, the influx from the north energised churches in the south and encouraged them to grow. On the other hand, in the Presbyterian Church, which made up 70 per cent of Korean Protestants in 1954, refugees from the north-west had taken over the church structure, purged what they perceived as a liberal church and deeply divided it as a result of disputes which originated in the north (IHCK 2009:116–21). Other Protestant churches also were subject to similar pressures, although not to the same extent. Now the majority of the churches in the south adopted the north-west style of Christianity – conservative, self-supporting, self-propagating, hard-working and vehemently anti-Communist. Politically, they were firmly behind the express American intention to defeat Communism and establish a liberal democracy and therefore electorally disposed to support the KDP (Heo Myung-sup 2009:94). But they were not merely anti-Communist, rather they were positively convinced, along with Rhee Syng-man, that if the nation was founded on Christianity not only would it survive the Communist threat, but it would prosper like other 'Christian' nations. Similarly, the US regime and Rhee received strong backing after 1945 for their tough stance against Communism from the Catholic Church, led by Bishop Noh Ki-nam, and for their policy of introducing democracy from the Maryknoll Fathers (Kim Nyung 1993:223).

When trusteeship arrangements broke down in 1947 and the United Nations was unable to organise nationwide elections, Rhee and the KDP insisted that elections should go ahead anyway in the south. However, the plan was strongly opposed by Confucianists and Cheondogyo leaders and by several Protestant nationalists who foresaw a permanent division of the country. The latter included Kim Gu and Kim Gyu-sik, both of whom were assassinated amid the heightened tensions (Wells 1990:162; cf. D. Clark 1997:179–80). Rhee, now an elder in Chungdong Methodist Church, actively courted the Protestant vote, and church leaders united in favour of separate elections and in support of the KDP. The Catholic Church was particularly supportive: Byrne, who was staunchly anti-Communist, was given full powers to act as apostolic delegate even before the decision to have a separate state was made; Bishop Noh cultivated links with Protestant pastors and encouraged Catholics to participate in the KDP; Catholic youth were mobilised, and the bishops issued a joint pastoral letter to urge believers to 'resist Communism in the spirit of martyrdom' (J. Kim and Chung 1964:538; Chérel-Riquier 2003:6; Choi Seok-u 1984:11).

With US help, church backing, tactics of intimidation and a boycott by the left and centre, the KDP still only scraped to victory in the election. Protestant support is indicated by the fact that more than a fifth of the members of the first assembly were Protestants. Afterwards, Bishop Noh offered a solemn mass in the presence of the whole Constituent Assembly and other dignitaries at Myeongdong Cathedral, and Rhee thanked the church for its help. The backing of the Catholic Church was particularly significant for the new nation: the Holy See was the first state to recognise the Republic of Korea when it was declared in August 1948. This action had been negotiated by Chang Myon, who was the chief Korean delegate to the

United Nations General Assembly in Paris in 1948 and had a private audience with Pope Pius XII before returning (Considine 1949:168; J. Kim and Chung 1964:339). In December 1948, Jang also secured UN recognition for the new republic. Now both the Protestant and Catholic churches were aligned with Rhee's unpopular, US-backed regime, which had divided Korea for the first time in thirteen hundred years. When Byrne was confirmed as apostolic delegate and at the same time consecrated bishop in 1949, his procession was led by the band of the Republic of Korea (ROK) Marine Corps (Kang In-cheol 2006:250–57; Kim and Chung 1964:339, 538).

Rhee's government presented itself as ethnically Korean but also strongly Christian. The new nation of South Korea displayed its claims to be the true Korea by adopting the Taegeukgi, the flag of the Joseon dynasty from 1883, which features Taoist symbols; by defining itself as the Republic of the Great Han People (Daehan Minguk); and by establishing a National Founding Day on the birthday of Dangun – the only other religious holiday apart from Christmas (Shin Gi-wook 2006:99). When, at his inauguration, Rhee declared, 'We are here because of the grace of God' (Heo Myung-sup 2009:242–43), both the God of Dangun and the Christian God were invoked. However, Rhee showed his primary Christian allegiance when he chose to be sworn in on a Bible and during the ceremony suddenly departed from the order and asked Yi Yun-yeong, a Methodist minister and assemblyman, to pray for his presidency. Protestants dominated in the leadership of Rhee's government. His vice-president, Ham Tae-yeong, was a Protestant minister, and Yi Yun-yeong was his acting prime minister at first (Park Chung-shin 2003:173–74). Whereas nine out of the twenty-one members of Rhee's first cabinet in 1948 were Protestants, only one was a Buddhist; four others were from new religions (IHCK 2009:41–43). There was no Catholic, but Bishop Ro had recommended about sixty people, mostly Catholics, to work in government, including Chang Myon, and Rhee met regularly with Bishop Byrne, and with other prelates (Chérel-Riquier 2003:6; Considine 1949:168; J. Kim and Chung 1964:339). Christian leaders repeatedly emphasised the Christian spirit as the founda-tion of the new nation, and Rhee was susceptible to Christian pressure to downplay the symbols of Korean traditions (IHCK 2009:44). For example, when Christian students objected to bowing in front of the Korean flag, arguing that it was reminiscent of Shinto worship, the practice was amended to putting a hand to one's heart (Heo Myung-sup 2009:242–53). Furthermore, Christian broadcasting was allowed a disproportionate time on the government network (Park Chung-shin 2003:111) and the republic adopted its national anthem from the hymnal that had been used by the

Provisional Government reset to a tune composed by Ahn Ik-tae, who was a graduate of Soongsil Middle School. In one of Rhee's most controversial decisions, he dispensed with the list of 657 collaborators drawn up by the investigating committee under the US regime. This could also be seen as a pro-Christian measure since the list included a large majority of Protestant leaders, but Rhee insisted that the reason was the priority to fight Communism. In 1949 he proposed Ilmin Juui – 'One People-ism' – as state policy and this was explicit that Christianity should be the basis of the nation, following what he believed to be the US example (Shin Gi-wook 2006:100–103). So although the new constitution included the separation of religions and the state, in practice politics was founded on 'three pillars: American aid, anti-communism and Christian churches' (Chérel-Riquier 2003:6).

The overriding priority to defeat Communism was also used to justify the violent suppression of any opposition. The years 1945–1950 saw increasing communal strife, civil disobedience and eventually armed rebellion in South Korea. Both the Americans and Rhee blamed the unrest on Communist infiltrators from North Korea, but many Koreans in the South were attracted to Socialism simply because issues such as land reform were not being addressed. Youth vigilante movements formed which then divided left and right to support different political figures and clashed frequently on the streets. Many of the latter were based on youth groups attached to the churches, which saw themselves as Christian freedom fighters. Among the most feared was the North-west Youth (Seobuk Cheongnyeonhoe), right-wing reactionaries who included Protestants among their leaders (Cumings 2005:208). They were used by the government and wealthy individuals to break up strikes and meetings, such as a YMCA meeting in 1946 in which church leaders from the left and centre were trying to forge an alliance (Park Chung-shin 2003:169). The Youngnak Church youth group was also involved in violence, and one of the reasons Han Kyung-chik started schools and building work was to occupy young people and keep them away from militancy (Kang In-cheol 2006:210–20; Lee Won-sul et al. 2005:130–33). When the people of Jeju Island rose up in 1947–1948, the North-west Youth inflamed the situation and then were allowed to join the police in suppressing the movement. This was partly the reason for a backlash against Christians during the Yeosu-Suncheon Rebellion later that year, following which Pastor Son Yang-won famously forgave and then offered to adopt the Communist killer of his two teenage sons (Blair and Hunt 1977:146–59; D. Clark 2003:337). Afterwards Rhee enacted the first National Security Law and a press control law. The increasingly

anti-Christian behaviour of the Communists and the kill-or-be-killed situation in which Christians saw themselves led most Christians to support
Rhee's using the police, the military and thuggish youth groups to violently
suppress Socialist-inspired outbreaks of civil unrest (Choi Seok-u 1984:11).
By 1949 public opinion in South Korea was overwhelmingly in favour of
Socialism yet the Catholic and the mainline Protestant churches were firmly
associated with the right-wing and oppressive policies of government and
accused of hindering unification (IHCK 2009:39). Not surprisingly they
faced harassment wherever Communists were dominant.

THE CHURCHES IN THE KOREAN WAR, 1950–1953

Since August 1948, Korea had been divided into two nations: the Republic
of Korea (the South) and the Democratic People's Republic of Korea (the
North). Each regarded itself as the legitimate government of the whole
peninsula, both presidents expressed their intention to unify the peninsula
by force and there were frequent border skirmishes. But whereas the
Communists had consolidated their control in the North, Rhee's regime
in the South was still unpopular. In this context when the United States
announced in 1949 its intention to withdraw from the peninsula, church
leaders were alarmed and the National Council of Churches in Korea
(NCCK) organised a demonstration against it which was attended by one
hundred thousand Christians. In January the NCCK launched the Save the
Nation campaign, using the latest evangelistic methods and with help from
groups of Christian youth from the United States (IMC 1951:8). The latter
may not have been aware that for the organisers national salvation was at
least as important as individual salvation.

Despite the tensions, the scale and timing of the attack by the North on
South Korea on 25 June 1950 was not expected. Significantly, considering
Christian experience of Communist tactics, it was a Sunday; so many
Christians heard the news of the invasion while they were in church.
South Korean Christians who were able joined the mass flight ahead of
the Communist armies which soon overran Seoul. Those who had come
from the North became refugees for a second time in less than five years.
Congregations regrouped in Daegu, Busan and other places within the
'Busan perimeter'. However, the Communist advance was so quick that
many were trapped in Seoul where they were watched, interrogated and
summoned to re-education classes. Most of the Protestant missionaries were
evacuated immediately along with their families, but Korean church leaders
in Seoul were identified and taken prisoner; these included most of the

NCCK staff. Foreign Catholic clergy and sisters, including Bishop Byrne, who mostly stayed at their posts in Seoul, were rounded up and held in a dank basement (J. Kim and Chung 1964:343–44, 537–60). Among others captured were the Salvation Army commissioner Herbert Lord (A. Clark 1971:281–82; P. Chang 2007); Mother Mary Clare, superior of the Anglican Society of the Holy Cross; and Mother Agneta Chang of the Sisters of Our Lady of Perpetual Help.

Internationally, church leaders and bodies mostly leapt to the defence of South Korea, which, after the Communist victory in China, appeared to be one of the last strongholds against advancing Communism in East Asia. Soon after the outbreak of hostilities, the International Missionary Council (IMC) and the World Council of Churches (WCC) openly supported the United States–led and United Nations–backed intervention in Korea, although they later moderated their stance under pressure from church leaders in China and Eastern Europe (Kim Heung-soo 2003a). The Roman Catholic Church exerted pressure in favour of South Korea, and in his 1951 encyclical Pope Pius XII lamented the situation of Korean and Chinese Christians under Communism.[2] Rhee felt vindicated now that the Communist threat was plain and treated the military campaign as a right-eous war. The Christian leadership was taken with the Communist army in its retreat and most were never seen again. On this and other occasions Christians were also among the intelligentsia the Communists singled out for punishment or liquidation. Sometimes these and other such prisoners were shot but more often they died of ill-treatment, starvation or cold. As the UN forces were repulsed from the Chinese border and armies marched back and forth over the 38th parallel, church leaders organised evacuations. For example, the Christian Union Wartime Emergency Committee helped twenty thousand Protestants and a thousand pastors to safety on Jeju and Geoje Islands and Bishop Noh arranged the evacuation of Catholics to Daegu and then, when that was no longer deemed safe, the transportation by air of one thousand eight hundred priests, seminarians and laity to Jeju Island (A. Clark 1971: 248; J. Kim and Chung 1964:351).

Numerous atrocities were committed during the Korean War. In some of these Christians appear to have been targeted particularly, but in other cases Christians were the perpetrators. Some of the North-west Youth formed particularly belligerent units of the South Korean army. In one of the worst incidents, on 10 October 1950 in Sincheon (Hwanghae province), Protestants took revenge on retreating Communists (Cumings 2005:247,

---

[2] *Evangelii Praecones* (*On the Promotion of Catholic Missions*), para. 27.

261). In another, seeing what they thought were advancing UN troops, young Catholics emerged from hiding to join in and 'Kill the Reds!' but the figures approaching turned out to be Communist forces who had not yet left and hundreds of Catholics were massacred (J. Kim and Chung 1964:373).

Soon after hostilities began, Protestant church workers of every denomination met in Daegu to organise help for the Christian community. They set up the Korean Christian National Relief (or Salvation) Association to work in cooperation with government agencies (A. Clark 1971:247; Lee Won-sul et al. 2005:149–50). As soon as the North Koreans were driven back across the 38th parallel again, Father Jang Geum-gu was sent to Seoul to take care of the Catholics who had remained there. Bishop Noh returned in June 1951 (J. Kim and Chung 1964:351). Han Kyung-chik and Youngnak Church members were also among the first to re-enter Seoul and begin relief work. As the war ground to a stalemate, and while North Korea continued to be pounded by US planes, South Koreans began drifting back to their homes, churches began cleaning up and resuming their activities and church organisations started rehabilitation and reconstruction work. By November 1951 the Christian Literature Society was back in business and had sold out of the new hymnal, the Korean Bible Society had moved back to Busan from Japan, Sunday school material was being prepared, theological schools were reopening and there were plans for expansion (*IRM* 1953).

At the end of the war both North Korea and South Korea were counted among the poorest countries in the world. First, in addition to the injured and sick, there was a huge refugee problem, especially in the South where the government estimated that two million people were homeless, many living in tents (Foley 2003:42–44). The second problem was the orphans or packs of destitute children. In South Korean in 1952 there were 280 orphanages looking after 30,471 children; many of these were run by Christians with help from the churches and government. The third priority was widows, who usually had no means of earning their own living. By 1953 there were an estimated 300,000 widows with 517,000 dependent children. Churches tried to house them and to provide training for the women – for example, in sewing, knitting or raising chickens – and education so that they could begin to support themselves. The South Korean government estimated that nearly half of South Koreans were in need of aid – food, shelter and clothing. This statistic called forth a great deal of international aid and relief work. The channels of aid to Korea were the UN, separate countries – mainly the United States – and NGOs which were overwhelmingly Christian. The church mission boards were already committed to

Korea and so were some specialist agencies already involved in relief work, including the Maryknoll Sisters, who had opened a clinic in Busan in 1950, and the Christian Children's Fund, which had an extensive programme of orphanages. Most funds were coordinated through two umbrella bodies based in the United States: Church World Service (CWS) and the parallel Catholic Relief Services (CRS); both continued their work into the 1960s. CRS, which had its headquarters in the Empire State Building in New York City, was by far the biggest single donor to Korea and was supported especially by Cardinal Spellman, who made annual Christmas visits to Korea. Monsignor George Carroll, M.M., the apostolic delegate, was the key organiser and administrator of the combined relief efforts of all the churches after the war (Kim Heung-soo 2003a:330–43; A. Clark 1971:265–66, 271–72, 285; D. Clark 1986:35).

As the situation stabilised more foreign missionaries, many redeployed from China, which was closed to mission work since the Communist victory, were admitted to South Korea and the number of different denominations and organisations increased still further. For example, the daughters of the earlier Australian missionary – Nurse Catherine and Dr Helen Mackenzie – began Il Shin maternity hospital in Busan in September 1952 (Brown 2009:429–35). New Catholic bodies included Misereor, the German Catholic bishops' development organisation and, through the influence of the first lady, Katholische Frauenbewegung Österreichs (RFKCH 2010:138). On the Protestant side, the Society of Friends made its first appearance in the shape of the Friends' Service Unit and the Mennonite Central Committee did relief and development in the Daegu area. The American Mission to Lepers took on the work founded during the colonial period. Severance Hospital ran a post-polio project and, with the help of CWS, a control service to address the problem of polio which was estimated to affect three million people (*IRM* 1953:6). Reuben Archer Torrey Jr., son of the famous American evangelist, started the Amputee Rehabilitation Project, which was centred at Daejeon (Clark A. 1971:285–87; Campbell 1957:111–16). In addition to these initiatives, a new generation of evangelical relief and development agencies was born in Korea during the 1950s which had the effect of undermining the dominance of the church mission boards and ecumenical bodies. Three agencies in particular were begun by Americans moved at the plight of war orphans: World Vision, founded in 1950 by Rev. Bob Pierce; Compassion Inc. (or International), founded in 1952 by Rev. Everett Swanson; and Holt International, the adoption agency founded in 1955 by Harry and Bertha Holt. By 1952 there were forty agencies working, not always in a coordinated way, in South Korea (Kim Heung-soo 2005:97–99).

Because the distribution of aid involved relating to Western agencies, graduates of Christian schools and individuals who had contact with missionaries were most readily employed. Leading Christians became key figures in the relief effort. The redoubtable Kim Hwal-ran took charge of the Red Cross work and later the Office of Public Administration (A. Clark 1971:416–23). Given the history in Korea of the use of a red cross as the symbol of a Protestant church, this group must have appeared as a Christian initiative. Furthermore, the churches were soon identified as providing effective networks through which this and other agencies could work. However, since churches also acted as self-support networks, they tended to look after their own first. Therefore being part of a church or at least having Christian contacts had tangible benefits in this period, and there were concerns about religious favouritism in the distribution of aid (Kim Sou-hwan 2009:159; Kim Heung-soo 2005:111).

The human displacement caused by the Korean War had the effect of spreading Christianity further across the South. This was partly the result of intentional and organised evangelistic activity. For example, displaced Youngnak Church members were encouraged to replace themselves with new Christians and leave behind a daughter church before returning to Seoul (Park Cho-choon 1983:202). Bible women, pastors and missionaries served in a civilian capacity among the wounded and in hospitals and refugee camps, where many conversions were reported. From late 1951, Rhee allowed and encouraged the appointment of Christian chaplains – mostly Protestant and some Catholic, but no other religion – to the Korean army and from 1952 these were paid by the government (Kang In-cheol 2006:347). They were allowed freedom to evangelise both personally and also through mass meetings. Evangelism among these impressionable young men, 'freed from the bondage of village tradition', had spectacular results (Heo Myung-sup 2009:242–45; Kang In-chol 2006:250–57; Campbell 1957:64–69). The US military allowed missionaries and Korean pastors to work among the more than one hundred and sixty thousand prisoners of war (POWs) – North Korean and Chinese – and they estimated that sixty thousand accepted Christ (A. Clark 1971:256; Kang In-cheol 2006:352).

Negotiations on a ceasefire dragged on, partly because of disputes about the forcible repatriation of POWs. The United States, supported by Korean chaplains and foreign missionaries, insisted that more than a third of the men held in UN camps did not wish to be repatriated – including those who had become Christians – while accusations were made that many had been tortured, brainwashed and even tattooed with anti-Communist slogans (Foley 2003:44–46). A deeper reason why the peace talks were prolonged was that Koreans had been fighting for unification of the peninsula and did not want a peace which would entrench the division but an outright victory (e.g. T. J. Lee 2005:113). On this issue, the leadership of the churches in the South agreed with the military and government that co-existence with the Communist North was not an option (Chung Shung-han 2003:203–17, 240–60). Even after the truce, Korean Protestants continued to express their opposition to any peace with Communists and their intention to march north and drive out Communist forces (Yi Mahn-yol 2006:239–40). Not only the US and UN commanders but also the world Protestant community – through the WCC and some of the US and European churches – put pressure on Rhee to agree to a truce (Kim Heung-soo 2003a:361–62; Fey 1993:273–74). Rhee resisted and even tried to sabotage the talks by releasing POWs. In the end the truce was agreed to but without the South Koreans.

There are no verifiable figures for the total killed in the Korean War, but it is estimated that 3 million Koreans (roughly 10 per cent of the population) were killed, wounded or missing as a result of it (Oberdorfer and Carlin 2014:8). By 1953, 40 out of 144 Korean Catholic priests were held in the North, killed or missing, along with many lay leaders. Of 153 foreign missionaries and religious, 57 were dead or unaccounted for (J. Kim and Chung 1964:343, 351). At least 202 – and perhaps 400 – Protestant ministers and seminarians were killed or imprisoned in the North (Yi Mahn-yol 2001:371–74). Presbyterians lost 619 church buildings, Methodists 239 and Holiness churches 106 (Kang In-cheol 2006:191). Millions had been displaced, and approaching 1.5 million North Koreans had moved south between 1945 and 1953 (Foley 2003:47–50). Among them were 80,000 Protestants and 15,000–20,000 Catholics, or about 40 and 25 per cent respectively of their church populations in the North (T. S. Lee 2010:65, 68, 176). Several million Koreans on both sides of the border found themselves permanently separated from their loved ones with no means of knowing whether they were even alive or of fulfilling their filial obligations (Foley 2003:47–60).

The result of the war was that the Communists got North Korea and the Christians got South Korea (Kang In-chol 2006:65–68). Their respective adherents were concentrated in each half of the peninsula, and both had purged any opposition. There was no middle ground. But the 1953 truce satisfied no one and left a sense of unfinished business. There was no peace settlement, only mortal enemies kept apart by a narrow strip of land – the Demilitarized Zone (DMZ) – maintained by the superpowers, whose Cold War policies aggravated the tension. The religio-ideological differences that divided Koreans before the war had become far more deeply entrenched and were now inscribed in the blood of a new generation of martyrs.

CHURCH RECONSTRUCTION AND POLITICS
IN SOUTH KOREA, 1953–1961

Within the space of fifty years, the Korean people had endured the political traumas of loss of nationhood, colonisation by Japan, liberation, division and civil war, and now both Koreas were facing tremendous readjustment. For the rest of the 1950s, South Korea remained desperately poor and almost entirely dependent on foreign aid, most of it from the United States. Most South Koreans were preoccupied with surviving, meeting bodily needs and coping with an onslaught of Westernisation (cf. Rutt 1973). Furthermore, they continued to live with domestic political instability and a pressing national security threat as North Korea made repeated attempts to destabilise the country (D. Clark 1997:182; Nahm 1989:409). Rhee exploited US strategic interests for maximum benefit to Korea and encouraged the growth of the large conglomerates known as chaebol. Other entrepreneurs got rich on the back of the war or by trading US goods on the black market (Kang Man-gil 2005:264–65; Cumings 2005:299–309).

Immediate post-war reflections by South Korean Christians were sombre. Some saw the war as a punishment of God on Korean Christians for their unfaithfulness, including their capitulation to Shinto worship and their divisions. Others understood the war as part of a sacrifice for the greater good of the nation in line with the sacrifice of Christ for the world. But the dominant interpretation by Christians in the South was that the war was the result of the Communist aggression and that this needed to be responded to with decisive force and vigour, on the one hand, and with prayer and mission towards the people of North Korea, on the other (S. C. H. Kim 2008b:166). Protestant anti-Communism was justified theologically using apocalyptic imagery of the Great Satan and Korea as the people chosen for salvation (Kang In-cheol 2006:65). All the leaders of the main churches, both Protestant and Catholic, were like the Rhee administration convinced that co-existence with the Communist North was impossible and that regime change was a prerequisite for peace and stability; in other words, the country must be unified either by force or by the evangelisation of North Korea (Chung Shung-han 2003:150–73, 203–17, 240–60; Yi Mahn-yol 2001:371–74; SCKCM 1952).

Rhee continued his repressive policies on the basis of a perceived threat from the North, and the churches continued to back him. Even though

Rhee declared martial law ahead of the 1952 presidential elections and intimidated the National Assembly to amend the constitution, the NCCK organised an election committee which actively campaigned for him and his preferred vice-presidential candidate, Yi Gi-bung, with particular support from the Methodist Church to which both belonged (Lim Hee-kuk 2013:260–66). Christians were encouraged to vote for Rhee because he had abolished the idolatrous greeting of the national flag and installed chaplains in the military and prisons. The campaign portrayed the election as Christians versus anti-Christians, likening Rhee to Moses and Yi Gi-bung to Joshua leading the people of God against the Canaanites. Furthermore, Rhee's right-wing policies increasingly suited the social composition of the Protestant church leadership after 1945. Clergy were now leaders of the society and by virtue of their cooperation with the government were attracting the social elite. These people, who generally put a premium on social and political stability for their business interests, supported the churches financially and tended to be appointed as elders. If the elders had called the pastor, he was also under pressure to do as they decided (Park Chung-shin 2003:95–97, 178–80).

A few Christians challenged Rhee's authoritarianism, such as the Catholic poet and journalist Ku Sang, who was promptly imprisoned (Ku Sang 2005). The Catholic politician Chang Myon had allied with Rhee initially and shared his anti-Communism (Nahm 1989:425). However, the two parted company in the early 1950s. From then on Chang became a powerful rival, and he and Bishop Noh (archbishop of Seoul from 1962) worked closely together against the regime (D. Baker 1997:149; Cumings 2005:350). Rhee accused Chang of being under the control of the church and tried to force Noh to resign (RFKCH 2010:144–46). In the late 1950s, the policy of the Catholic Church shifted under John XXIII from outright anti-Communism to a greater emphasis on maintaining an independent diplomatic position to mediate between the superpowers, and so it was able to be more critical of Rhee (Hanson 1980:9). He became increasingly dictatorial, his policies became more extreme and he made repeated threats to march north. After his re-election in 1956, Rhee increasingly justified his actions on the basis of his agenda that Christianity was the only sure foundation for Korea and on his own reading of scripture. Foreign observers worried that his religious convictions gave him an 'almost messianic' perspective which clouded his political judgement (Kim Heung-soo 2003a:372; Cumings 2005:345–46). When in 1960 Rhee, who was eighty-five years old, was obviously rigging the election to win a fourth term, popular patience was exhausted. There was a growing number of demonstrations until, after the shooting by the police of well over a hundred student-demonstrators on 19 April – the so-called April Revolution – Rhee was prevailed upon to step down (Kang Man-gil 2005:198–99; Nahm 1989:433; Cumings 2005:344–51). Kim Jae-jun called for the church to be held responsible for the misdeeds of Rhee, and the Methodists and NCCK were forced to apologise for being part of corrupt politics (Park Chung-shin 2003:180–82). Yun Bo-seon (Yun Po-sun), a Presbyterian elder, was elected president, but under the new parliamentary-style constitution, greater power rested with Chang Myon after he was elected prime minister, so he may be counted as the first Catholic to lead Korea.

With the military threat from the North in abeyance, Christians focused on the task of evangelisation, laying the faith foundation they believed South Korea needed and that they hoped one day to extend to the North as well. A very important aspect of life in South Korea for Christians (Protestant and Catholic), and a sign of their religious freedom, was the opportunity to affirm and celebrate their faith in a public way. After the Korean War, the NCCK organised Easter sunrise services which were attended regularly by more than ten thousand Christians and were held, highly symbolically, on the site of the former Shinto shrine on Namsan (South Mountain) (A. Clark 1971:250). Another sign of the public nature of South Korean Christianity was the construction of buildings. Not only were churches rebuilt but many new ones were erected. In 1941 there were forty churches of all denominations in Seoul, but by 1958 there were four hundred, and similar trends in the construction of churches, schools, colleges and other institutions were seen in other cities (A. Clark 1971:251–52). Increasingly Christianity took on the form of a civil religion, encouraged by the conditions of US hegemony and Rhee's government (Kim Byong-suh 1985:63–64).

In a democracy, a Christian foundation necessitated increasing Christian numbers so proselytising was imperative for the churches. At first the Protestant denominations worked separately: the Presbyterians set 1952 as a special year of personal evangelism; the Holiness churches began a big evangelistic movement led by Lee Seong-bong, who established Emmanuel Special Force (using Communist terminology), a militaristic Christian organisation which toured the country in 1954–1955 founding churches and battling against Satan; and the Methodists took the opportunity presented by the 250th anniversary of John Wesley's birth to make 1953 a special evangelistic year (A. Clark 1971:249). In 1954, Presbyterians and Methodists both celebrated the 70th anniversary of mission work in Korea. As the Communists in the North devised three-, five- and seven-year development plans, the Presbyterians worked out a five-year plan to start a new church in 490 townships without an existing congregation and the Methodists similarly planned to establish a hundred new churches. Han Kyung-chik and the Presbyterians from the north-west also encouraged larger events featuring US evangelists coordinated across the denominations. The 1953 revival led by Bob Pierce in Daegu attracted people in 'swarms'. Billy Graham led a 'crusade' in Busan in December 1952, and when he came a second time in February 1956, he preached in Seoul Stadium to an audience of eighty thousand, including Rhee and some government officials (T. S. Lee 2010:85, 90–91; Lee Won-sul et al. 2005:155–66). Such large campaigns were conspicuously different from the practices of other Korean religions of the period and many thoughtful people found them off-putting, but they seemed to be effective in increasing membership (Kim Byong-suh 1985:63–64). By the late 1950s the number of Protestants had doubled and reached around 5 per cent of the population (T. S. Lee 2010:85), and as they saw the churches growing, Christians became more and more confident.

Joining a Christian community through such events made strategic sense in the new situation of South Korea for a number of reasons: first, because it offered an interface with the wider context of Western modernity and was a step on the path of self-improvement in terms of access to aid and welfare and possibilities for education. Most of the evangelists invited were not only ministering to souls but were engaged in relief and development work as well. Second, in a fragmented situation Christian churches were among the few organised bodies. They were run by relatively well-educated people who had good networks and a connection to the United States. Furthermore, they offered a variety of forms of religious expression which were not very demanding in a society now supportive of Christian culture. Third, the nationwide campaigns were explicitly anti-Communist and nationalist in their slogans and the churches promoted a focused alternative society after the example of the United States, which was seen as a beacon of stability, democracy and freedom (cf. Kang In-cheol 2006:250–57). They provided a welcome, particularly for those who were persuaded that politically Christianity was the way forward.

Alongside the nationally organised campaigns, there were many other revivalists who focused less on national salvation but held out hope of personal reconciliation, spiritual blessing and healing. Post-war South Korea was fertile ground for evangelists and church planters, both Koreans and foreigners. With so many displaced, confused and desperate people looking for ways to meet physical and psychological needs in the grim reality of the current situation, it was relatively easy to gather a crowd and persuade them to join a new movement (Min Kyoung-bae 1982:470–71; S. C. H. Kim 2008a:134–38). A common pattern for Protestant or Pentecostal revivalists and evangelists in this period was to erect a tent for large meetings. Tent meetings were appropriate in a country full of military camps and where many were still living in refugee shelters and makeshift accommodation (Kim Ig-jin 2003:112). The team, which would include women as well as men, would then print some posters or leaflets and go door-to-door to encourage people to attend. Meetings scheduled in the evenings continued long afterwards into the night as those who responded to the call were prayed with until they came to faith. Many who were traumatised received rudimentary counselling in this way, as well as practical advice to help them rebuild their lives. Some revivalists and their teams practised healings and exorcisms as well. People who came from a distance would sleep in the tents on the straw floor, and a makeshift kitchen would be set up to feed the mission workers and those who attended meetings. Koreans who became Christians during these meetings usually joined local congregations, and these offered a new community that was appealing, especially to refugees (Kim Byong-suh 1985:63–64). Probably the most numerically successful revival meeting of the 1950s was the one held at Namsan Park Plaza in Seoul in March-April 1955, at which Everett E. Swanson preached (T. S. Lee 2010:91). But the greater draw was Swanson's co-preacher, Elder Park Tae-seon, who was known for his healing and supernatural visions. Those who were promoting Christianity as a public religion were nervous about this development, and shortly afterwards Park was castigated as a heretic for 'flaunting his paranormal inclinations and making unorthodox claims' (T. S. Lee 2010:92). But Park took large numbers with him to form a new movement.

Apart from centralised evangelistic events, churches continued locally with the tried and tested methods of handing out tracts, visiting homes (especially those of the relatives of believers) and seasonal revival meetings. But new technologies were also available, especially media resources since the US forces were using these to encourage the spread of American popular culture (Heo Myung-sup 2009:110–25). The NCCK set up mobile audio-visual units using film strips with slides, flannel graphs, pictures and drama, and Hollywood biblical epics became very popular (A. Clark 1971:263–65, 294–95). Radio communication was now employed as well, at first by using airtime on the government network. In December 1954 plans laid before the war for a private NCCK station were realised when what became the Christian Broadcasting System (CBS) went on the air. The NCCK gave radios to country church workers, but they were tuned only to that station. Certain broadcasts were aimed at the North to try and reach inside with the Christian message. The Evangelical Alliance Mission (TEAM), which arrived in 1953, set up a second station in 1956 at Incheon from which it broadcast in Korean, English and several other languages to reach further into Asia. The appointment of chaplains to the armed forces, police departments and prisons was also taken as an opportunity to proselytise. The percentage of Christians in the military grew spectacularly, from 5 per cent in 1951 to 15 per cent in 1955. By that time there were 329 army chaplains, almost all Protestants, and in 1960 there were chaplains in more than twenty prisons (A. Clark 1971:255–56).

Education continued to be an important part of evangelisation. There were now six Presbyterian high schools and five Methodist ones in Seoul, each with one thousand to two thousand five hundred pupils. Ewha and Yeonhui (Joseon Christian College) colleges reopened under principals Kim Hwal-ran and Paik Lak-geoon, respectively, both of whom served in government as well. Han Kyung-chik raised funds for the re-establishment of Soongsil College in the South, and several new colleges were founded in other cities (Lee Won-sul et al. 2005:155–66). There were eight theological seminaries of different denominations in Seoul alone, and Bible institutes of various sorts and quality mushroomed (A. Clark 1971:251–53). The hunger for education and the reduced incomes of most of the population increased the popularity of night schools, many of which were started by churches. There were also popular Bible correspondence courses run by different bodies for those who could not attend classes, including soldiers and prisoners. For children whose parents could not afford to pay school fees, there were 'Bible clubs' run by the Presbyterians and TEAM, and 'Wesley clubs' by the Methodists, which taught reading and writing using the scriptures (Lee Won-sul et al. 2005:155–66). For adults lacking basic literacy, the NCCK organised the Christian Literacy Society in 1954, which provided primers and graded readers and encouraged the formation of reading groups (A. Clark 1971:257, 261–63). The importance attached to the agenda of evangelisation can be gauged by the fact that the effort continued largely uninterrupted by the organisational splits in the Protestant churches in the 1950s.

Despite the conscious proselytising of the Protestant churches, Catholic Church growth statistics outstripped them in the 1950s without, apparently, the same kind of effort. Total Catholic numbers increased annually by more than 16 per cent between 1953 and 1962 (RFKCH 2010:140–41). By 1955 Catholics had reached 1 per cent of the population, and between 1955 and

1962 that proportion doubled. This spectacular growth was experienced in a decade – the 1950s – when, owing to the depletion of Korean clergy during the war, the priests were largely foreign (D. Clark 1986:34; D. Baker 1997:148–49). A number of reasons can be suggested for this: the church's growing respectability and its anti-Communist stance, its institutional outreach, its proselytising activities and organisational development and its spiritual life (Choi Seok-u 1984: 12; D. Baker 1997:152). The church's increasingly public voice and its critical support for the new republic gave the formerly outlawed community a new respectability, while the Protestant churches' close relationship with Rhee and implication in various scandals badly affected their credibility towards the end of the 1950s (Kang In-cheol 2006:224). Respectability was indicated and further helped by the conversions of prominent persons to the Catholic Church in this period (J. Kim and Chung 1964:339–40). These included Yi Gang and Yi Eun, descendants of the royal family. Respected intellectuals and anti-Japanese activists also became Catholics, including Choi Nam-seon, as did some prominent politicians, including Kim Dae-jung, and also literary figures such as Kim Chi-ha (Kim Ji-ha) and educators such as the former Protestant businessman Kim Seong-su (D. Baker 1997:151).

The active relief activities of CRS certainly drew people towards the Catholic Church. In addition, credit unions were set up beginning in 1952 and education programmes were run for war widows, the unemployed and others. There was also a big drive to establish Catholic institutions. Before the Korean War, the Catholic Church had a relatively low institutional presence compared with the Protestant churches and with other Catholic mission fields. There were only five high schools and no colleges, few social welfare institutions and only one periodical (Considine 1949:168). This was due to the relatively short church history, the circumstances of persecution and the limited mission investment. Now, especially with the support of US Catholics, the number of schools and institutions increased rapidly, although still relatively low by global standards. The former theological seminary became Seongsim (Sacred Heart) College in 1947 and was renamed the Catholic College in 1959. Other institutions founded in this period include the Catholic Medical College (1954), Sacred Heart College for Women (1964), Hyoseong Woman's College in Daegu and Sogang College (1960). There was also a programme of hospital and medical clinic construction in the 1950s (D. Baker 1997:151–52). The church commissioned modern, indigenous and traditional religious works to adorn the new buildings, and the Catholic artists' network based around Seoul National University flourished (Yi Ku-yeol 1984:58). These projects gave the church a new visibility, especially in urban areas, and enhanced its voice in public affairs.

The Catholic Church also began evangelistic programmes, developed the church organisation, increased the numbers of priests and welcomed many foreign missions (Choi Seok-u 1984:12). New vicariates were established at Chuncheon (1955), Gwangju, Jeonju and Busan (1957), Daejeon and Cheongju (1958) and Incheon (1961) (RFKCH 2010:140–41). The main foreign missionary societies which were active in Korea before 1950 opened new works in the South after the war. By 1962 the Columban Fathers were working in Gwangju and Seoul (J. Kim and Chung 1964:694). The Maryknoll Fathers took up work in the dioceses of Cheongju, Incheon and Busan, and they worked especially with Monsignor Carroll and CRS. In 1952 those Benedictine monks who survived from Deokwon Abbey in North Korea founded a new monastery of Waegwan, Gyeongsangbuk-do, which was raised to the status of an abbey in 1964 and continued the printing work associated with Deokwon (J. Kim and Chung 1964:707). In 1956 the Benedictines took charge of the missionary work in the northern part of the vicariate of Daegu. The Order of Friars Minor (Capuchins) returned, the Society of Jesus (Jesuits) arrived in 1954 to start Sogang College and many other orders of men followed. Korean women's orders grew and thrived, and other communities of nuns returned or entered for the first time from overseas. The Sisters of Our Lady of Perpetual Help re-established their headquarters in Seoul in 1955. By the early 1960s, the Sisters of St Paul de Chartres had a mother house in Seoul and forty-seven branch convents, together with Gyeseong Girls' Middle and High Schools in Seoul; schools in Nonsan and Gyeongju; a kindergarten; several orphanages; hospitals in Seoul, Incheon and Daegu; and a clinic in Seoul (J. Kim and Chung 1964:703–51).

RELIGION IN NORTH KOREA, POST-1953

In North Korea, Kim Il-sung survived the Korean War with even greater popular support, having ensured the loyalty of his comrades and purged any opposition, including Christians. Although the philosophy of Juche was not promulgated until after 1955, from the beginning, Kim made self-reliance and self-sufficiency priorities for the North Korean government in continuity with the nationalism of the colonial period (Shin Gi-wook 2006:49, 80). The result was a highly distinctive form of Socialism which kept itself aloof even from its nearest neighbours and became one of the most totalising regimes of the twentieth century (Armstrong 2007b:189; Shin Gi-wook

2006:83–86). Nevertheless, as far as material development was concerned, inspired by first Stalinist and then Maoist models, the North rebuilt and developed much faster than the South (Armstrong 2007b:196; cf. Cumings 2004; Kim Byoung-lo 1992). From the 1950s North Korea was a leader, and regarded as a shining example, in the Third World (Hoare and Pares 2005:44–45, 115; Cumings 2005:434–47).

Despite the country's spectacular strides in development, the North Korean leadership did not feel secure when the United States was ranged against it, continuing Russian commitment was by no means assured and the Chinese withdrew their troops in 1958. From 1957 universal compulsory military service was extended and North Korea took on the nature of a 'garrison state' (Cumings 2004:1). All other sectors of society were also mobilised, and the whole nation was constantly on a war footing (Nahm 1989:409). Not only was the North Korean state dominant, it was also hegemonic, maintaining a very high level of official surveillance and penetrating deep into family life (Armstrong 2007b:189). The press was strictly censored, and access to foreign media or literature was not permitted. There was no freedom of movement or freedom of assembly. Much time was given to propaganda and 'moral rectification' campaigns, and artistic and musical expression was directed to serve the party (Hoare and Pares 2005:95–97, 105–7; Pratt 2006:279–303; Nahm 1989:378–420). Party membership was prized but attainable only after a long screening process and following detailed study of the teachings of the 'Great Leader' and self and mutual criticism (Kim Hyun-sik 2008:23–24). And it was not possible at all for those who belonged to the wrong social division or seongbun or 'attitude'. Seongbun was a measure of ideological purity – 'core', 'wavering' or 'hostile'; however, it was not based on individual qualities alone but also on family background. Its three-part structure both replicated and reversed the social hierarchy of the Joseon era since peasant heritage was now generally privileged and yangban relations despised (Armstrong 2007b:191; Schwekendiek 2011:38–46; IHCK 1996:378). About 20 to 30 per cent of the population was identified as having the wrong seongbun and were beaten, executed or exiled to one of the country's notorious prison camps (Nahm 1989:378–420; Cumings 2005:431–33). Among these were most Christians because of ideology or because they were themselves, or were related to, landowners or collaborators (Kim Heung-soo and Ryu 2002:99–103).

Along with other freedoms, religious freedom had also been completely suppressed by 1949 (D. Clark 2007:172–74; Hoare and Pares 2005:88–91). Religious organisations and buildings were expunged, and all other social manifestations of religion, such as traditional customs and holidays, were also removed (Nahm 1989:409). Religions continued to be criticised according to the usual formulas, but US and South Korean aggression during the Korean War, which was perceived to be Christian, had given Christianity an even worse reputation. Precise figures are not available, but the intensive bombing ruined the cities and industries of the North and the use of napalm especially destroyed its environment. It is possible that three million or more North Koreans died (Cumings 2004:40). Furthermore, US bombing of churches led to tremendous loss of life because people assumed that they were safe in the buildings; for example, in November 1950, on a Sunday, two hundred and fifty people were killed in Jeil Church in Sinuiju. The behaviour of US troops and of youth gangs which called themselves Christian further soiled the reputation of Christianity, and there were rumours that missionaries were involved in atrocities (IHCK 1996:403, 410–18, 430–33). With such experience, there was little need for the government to campaign against Christianity after 1953. As a result of social pressure and active suppression, the number of Christians rapidly declined and was estimated in the 1960s to be only between ten thousand and twenty thousand. Christians met in house churches rather than in public buildings. Others hid their faith altogether; such was the level of social control that they could not even talk about it to their children, leading to ignorance in the next generation (IHCK 1996:433–35).

In place of religion, functional substitutes were created as the state tried to 'cater for everybody's spiritual as well as material needs' (Pratt 2006:290). Quasi-religious beliefs and practices were related to one or other of the two strands of ideological development which came together to make Juche-Kimilsungism, the political philosophy of self-reliance and the cult of personality around the 'Great Leader', Kim Il-sung. The cult began as early as 1948 and grew after Stalin died (Armstrong 2004:222–23; Kim Hyun-sik 2008:24). Kim attained the stature of and generated the loyalty due a 'feudal warlord' or a messianic figure, and his biography was embroidered to identify him more closely with the struggles of the nation (Cumings 2005:420). For example, a certain Kim Eung-u who supposedly led the people of Pyongyang against the ship *General Sherman* was identified as Kim's great-grandfather. Kim's father was described as a great anti-Japanese nationalist who organised the March 1st uprising, and Kim himself, age seven, was said to have taken part in it (Hoare and Pares 2005:35). Time and landscape were reconfigured to celebrate Kim's life story with new holidays and ceremonies, and with new art, shrines and monuments (Yoon Min-kyung 2012:71).

Kim was soon being called and portraying himself as the 'fatherly or parental leader' (suryeong), 'sun of the nation' and 'present-day Dangun'. Each of these titles may be connected with East Asian religious influences on Korea, but they have resonances for Christians as well. Although the title of fatherly or parental leader relates most closely to the Confucian heritage of Korea and to the Dangun legend, the appellation of Kim as 'dear father' and even 'our father' is strikingly reminiscent of the Lord's Prayer and of the way God is addressed in supplication in Protestant prayer meetings (Shin Gi-wook 2006:85–95). Although the extended Confucian family system of ancestors was dismantled, filial piety was retained but directed towards Kim and the party (Nahm 1989:378–420). The ascription 'sun of the nation' to Kim most obviously relates to Shintoism, and ironically, the cult of Kim Il-sung is not unlike the cult that surrounded the Japanese emperor which it displaced (Cumings 2005:147, 420). But the sun was also the symbol of Rome and is a Christian symbol of Easter and the resurrection of Christ. In South Korea, it is the churches which have largely replaced the Shinto shrines. The Festival of the Sun, on Kim Il-sung's birthday – 15 April – occurs at the same time of year that the churches in the South are holding Easter sunrise services. After Kim Jong-il was confirmed as his father's successor in 1973, he pleased his father by exalting his name still higher and ascribing to him absolute authority. Kim's 'Ten Principles of Life' appear as the North Korean equivalent of the Ten Commandments or the Creed (Kim Hyun-sik 2008:22–23). Alongside this peudo-religious cult, Juche thought was developed as an ideological substitute for theology (see Chapter 6).

PROTESTANT PLURALITY AND NEW MOVEMENTS IN THE SOUTH, 1948–1961

In the context of religious freedom in South Korea, six religious bodies were recognised by the government: Buddhism; Confucianism; two Korean new religions – Cheondogyo and Daejonggyo; and two distinct forms of Christianity – Catholicism and Protestantism. In the post-Liberation period there was also increasing plurality within each faith, especially Protestantism. The breakdown of the comity system, mass migrations and the entry of new churches meant that in many places, especially in the growing urban areas, several different churches co-existed. This plurality was increased further by splits in Protestant denominations in the 1950s. As well as theological disputes and personality issues, these splits involved regional differences, the fall-out from colonisation and national partition, and relations with foreign bodies.

The denomination most affected by division was the largest, the Presbyterian Church, which by 1960 had fractured into four different denominations in the South. By 1950 the church had three factions: a conservative mainstream strongly influenced by migrants from the north-west led by Han Kyung-chik and supported by PCUSA missionaries who patronised the new Presbyterian Theological Seminary; a liberal wing centred on Joseon Theological Seminary led by its principal Kim Jae-jun, who was supported by north-easterners and the Canadian Presbyterian mission; and an ultra-conservative wing based around the Goryeo Seminary in Busan and supported by the Orthodox Presbyterian Church. When the General Assembly of the Presbyterian Church, due to meet in autumn 1950, finally met in 1951 – in Busan because of the war – the Goryeo group was excluded and few if any were prepared to defend them. Rhee's government had dropped the issue of collaboration, and in wartime conditions the church was anxious to toe the government line (Park Chung-shin 2003:102). The Goryeo group, together with many congregations of the Restoration (Jaegeon) group led by the 'released believers', responded by founding a new Presbyterian denomination known as Koshin (Goshin; now the Presbyterian Church in Korea). On the basis of resistance to Japanese oppression, it stood for a 'pure faith' and against liberal theology and theological leftism (Oh Pyeng-seh 1983:227–28). In 1952 it held its first meeting of synod leaders, and in 1954 the new denomination joined Carl McIntire's fundamentalist International Council of Christian Churches. In 1956 when Koshin held its first general assembly, it had three hundred and fifty churches and sixty pastors in six synods, mainly in the south-east (IHCK 2009:90–96).

The 1951 General Assembly was asked to resolve the problem of the existence of the two rival Presbyterian theological seminaries in Seoul. It decided to revoke its recognition of both institutions and to build a new theological seminary in Daegu. The new seminary opened in wartime with no proper facilities and few qualified professors but with many eager students. Some had escaped from the North, and all had survived war and persecution of different kinds (Campbell 1957:97). But although the General Assembly intended the new seminary to be a clean start to over-come theological division, in fact it was staffed mostly by former faculty members of the Presbyterian Theological Seminary in Pyongyang, who were overwhelmingly from the north-west, and overseen by a conservative American principal (Kang In-cheol 2004:163–65; Campbell 1957). The north-westerners utilised the anti-Communist atmosphere of the time to accuse the Kijang group of treachery by staying in Seoul during the first Communist occupation of the city, and they criticised its social activism for leaning towards Communism. Structurally, the northerners gained dominance in the General Assembly by insisting on dual representation in the assembly of both the (by now nominal) synods in the North and the northern presbyteries in the South, according to the 'emergency measure' of 1952. As a consequence of this, by 1952–1953 the northerners accounted for 40 per cent of the assembly representatives (Kang In-cheol 2004:166–68; Kang In-cheol 2006:451). Whereas before the Korean War the moderators of the southern assembly had all been of Gyeongsang origin, in the General Assembly of 1953 Myeong Sin-hong and Han Kyung-chik, both from southern Pyeongan province, were elected as, respectively, moderator and vice-moderator; another north-westerner became the director of the judicial board, which then removed Kim Jae-jun from his position as a minister. For some in the South, this felt like a second attack from the North by extremist forces (cf. Jang Suk-man 2004:139–40). Since the graduates of Joseon Seminary were not recognised by the rest of the church and there was no prospect of reunion, a new denomination, Kijang (Daehan Gidokgyo Jangnohoe; Presbyterian Church in the Republic of Korea), was started in June 1953 with six hundred churches, many in the Jeolla provinces, and with financial support from the United Church of Canada (Kang In-cheol 2006:492).

Koshin and Kijang were splinter groups – the majority of the church stayed together – but in 1959 the mainline church was split in two by another controversy. This schism, at the General Assembly in Daejeon, concerned mainly the issue of whether the denomination should join the World Council of Churches. Kim Gwan-sik, then general secretary of the NCCK, had attended the formation of the WCC in 1948 in Amsterdam and recommended joining, and the General Assembly at that time had accepted the proposal, although conservatives were sceptical because the WCC included churches in Communist countries (Kang In-cheol 2006:76). Of three representatives from Korea who attended the second assembly at Evanston, Illinois, in 1952, one reported negatively that the WCC was pluralistic in theology and pro-Communist. The heightened anti-Communism of the post–Korean War context, the express views of Rhee against association with the WCC (e.g. Park Chung-shin 2003:177–78) and the fact that the WCC had retracted its initial support for the South in the Korean War all strengthened the hand of those who wished to stay out of the organisation. In particular, Park Hyeong-ryong and others who established the Korean Association of Evangelicals which joined the ultra-conservative (US) National Association of Evangelicals (NAA) in 1955 would not agree to membership. The report of a committee formed to discuss becoming part of the WCC recommended selective participation; however, additional issues arose between the factions and the 1959 General Assembly that was to decide on the matter broke up acrimoniously (Lim Hee-kuk 2013:227–31). Both groups started separate meetings at different churches which then founded two separate denominations of more-or-less equal membership: Tonghap (Presbyterian Church of Korea) and Hapdong (Presbyterian Church in Korea). The seminary also divided into two schools, and the foreign relations of the church were reconfigured. The mission boards which had founded the denomination (the two US Presbyterian denominations, the Australian Presbyterians and the Canadian Presbyterians) were all committed to the WCC and therefore supported Tonghap. Missionary attempts to mediate between Tonghap and Hapdong were swept aside. It now being clear to them that the Korean Presbyterian Church was independent, the boards dissolved the mission and established a system of cooperation instead (Suh Kwang-sun 1986:13; D. Clark 1986:19). Hapdong raised support from the NAA and from private individuals. Further attempts to bring the two new denominations together failed.

Two other dimensions of the split are also worth mentioning. First, the WCC was portrayed by its detractors as an elitist, world-dominating power and the Tonghap faction took with it the long-standing missionary organisations and most of the institutions and prestigious churches. Therefore the membership of Hapdong was more representative of the tradition of independency strongly ingrained in the Korean churches and of political resistance (cf. Park Chung-shin 2003:75–78). Second, although the split into Hapdong and Tonghap appeared to be issue based, looked at regionally, it also largely separated the north-west clergy from the two provinces of Hwanghae and Pyeongan, respectively (Kang In-cheol 2004:168–70). The antagonism should also be considered in the context of the division of Korea itself, the history of factionalism in Korean society and the levels of violence to which the protagonists had been exposed in the previous decades. Factors in the mission background could be regarded as exacerbating the divisions, for example, the theological isolation produced by the comity system, the independency fostered by the Nevius method and its ecclesiological weakness, the limited theological diversity among the missionary community, the encouragement by dominant missionaries to conservatism and emphasis on orthodoxy over ethics and the influence of the fundamentalist–liberal controversy in the West, which was itself linked to the struggle between Communism and emerging liberal democracy (cf. J. Smith 1961:322–24).

The Presbyterian Church was not the only church beset by division in this difficult period. In 1950 the Methodists faced a second contested election for bishop, and the differences were not resolved until 1959, when they finally managed to establish the single seminary they had planned (D. Clark 1986:17; D. Clark 1997:174–75). The differences over collaboration surfaced again in the 1970s, leading to a four-way fracture in 1974 that was healed four years later (Lim Hee-kuk 2013:233–36). The Holiness churches split in 1955 over whether to join the ecumenical instruments (NCCK and WCC) or the NAA. They joined both organisations initially, whereupon the conservatives split off to form two denominations of the Korea Evangelical Holiness Church, named after Christ (Ki) and Jesus (Ye): Kiseong joined but Yeseong did not. The Baptists, whose leadership was a combination of the old Fenwick Baptists and others trained by the Southern Baptists, split largely along these lines in 1959. Two regionally based denominations resulted – Daejeon and Pohang – which eventually reunited in 1968 (cf. A. Clark 1971:288–91).

The splits in the Protestant churches were not solely due to differences in theology, but a growth in theological diversity was an important factor and the new groups defined themselves in distinction from one another primarily by theological arguments. The period from the 1930s through to the 1950s can therefore rightly be called 'the period of the establishment of Korean theology' (Ryu Dong-sik 2000:135–262). Since the theological differences were rooted in the same contemporary historical experience, they crossed the divides of the denominations introduced by the missionaries, and the framework for theological formation was shaped by movements under Korean leadership. At this point five main strands can be identified. The first was fundamentalism, represented by Koshin and the Baptists, both of which had links to US fundamentalism. Second was conservative evangelicalism, represented by Hapdong and the Holiness churches, which had links to US conservatives who engaged with public life but prided themselves on their tradition of independency. Third was mainstream evangelicalism, represented by Tonghap and the Methodists, which was theologically conservative but was open to working through the ecumenical movement with Christians who differed theologically. Fourth was progressive Christianity, represented by the Kijang group, and fifth was liberal existential thought, represented mainly by Methodist intellectuals. Park Hyeong-ryong moved between fundamentalism and conservative evangelicalism, as we have seen. Han Kyung-chik represented mainstream evangelicalism. Kim Jae-jun was the leading progressive, and Jeong Gyeong-ok can be regarded as the chief example of the liberal existentialists.

The other pre-Liberation churches also faced challenges during the reconstruction era. From 1941 the Anglican Church had been under a Japanese bishop who left in 1945. Bishop Cecil Cooper returned in 1946 to find a scattered almost unsupported flock. But in 1950, while trying to rebuild the church, he and two other English priests and a sister were captured by Communists and only he survived. Three Korean priests were also reported missing, presumed dead. Anglicans were still concentrated on Ganghwa Island, and churches on the mainland were mainly composed of migrants from there; almost all were poor. The church struggled on under serious financial problems, serviced by voluntary deacons but depending mainly on English priests for the sacraments while more Koreans were in training overseas. Eventually, by the initiative of Bishop John Daly, who was enthusiastic about indigenisation, the church ordained several lay ministers as presbyters to administer the sacraments, again on a voluntary basis, encouraging the local churches to support them (Lee Jae-jeong 1990:242–45). Despite the difficulties, numbers increased by 10 per cent per year during the 1950s. In 1957 St Michael's Theological College was re-established in Seoul with Reuben Archer Torrey III as rector (Whelan 1960:157–66).

Hieromonk Polycarp Priimak had served as head of the Korean Mission of the Russian Orthodox Church in Seoul under the jurisdiction of the Moscow Patriarchate since 1936. He had distanced the church from Japan after the Liberation, but the link with Russia was equally problematic in the new South Korea. In 1949 he was arrested by the South Korean police on charges of being a Soviet spy; he was deported, and the mission was closed. During the Korean War, a Greek army chaplain serving under the United Nations made contact with the small remaining Korean Orthodox community and renovated the ruined church of St Nicholas in Seoul with funds raised from among Greek soldiers. In 1954, Moon Yi-han (Boris) from Seoul was ordained as a priest by the archbishop of Tokyo and became the fourth indigenous Korean priest. For some years the church was cut off from other Orthodox churches until it agreed in 1955 to put itself under the jurisdiction of the Ecumenical Patriarchate of Constantinople (K. Baker 2006:205–6). In 1967–1968, Moon Yi-Han rebuilt the Church of St Nicholas in Mapo-ku. A second priest, Na Chang-gyu (Daniel), was ordained in 1977 and from then on Orthodox churches were gradually established in other parts of the country.

The diversity of Korean Christianity was further increased in the 1950s owing to the influx of people and the help of outside agencies, mostly from the United States, who heard about Korea because of the war (D. Clark 1986:18). Church of Christ refugees from the North established churches in the South – seventeen by 1959 – and from 1954 they were supported by missionaries from the United States. They operated an orphanage in Daejeon, an old people's home in Gwangju and a widow's home in Busan. The Korea Christian Mission had been founded through contacts with missionaries in Japan, and in 1936–1940 a US missionary helped establish six churches in Korea. The work was taken up again in 1948, and in 1954 a seminary building was constructed. The mission was very much involved in relief work, and in 1959 it had eighty congregations. The Nazarene Mission began work in 1948 when a group of Korean Christians led by Jeong Nam-soo (Robert) united with them to form nine churches. The first US missionaries arrived in 1954 and established a Bible school just outside Seoul (A. Clark 1971:291–93). Towards the end of the Korean War, at the urging of Korean students in the United States, the Lutheran Church-Missouri Synod agreed to open a work. Missionaries, including an ordained Korean, Won Yong-ji, arrived in 1958 – the first Lutherans recorded in Korea since Karl Gützlaff in 1832. They developed media and literature programmes and social outreach work, and set up a theological school. In 1958, Scandinavian Lutherans, working through their national governments, established a medical centre in Seoul which in 1968 became the National Medical Center. The Lutheran Church in Korea was constituted in 1971 (Won Yong-ji 1988).

Having been founded by private women missionaries, the Pentecostal churches had never been formally registered nor linked into an international denomination. In 1945 the three leaders of the pre-war Pentecostal congregations – Park Seong-san, Heoh Hong and Bae Bu-geun – all resumed part-time ministry. A Korean Pentecostal Church had been founded in Osaka, Japan, in the 1930s by Gwak Bong-jo. He trained a number of fellow Koreans from the south-west, including Park Heon-geun, and through these men a 'second wave' of Pentecostal churches was planted in South Jeolla province in the 1940s and 1950s (Kim Ig-jin 2003:69–77). Another group of churches in Jeolla grew rapidly under the ministry of Park Gui-im, a woman evangelist and powerful healer who was also noted for dancing while preaching. Park had been baptised in the Spirit through the ministry of Holiness church revivalist Lee Seong-bong and a group of women in Mokpo who had connections with the Osaka church. She founded Suncheon Church in 1948 – the first local church to be called

'Pentecostal' (Osunjeol) – and Park Heon-geun came to help with the ministry she had established. The Pentecostals in Jeolla province antagonised some of the mainline churches by proselytising among their members and because of their loud worship. Their untrained women leaders like Park were despised, and sometimes their meetings were interrupted by youths from other churches (Kim Ig-jin 2003:91–92).

During the Korean War, Bae Bu-geun met an Assemblies of God chaplain who alerted the US churches to the need in Korea and the first official missionary from that denomination, Arthur B. Chestnut, was sent in 1952. The following year he presided over the inaugural general meeting of the Korean Assemblies of God from a loose federation of the three groups formed just before war had broken out. The denomination began with eight churches and five hundred members. A seminary, which was given the name 'sunbogeum' – 'full' or 'pure gospel', a term used by pre-1945 Holiness preachers – produced its first graduates in 1955: five men and two women. The church grew rapidly to forty-four congregations by the end of 1955, but serious tensions soon emerged which led to schism; Heoh Hong and Park Gui-im and a group of churches left (Kim Ig-jin 2003:94, 107–11). Meanwhile a spiritual awakening took place at the seminary that was to lead to the development of the distinctive Korean Full Gospel Pentecostalism. The main roles in this awakening were taken by Cho Yong-gi and his future mother-in-law, Choi Ja-sil, who were both students at the seminary in 1956–1958, and whose biographies helped to define the theology. Choi had been a nurse, a church and local political leader and a businesswoman, but after a series of personal tragedies and businesses failures, she hid herself on Samgak Mountain near Seoul hoping to die. However, she was persuaded to attend a revival meeting led by Lee Seong-bong at which, in an intense experience of weeping, shaking and self-harm, she was released from her guilt, received baptism of the Holy Spirit and began to speak in tongues (Kim Ig-jin 2003:116–20; Lee Young-hoon 2004:3–20). Cho's biography includes a fear of various ghosts and spirits, illness, a vision and healing from tuberculosis. His education was interrupted, but he taught himself English and had some medical training during which he encountered different theories of psychological healing, including the work of Hermann Hesse, which later informed his ministry. In 1956 he began attending the Pentecostal church in Seoul founded by the independent missionary Louis P. Richards. One night, after three days of fasting, he had a vision of Christ, which included a call to preach God's kingdom, and he started speaking in tongues (Kim Ig-jin 2003:120–26; Lee Young-hoon 2004:3; 2009:93–95; Cho Yong-gi 1979:xi–xix). Choi and Cho met at

Sunbogeum Seminary in winter 1956 and in the summer of 1957 Choi, assisted by Cho, led a revival on Samgak Mountain which was characterised by 'triple prayer': prayer in tongues, overnight prayer and prayer with fasting, in addition to regular morning prayer. The pair also helped organise crusade meetings with visiting Assemblies of God evangelists. In 1958, Choi set up a tent church in the western suburbs of Seoul (Daejo-dong). Cho soon joined as minister, and they formed a partnership ministry.

It was in this context of ministry to a destitute congregation in the aftermath of the Korean War that Cho began to develop the Full Gospel theology that gradually took over the Korean Assemblies of God (Ma Won-suk, Menzies and Bae 2004:36–41; Anderson 2004b:148–50). Lacking the means to offer practical help, and convinced that the spiritual world holds power over the material, Cho emphasised spiritual healing and prayer as the means to solve human problems. He proclaimed hope for the suffering by his message that 'God is good' and addressed poverty by his doctrine of blessing and sickness by his healing ministry (Ma Won-suk et al. 2004). There were numerous testimonies to lives turned around through contact with Cho and his congregation (e.g. Elliott 1989:20–21). After the denominational split in 1958, Cho emerged with the trust of the missionaries and joined the church leadership. The American denomination was channelling special funds to evangelise Korea, which it had identified as strategic for its 'Global Conquest' project, and as part of this in 1961, a month of highly successful revival meetings was held at Seodaemun rotary in central Seoul (Kim Ig-jin 2003:111–14, 140–45). Two developments stemmed from this: first, while interpreting for the guest preacher, Cho learnt from him about the prosperity teachings of Oral Roberts and others; second, afterwards, the missionary John Hurston persuaded Cho and Choi to lead a second church – the Full Gospel Central Church (FGC) – and this soon became their main ministry (Kim Ig-jin 2003:146–48). In 1962, Cho was ordained in the Assemblies of God, and in 1965 he married Choi's daughter, Kim Sung-hae (Kim Seong-hye). The FGC grew rapidly, far outstripping other congregations. Nevertheless, by the early 1970s Pentecostalism in Korea was still only about a thirtieth of the size of Presbyterianism (Kim Kim Ig-jin 2003:125–36, 154–55).

The messages preached in the revivals in the 1950s were, unlike those of the 1920s and 1930s, less about eschatological hope and more about health and prosperity, which were the primary concerns of people who had recently come through life and death challenges and were trying to reconstruct their lives. Many new religious movements were derived from such revivals, and revivalists sometimes started their own churches or denominations. Na Un-mong had seen a vision of Christ while he was seeking the Buddhist goddess of mercy on Yongmun Mountain, not far from Seoul, in 1942. He became the Methodist elder and revivalist and gathered a following for his message of a second experience of filling with the spirit. There were healings, tongues and trances at his meetings, one of which in 1954 drew thirty thousand people. But in the 1960s most denominations stopped inviting him, especially because of his attempts to harmonise Buddhism and Confucianism with Christianity. Nevertheless, by then Na's ministry had helped to open up the mainline churches to Pentecostalism and Pentecostal-style revivalism (Kim Ig-jin 2003:47, 102, 139).

Much religious activity centred on 'prayer mountains' (gidowon), which mushroomed after the Korean War. In this period, they were largely independent of the established churches and denominational structures and were associated with charismatic figures. Prayer mountains drew on the traditional association of the mountains with the dwelling of Haneunim/Hananim and were also a response to the encouragement of the Dangun tradition by ethnic nationalism. Many of the leaders of the prayer mountains were women who lacked theological training or even basic formal education but interpreted the Christian faith from within a traditional Korean spirituality (Lee Yeon-ok 1983). They comforted people with 'the advent of a future world, paradise on earth, faith in a saviour, the notion of a chosen people, faith in Jeonggamrok, and Shamanistic faith' (Shim Il-sup 1985:103). They practised healing by laying hands on people's heads as a way of conveying blessing or spiritual power, or by laying hands on the site of the sickness. Other supernatural events were often reported from prayer mountains, together with gifts of the Spirit – especially speaking in tongues. Some people wandered from mountain to mountain to see well-known miracle workers or revival preachers. These activities were generally criticised by the established (and male-led) churches, and most of the movements are forgotten, except for a few which became linked with new religious movements associated with charismatic men (Kim Kwang-ok 1997:220). The largest example was Jeondogwan (Hall of Evangelism; also known as the Olive Tree Movement), which was founded by Park Tae-seon, the Presbyterian elder who had been the popular partner of Swanson in 1955. He claimed to actualise the millennial kingdom by his healing miracles and by establishing several new model towns. These 'faith villages' in Gyeonggi province and near Busan, which were self-supported by agriculture and light industry, grew to twenty thousand to fifty thousand people each. However, subsequent scandals and Park's claims to be 'the Heavenly Father' (Cheonbu) led to the near complete demise of the movement by the 1980s (Grayson 2002:207–9). A more recent millienni-alist sect, Shincheonji, was founded in 1984 by Lee Man-hee, who had been influenced by Park and other new movements. At the time of this writing it is regarded as a serious threat to mainline churches (Lim Hee-kuk 2013:237–43).

Tongilgyo or the Unification Church, founded in 1954, is the best-known new religious movement of this era because it has grown consid-erably outside Korea. The story of its founder Sun Myung Moon (Moon Seon-myeong) weaves together many new movements. Moon grew up in a Presbyterian family in the north-west, but after a vision at Easter 1935 he accepted what he believed to be a special call from Christ to complete his mission, which had been cut short by his crucifixion. From 1945 he led a group associated with the movement started by the revivalist Yi Yong-do, and he had links with two sects founded in rural areas by women (Chryssides 1991:93–101; Grayson 2002:209–12). The Unification Church shared many of the beliefs and characteristics of the popular Korean Christianity and the new religious movements of the 1930s and 1940s. Moon's personal testimony was like that of many pastors of his generation who endured physical suffering, spent days in prayer and saw visions. His teaching of 'blessings' echoed that of Holiness and Pentecostal churches. His attention to scriptures and prophecy was similar to Korean evangeli-calism and revivalism, with its dispensationalist and eschatological empha-sis, and its conviction that Korea holds a special place in world history. However, the doctrines of the organisation, which although it claimed to be Christian also derived from the indigenous religions of Korea, gave Moon messianic status and, unlike the mainline churches, the Unification Church channelled little prosperity back to individual members (Brouwer, Gifford and Rose 1996:123). Although it actively proselytised in Korea, it met with relatively little response. In 1970, Moon moved his headquarters to the United States (Chryssides 1991). The Korean churches regard it as a sect and actively campaign against it.

Church splits, the planting of new congregations by refugees from North Korea and huge financial support from foreign missionary societies all contributed to the 'chaotic spiritual atmosphere' in Korea in the 1950s, a decade which was characterised by new movements and much 'abnormal religious activity' (Kim Ig-jin 2003:103; Ji Won-yong 1965:5–6). The growth of sects on the one hand, and the theological controversies on the other, helped to define the shape of Korean Protestantism, marking the limits to diversity and at the same time confirming its indigeneity.

CHAPTER 6

Growth, Thought and Struggle, 1961–1988

South Korea in 1961 was still poor and heavily dependent on US aid. It had fallen badly behind the North in economic and technological development, and most people were mired in poverty. Chang Myon's new government proved unstable, and Protestants called continually for Chang to step down (Park Chung-shin 2003:181). Fearful for national security, a group of colonels led by Park Chung-hee (Park Jeong-hui) deposed Chang and his government in a largely bloodless coup on 16 May 1961. Chang fled from the Blue House to the Carmelite Convent while trying in vain to contact the US embassy. From a Catholic point of view, Chang may have been a political martyr (T. J. Lee 2005:168), but the return to law and order was greeted with relief by many Koreans. The church reassessed its role in political life, and the *Kyunghyang Shinmun*, which had become virtually a mouthpiece of the Chang government, became independent of the church in 1962 (D. Baker 1997:150).

Park, a Buddhist, treated the main religions impartially. He won strong backing from Christians for his staunch anti-Communist stance and the Holy See was the first foreign state to recognise his government. Park knew the importance of Christian support and sought cooperation for his ambitious plans for industrialisation. During his rule, Park encouraged ethnic nationalism in order to develop a national spirit of self-reliance or jaju, which had much in common with the Juche philosophy of North Korea (Shin Gi-wook 2006:100–106; Wells 1990:163). Park was popular enough to win elections in 1963, 1967 and 1971, but he increasingly relied on military force and the terror created by the Korean Central Intelligence Agency (KCIA) to hold on to power. He was to preside over massive economic growth in the 1960s and 1970s and great improvements in rural standards of living, but this was at great cost to human and civil rights.

CHRISTIANITY IN SOUTH KOREA IN THE 1960S

While the North Korean regime had suppressed religion altogether, church communities of all kinds were thriving in 1960s South Korea. They offered not only religious comfort but also practical help through mutual support and cooperative ventures. Christians continued to gain social advantages, to be better educated and to have a higher standard of living than the average Korean, but Protestants were doing better than Catholics in this regard (Biernatzki et al. 1975:28). However, at the height of the Cold War, Korean Christians were caught in the ideological struggles which were translated theologically into 'liberal' versus 'fundamentalist', politically into 'progressive' versus 'conservative' and missionally as 'social action' versus 'evangelism' in the sense of a conversion agenda.

In 1962 Pope John XXIII established the local hierarchy of the Catholic Church in Korea with three archdioceses: Seoul, Daegu and Gwangju. The establishment of the Korean Catholic Church was celebrated with a fully illustrated compendium which demonstrated the diversity and vibrancy of its growing institutional life, celebrated its global connections and recorded in full its martyr heritage (J. Kim and Chung 1964). Growth was at 5–6 per cent per year, and by the early 1970s, the number of Catholics had reached eight hundred thousand – nearly 2.5 per cent of the South Korean population – in fourteen dioceses and four hundred parishes, and with almost a thousand priests. It was a very young church – both in age and in faith. An estimated four-fifths of the faithful were either converts or the children of converts who were still learning the tradition (Biernatzki et al. 1975:xi–xiii). Many of the remainder came from the families of 'old Catholics' who had survived the Confucian persecutions. Priests, seminarians and sisters tended to be drawn from the latter population. Most of the religious life revolved around public services or masses led by parish priests rather than emphasising private prayer, monastic practices or social movements, which reflected the fact that Korea had been evangelised by MEP missionaries who were diocesan priests rather than by members of religious communities (Biernatzki et al. 1975:61, 116, 138). Clergy were highly educated and professionalised; two-thirds of them were foreigners. They tended to dominate and were treated with great deference, and despite the history of the church as a lay community, lay people had limited access to decision making. The hierarchy tended to focus on the numerical growth and the well-being of the church and its related institutions, leaving the religious communities to deal with social issues. For pastoral needs, the rapidly growing church was dependent on lay catechists and the Korean sisters (Biernatzki et al. 1975:23, 113–14, 139).

Amid suffering, hardship and grieving over the traumas of the past decades, the martyr history continued to have a profound impact on the character of the Korean Catholic Church, and it was the martyrs who were venerated rather than the saints. Another important influence was the official Catholic prayer book *Seonggyo Gonggwa*, dating from 1886. The ascetical and devotional nature of this and other Catholic publications combined to encourage the martyr virtues, emulating the passion of Christ and the sorrows of Mary, and longing for heaven (Biernatzki et al. 1975:6–7, 9–11). In other words, despite out-of-date, foreign literature, and the continued high level of foreign personnel, Korean Christianity was still showing distinctively Korean features: pride in the martyrs, emphasis on filial piety and willingness to make personal sacrifices (cf. Rausch and Baker 2007:377–78).

In 1962 the Catholic Church in Korea took its place within a rapidly globalising Roman Catholic Church at a crucial point in its history: the Second Vatican Council (Vatican II). As a new church, it was formed by the council in many respects and the council's recommendations were more fully implemented in Korea than in many other contexts. On 1 January 1965 Korean was first used officially in the mass. The following year the Korean church published its own order of mass, and a Korean catechism was produced in 1967. The old prayer book was revised and updated, and it was republished in 1968. As part of its general encouragement of incultura-tion, Vatican II reaffirmed the tolerant attitude towards ancestor veneration since the 1930s while at the same time linking it theologically with the Communion of the Saints.[1] Ancestral rites were thus affirmed as an impor-tant part of Korean Catholic faith and practice (Biernatzki et al. 1975:46). But Korean Catholics did not attempt to formally incorporate local customs and culture into Catholic liturgy other than what had already become the norm, such as traditional bows and forms of greeting, responses in a distinctive Korean chant and the white mantilla worn by women. Partly because in the 1960s and 1970s the nation was embracing modernity, and also because the church was celebrating its recognition within Korean society and the global church community, Korean Catholics were proud to identify with what was the norm in Rome and other parts of the world. Moreover, most new church buildings were symbols of modernity (Rausch and Baker 2007:376–77; Biernatzki et al. 1975:61–62).

The enhanced role given by Vatican II to the role of the laity and the theological emphasis on the church as the 'people of God' would hardly

---

[1] *Dogmatic Constitution on the Church* (*Lumen Gentium*), 1964, para.51.

seem necessary in a country in which the church had for many decades survived either without priests or with priests who were foreign and dependent on local people for basic communication. Indeed, unusually, in Korea lay councils at parish and diocesan levels were formed with alacrity in almost every parish and diocese (RFKCH 2010:150). New lay organisations introduced into the country were also enthusiastically received. The Legion of Mary was established in Korea in 1955 by Kim Ig-jin (Francis) and Bishop Harold Henry. The JOC (Jeunesse Ouvrière Chrétienne), also known as 'Jocists' or Young Christian Workers, entered in 1956. Other popular lay movements included Cursilio, which was introduced in 1967 by Filipino Cursillistas, and Focolare, which started in 1969. Following Vatican II, the introduction of base ecclesial communities for Bible study and social action was encouraged. However, the extensive Korean Bible study movement resulted more directly from the Catholic Bible Life Movement, which was started in 1972 by the Sisters of Our Lady of Perpetual Help after they learnt that many of the young Catholics who wanted to study the Bible were attending Protestant Bible studies, which often led to heated arguments. The method was soon extended by religious communities and lay people to include all age groups and most parishes (Yoon In-shil 2007:363–64).

When given a voice, the laity, it transpired, was especially keen that the martyrs should be canonised and after a further twenty-four were beatified in 1968, that movement intensified. But the changes brought about by Vatican II led to criticism of the martyr tradition in some quarters and of Korean ascetical and devotional spirituality for having more in common with Vatican I, for being other-worldly and for lacking in social concern. Popular Catholicism was accused of accommodating itself to Korean religious traditions which were perceived negatively and stereotypically. These included, for example, Confucian 'conformity' and 'hierarchy' and a shamanistic utilitarian approach to faith or the manipulation of the divine (Biernatzki et al. 1975:10–24). There were also unfavourable comparisons with Protestantism as being more successful in terms of both social transformation and growth (A. Finch 2000:561–62). However, given its involvement in government in the 1950s and 1960s, its growing institutional presence and its long tradition of lay agency, descriptions of the church as having a 'ghetto' or 'catacomb mentality' until the 1970s are overstated (Biernatzki et al. 1975:5, 8; D. Baker 1997:159; Grayson 2002:171).

Lay people were active in community development work in their parishes, and church organisations were involved in medicine, relief, education, counselling and mass communication. There was overwhelming agreement on the potential of Catholicism to promote social and economic development in line with the Second Vatican Council, and the bishops set up the Committee for Justice and Peace (Biernatzki et al. 1975:91, 160; Choi Seok-u 1967). This express social concern was accompanied by an influx of Catholic development agencies from overseas and the founding of many national organisations for social justice, such as Caritas Korea, which was established in 1975 (Yoon In-shil 2007:364–65). The increasing social involvement of the Catholic Church can be attributed to the influence of Vatican II, the Koreanisation of church leadership and the urbanisation of laity but it also owed something to 'the example and stimulus of the large and active Protestant community' (Grayson 2001:72, n. 6). Moreover, like their Protestant neighbours, the Catholic laity were noted for their involvement in proselytising and the clergy very much encouraged this (Biernatzki et al. 1975:139).

The affirmation by the council of the good in others and the opening towards other Christians and people of other faiths was taken seriously in Korea through private discussions and open dialogue on the radio. In the interests of ecumenism, *Catholic Korea* included a history and introduction to Korean Protestantism (J. Kim and Chung 1964:561–68). The first Anglican bishop, Yi Cheon-hwan (Peter), installed in 1965, was known for his ecumenical work and helped to bridge both the Catholic and Protestant churches (Lee Jae-jeong 1990:267–69). The most serious organised attempt to work together towards unity was on a new translation of the Bible. The Common Translation of the New Testament was published in 1971 and the whole Bible in 1977. One of the main obstacles to Catholic-Protestant unity, and one of the chief problems facing the translation project, was the term question. Spelling reform in the 1930s had forced Protestants to decide been the alternatives of Hananim and Haneunim, and this had the effect of driving a wedge between Protestants and Catholics, respectively, as the Presbyterians particularly insisted on the former, meaning 'one Lord', and not the latter, which could be regarded as the Korean version of Cheonju, or 'Lord of Heaven', as used by the Catholics. The translation project agreed to use Haneunim as a compromise, but this was one of the main reasons why most Protestants objected to the new version. Few Catholic congregations chose to use it either, but it was adopted by the Anglicans and the Orthodox (Lim Hee-kuk 2013:214–17).

When the archbishop of Seoul, Kim Sou-hwan (Stephen), was elevated to cardinal in 1969, this was a sign not only that the Korean Catholic Church was deemed a mature member of the global Catholic Church but also that it could offer leadership to it. At the time Kim was the youngest member of the House of Cardinals. Having studied in Europe before and during the Second Vatican Council, including sociology in Münster where Joseph Höffner introduced him to Catholic social teaching, Kim was said to embody the council. At the same time he represented the 'old Catholic' tradition in Korea. His grandfather, Kim Bo-hyeon (John), had been martyred in prison in 1868, and his father had peddled pottery. In keeping with expectations of the first generation of indigenous archbishops and cardinals in the global South, Kim was seen as religiously, not politically, motivated. He was a deeply spiritual man, devoted to the Eucharist and the Virgin Mary, and faithful in parish and diocesan ministry. But theological traditionalism does not necessarily equate with political conservatism, and Kim was to become a courageous leader of the Korean Catholic Church through the next two turbulent decades of struggle with the military regime (Linden 2009:35–36; Hanson 1980:103).

Despite the splits in the Presbyterian Church, the main differences between the Protestant churches in the 1960s were not along denominational or organisational lines but across them in terms of three distinct forms of spirituality, each of which appeared distinctively Korean: Bible Christianity, gibok sinang (faith seeking blessings), and cultural or indigenous theology in relation to ethnic nationalism. In the 1970s and 1980s a fourth strand of Korean Protestantism became apparent in radical social activism. Korean Bible Christianity, with its origins in Confucian-style reading of scripture and its application to public life in the 1907 revival and 1919 March 1st Independence Movement, was continued by Han Kyung-chik and other leaders of mainline denominations. It was pressed into service to support anti-Communism, in the sense that religious belief based on the Bible was the antidote to Socialist unbelief. The popular gibok sinang, which stretched back to the 1903 Wonsan revival and Holiness healing ministries, was a feature of revival meetings and was also practised in prayer and small group meetings at the local and lay levels even in conservative churches. For example, from 1977 the Pentecostal leader Park Gui-im worked with cell groups in a Kijang church in Gwangju (Kim Ig-jin 2003:81). Cho Yong-gi's Full Gospel theology, which was fully formed by about 1964, emerged in continuity with this 'maternal' revival tradition (Kim Ig-jin 2003:150–51). In this form of spirituality, the Holy Spirit received special attention as the power of revival and a greater power than any other. This made sense in the context of Korean shamanistic cosmology and linked the church with popular religiosity as shown by the testimony of Deaconess Chang, a shaman who became a Christian (Harvey 1979:205–34; cf. D. Clark 1997:192–94). Charismatic Christianity was introduced into Korea by Reuben Archer Torrey III, who founded Jesus Abbey in the

Taebaek Mountains in 1965 as a community of prayer which also combined physical labour as a form of spirituality. Thousands of mainly young people from across the churches were attracted to the abbey and took its style of worship back to their respective churches.

In the 1960s, a combination of ethnic nationalism, lively intellectual life and the global growth of the culture concept encouraged a flowering of Korean culture and the recovery of interest in Korea's folklore and religious traditions. Methodist theologians especially, building on the work of those who had attempted cultural and inter-religious theologies in dialogue with German and Japanese theology in the 1930s, developed indigenous or folk Christianity in this period. These aimed to integrate the Christian gospel with Korean culture and religiosity, both as a means of national evangelisation and to bring about national unity. The foremost theologians in this field were Yun Sung-bum (Yun Seong-beom), Byeon Seon-hwan and Ryu Dong-sik. Yun explored the religious meaning of the Dangun myth in the light of the Bible, drawing out its Trinitarian structure. He also insisted that Confucianism should be an indispensable tool for Korean theology and, using Confucian sources, developed a 'theology of sincerity (seong)' which he argued could integrate dualisms such as law and gospel, sacred and secular (Yun Sung-bum 1998a:313–62; 1998b:15–45). Byeon built on the legacy of the first Korean Protestant theologian, Choi Byeung-hyeun (Taksa). He likewise insisted on inter-religious dialogue but went much further towards religious unity, advocating 'Mahayana Christianity', describing Buddha as Christ incognito and asserting that there are many ways to salvation (Choo Chai-yong 1998:361–80). Ryu promoted the use of Tao or the Way to convey the Christian message (Logos) in Asia. He also made attempts to unify the different strands of Korean Protestantism. In his pungnyu or 'wind and flow' theology he evoked the golden era of Korean philosophy when its ancient spirit (eol) emerged in the three forms of oneness (han), beauty (meot) and life (sam) and suggested that contemporary Korean theology was a similar unity in diversity (Ryu Dong-sik 2000:14–35; Adams 2012:58–70).

Another original Christian thinker was Ham Sok-hon, a graduate of Osan School and an independence activist who had been involved in the Sinuiju incident in 1946, after which he escaped south. He became an influential writer and speaker, who synthesised Christian theology and ethnic nationalism although, influenced by Uchimura and critical of the churches, he later rejected any particular religion. In the 1960s, Ham joined the Society of Friends, which had a small Korean meeting in Seoul. The Quakers appreciated Ham's non-violent activities to bring about grassroots democracy and world peace, together with his pioneering of dialogue between religions in Korea in the 1970s and 1980s, and in 1985 they nominated him for the Nobel Peace Prize. The title of Ham's book *The Queen of Suffering* (1985 [1933]) was intended as a description of Korea, whose tragic history he traced. Ham taught that Koreans' crucifixion-like experience gave them a special Christ-like responsibility to bring about world peace by themselves giving birth to the Messiah as a seed-kernel (ssial) gives forth a plant (Park Jae-soon 2000:134–74; Adams 2012:220–28).

These theologians were pushing the boundaries of what was acceptable in the conservative theological context of Korea. Any divergence from the received tradition tended to be perceived as a threat to the identity of both church and nation. So, for example, when in 1966 President Park Chung-hee ordered the erection of a large statue of Dangun in Namsan Park as a unifying national symbol, conservative Protestants, who otherwise supported him, vigorously protested, fearing that Dangunism could become a new civic religion similar to Shintoism (T. S. Lee 2009:91). Conservatives would not tolerate compromise with Buddhism either. After Byeon Seon-hwan spoke in a Buddhist–Christian dialogue meeting in 1982, the Methodist Church condemned him. He retracted, apologised and reaffirmed his Christian faith only to be condemned again in 1990 for his address to a Catholic-organised inter-faith dialogue and this time excommunicated (Ryu Dong-sik 2005b:995–1010). Intentional attempts to inculturate the gospel in Korea were generally rejected by mainline church leaders as 'liberal' or 'radical'. Instead, conservative Protestants aimed to replace Korea's traditions with Christianity. The conviction that only a decisive break from the past could save Korea was evident in the continuing resistance by conservatives to ancestor veneration. Byeon Seon-hwan might regard ancestor worship as simply 'a social product of a large-family system' but for many converts ceasing to participate in ancestor rituals was a crucial marker of their new identity (Park Chang-won 2011:160–62; Lee Jung-young 1988a). Nevertheless, to ease the strains in the families of converts, the Christian alternatives became more widely practised. Methodists had included memorial rites (chudoyebae) in their book of *Doctrines and Discipline* from 1935, and Holiness churches and the Salvation Army followed suit in 1955. Presbyterians were less prescriptive about their liturgy, which depended very much on the particular pastor, but after 1978 guidelines were made available by most Presbyterian denominations, and similarly by the Baptists and the Assemblies of God, although they were hedged around with warnings about paganism (Grayson 2007).

CHURCH GROWTH AND ECONOMIC DEVELOPMENT IN THE SOUTH, 1960s–1980s

To achieve his ambitious plans for South Korean industrialisation, Park Chung-hee began normalisation of relations with Japan. But less than two decades after the end of colonial rule this provoked huge public protests in 1964–1965 (Cumings 2005:309–12). Youth movements were at the forefront of the protests, and the Korean Student Christian Movement (KSCM; founded in 1955), the YMCA and the YWCA wrote a joint open letter to Japanese Christians protesting that the treaty was unjust (Zoh Byoung-ho 2005:81–83). Park dealt with the opposition by imposing martial law in June 1964, but before the treaty could be ratified by the National Assembly, 215 Protestant church leaders, including both Han Kyung-chik and Kim Jae-jun, issued a statement against corruption, injustice and dictatorship which urged assembly members to vote against it; it was passed nonetheless (IHCK 2009:236–37). After this the United Church of Christ in Japan tried to heal relations by sending a letter addressed to President Park, to the chair of the National Assembly and to the NCCK apologising for wronging the Korean churches. As a sign of this apology they paid to restore Jeamni Church, where the most well-recorded massacre had taken place. But for many Korean Christians this gesture could not disguise the fact that Japan was once again taking advantage of Korea's relative weakness (Kim In-soo 1997:652–53).

In economic terms Park's plan was successful. With the new investment from Japan, and also because of the opportunity to supply the Vietnam War, the Korean economy showed healthy growth in the years 1965–1971. But in 1972, under economic and political pressure, Park borrowed heavily to invest in a series of five-year plans for industrialisation and pushed through the repressive Yushin constitution, which trampled on workers' and human rights and involved the widespread deployment of KCIA agents (Cumings 2005:361–68). Park's 'Korean model' is credited with transforming South Korea from an economic basket case propped up by foreign aid to an industrial powerhouse. The 'miracle on the Han' set South Korea on the road to becoming one of the world's largest economies by the end of the century, giving it the independence and self-reliance that were so long craved. So despite their initial protests at the political repression, the churches, for the most part, backed Park's national security and economic policies as in the national interest and commensurate with their vision of a strong nation that could resist Communism.

The period of rapid economic development under Park coincided with spectacular church growth, particularly in the number of Protestant churches. These now lit up the city at night with neon versions of the Sorae red cross. In the 1950s, the Protestant population doubled, and it did so again in the 1960s and in the 1970s (IHCK 2009:116). The Catholic Church also grew rapidly in the three decades to 1980 but in 1985 was only about a quarter of the total number of Christians (D. Baker 2006b:296–97). Overall in the period under military rule, Christian growth greatly outstripped population increase, taking Christians from about 6 per cent in 1960 to 20 per cent of the population by 1985. The correlation between church growth and economic growth was not accidental, as we shall show.

The aim of increasing the Christian population and the practice of target setting for numerical growth had been well established in the Protestant churches since the missionary period, but in the new context of South Korea it became the chief interpretation of the mission of the church. Evangelism was no longer left to revivalists and Bible women; the whole church membership was mobilised into a variety of activities towards this end. Some of the activities which led to church growth were simply corollaries of the nature of the Protestant churches. Communitarianism in the churches, a legacy of the Nevius method encouraged by Korean traditions of loyalty, was especially conducive to local growth (Lee Won-gue 2000:177–86; A. Min 2009:206, 211). Members of local congregations were committed to their own church community, even to the extent of displaying their allegiance on their doorposts, and convinced of the qualities of their pastor, chiefly his sermons, which were equated with the Word of God. Members persuaded their families and friends to 'receive grace' through hearing the sermon and brought to the church those facing problems, expecting that the pastor or church could solve them, and pastors praised the members for doing so. Each of the different groups into which members were divided according to age, gender or (in urban churches) profession was proselytising (cf. Park Cho-choon 1983:208). Christians also used sport – taekwondo and football especially – as vehicles of evangelism. Church professional football teams, such as Hallelujah (1980) and Emmanuel (1981), were formed which played nationally and internationally and trained youngsters (Ro Bong-rin 1983:160, 167). Other people were reached through door-to-door visiting in the neighbourhood and street preaching (Park Cho-choon 1983:208–10). Evangelistic methods could be very aggressive. A common slogan offered a stark choice: 'faith – heaven: unbelief – hell'.

Between 1960 and 1990 the urban population of South Korea grew from a little more than a quarter of the whole to three-quarters, and the number of cities nearly trebled mainly due to migration from the countryside (T. S. Lee 2010:88). The context of rapid urbanisation facilitated the appearance of 'megachurches'. In South Korea these are defined as having a congregation numbering more than ten thousand (Lee Kwang-soon 2005:30–38). The growth of megachurches was often by 'poaching' from other churches as people preferred one church over another and made 'horizontal moves'. The quality of the sermons was the primary consideration in choosing a church; after this, large churches could offer a greater variety and quality of pastoral and educational programmes. Large churches developed their own distinctive characteristics and membership in them conferred status, similar to that gained by membership in a 'prestigious club', or employment in a chaebol rather than a small company (Lee Kwang-soon 2005:94–124; Han Gil-soo, Han and Kim 2009:345–47). In addition to these factors, the draw of large urban churches reached deep into the countryside. This was not only because of their general fame, but also because they planted daughter churches in villages and migrants to the city then gravitated towards the mother church (Park Cho-choon 1983:209; Kim Chang-in 1983:251). In many respects, the megachurches exemplified the 'McDonaldization' of late modernity, but at the same time they resisted modern rationalism by charismatic enchantment of the world, attractive religious experiences and doctrines of certainty (Hong Young-gi 2007: 242–47).

The most spectacular example of a Korean megachurch was Yoido Full Gospel Church (YFGC). By 1965, Cho Yong-gi's Full Gospel congregation had reached four thousand members and was second only to Youngnak Church in size. But following the opening of a large and impressive new building on Yoido – a sandy and undeveloped island in the Han River – reported growth accelerated to one hundred thousand in 1979 and six hundred thousand in 1986. (These numbers included 'satellite' churches in other parts of the country.) By the 1970s YFGC was autonomous and had taken leadership of the Pentecostal faith in the Korean church. Furthermore, its characteristic expression of gibok sinang had pervaded almost all the Protestant churches, as measured by the spread of speaking in tongues by 1970 (Kim Ig-jin 2003:137–38, 157). In the late 1970s YFGC further extended its reach through television broadcasting and the weekly *Full Gospel News* church bulletin. And in 1988 YFGC began to publish *The People's Daily* (*Kukmin Ilbo*), a national newspaper. When Cho undertook a two-month preaching tour in the United States in 1964, he found that 'the Korean way of faith' was attractive globally and he made plans to export it through a world revival beginning from Korea (Kim Ig-jin 2003:131–32). The Korean Full Gospel Businessmen's Fellowship, established in 1976, became a powerful supporter of these missionary activities. In 1973, at a time when South Korea received few foreign visitors, YFGC hosted the first of many global events: the Pentecostal World Conference. In 1976, Cho started Church Growth International to disseminate YFGC experience and methods, and the doyens of church growth studies featured Korea as their outstanding and most dramatic example (McGavran and Wagner 1990). Cho was now an international figure with significant political influence at home (Kim Ig-jin 2003:158–59, 163–70; T. S. Lee 2010:101).

Although the church was soon on a different scale even from other 'megachurches', the worship and ministry of Yoido Full Gospel Church shared many characteristics common to Korean Protestant churches. It differed in its emphasis on 'triple prayer', Spirit-baptism and divine healing. In 1973 the church built a mountain retreat or 'fasting prayer house' in Osanli Hills, which became an integral part of the church's work – a pattern that was later followed by most other large churches (Kim Ig-jin 2003:167–68). Also distinctive was the cell system of church organisation. The practice of meeting in small local groups for 'family worship' was widespread in Korean Protestant churches and dates back to the Nevius method, but Cho adapted and systematised these as 'cell groups' to which he devolved much pastoral responsibility. Seoul was divided into 'districts' overseen by pastors, 'sub-districts' with sub-pastors, and 'sections'. Each member in a locality was included in a group made up of five to seven families which met once a week in each other's homes for worship services, discipleship training and pastoral care. Cho regarded the cell groups using informal grassroots evangelism by personal witness in the power of the Spirit as the main mechanism for church growth (Cho Yong-gi 1989:20–29). By the cell analogy, when the group reached ten families, it would divide and the assistant leader would take on the new group. The system was so successful that cell groups became an 'internationally registered mark of YFGC' (Lee Young-hoon 2004:3–20; Kim Ig-jin 2003:136–37; Hurston and Hurston 1977). Arguably what is most distinctive about YFGC is not that Cho utilised cell groups but that he recognised that leading these was largely a women's ministry. Inevitably most of those who attended these groups were women since cells met in the home, which was the woman's sphere; working men were out for long hours; and most groups were organised and led by women. This was the case across the churches, but unlike in most Protestant churches, which followed Confucian leadership models, Cho gave public recognition to these women as church workers alongside the (male) pastors. Furthermore, Cho was not ashamed to recognise his mother-in-law, Choi Ja-sil, as co-founder of the church. Kim Seong-hye, Choi's daughter and Cho's wife, was referred to as 'honorary pastor', and also had her own global ministry.

Numerical growth was fostered by national interdenominational evangelistic campaigns as well as by local evangelism and the building of megachurches. These campaigns increased in frequency and scale up to the end of the 1980s (T. S. Lee 2010:90). Not only were these more sustained and inclusive of different churches than earlier campaigns but they were more in the tradition of gibok sinang, that is, more populist in their revivalistic style and in their emphasis on the power and gifts of the Holy Spirit (Kim Ig-jin 2003:139, 157). However, they retained the nationalistic agenda of 'total evangelization' to convert the whole nation and thus to save it from Communism in the belief that this would result in 'amazing blessing' (Adams 1995; Kim Joon-gon 1983:23). The mass rallies were mainly a feature of Protestantism, but Catholics kept a keen eye on Protestant growth rates and evangelistic activities (Biernatzki et al. 1975:xi) and they too organised large-scale events in this period which demonstrated the popularity and power of the Christian movement.

The first truly nationwide evangelisation campaign was initiated by Kim Hwal-ran, who invited seventy-five church leaders to what was now Ewha Women's University, including Han Kyung-chik and Hong Hyeon-Seol, the principal of the Methodist seminary, to plan the eightieth anniversary of the Korean church in 1965. Eventually seventeen denominations were involved, and even more remarkably, and for the only time, these included Catholics and Anglicans. The slogan for the campaign was 'Thirty million to Christ!' – a figure representing the population of South Korea at the time. The campaign took place in several phases, starting with more than two thousand preparatory meetings in different locations across the whole country, in both rural and urban areas, and also involving schools and colleges. In May-June, the Hong Kong evangelist Timothy S. K. Chao addressed more than one hundred revival meetings in different cities. The campaign continued through the rest of the year, concluding with a rally at Seoul Stadium in November. The organisers counted a total attendance of more than two million, of whom forty thousand made a commitment to Christ (T. S. Lee 2010:92–93; A. Clark 1971:416–23).

Such large gatherings became a feature of the 1970s, the main venue being Yoido 'Plaza' near the site of the new YFGC. In the 1960s this was a reserve airfield on which the military allowed the Christians to pitch tents in the summer for meetings and accommodation. In the early 1970s it was turned into a huge paved potential landing strip which doubled as a place for military and other displays, rivalling the spectaculars in North Korea.

The Christian organisers of large-scale events similarly had an agenda to demonstrate to the North the strength of Christianity in the South. The next one was the 1973 'Crusade', jointly organised and funded by Korean Protestants and the Billy Graham Crusade, and coordinated by Billy Kim (Kim Jang-hwan). This time the target was 'Fifty million to Christ', a figure signifying the intention to evangelise the North as well. Graham had a particular concern for the North because his wife, Ruth, whose parents were missionaries in China, had studied in the 1930s at the foreign school that operated in Pyongyang. Graham addressed crowds which were claimed to reach over a million people of all ages and backgrounds. They sat cross-legged on the ground, picnicking and even sleeping on the tarmac between meetings. Many made 'first-time decisions for Christ' (T. S. Lee 2010:94–95). The government backed the campaign: it was held on military land with logistical support, the army construction corps erected the scaffolding for the cameras and a stand for the six thousand-strong interdenominational choir, and the military academy brass band played the hymns (Kang In-cheol 2006:206). Much of the meeting time was spent in prayer for the nation and for the unification of the peninsula. No criticism was made of the Yushin constitution, even though other Christians were in prison under torture at the time for supposed Communist activities. Instead, Protestants seemed to share the Park regime's 'obsession with statistical . . . growth . . . at the expense of broader social concerns' (Eckert et al. 1990:368).

The church growth resulting from these and further campaigns and the evidence of government favour added to the confidence of Protestantism, as well as to its attractiveness to others (T. S. Lee 2010:89–90). While their leaders and business backers may have had a political agenda to support anti-Communism and the alliance with the United States, the faithful church members who were active on the ground understood that to help someone become a Christian was good for them, even the highest expression of Christian love (Kim Joon-gon 1983:24). The success of these events depended on an army of lay volunteers. They believed that they were in a spiritual struggle in which fasting and all-night prayer in the mountains and in homes was integral to their work (Kim Joon-gon 1983:50; Han Chul-ha 1983:51–58). If we consider that men and young unmarried women made up most of the labour force in the South, which by the 1970s had the longest average working week in the world (Eckert et al. 1990:403), and that a young married woman was busy caring for her children, her husband and maybe also his parents, it is obvious that apart from clergy and professional church workers, those making the campaigns possible were middle-aged women and students. Women, estimated to be up to three-quarters of church membership, and especially those women whose children were older, were 'strong in the spirit of evangelism and . . . devoted to service' (Lee Yeon-ok 1983:238, 241). They were praised for having two great 'weapons' in the 'battle for the soul of Korea': efficacy in prayer and the ability to raise funds (Kim Joon-gon 1983:29; Lee Yeon-ok 1983:236–37). Moreover, church women's organisations had always had a focus on evangelism and this continued to be their priority through the 1960s and 1970s, although with little methodological development or reflection on its appropriateness or efficacy (Yi Hyo-jae 1985:98–100).

Because of the demographics of South Korea in this period and rising educational levels, student movements were extremely important in national life, as shown by their involvement in the overthrow of Rhee Syng-man. All the churches had youth movements, and student groups emerged in the 1950s and grew rapidly. Church leaders were challenged to control them and direct their energies. Cold War divisions and the Kijang split led to a clear division between liberal and conservative students: the former were found in the progressive KSCM, YMCA and YWCA, and the latter in new Bible study–oriented student organisations founded in Korea in the late 1950s. The earliest of these were home-grown: JOY Mission (founded in 1958), the University Bible Fellowship (1961), and the Student Bible Fellowship, which separated from the UBF in 1976. At the same time branches of US-based international student organisations were established in Korea with a mission to build up the Christian testimony of Korean students: the Inter-Varsity Christian Fellowship (IVF) in 1959 and the Navigators in 1966 (Zoh Byoung-ho 2005:61–71, 137–39; Chung Chin-hwang 1983:324–28). Still other groups put evangelism before discipleship, such as Youth for Christ, which started in Korea in 1960, and especially Campus Crusade for Christ (CCC), which rapidly took over as the focal point for evangelical students. The methods of 'personal evangelism' introduced by the CCC, IVF and other groups spread to the churches in general (Park Cho-choon 1983:204).

The Korean branch of Campus Crusade for Christ was founded in 1958 by Kim Joon-gon, who was vehemently anti-Communist because both his wife and father had been murdered during the Korean War in his native North. After seeing the perpetrator of this violence converted to Christianity, Kim developed a strong and distinctive theology of the filling of the Holy Spirit. The CCC specialised in training thousands of young people in proselytising, using a 'how-to' approach based on the 'Four Spiritual Laws'. The Korean programme was intensive – a hundred hours over five days – and followed a biologically inspired vision of exponential growth. Kim had long entertained a vision for the evangelisation of the whole peninsula (Kim Joon-gon 1983:18–24, 37–50). He supported the Yushin reforms and gained government support for many CCC activities. With the help of the Christian Businessmen's Association, he started the annual 'Presidential National Prayer Breakfast' in 1966 and through these got to know President Park personally (Kang In-cheol 2006:358; Lim Hee-kuk 2013:306–11). In the context of the discovery of tunnels from the North under the DMZ and other acts of terrorism, the CCC organised the Korean 'Explo '74', one of a global series of meetings celebrating the 'Jesus Revolution' and 'the Holy Spirit's Explosion'. It was not like a traditional revival but more a 'massive study camp' which aimed to train three hundred thousand students and other churchgoers – or one-tenth of Korea's Protestant population – as evangelists (T. S. Lee 2010:96–100). The North Korean assassination attempt on President Park, which killed his wife, took place while Explo '74 was going on and strengthened the organisers' call to overcome the Communist challenge by prayer (Kim Joon-gon 1983:27). They claimed that the impact of the campaign could be measured in the rise in Christian numbers over the next four years (Kim Joon-gon 1983:28). Although Han Kyung-chik endorsed it, the aggressive, corporate and charismatic style of Explo '74 did not win the support of all the Protestant churches. And at a time when progressive Protestants were under arrest for participating in an alleged Communist plot, their supporters were incensed when CCC founder Bill Bright claimed publically that there was 'more freedom to preach the gospel of Jesus Christ in Korea than there is here in the United States' (Turner 2008:152–53).

For many the Billy Graham Crusade and Explo '74 were too foreign dominated so in 1977 the revivalist Shin Hyeon-gyun led a Korean-sponsored and Korean-led campaign (T. S. Lee 2010:95). It was held symbolically seventy years after the Korean Revival and began on 15 August, Liberation Day, to emphasise the Korean church's unique identity and its place in the political agenda. It was intended 'to evangelize the Nation, by Koreans and Only through the Holy Spirit' and to address the issues which concerned them all, which at this point were chiefly the stated intention of President Jimmy Carter to withdraw US troops from South Korea and worsening social unrest. The assembly was described as a 'patriotic event' which every Korean should attend, in Korea and in the diaspora. The intensity of feeling was such that possibly a million participated in a three-day fast (T. S. Lee 2010:102–4). Although the stated target group was the nation, the revivalists increasingly expressed their growing sense of the nation's manifest destiny to evangelise East Asia after their deliverance from the Japanese, Kim Il-sung and the Korean War (D. Clark 1997:184). As they looked around, they saw only pagan nations and South Korea alone as a light, a city on a hill. The 1980 'World Evangelization Crusade' made this reorientation – from object to agent of evangelisation – explicit in its title and in a call for volunteers for world mission during the event. Kim Joon-gon was the executive chairperson of the crusade, and this time all the Protestant churches worked together. Extensive use was made of advertising, and there was unprecedented media coverage. In terms of numbers, this was the greatest of all the evangelistic campaigns. Organisers recorded 2.7 million in a single evening, more than a million staying each night, all night, for prayer, and more than 17 million total attendance over four days. Many of these people were bussed to Seoul from the countryside especially for the event. But although the horizon was the world, the focus was still on the needs of Korea (T. S. Lee 2010:104–10). On the final day, Liberation Day, Han Kyung-chik preached on the 'Evangelization of the Nation and National Unification', and the serious-ness and magnitude of the campaign needs to be seen in light of the unstable political situation following President Park's assassination and during the bid for power of Chun Doo-hwan (Kim Joon-gon 1983:31–32).

Although Catholics did not hold similar mass evangelistic meetings, in 1981 a National Faith Conference was held to mark 150 years since the foundation of the vicariate apostolic of Korea. This attracted eight hundred thousand people for a one-day celebration of faith on Yoido Plaza. In his address, Cardinal Kim remembered the history of the church, and urged the faithful to become both yeast to transform the people's present and a light to shine for the future. The occasion was also memorable because a cross was said to have appeared in the clouds above Yoido just as the bishops and priests approached the platform (Kim Sou-hwan 2009:338–41).

The year 1984 was highly significant for both Catholics and Protestants. It marked the bicentenary of the founding of the first Catholic lay com-munity and was taken as the centenary of the Protestant mission as well. For Catholics the year was even more special because the Holy See agreed to the canonisation of the 103 Catholic martyrs for which the Korean church had campaigned for so long (RFKCH 2010:150). One of the difficulties for the process had been that there were not always clear records of a miracle connected with each martyr. However, Cardinal Kim argued successfully that it is natural during times of persecution that miracles cannot be documented, but that the Korean Catholic Church's rising from the ashes of persecution to the point where it was baptising one hundred thousand children and adults every year was a miracle which should be attributed to the blood of the martyrs (Kim Sou-hwan 2009:355–60). Pope John Paul II departed from tradition when instead of holding the ceremony in Rome he chose to come to Korea for the occasion. The first visit of a pontiff to the country attracted a million people to Yoido Plaza on 6 May (RFKCH 2010:156–57). In his four-day trip the Pope also visited the leprosarium and addressed representatives of those who could be regarded as struggling under the Chun regime: workers, intellectuals and artists, and young people. He made a point of visiting Gwangju, still reeling from the brutal suppression of the uprising in 1980, where he expressed his awareness of 'deep wounds' and his sympathy for those suffering as a result of the recent 'unfortunate events'.[2]

The same year, 1984, was appropriate for the Protestant centenary because it marked both the arrival of the first missionary (Allen) and the founding of the first indigenous church at Sorae (Kim In-soo 1997:677–79). Ironically, the prospect of the centenary had not increased church unity; instead, it encouraged the different denominations to hold a number of separate evangelistic campaigns from 1975 onwards in order to increase their membership to specific round number targets by 1984. Nevertheless, twenty major denominations and twenty-five Christian organisations were involved in the main thanksgiving event which took place on 15–19 August on Yoido Plaza. Billy Graham was the only foreign preacher participating in what was emphatically a Korean event (T. S. Lee 2010:101–2, 110). But as a sign of their gratitude to the foreign missionaries, the Protestant denominations constructed a fine building adjacent to the graveyard by the Han River at Yanghwajin granted by King Gojong in 1890 for use by foreigners. It was intended as a place of worship for Seoul Union Church – a congregation of expatriates which had been meeting on and off since 1886. Protestants, believing like Catholics that 'the blood of the martyrs is the seed of the church', also reflected on the martyr history of the church, first, by claiming the Catholic martyrs in their telling of the churches' story (e.g. Park Cho-choon 1983:203), and second, by identifying their own martyrs: 851 of them, 90 per cent of whom were killed by Communists (Kang In-cheol 2006:143–49; cf. Lim Hee-kuk 2013:138–46). These were commemorated with statues, plaques, shrines to leading figures like Ju Gi-cheol, special services and also a museum, Yongin Martyrs Memorial Hall, which was a white mausoleum-type structure erected in 1989.

---

[2] Homily of Pope John Paul II, Gwangju, Friday, 4 May 1984.

While economists were extolling South Korea's economic success, start-ing in the 1970s the Korean example of church growth was being propagated as a model for other Asian nations. For example, the Asian Center for Theological Studies and Mission (ACTS), founded in 1974, brought pastors from other parts of the continent to Korea to study and observe (Han Chul-ha 1983:62–68; Nelson 1983:94–97). On the occasion of the Protestant centenary it tried to account for the 'Korean church growth explosion' (Ro Bong-rin and Nelson 1983). This was done primarily in terms of a movement or outpouring of the Holy Spirit resulting from fervent prayer and leading to evangelism – a view which interpreted the revival of 1907 as 'the Korean Pentecost' (Blair and Hunt 1977). A second set of reasons concerned such matters of strategy as evangelistic activity, Bible study, training in evangelism and, chiefly in this period, the cell group method. A third reason was also proffered: the example of the 'godly living' of Christians. 'Situational factors' – regarded as providential – that promoted growth were also recognised, and sociological and psychological methods were used to explain patterns of receptivity. However, already in the 1980s there were internal criticisms of the church growth model and its fixation on numerical growth. Kim Byong-suh, a professor of sociology at Ewha University, complained that the rapidly expanding urban churches were bureaucratic; dominated by charismatic, wealthy and powerful leaders; and embroiled in the money economy (1985:71–72), and even Han Kyung-chik lamented the in-fighting in the churches, duplication of theological semi-naries and preoccupation of members with their local church at the expense of support for the denomination or national church (1983:348–70).

The spectacular growth of the churches in Korea has naturally attracted much attention from missiologists and sociologists of religion. Chief among the theories are those suggesting that it is to the background of social change and market competition that we must look to understand the rapid growth in church membership in the three decades from 1960. Durkheimian theorists point to the turmoil of colonisation, conflict and rural–urban migration which contributed to the destruction of traditional hierarchies and the weakening of the extended family structure and led to rootlessness and the need for community support (Lee Won-gue 2000:177–86). In a hostile and cut-throat economic environment, the churches provided social facilities, practical help, welfare support, advice, healing and encourage-ment, especially for new arrivals from the countryside. Amid 'unrest, chaos, tension and instability', the churches gave self-identity, offered a haven of stability and functioned as 'a reference group' (Kim Byong-suh 1985). Most of all they engendered a sense of togetherness in striving and suffering. In

Protestant churches this was felt especially through the dawn prayer meetings and in the Friday night prayer meetings which lasted through the
military curfew.

While theories of anomie suggest that the churches grew as a refuge from
the negative effects of economic policy, supply-side theories portray the
churches as benefitting from immersion in the market. After the end of the
comity arrangements, without a parish system and in the context of urbanisation and social Darwinism, the Protestant churches were increasingly
situated cheek by jowl and in competition with each other for members. In
the religious marketplace created by the city and urban transport infra-
structures, popular churches could potentially attract people from across a
whole   conurbation   and   become   megachurches   (Lee   Kwang-soon
2005:94–124). Furthermore, from the 1960s into the early 1980s religious
demand was met by an increasing supply and this convinced some that this
competition actually produced growth. The supply was driven by religio-
economic entrepreneurship on the part of clergy who expected to plant,
market and grow churches for consumers of religious goods and services
(Han Gil-soo et al. 2009:338–41). Some theological seminaries even made
planting a new church a prerequisite for graduation. In the age of the
chaebol or mega-companies, Protestant pastors also looked to develop
'megachurches'. The 'bigness syndrome' measured size not only by congregation but also by church buildings (Kim Byong-suh 1985:71). Urban
churches invested heavily in the latter in anticipation that they would pay
dividends in terms of growth. That this expectation was not always fulfilled
accounted for a number of empty concrete shells in Seoul and other cities by
the 1980s. Despite a Christian history of struggle in adversity and resistance
to the majority, size and success tended to be taken uncritically as signs of
divine blessing. The motive for church growth was not only in order to
achieve the goal of Korean or world evangelisation; growth had become an
end in itself. By extension of the biological language, growth was a sign of
health, and unless it kept growing, it would not be a healthy church.

In addition to the imperative of growth and the incentive of size, an
'achievement- or success-orientation' was shared by clergy and laity, especially the eldership. Following the Nevius method and the congregational
polity, the local church chose the pastor and invested to maintain and
expand the congregation (Han Gil-soo et al. 2009:339–42). In most
denominations the Protestant pastor's salary was paid by the offering of
the congregation and not from a denominational fund, so his salary
increased with the size of his congregation. Whereas a successful pastor
could stay on indefinitely and build up a power base, unpopular pastors

could be intimidated to make them leave. Large churches were more able to appoint gifted pastors, further increasing the disparity among churches. By the early 1980s local churches had become 'highly stratified': the salary of an urban church pastor could be twenty times that of a rural one (Kim Byong-suh 1985:71; Han Gil-soo et al. 2009:343–46). The market context encouraged further splintering of denominations. The prevailing philosophy offered few strictures against those who split to form new churches and even condoned church splits on the basis that competition fuelled growth (McGavran and Wagner 1990:4). Cell groups, which were widely adopted by other churches, were another way in which splits were seen as a virtue since dividing cells were the mechanism for growth. Establishing a new subdenomination not only could result in control of considerable income and a stake in valuable land and property but it also could elevate the pastor to the status of a theologian and enable the church to found a seminary which would employ professors and spawn graduates who would found daughter churches, and so on (D. Clark 2007:181; Han Gil-soo et al. 2009:347–48).

A further link between church and economic growth was that churches directly contributed to economic success by helping individuals and families and by servicing the workforce through this challenging period. Furthermore, Protestants, particularly those who had fled from the North earlier, inculcated capitalist thinking and encouraged the entrepreneurial skills and business acumen that were advantageous in the flourishing economy of the 1970s. Especially in urban areas, churches offered networks for business purposes, and larger congregations even published a church 'Yellow Pages'. At the same time, Protestant pastors of the Bible Christianity tradition instilled in their congregations their responsibility to work hard for the sake of God, nation and family, and encouraged church members to support Park's economic push as part of their Christian duty. Christian workers felt a responsibility to outdo their fellow labourers in productivity and to put in even longer hours than others in order to set an example of hard work, demonstrating their loyalty to God and the superiority of Christianity. Remembering the suffering of Jesus Christ on the Cross, which they believed lifted the burden from their own backs, Christians were willing to make sacrifices for the national good (Ogle 1977:31).

However, Max Weber's Protestant work ethic theory ([1905] 1974) only partially applies in Korea since the argument presupposes a large mass of practising Christians whereas around 1970 Protestants numbered only about 6 per cent of the population (IHCK 2009:116). The Park Chung-hee government's work ethic was drawn partly from military discipline and partly from the Confucian virtues which were complemented by, but not based on, conservative Protestant morality (Grayson 1995). Park's Saemaul Undong or New Village Movement launched in winter 1971–1972, which epitomised his cultural agenda, was greatly influenced by the rural church and mission programmes of the 1920s and 1930s, and many of the successful examples cited were drawn from the experiences of Christian rural workers (Park Keun-won 1985:55). As this example shows, the influence of Christianity in Korea in this period was via the leadership it offered rather than by its widespread practice. Through their sermon illustrations, many drawn from a Western context, pastors opened up new vistas and raised up a vision of a Christian nation, and the Holy Spirit movements injected a new energy that enabled Koreans to revitalise their society (K. Kim 2010).

Another respect in which churches contributed to economic success – at least for Christians – was that gibok sinang or the 'faith of seeking blessings' of both evangelicalism and Pentecostalism provided legitimacy for the accumulation of wealth (Jang Suk-man 2004:140–41). In the context of government campaigns for economic growth at all costs, gibok sinang shifted its predominant concern from health to wealth, and as the economy and the churches grew simultaneously, many South Korean Christians came to regard faith and material blessing as two sides of the same coin (S. Kim 2007:43–50). The Full Gospel theology of Cho Yong-gi and Yoido Full Gospel Church was the most influential prosperity theology. The central message of the church, the 'fivefold gospel' was derived from the 'fourfold' gospel of the Holiness movement and the 'four cardinal doctrines' of the Assemblies of God, but Cho included a fifth doctrine, 'the Gospel of Blessing'. This was expanded in Cho's teaching of 'threefold blessing' – 'spiritual well-being', 'bodily health' and 'general well-being' – which was indebted to the teaching of Oral Roberts and other North American Pentecostal evangelists. 'General well-being' referred to the expectation that all the worldly activities of the believer would prosper. Cho reasoned that the world was created for the enjoyment of human beings and that Jesus' poverty was so that humanity might be rich. As South Korea became more prosperous, Cho's original gospel for survival and healing developed into a gospel for success through a spiritual version of positive thinking. He taught his disciples to 'see by faith' in a 'fourth dimension' what they wanted to achieve and then pray it into becoming a reality (Cho Yong-gi 1977; 1979; 1989; Ma Won-suk et al. 2004:36–41; Anderson 2004b:148–50). Cho's theology of blessing was linked to extensive business operations carried out by the church. It also chimed well with the government's Better Life Movement (Jalsalgi Undong) and attracted government support (Kim Ig-jin 2003:152).

However, Cho's approach was strongly criticised and even condemned by many other Christians (e.g. Lee Hong-jung 1999:149, 157). There was also a wider criticism of gibok sinang and the revivalist streams in the mainstream churches going back to the 1920s, and this was reiterated by North Korea, for example, after the 1973 Billy Graham Crusade (Kang In-cheol 2006:129). The main criticisms of gibok sinang were, first, that it was unbiblical and basically shamanistic (Kim Ig-jin 2003:195–98). As YFGC became known globally, Western observers also repeated the same concerns about syncretism (e.g. Cox 1996:226). Second, it was blamed for contributing to what was seen as a lack of social participation by the Korean church. This was especially the view of minjung theologians, who sought to address the problem of poverty by political action. Third, critics seized on the excesses and unethical methods of some Full Gospel preachers, such as borrowing money in 'faith' that God will fulfil his promise. In addition, critics – especially those with a martyr theology – took issue with Cho's teaching that material wealth and physical healing are signs, or even proofs, of God's blessings, and the corollary that poverty is a curse, the result of wrong actions and attitudes towards God.

The American Assemblies of God put pressure on Cho to drop the fifth doctrine, but rather than do so, Cho withdrew his church from the Korean Assemblies of God in 1981, leading to a three-way split in the denomination. In 1983 the Presbyterian Church of Korea declared that Cho had heretical tendencies and that members should not associate with him. Debate continued for a decade (Lee Young-hoon 2004:16–19; Kim Ig-jin 2003:175–87). Cho continued to insist that his view was biblical and that, furthermore, it appeared to have worked, not only in his church but also in the post-war history of Korea. His supporters, especially the Pentecostal theologian Pak Jeong-geun, vigorously defended Cho against accusations of shamanism by pointing out that he explicitly rejected 'the evil spirit world' and had not adopted any of the language or cultural symbols of shamanism (Anderson 2004b:139–43). Although during the 1970s and 1980s the YFGC did not take the kind of political action that minjung theologians would have liked to have seen, it was certainly socially and politically involved. For a start, YFGC was itself a community development project which produced upward social mobility. Furthermore, as part of the planting of new churches, church members were urged to engage in charity work and to establish schools and hospitals (S. C. H. Kim 2007). Regardless of their validity, the criticisms clearly revealed the tension between the 'paternal' spirituality or Bible Christianity of the elite on the one hand and the 'maternal' faith and gibok sinang of the masses on the other. The critics appeared to be condemning the traditional religiosity of the people, and those who by and large enjoyed material blessing were criticising those who aspired to it (S. C. H. Kim 2008a:134–38).

Not only Pentecostal but also Holiness preachers encouraged the belief that the outpouring of God's Spirit was responsible for both church growth and material blessing. From the 1960s Holiness churches, especially the Kiseong branch, grew rapidly; by 1970 Holiness churches had reached three hundred thousand members and become the third largest Protestant denomination (after the Presbyterians and Methodists). The Holiness leader Chung Jin-kyung (Jeong Jin-kyeong) worked to integrate Holiness churches with other denominations, and the movement became part of the main line. So even within mainstream Protestantism, the link between numbers and grace was commonly accepted. The growing prosperity of South Korea was taken as evidence of the truth of God's promises and justification of church support for the government's drive for modernisation and economic development. Han Kyung-chik and other mainline pastors similarly regarded material well-being to be the result of faith and the fellowship of the church, although they were more likely to talk about God's 'provision' than about 'wealth' and they placed relatively more emphasis on right living, hard work and education as important to economic well-being and encouraged work for social justice (Lee Won-sul et al. 2005:99–106, 284–92).

CHRISTIAN SUPPORT FOR NATIONAL RECONSTRUCTION, 1960s–1980s

Christian attitudes towards the military regime of Park Chung-hee can be classified in one of three ways. On the whole, conservative Protestants or evangelicals conformed and some actively supported it. Others, such as the Catholic Bishops' Conference, more reluctantly adapted themselves to the circumstances. Those who actively resisted were the more left leaning and progressive Protestant and Catholic groups, especially those close to farmers and workers. Until very nearly the end of the 1980s, despite its practice of political repression and the surveillance, arrest, torture and imprisonment of a significant number of Christians, most churches and Christian organisations supported the 'symbiosis' of church and military government (D. Clark 2007:175). Several reasons are suggested for this.

Minjung theologians and other progressive Protestants accused the Protestant mainstream of failing to join them in resisting oppression owing to an 'emotional, conservative, individualistic, and other-worldly' or 'fundamentalist' theology (Suh Kwang-sun 1981:20–21). However, the conservatives were not apolitical; their support for the Park regime was active not passive and included working with the government to discredit minjung leaders (Park Chung-shin 2003:50–94). Another reason put forward for their disinclination to criticise the government is the self-interest of middle-class church leaders who valued economic stability and did not want to risk their positions. On top of this disincentive, unless he had founded the church, if the pastor wished to protest against the government, he would first have to convince the elders who supported the church from their own personal wealth (cf. Park Chung-shin 2003:95–97, 108–12, 188). But while self-interest may have been a factor, majority Christian support for successive military regimes is more obviously explained by the shared agenda of anti-Communism which bound churches and government together and, until the end of the 1980s, also held together progressive and conservative Christians. The more conservative Protestant denominations and local churches provided direct support for the regime's anti-Communist agenda through the Korean Christian Association for Anti-Communism, founded by Kim Jong-geun in 1965 (Kang In-cheol 2006:251–53). Furthermore, the anti-Communism argument also applied to the Catholic Church, against which the accusation of commercial self-interest on the part of the leadership is harder to level. The Bishops' Conference was consistently anti-Communist, gradualist, and for the separation of church and politics (Im Hyug-baeg 2006:151).

In the polarised context of the Cold War, support for the South Korean government meant not only strong anti-Communism but also pro-Americanism. It was for both these reasons that the churches – Protestant and Catholic – manifested strong and united support for the Vietnam War, in which fifty thousand Koreans were fighting on the side of South Vietnam by 1971 (Cumings 2005:364). The Christian press and churches – even the progressive ones – agreed that Koreans had a duty to support their South Vietnamese allies (Ryu Dae-young 2004:197). They described the war in terms of an eschatological struggle between good and evil and included exaggerated reports of Korean victories from army chaplains travelling with the troops. The army itself was estimated to be 20 per cent Christian in 1970 – the overwhelming majority Protestant. After the Korea Christian Officers Association started the Movement to Make the Whole Army Christian, for which Kim Joon-gon claimed to have obtained the backing of President Park, this proportion rose to 48 per cent (1973). In April 1972 more than three thousand Korean soldiers were baptised in a single baptism ceremony (Kim Chang-in 1983:252; Kang In-cheol 2006:354–58).

The NCCK asked all the churches to pray for the servicemen in Vietnam and in August 1966 organised an official farewell service for the White Horse Division at its barracks in Yoido. The service was led by Kim Hwal-ran and leading clergy across the Protestant denominational spectrum officiated, ranging from Lee Cheon-hwan, the first native Anglican bishop, to Jang Un-yong, the Salvation Army general. Kim Hwal-ran called the soldiers 'crusaders' fighting for the freedom and dignity of humanity and simultaneously repaying the debt of Korea to its allies. Gil Jin-gyeong, the acting NCCK general secretary, claimed that the 'Immanuel' battalion, which was commanded by Christian officers, was an army for justice and would sanctify the rest of the troops. Yu Ho-jun, the general secretary of the Presbyterian Church (Tonghap), said that defeating Communists was an act of 'humanitarian love', and Kim Joon-gon justified the war as a necessary evil in order to liberate those enslaved by Communism. Christian solidarity around the war continued for the duration, and the 'anti-Communist mentality' allowed for little critical assessment. It was also linked by, for example, Hong Hyeon-seol, the president of the Methodist Theological Seminary, to the need for the continuing presence of US troops in South Korea, which was periodically called into question, but on which there was also pan-Christian agreement (Ryu Dae-young 2004:200–205, 214–15).

Although the threat of Communism was a major motive for proselytising in the post-war period and the churches' anti-Communist stance increased their attractiveness in the context of the threat from the North, it would be an exaggeration to say that fear was the main driver of conversions in this period. Politically Christians were not merely anti-Communist but were *for* Korean independence; like other Koreans, they saw the nation's independence as safeguarded by the national security and economic growth which the regime provided (cf. Kim Djun-kil 2005:123). As we have seen, the vision of a Christian nation, hope of prosperity, support and comfort from the church community and the powerful story of the identification of Christ with suffering were all important factors in drawing people to faith.

Christianity not only contributed to national development but it also was at the forefront of South Korea's increasing global orientation and involvement through the diaspora churches and mission movements. The diaspora in the West was predominantly Protestant and was held together and connected with Korea itself by church links as much as by business and government. Diaspora churches were linked by missionaries from Korea, who both served the diaspora and pioneered new territories, sometimes alongside and sometimes ahead of other Koreans. Korean Protestants had been sending missionaries since the establishment of the first Korean denominations. For most of the twentieth century, the circumstances of Korea were hardly conducive to maintaining an overseas missionary movement, but even though the Shandong work of the Presbyterian Church had to be terminated following the Communist victory in China, foreign missionary activity was continued by the sending of two couples to work with the United Church of Christ in Thailand in 1955 (A. Clark 1971:258). In the 1960s and 1970s a small number of Koreans worked with other churches through global church exchange programmes or international mission organisations, and a few large churches founded overseas mission organisations – for example, Chunghyeon Presbyterian Church in 1968 (Kim Chang-in 1983:255). From the 1960s overseas missionary sending began to increase (D. Clark 1997:184–85; see Chapter 7). YFGC was at the forefront of this initiative and, ambitious to reach the centres of global power, included the United States and Europe as mission fields. In 1973 the All-Asia Missions Consultation, an initiative of Han Kyung-chik and Cho Dong-jin (David), was convened in Seoul and more mainline church leaders began to see Korea as a 'light to Asia' and even a global mission force (Cho Dong-jin 1983:117). By 1982 there were 323 Protestant Korean missionaries and their wives working in thirty-seven countries, 143 of them cross-culturally. Most were sent through eight mission agencies which had good ties to the government and were supported from the offerings of the local sending congregations (Nelson 1983:90). At the 'World Evangelization Crusade' in 1980 Kim Joon-gon, the chair of the organising committee, made clear his intention to 'start a Korea-modelled and Korea-led [world] missionary movement' and launched a programme to send one hundred thousand missionaries and volunteers overseas in the next decade (Kim Joon-gon 1983:35; T. S. Lee 2010:107–10). The growing number of Protestant missionaries saw themselves as ambassadors for South Korea and exported not only a Korean gospel but also Korean culture and products wherever they were sent.

The missionary connection also continued in the opposite direction – into South Korea. Although as the economy grew, the need for relief work lessened and development work was handed over to local control, a number of organisations maintained their missionary sending but now most were invited by Korean churches to do tasks they were not able to manage or to train Koreans. For example, the Maryknoll Fathers deliberately worked in remote rural areas which the indigenous priesthood could not stretch to cover (Hanson 1980:246), human rights campaigners helped set up new organisations, others taught new methods of Bible study and some offered specialist medical skills. The continuing presence of foreign missionaries from the West had several advantages for the Korean churches and national reconstruction: first, as a link with the wider world, especially when ordinary Koreans had restricted travel opportunities and the Korean press was heavily censored, and second, as a source of funding for projects. Third, through missionary contacts and organisations, some Korean Christians were enabled to study overseas and many of these took up leading roles in international organisations on their return. Fourth, missionaries were a source of foreign-language tuition – especially in English – and conversation practice since there were few other proficient speakers living in Korea. Mastery of English in particular opened many doors and allowed Korean voices to be heard internationally. Fifth, missionaries were the chief means of propagating distinctive Korean innovations such as minjung and Full Gospel theologies and helped to spread the word of Korean growth.

CHRISTIAN ACTIVISM IN LABOUR AND FARMERS' MOVEMENTS IN THE 1970S

The decades of the 1970s and 1980s, which saw such numerical growth in the churches, are also known as the era of struggle for civil and human rights and for democracy, in which Christians – Catholic, Protestant and Anglican – worked together and played a leading role. While the majority of Christians were mobilised to build up their local church and increase the Christian population, activists formed minjung (grassroots or people's) movements to struggle for the civil and human rights of farmers and industrial workers and for democracy. It is convenient to divide these movements into two decades. In the 1970s, the catalyst was at first the conditions of labour and later the repressive Yushin constitution that President Park Chung-hee imposed backed by corporate business interests. The action against the regime was led mainly by a coalition of workers, students and Christian activists. In the 1980s, the catalyst was the brutal suppression of the Gwangju Democratization Movement in which Park's successor, Chun Doo-hwan, was implicated. This provoked wider calls for an end to dictatorship, for democratisation across a much broader social spectrum and for a more just policy of development. In this period, Christian activists partnered with a wider coalition. In both decades, there was 'a well-developed Christian social movement' made up of a network of Christian organisations and supported by minjung theology and art (P. Chang 2006).

Globally, in the 1960s, Christians became more aware of the need for social justice, although they were divided as to the priority this should be given in Christian mission. Influenced by the social teaching of the Second Vatican Council, the Korean bishops began in 1967 to raise pastoral concerns about socio-economic issues. Among the laity, the expansion of Catholic education and simultaneously of service to the poor through hospitals and other institutions also contributed to 'an awakening of the Catholic social conscience' (D. Baker 1997:152). Archbishop Roh had discouraged political protest, but it became a possibility after Kim Sou-hwan replaced him in 1968, although the hierarchy were divided on the issue and Cardinal Kim was at first reluctant to speak out. As they were doing in other parts of the world at the time, the Maryknoll Fathers particularly encouraged Catholics to engage more with social issues and urged the bishops to use the church's 'position of moral leadership' to make 'objective non-political statements on the social issues of the day' (Hanson 1980:246–47; Biernatzki et al. 1975:171). Paik Lak-geoon, Kim Jae-jun and Kang Won-yong were delegates at the seminal World Council of Churches conference, 'Church and Society' in 1966, and in the late 1960s the Kijang denomination particularly, as well as leaders of organisations with links to the WCC, began to take a more radical position on social justice. It was in this context that Kim Jae-jun penned the well-known hymn:

> Unto hearts in deep night pining,
> And a world captive under darkness' hand,
> The morning star, shining upon the East,
> Brought a new dawning to this land.
> In this Land of the Morning Calm,
> Lives [are] now in light made new.
> With this light shining through our lives,
> A tower of life is being built in this land.
>
> (Korean Hymnal Society 2007:no.582; our translation)

However, even in Kijang churches, congregations tended to be conservative theologically and pro-government politically so it was mainly those clergy who worked in church-related agencies and seminaries (gigwan moksa) and Christian intellectuals who engaged in activism (Park Chung-shin 2003:192–98). The NCCK mouthpieces of the monthly journal *Gidokgyo Sasang* and the Christian Broadcasting Station were available to these various groups. Furthermore, they had close links with churches overseas and received moral support and financial assistance especially from the United States, Japan, Canada and Germany (D. Baker 2007b).

In the 1970s South Korean workers were exploited by multinationals, by Korean conglomerates and by medium and small businesses under pressure to supply the others. Light industry predominated, and much of the workforce was fresh from the countryside and living in dormitories, slum housing or shanty towns. In the workplace, training was poor, and health and safety were grossly overlooked. Social security was virtually non-existent, and management was rough and sometimes brutal. Although collective bargaining was practised, unions were generally organised or manipulated by employers rather than representing the interests of employees (Ogle 1977). Besides their personal grievances, the growing working class observed that the rewards for their labour seemed to be disproportionately benefitting the Korean business elite and that powerful Japanese and American business interests were increasingly dictating domestic policy. Industrial unrest grew, and in 1968 it resulted in the first large-scale strike (Cumings 2005:372–74).

Christians sought to address the needs of industrial workers in several different ways. Christian owners employed industrial chaplains, who had mainly evangelistic and pastoral roles; other Christians did social work such as running night schools and kindergartens; and some directly tried to improve conditions for the workers and challenged management (Koo Ha-gen 2007:76; Ogle 1977:67–68). Foremost among the latter category were the UIM and JOC. The UIM (Urban and Industrial Mission) was a project of the WCC which built on the Protestant social gospel tradition and the theology of Reinhold Niebuhr, and was also inspired by the Catholic worker-priest movement. It had been active in Korea since 1958. UIM workers were mainly young graduates who had disguised their identity and deliberately took factory work to discover what it was like and to make workers aware of their rights (Ogle 1977:33–65). Although it tended to be the theologically radical who were most vocal in support of the UIM, mainstream churches and leaders in the NCCK also backed it. In addition the UIM received funds and personnel from foreign church agencies, such as the Australian Presbyterians who supported the work at Yeongdeungpo from 1964. The JOC was a Catholic Action movement founded in Belgium by Joseph Cardijn which received papal approbation in 1925 for its work for labour justice and in encouraging Catholic trade unions. In 1967, the JOC was involved in a successful action against the Ganghwa Island Simdo garment company (Kim Nyung 1993:241). This resulted in a statement by the Bishops' Conference in February 1968 which declared that 'the Church has a right and responsibility to teach Christian social justice' and to uphold the dignity of workers (Kim Sou-hwan 2009:199–202). The Bishops' Conference formed the Justice and Peace Committee in 1970, and the following year it issued a pastoral letter saying that economic and social development should go hand-in-hand (Hanson 1980:102). The JOC in

Korea also had an agricultural wing that, in 1972, became the Korean Catholic Farmers' Movement.

Both the UIM and JOC worked by forming small groups for leisure activities, problem sharing, conscientization and Bible study (Koo Ha-gen 2007:75). They played an important role in politicising labour, linking the intellectual community with the workers and broadening the social background of participants in the labour movement (Sohn Hak-kyu 1989:180). Using media, street demonstrations and other protest methods, they drew attention to the cause. When industrial workers found their own struggle for labour justice suppressed, they tended to gravitate towards the Christian progressives because of their organisational structures and international connections, and also because they were less susceptible than intellectuals to accusations that they were Communist. Both the UIM and JOC drew membership from among Christian students, especially after the tenth anniversary of the student revolution that overthrew Rhee Syng-man suggested contemporary parallels (Koo Ha-gen 2007:74–78). Most of the student support came from the progressive groups, the KSCM, YMCA and YWCA, that had united as the Korean Student Christian Fellowship (KSCF). The KSCF was part of the international Student Christian Fellowship movement and also linked up with Catholic groups. Together they declared they would fight against dictatorship and corruption and for those oppressed (Zoh Byoung-ho 2005:60–65).

One single event – the self-immolation of Jeon Tae-il in November 1970 – 'marked the beginning of South Korea's working-class formation', 'awakened the intellectual community to the dark side of the export-oriented industrialisation' and stirred Christian consciences into action (Koo Ha-gen 2001:70–74). Twenty-two-year-old Jeon worked as a tailor under sweatshop conditions in the (strangely named) Peace Market in Cheonggyecheon in Seoul, which was full of garment factories employing mainly young women workers. He was also a Sunday school teacher at Changhyeun Methodist Church, which was started among people displaced by slum clearance. Jeon documented how young women, fifteen to eighteen years old, were spending fifteen-hour days in exceedingly cramped conditions with no sunlight for very low payment even by the standards of the time. In 1969 he started a workers' group and began to campaign for better pay and conditions for the women. After letters to the relevant government ministry met no response, and peaceful protests were forcibly broken up, Jeon set himself on fire outside the market, shouting, among other things, 'Abide by the Labour Standard Laws', 'We are not machines!' and 'Let us rest on Sundays!', and leaving a letter to the president (Rhie and Cho 1997:306–9).

Jeon's self-immolation was widely reported and shocked the nation. After his funeral at Changhyeon Church, multiple memorial services were held at churches and university chaplaincies. Jeon Tae-il had asked his mother, Yi So-seon, who was a deacon, to carry on his work. Known as the 'mother of all workers', she became the figurehead of Korea's first independent trade union, the Cheonggye Garment Workers' Union. Despite government repression, women textile workers particularly continued to form unions and struggle for their rights, including Sundays as a day off (Ogle 1977:109–10; Sohn Hak-kyu 1989:34–38). In almost all cases the workers were educated and encouraged by progressive church leaders (Koo Ha-gen 2001:74) such as Cho Wha-soon, a (woman) Methodist minister working with the UIM in Incheon (Ogle 1977:115–18; Lee Sun-ai and Ahn 1988). Korea Church Women United, which was constituted in 1967 with Lee Yeon-ok as president as an umbrella organisation for local and denominational women's movements, joined the protests and helped those arrested and their families as well as campaigning for women's rights (Lee Yeon-ok 2011:229–34; Yi Hyo-jae 1985:93–102). The progressive churches facilitated workers' organisation, offered some protection against state oppression and mobilised alliances (Koo Ha-gen 2007:99). In September 1971, Protestant bodies and the Catholic Church came together to form the Korea Action Organisation for Urban Industrial Mission (Kim Nyung 1993: 242).

After President Park had amended the constitution and was standing for a third term in 1971, the opposition united behind Kim Dae-jung, a populist politician who took up the cause of Jeon Tae-il. Kim had been encouraged as a politician by Chang Myon, and, after the sudden death of his first wife, he converted to Catholicism, taking the baptismal name Thomas More. He later married Lee Hee-ho, a Methodist and NCCK activist. Kim publically expressed his personal faith alongside his belief in justice in history.[3] Despite Park's huge election budget and corrupt electoral practices, Kim Dae-jung polled 46 per cent of the vote but this was not enough to oust Park who now gave up any pretence of democratic rule. Meanwhile, the International Monetary Fund stepped in to deal with Korean debt, which intensified pressure on workers and resulted in widespread unrest. After Park's 'garrison decree' in December 1971, politicians, journalists, professors and students were effectively silenced and church services and prayer meetings became the major forum for anti-government protest (Sohn Hak-kyu 1989:38–40). At Christmas midnight mass in Myeongdong Cathedral at the end of 1971, Cardinal Kim warned the president that his action would

---

[3] For example, in his Nobel Lecture on 10 October 2000 in Oslo, Norway.

'help widen the already existing gap between the people and the government' and asked him to withdraw the measure. At this point KBS, the government station, stopped broadcasting. After a further intervention in August of the following year, Kim believed that the government began to try to discredit him but his simple lifestyle made it impossible for the KCIA to charge him (Kim Sou-hwan 2009:219; Hanson 1980:101–3). Whereas the Protestant churches remained ideologically divided for most of this period, the Catholic Church, although also encompassing diverse opinions, was able through Cardinal Kim to speak with one voice at crucial points in the struggle which eventually resulted in a democratic South Korea.

Park's dictatorial actions had succeeded in uniting against him the labour movement and the movement for democracy. He nevertheless brought in the Yushin (Restoration) Constitution in October 1972, justifying it to the population on the basis of the threat from the North. Under it, Park ruled by emergency decree, with each one more restrictive than the last. Not surprisingly, Christians found that they were subject to increased surveillance and interference in church affairs to the extent that even conservatives were alienated (T. S. Lee 2010:186). South Korea was economically, politically and militarily dependent on US and Japanese support. Although these governments had largely turned a blind eye to worker exploitation and the Yushin constitution's attack on human rights, in the Cold War climate, attacks on civil and political rights and lack of democracy drew international interest (Hanson 1980:106). For example, on Easter Sunday 1973, Park Hyeong-gyu, a Kijang Presbyterian minister and UIM activist, was arrested on a trumped-up charge of planning to lead the eighty thousand Christians assembled at the sunrise service in a march on government agencies. After the NCCK, Korea Church Women United, and other organisations gained international support for their protests, Park was released (T. K. 1976:11, 49–50; Sohn Hak-kyu 1989:58–59; P. Chang 2006:212–14).

In the 1970s a Christian theological response to the injustices done to workers and the lack of political freedom emerged as a distinctive Korean liberation theology in solidarity with the minjung, or masses – as opposed to Park Chung-hee, who claimed to lead the minjok or people (P. Chang 2006:214–15). Minjung theologians were Protestant writers and university teachers who positioned themselves in solidarity with the social activists, in support of justice and human rights. In common with other political or liberation theologies of the period, minjung theology addressed the structural evils of capitalism and dictatorship and was concerned about changing the social processes and systemic conditions believed to be the cause of the oppression of the minjung. It owed its method to the political theology developed by Johann-Baptist Metz (Catholic) and Jürgen Moltmann (Protestant) in Germany and the civil rights movement in the United States of the 1960s. As the movement wore on, the works of Dietrich Bonhoeffer also inspired a minjung church 'for others'. In many cases their opposition to the government led to minjung activists being arrested, dismissed from posts, imprisoned and tortured by the government. In the context of the divided peninsula, they were inevitably labelled as Communists but because the works of Marx and other Socialists were banned in Korea, minjung theology was not directly a dialogue with Marxism, and where it did engage with Communism, it was of the North Korean variety. Minjung theologians derived their inspiration from Korean traditions and historical events such as the Donghak Peasant Revolution and the March 1st movement which resonated with their reading of the Bible in the context of the political struggle. Key texts included the fratricide of Abel by Cain, the suffering of Israel in Egypt and of the prophets, the arrests of John the Baptist and other apostles and, above all, the passion of Jesus (Kim Yong-bock 1981b; Lee Jung-young 1988b).

Unlike the Latin American liberation theology to which it is often compared, minjung theology was mainly a Protestant creation. In the Catholic Church there was no minjung school of theology as such, but minjung thought was expressed in art, literature and practical solidarity. It was founded in the appeal by Cardinal Kim and others to Catholic social teaching which affirmed the option for the poor and also in the struggles of the Korean martyrs for religious freedom (cf. D. Clark 2007:182). The Catholic writer and artist Kim Chi-ha was the inspiration for much minjung thought, and he became the 'poet laureate of a protesting nation' (Cumings 2005:373). A dissident and social activist, Kim was tortured for being a Communist and eventually sentenced to life imprisonment by the military regime. His pictures, writings and plays vividly portray the Korean Christ who is brutally treated and suffers with the minjung, who is crowned and at the same time disempowered by the church, and for whose release and revitalisation the poor long and struggle. Evoking the Eucharist, Kim famously expressed Christian solidarity as 'sharing food' in his poem 'Food is Heaven' (Kim Chi-ha 1978:xiii, 30).

Two Protestant theologians are regarded as the originators of minjung theology: Ahn Byung-mu and Suh Nam-dong. Both were Kijang pastors who were prompted to join the minjung movement by the death of Jeon Tae-il. Ahn Byung-mu taught New Testament at Hanshin University and, while working with the activists at the Peace Market edited the journal *Sinhak Sasang*, a leading progressive mouthpiece. Ahn explained the minjung as equivalent to 'the crowd' in Mark's gospel, a 'marginalized and abandoned' group (Ahn Byung-mu 1981:150.). He went on to assert that Jesus is the minjung and the minjung are Jesus since he shared his life with them and that the event of the Cross is the climax of their suffering (Ahn Byung-mu 1990:31–37). Suh Nam-dong was dismissed in 1975 from his post as professor of systematic theology at Yonsei University and imprisoned three times for his political activism. He identified 'han' as a metaphor for the predicament of the Korean people. He construed this as a psychological concept from minjung history meaning a 'just indignation' or 'feeling of repression', which also gives rise to the energy for life that breaks out in movements of liberation (Suh Nam-dong 1981:51–65). He and other minjung theologians related han to Jesus Christ, the Suffering Servant, who was a 'servant to the aspiration of the people for liberation' (Suh Kwang-sun 1981:33). The minjung portrayal of the suffering Christ picked up on a deep theme of suffering and martyrdom in Korean spirituality. But rather than dwelling on the minjung's need and victimhood, the theologians regarded the minjung as the 'subjects of their own liberation' and the Christian message as one of transformation in history (CTCCCA 1981). To convey their message, they developed minjung art and utilised folk culture and the symbols of ethnic nationalism, including plays, masked dance, traditional instruments and some shaman rituals, which enabled them to build up a broad base of support across society for the labour and democracy movements (Lee Nam-hee 2007; Küster 2010:115–24; cf. Kendall 2009:22).

In May 1973 an anonymous group of Protestant ministers issued 'The Korean Christian Manifesto' which condemned the Yushin constitution as a 'betrayal of the people' by a minority who wanted to 'rule and profit' and criticised Park for ruling by 'power and threat' instead of 'law and dialogue'. They called for rejection of the Yushin constitution and unity for democratisation, for renewal of the church to serve the poor and oppressed and for support from the world church. The clergy cast their manifesto as a continuation of the liberation movement during Japanese rule and used the messianic and liberationist language that became characteristic of minjung theology. For example, 'We believe that Jesus, the Messiah proclaimed that the evil power will be destroyed and the kingdom of Messiah will come, and this kingdom of Messiah will be the haven of rest for the poor, oppressed and despised' (Rhie and Cho 1997:270–76; our translation). The 1973 declaration was the beginning of a labour and human rights movement led by minjung theologians, but it also signalled the polarisation of political positions among Protestants, the majority of whom were aiming to bring social transformation by evangelism and conversion instead.

The NCCK held a 'consultation on human rights in Korea' in November (1973), and soon the NCCK and YMCA buildings and leading liberal churches in Seoul – Tonghap, Methodist and Kijang – became recognised centres of anti-government activity (Park Chung-shin 2003:194; cf. KDF 2009:359–71). The activists also built up international support. Between 1972 and 1988, 'T. K.' (later to be revealed as Chi Myeong-gwan) wrote 'Letters from South Korea' in the Japanese magazine *Sekai*. T. K. worked with Oh Jae-sik of the Christian Conference of Asia and the Documentation Centre for Action Groups in Asia (DAGA); the minjung theologian Kim Yong-bock; Pharis Harvey, a Methodist missionary close to Kim Dae-jung's wife; and others. Overseas Koreans and foreigners founded pressure groups, funded by Korean Christians in North America and the WCC, which initiated the International Christian Network for Democracy in Korea, a group that also provided financial support for opposition activities and for victim's families. West Germans, who identified with a divided Korea, were particularly involved: Bread for the World and the Evangelical Church of Germany supported the NCCK and the Christian Academy. The academy, founded by Kang Won-yong in 1959, was critical of the government and trained leaders, especially in industrial and agricultural work and on women's issues (Park Chung-shin 2003; P. Chang 2006; Yeohae Ecumenical Forum 2013).

In April 1974, Park arrested 1,024 members of the newly formed National Federation of Democratic Youth and Students (NFDYS; Mincheong Hakryeon) and then issued Emergency Decree No. 4, which subjected NFDYS members to arrest without warrant and made it a crime to support the organisation. The government then tried to connect some of the students to an alleged Communist ring, supported by North Korea, and, warning of Communist infiltration into church circles, charged several hundred more, including leading Christian dissidents. Among them were the Catholic bishop Chi Hak-soon, Kim Chi-ha, the staff and key members of the KSCF, Park Hyeong-gyu, Kim Dong-gil and former president Yun Bo-seon. The arrest of a bishop reminded Catholics of the tradition of the martyrs and galvanised the whole church into action – even the more conservative bishops and laity. The protests took the form of masses and vigils at which the Beatitudes were read, prayers were said 'for the fatherland, for justice and peace, and for the incarcerated bishop' and the hymns of the martyrs were sung along with modern protest songs such as 'We Shall Overcome' (Kim Sou-hwan 2009:259–64). Bishop Chi was an unlikely Communist. He had been tortured in his native North Korea and was working for the poor by encouraging them to participate in Park's New

Village Movement. He also had been commended for organising flood relief in 1972 (Sohn Hak-kyu 1989:74).

The bishop's arrest led directly to the formation of the very active Catholic Priests' Association for Justice (CPAJ; Cheonjugyo Jeongui Guhyeon Jeonguk Sajedan). The priests were generally more radical than the bishops and more than half of them joined. In September 1974, encouraged by Vatican II that the church should pass moral judgement on social issues and drawing on Catholic social teaching about the right and duty of the church to protect human dignity and vocation, the association made the first of several declarations. It called for the end of the Yushin constitution, the release of those arrested, a guarantee of the people's right to life and basic human rights, freedom of speech and meeting and a basic minimum living standard (Myeongdong Cathedral 1984:133–38). After a great open-air mass celebrating Holy Year, five bishops (including three foreigners), a hundred priests, three hundred nuns and three thousand lay people marched to demand Bishop Chi's release. Tear and pepper gas were used to disperse them (Hanson 1980:103–4). At his trial, the bishop admitted complicity in the NFDYS demonstrations and also helping the banned poet Kim Chi-ha when he had been suffering from tuberculosis and the effects of torture. He was sentenced to fifteen years' imprisonment but released in an amnesty in February 1975. The bishop's 'declaration of conscience' and his 'message from prison' became key documents for the Catholic democratisation movement (Sohn Hak-kyu 1989:74).

Other denominations also made anti-government declarations. Anglican priests made their first declaration against the regime in December 1974 (Lee Jae-jeong 1990:342–44), as did Kijang, Tonghap and Methodist denominations, and sixty-six Protestant theologians justified their involvement in politics in a 'Theological Statement' issued on 18 November 1974 (Rhie and Cho 1997:279–86). Leadership of the supposed People's Revolutionary Party was eventually pinned on eight men, none of whom were Christians, but they and their wives were supported by activists and missionaries, two of whom – George Ogle of the UIM and the Catholic priest James Sinnott – were deported for their pains (Ogle 1977:133–79; Hanson 1980:99). On Christmas day 1974 a broad coalition of politicians was formed, including Kim Dae-jung and Kim Young-sam (an opposition politician and elder of Chunghyeon Presbyterian Church), civic leaders and church people. It was supported organisationally and financially by the Catholic Church under the leadership of two Catholic priests, Yun Hyong-jung and Ham Se-ung. But in April the government moved against the coalition and other Christian leaders before closing down any criticism of the constitution indefinitely by Emergency Decree No. 9 in May 1975 (Sohn Hak-kyu 1989:75–85, 89). After a sham trial, the eight supposed revolutionaries were executed.

Meanwhile, Park set the nation on a war footing with a military build-up, mass mobilisation and further repressive legal measures. As the regime in the South increasingly resembled that in the North, KCIA agents infiltrated churches and organisations both in Korea and in the diaspora (Hanson 1980:107). The general anxiety about the future was such that four hundred thousand Protestants from across the theological spectrum gathered on Yoido Plaza on 22 May 1975 for a prayer meeting for national salvation. With the opposition 'emasculated' and public protest well-nigh impossible, political protest was made in religious language through the churches. Christian intellectuals, especially dismissed university lecturers and theologians, articulated their concerns at the regular NCCK-organised Thursday Prayer Meeting for the Restoration of Democracy (Lim Hee-kuk 2013:300–305). The Protestants held prayer meetings and the Catholics held masses, and many services were attended by leaders of both churches (Sohn Hak-kyu 1989:93–94).

In 1976 a joint Catholic-Protestant service was held on the highly significant date of 1 March in Myeongdong Cathedral, which was rapidly becoming the main centre of anti-government activity. It was attended by the Christian civil leaders who formed the core of the opposition: political leaders Kim Dae-jung and Yun Bo-seon, religious leaders including Ham Sok-hon, NCC General Secretary Kim Gwan-seok, and theologians Ahn Byung-mu and Suh Nam-dong. Twelve leaders had prepared the Declaration for the Democratic Salvation of the Nation, which was read out during the service by Yi U-jeong, a professor at Seoul Women's University and the president of Korea Church Women United. The 1976 declaration used secular liberal democratic concepts of freedom and rights for their broad appeal, and it posed a significant intellectual challenge to the rationale for the Yushin constitution by pointing to the need to deal with the underlying economic context and North–South tension in order to release funds and resources to achieve democracy and social justice. After the service, twenty-seven participants were arrested, including Kim Dae-jung, and some were jailed and harassed for years afterwards. The churches responded quickly, and international governmental support was also forthcoming (Rhie and Cho 1997:288–92; Sohn Hak-kyu 1989:96–108, 180–81, 228; D. Clark 2007:177; Oberdorfer and Carlin 2014:73).

Meanwhile, workers and farmers continued to struggle for their rights. Several long-running labour disputes had come to a head in 1976–1977, all involving women workers. These included the Dong-il Textile Company in Incheon, at which the UIM had been involved since Cho Wha-soon had been a worker there in the 1960s. The treatment of desperate, protesting women at the hands of police, management and male workers was so shocking that it called forth further declarations and charters. But despite protests during live broadcasts, including the Easter sunrise service in Yoido Plaza, a hunger strike in Incheon and also at Myeongdong Cathedral, and the best efforts of the Christian leadership, the women lost their jobs (Koo Hagen 2007:79–89; Sohn Hak-kyu 1989:94–96, 131–42; P. Chang 2006:215–16).

Another joint Christian initiative, the Charter for the Democratic Salvation of the Nation, was issued the year after the March 1st declaration and on the day of the sentencing of those arrested, 22 March 1977. The charter clearly linked the pro-democracy movement with basic rights of survival which were seen as inhibited by both social injustice and a development policy which favoured the few. Its release occasioned the first search of the office of the NCCK Human Rights Committee. In December 1977 the National Coalition for Human Rights was launched; it brought together the NCCK, the Priests' Association and many other organisations. It was chaired by Ham Sok-hon, and the activist Kijang clergyman and theologian Moon Ik-hwan was one of its vice-chairs. This coalition was more radical than earlier ones and showed a greater affinity for Marxist ideology in that it argued for distributive justice and attention to injustice caused by social, political and cultural structures. Furthermore, it addressed its concerns to both Koreas rather than just to the South and argued that unification was a prerequisite for the achievement of human rights. Those attacked as 'Communists' were also questioning the ideology of anti-Communism, promoted so strongly by fellow Christians, which acted in the name of 'the free world' yet suppressed basic freedoms (Sohn Hak-kyu 1989:124–33, 181).

Park was re-elected by an electoral college in 1978. He released Kim Dae-jung, who on 1 March 1979, along with Yun Bo-seon and Ham Sok-hon, re-launched the coalition, which had foundered since Moon Ik-hwan had been imprisoned again. This time the executive included radicals such as members of the Democratic Youth Council and dissident writers. For the first time since the introduction of the Yushin system, students had started demonstrating again, including Christian students, even in the centre of Seoul. Regime brutality increased further: there were even more arrests of leaders, including staff of the Christian Academy, who were accused of being pro-Communist. People were stopped and searched, and some Christians were prohibited from attending prayer services (P. Chang 2006:216). Eventually another labour incident involving women workers proved to be the spark that precipitated Park's downfall. Young female employees of the Y. H. Trading Company who took shelter in the headquarters of Kim Young-sam's New Democratic Party were evicted by police using such extreme violence that they killed a woman worker. More than ten thousand people attended a prayer service 'for justice and peace' at Myeongdong Cathedral, organised by the Justice and Peace Committee. Kim Young-sam's arrest and expulsion from the National Assembly led to widespread unrest even in Park's home province and power base, and the end of the regime came in October 1979 when Park was assassinated by his head of security.

It has been calculated that an average of 44.5 per cent of the participants in key events in the 1970s were people prominent in Protestant or Catholic churches. Furthermore, the most high-profile religious and political leaders were Christians and the minjung ideology was shaped by Christian thinkers (Sohn Hak-kyu 1989:179). By 1979, the repression had brought about a solidarity between Catholic and progressive Protestant leadership, and with other religious leaders, expelled politicians, fired professors, journalists, union workers and grassroots activists, that was to be characteristic of the democratisation movement of the 1980s (Park Hyung-kyu 1985:46; Koo Ha-gen 2007:82–83; Sohn Hak-kyu 1989:131–42).

CHRISTIAN LEADERSHIP IN THE DEMOCRATISATION MOVEMENT, 1980–1988

In early 1980, after the death of Park, the government relaxed restrictions on freedom of speech and assembly as preparations were made for a new constitution. The political rights of Kim Dae-jung and other politicians were restored, dismissed professors were reinstated, and expelled students returned to study. Seizing their opportunity, workers struck for long overdue wage increases in the context of rampant inflation and students demonstrated in support of democracy until, on 17 May, General Chun Doo-hwan used the public unrest as a pretext for staging a coup. He declared martial law, closed universities, banned political activity and arrested thousands of political leaders and dissidents, including Kim Dae-jung. Faced with overwhelming force, the protests stopped across the country, except in the city of Gwangju.

Gwangju had a population of eight hundred thousand people. It was the educational and an administrative centre of the Jeolla provinces and the seat of a Catholic archdiocese. The south-west or Honam region had a long tradition of rebellion and resistance. It had been a base for the Donghak

Peasant Revolution of 1894, for resistance armies against the Japanese, for the Gwangju Student Independence Movement of 1929 and for left-wing guerrilla activity in 1946–1949 (Kang Man-gil 2005:195). In the recent regional politics of Korea the Jeolla provinces had been left out of power, bypassed by transport infrastructure and denied development, and their people were stereotyped as 'backward, shifty, and slow' (McCann 1988:30). President Park had made matters worse by favouring his home region of Gyeongsang and the city of Daegu in the south-east. The south-west had developed a communal and egalitarian tradition which was wary of central government and this was the inspiration for much minjung art and thought, including that of Kim Chi-ha and Suh Nam-dong, who were both born there (McCann 1988:30–31; Katsiaficas 2012:191–92). The opposition leader Kim Dae-jung was also a native of Jeolla and drew a large measure of his support from the region. Since a large proportion of South Korea's urban workers were inevitably migrants from the south-west, regional and class disaffection tended to overlap (Eckert et al. 1990:369).

On 18 May 1980 a few hundred students of Gwangju's Chonnam (Jeonnam) University defied the curfew within view of the Provincial Building. The military response was heavy-handed, in keeping with the history of the region: General Chun sent in 'Black Beret' paratroops who attacked the students indiscriminately and then harassed the townspeople. Incensed by their arrogance and brutality, citizens rose up in support of the students and forced the soldiers out of the city (by 21 May). They then took over the administration and managed it through a citizen's council until on 27 May the army moved in to retake it. Before the revolution was finally crushed on 29 May, an unknown number of citizens were killed. In 2005 a total figure for the dead of 606 was announced by a combined group of civil society groups, but estimates ranged much higher and thousands of claims for compensation were brought by victims and their relatives (Katsiaficas 2012; D. Clark 1988; KDF 2010:487–521).

On the ground in Gwangju during the uprising, the churches were faced with a rapidly evolving situation. The Catholic Centre on the main street was the initial rallying point for protestors. The YMCA and YWCA buildings and Namdong Catholic Cathedral became focal points for activists. Christians were very involved with the relief work, especially at Gwangju Christian Hospital and the University Hospital. Along with other religious leaders they also organised funerals and gathered statistics on the number of dead. Gwangju activists called on religious groups to endorse their action, but the groups were reluctant to do so. After an initial silence, on 25 May Archbishop Yoon Gong-hui issued a pastoral letter to Christians; he did not criticise or condemn army action but expressed sadness for the killings and claimed that no sacrifice would be in vain. He asked everyone to help the injured. Most Gwangju priests, however, were already actively involved in events on the side of the people but were divided about whether to take up arms. Archbishop Yoon and several Protestant pastors were among many leading citizens who tried to mediate with the military as part of the Citizens Incident Settlement Committee of about twenty city leaders. Their main concern was to put an end to the stand-off to minimise bloodshed, and they were also mindful that North Korea was exploiting the situation. A Catholic priest, Kim Seong-yong, managed to escape from Gwangju and went to Myeongdong Cathedral to ask Kim Sou-hwan for help, but the cardinal hesitated to respond publically at that point because there were conflicting rumours; furthermore, the situation in Seoul was unstable, and he feared to escalate it (Kim Sou-hwan 2009:327–28). However, the Jeolla-do priests belonging to the Priests' Association were active outside the city and on 23 May in Jeonju sixty priests and three hundred laity gathered for a special mass. On 25 May NCCK representatives made a declaration in Mokpo stating that this was a 'civil revolution' and calling on those responsible for the atrocities to be punished. Missionaries and other foreigners smuggled news out of Korea. Arnold A. Peterson, a Baptist from Florida who was in Gwangju for a regional campaign ahead of the World Evangelization Crusade, was one of the first to report to the wider world that in Gwangju 'the military committed unprovoked atrocities against the people', and other missionaries, including C. Betts Huntley and Martha Huntley of the PCUSA, were able to alert the North American Coalition on Human Rights in Korea (T. S. Lee 2010:107; Cumings 2005:382–83; Lewis 1988:19–21; Katsiaficas 2012:162–220).

After the city was retaken, some Christians began to address the injustice. On 1 June the Gwangju branch of the Priests' Association published a leaflet, *The True Facts about the Gwangju Incident*, which they delivered to all dioceses. It claimed that the brutal suppression by the army had caused the uprising and criticised the government version of events. On 25 June 1980, Cardinal Kim Sou-hwan asked for an investigation to discover the real facts (Kim Sou-hwan 2009:325–30). But uncovering the truth was impossible under Chun Doo-hwan's new military regime, which was even more repressive than that of Park. Chun purged or restricted the activities of eight hundred politicians and eight thousand government officials and businessmen. Hundreds of professors and students were expelled, and thirty-seven thousand journalists, students, teachers, labour organisers and civil servants were sent for re-education to 'Purification Camps' in remote mountain areas. Any Communist-like groups or anyone praising North Korea could now be punished by death or life imprisonment (Cumings 2005:384). In Gwangju people continued to be arrested, including the members of the Settlement Committee and others like Cho A-ra, the head of the Gwangju YWCA, and Kim Seong-yong, the priest in charge of Namdong Cathedral. Amnesty International and other overseas observers were refused visas to witness the crackdown (L. Lewis 2002:66–67).

Christians who supported the opposition were angered that conservatives continued to support the government. The massive World Evangelization Crusade went ahead as planned on Yoido Plaza on 12–15 August with the government even lifting the curfew in that area to allow people to stay for overnight prayer. Another sore point was that on 6 August, Han Kyung-chik and other evangelical leaders were invited by General Chun to breakfast at the Lotte Hotel in Seoul with government and military officials and Han was asked to preach. The meeting was televised and aired repeatedly on the national television stations. Although they had little choice but to attend and comply with the requests, and Han's sermon was a challenge to govern justly, this apparent endorsement of the regime was heavily criticised by many, even by members of Han's own church (Yoo Jang-choon 2010:230–34). On 27 August, Chun was elected president by an electoral college, and in December, Kim Dae-jung was sentenced to death. Pope John Paul II sent a letter to Chun on 11 December 1980 asking for clemency for Kim, and under international pressure, Chun commuted the sentence to life imprisonment.

Now that the students of Gwangju had defied martial law and paid for it with their lives, there were many others who were prepared to do the same and the activities of radicals became more extreme (Katsiaficas 2012:246, 293). Park Gwan-hyeon, who had been the student president of Chonnam National University and a leader of the pro-democracy movement in 1980, died in prison of a hunger strike and was given a Catholic burial. Families and religious and human rights groups began a long struggle to obtain truth and justice, which culminated on the 18 May anniversary each year and raised political tensions (Katsiaficas 2012:246; L. Lewis 2002). What came to be known as the Gwangju Democratization Movement was a turning point for the opposition Christians. The spirit of the martyrs had been evoked, and minjung artists used Christian themes, especially images of the crucifix and pietà, to associate the sufferings of the people with those of Christ and his mother (Küster 1994:120–24).

After Gwangju the whole country entered a most severe 'political winter' (Park Hyung-kyu 1985:47). Even members of churches active in human rights in the 1970s had to keep quiet under threat of imprisonment or even death, and there was surveillance and repression of worship services in a way reminiscent of the Japanese colonial period (D. Clark 2007:178). The minjung movement took concrete form in this period in a group of 'minjung churches'. Church members, mainly from the Kijang, Tonghap and Methodist denominations, lived in community with poor people and worked for their welfare. They celebrated communal meals and used Bible study and 'base communities' inspired by liberation theology to raise socio-political awareness. They also set up local community services, such as evening classes in Korean history and labour rights, health education classes and clinics, day-care centres and after-school programmes (Hwang Hong-eyoul 2003:85–86; Lee Sun-ai Park 1992:271–72). In 1986, the Anglicans established their first 'House of Sharing', which had a similar ministry (Lee Jae-jeong 1990:361–63).

Despite the oppression, Chun's handling of the economy won plaudits from his economic backers and the 1988 Olympic Games were awarded to Seoul. He continued to take a hard line with strikes, and he drove down wages, increased working hours still more and opened up the economy to some US and Japanese goods and services. Despite repressive measures on their campuses, and emboldened by international interest in South Korea ahead of the Olympics, demonstrating students became ubiquitous on the streets of Seoul and other cities, together with lingering tear gas (Lee Nam-hee 2007; Eckert et al. 1990:380). The students called for democracy and frequently demanded justice for the victims of Gwangju. Perceived US complicity with the suppression of the Gwangju Democratization Movement produced anti-American slogans as well (Cumings 2005:389; Oberdorfer and Carlin 2014:129). Along with this suspicion of the United States went an open exploration of Western neo-Marxist thought, depend-ency theory and the North's Juche philosophy, whereas alternatives to capitalism had been expressed earlier in biblical or general socialistic terms (Eckert et al. 1990:379; Cumings 2005:385).

The alliance of students and labour forged in the crucible of the 1970s and at Gwangju continued, but the churches' influence on the labour movement declined for several reasons: first, the leadership shifted to heavy industry into which it was harder for churches to penetrate; second, church leaders tended to see the struggle as primarily one for political democracy rather than labour rights; and third, labour leaders found Christian approaches too mild in the face of the oppressive regime (Cumings 2005:385; Koo Ha-gen 2007:77–78). However, Christian influ-ence was strong in the United Mass Movement for Democracy and

Unification, a very broad coalition of the early 1980s led by Rev. Moon Ik-hwan. In this period, the Catholic Church emerged as the leading religious opposition to the government. This opposition was expressed first in the person of Cardinal Kim and second in the use of Myeongdong Cathedral in Seoul, which became a 'liberated space' and the focal point of the democratisation movement (Kim Sou-hwan 2009:367). In the 1985 elections an alliance was formed between civil society campaigners and Kim Dae-jung's New Korea Democratic Party, and it continued in the shape of a new national umbrella: the People's Coalition for Democracy and Reunification. The coalition brought together urban labour, landless peasants, students and intellectuals, Christians – Protestant and Catholic, clergy and lay groups – and Buddhists. In March 1986 Protestant pastors called for a new constitution, and with Kim Dae-jung and Kim Young-sam sitting prominently in his cathedral, Cardinal Kim declared that 'democratization is the best way to make peace with God' while at the same time warning students against left-leaning ideology (Kim Sun-hyuk 2007:54–56; Hanson 1980:332).

Student demonstrations and mass rallies, increasingly drawing support from other groups, continued into the next year (1987) when two significant events helped the opposition maintain the pressure on the government (Kim Sun-hyuk 2007:57; Eckert et al. 1990:383). First, proof emerged that Park Jong-cheol, a student who had died in police custody, had been tortured, implicitly confirming suspicions in many earlier cases. Park was a Buddhist, but a commemorative mass was held for him on 26 January at Myeongdong Cathedral. At this event, Cardinal Kim Sou-hwan challenged the government with the words: 'Are you not afraid of God? . . . God is now asking where is Park Jong-cheol – your son, your student, your citizen – just as he asked Abel who killed Cain' (Kim Sou-hwan 2009:368) (Fig. 9). Second, in April, President Chun tried to unilaterally terminate discussion on a new constitution until after the following year's Seoul Olympics. This resulted in more declarations, including statements from the NCCK and Cardinal Kim. Thirteen Catholic priests in Gwangju began a hunger strike to call for direct elections. On 17 May, Oh Chung-il, a progressive Protestant pastor, announced the formation of the National Coalition for a Democratic Constitution, a central symbolic body of sixty-seven representatives from all sectors of society and most major religious bodies, with its headquarters inside the NCCK building (Katsiaficas 2012:284). The coalition called for demonstrations on 10 June. On that day, Oh Chung-il, coalition leaders and Kim Young-sam went to the Anglican Cathedral ahead of President Chun's anticipated announcement that he was going to

9. Memorial gathering at Myeongdong Cathedral in 1987 for the student Park Jong-cheol, who died while in police custody. Korea Democracy Foundation.

formally confirm General Roh Tae-woo as his successor and rang the bell as if for a funeral (Lee Jae-jeong 1990:340–45). Protests erupted in all cities. Student demonstrators, chased off the streets by police in Seoul, occupied Myeongdong Cathedral, where on Sunday 14 June a large outdoor meeting was held. When the chief of police told Cardinal Kim that the police were going to enter the cathedral to arrest the students, he famously replied, 'If the police come to the cathedral ... to arrest the students, you must first tread over me, then the priests and then the nuns [behind me]'. The police withdrew, after which people called the cathedral 'the sanctuary of democratization' (Kim Sou-hwan 2009:370; our translation). On Monday 15 June, the one hundred and twenty or so protestors in the cathedral agreed to end their sit-in and left with the worshippers after evening mass. One hundred thousand demonstrators carried candles and made public the police failure (Katsiaficas 2012:287–91).

The next initiative came from Church Women United, which called for 18 June to be a national 'Day Against Tear Gas'. They distributed leaflets showing the harmfulness of tear gas to health, gave riot police red flowers and pinned ribbons on protestors. On 22 June Presbyterian ministers held a nationwide prayer meeting for the survival of the nation. By 26 June there were estimated to be more than a million people on the streets of Seoul and thirty-four other cities. By now they included office workers, middle-class professionals and even Christians from conservative churches (Kim Myeong-bae 2009:268). Huge demonstrations continued until eventually, on 29 June, President Chun's chosen successor Roh Tae-woo announced that there would be direct elections for the presidency and other freedoms, whereupon the protests subsided. The funeral on 9 July in Seoul of Lee Han-yeol, a Yonsei University student from Gwangju who had died of injuries he sustained in a demonstration, brought up to a million people together; they remembered countless other sacrifices, and Oh Chung-il compared Lee to Jesus in that he gave his life for the people (Katsiaficas 2012:298). Peaceful and fair elections were held in December of 1987, but progress towards full democracy was held up because the opposition was split between Kim Young-sam and Kim Dae-jung thereby delivering victory to Roh Tae-woo. It took another decade before there was a complete change of power and the corruption and injustices of the period of military rule, including the grievances of Gwangju, began to be addressed.

Christian leaders – both religious leaders and politicians – were less prominent in the 1980s democratisation movement than in the workers' movements of the 1970s because the coalition that was needed to achieve democracy was necessarily very broad and the vocabulary of resistance was increasingly Socialist rather than theological. Nevertheless, Christian networks continued to inspire, support and facilitate protest activity; Christian buildings – churches and organisational headquarters – continued to feature as venues for opposition activities; and Christian occasions – Easter, Christmas and memorial services – continued to be among the key moments in the protest calendar. Christian organisations and their overseas contacts especially kept the memory of Gwangju alive and Christian artists transformed it into a key symbol of the struggle. However, it is important not to lose sight of the fact that it was not the Korean church as a whole which supported the labour, human rights and political democratisation movements but – at least until just before the fall of Chun Doo-hwan – only a small minority (Park Chung-shin 2003:183–84). Because Protestant opposition activities were carried out under the NCCK, the opposition claimed to speak for all the Korean churches, but in fact it consisted of only ten denominations. These included the large Tonghap and Methodist churches in which, although there were radical elements, the vast majority supported the military government and the evangelisation programme. In practice, the NCCK was dominated by the progressive but small Kijang denomination and left-leaning staff, and few of its resolutions were widely owned at congregational level. The Catholic Church was also divided. Among the hierarchy were strongly conservative figures such as Archbishop Rhee Moon-hee (Paul) of Daegu, President Park's hometown, who was a staunch supporter of his regime. The priests were more or less equally divided between those who supported political action and those who focused on congregational life and growth, and surveys suggested that lay people were more conservative. However, the fact that Cardinal Kim became the religious figurehead of the democratisation movement, that Myeongdong Cathedral was the centre of protests in the 1980s and that the leader of the political opposition, Kim Dae-jung, was a Catholic gave the impression of opposition by the whole Catholic community (cf. D. Clark 2007:176). For those active against the government, the differences between Christians were not Protestant versus Catholic but whether they supported military rule. Despite their different origins, completely separate organisations and rivalry for converts, representatives of these two dominant forms of Christianity in Korea cooperated to a remarkable extent in the 1970s and 1980s in the cause of justice and peace.

Minjung theology caught the interest of political theologians in the West, especially German Ecumenicals and Maryknoll supporters. It was promoted as an authentic non-Western theology and used by activists to raise international awareness of human rights abuses in Korea (e.g.

CTCCCA 1981). However, whereas the first generation of minjung theologians in the 1970s had a high level of credibility because of the extent of
their identification with the minjung through hardship and imprisonment,
for the second generation, who participated in the democratisation movement in the 1980s, this claim is not so firmly founded. First, particularly
after the Gwangju Democratization Movement, minjung theologians
shifted their attention to ideological issues and as leftist literature and
ideas became more known, they became sympathetic to Marxism (e.g.
Suh Kwang-sun 1991; Noh Jong-sun 1994). But this openness to
the North meant that they attracted only minority support even among
the minjung and laid minjung theology open to being co-opted into the
North–South ideological combat. Second, the fact that many articles were
devoted to defining the minjung indicates that minjung theologians had
difficulty identifying this term with a concrete and tangible group; the
minjung seemed to be only a conceptual group created by theologians for
the purpose of their argument. Minjung theology appeared as an elitist
movement seeking to change society for the people rather than with them,
co-opting them into a Christian-Socialist framework and using them to
Koreanise political theology (Ryu Dong-sik 2000:437–38). In addition, in
the rapidly changing social context, people found it difficult to identify
themselves with this static and heavily loaded term without definite or
immediate benefits. As Koreans became more prosperous, they hoped to
rise out of the minjung, as the growth of neo-Pentecostalism illustrates.
Third, feminist theologians accused minjung theology of being 'androcentric' and preoccupied with anti-colonial and socio-economic categories
that do not take patriarchal oppression seriously. Furthermore, women were
not the 'doers' of minjung theology, and so their experience and spirituality
were not recognised, yet they were included among the minjung whom
theologians professed to be hearing (Choi Hee-an 2005:4–5, 98; Chung
Hyun-kyung 1991b:109–11). As far as the mainstream Korean church was
concerned, minjung theology's critical approach to the Bible and its use of
traditional Korean religious symbolism put it beyond the pale of Christian
orthodoxy. What is more, its challenge to church and government authority
and the similarity of its agenda to Socialism made it politically unacceptable
(S. C. H. Kim 2007). Nevertheless, minjung theology did represent and
provide resources to much of the activism which helped to bring about
Korean democracy, and in the long view, even a relatively conservative
scholar cannot help but be proud of its 'uniquely valuable' contribution to
Korean theology and its international recognition (Han Soong-hong
1996a:661).

NORTH KOREA, JUCHE-KIMILSUNGISM AND THE CHOSŎN
CHRISTIAN FEDERATION, 1961–1988

While Christianity in various forms was thriving south of the border, there was no sign of it, or of any other traditional religious activity, to the north. Not only the Chosŏn Christian Federation (CCF) but also the Federation of North Korean Buddhists and the Cheondogyo Association had disappeared by about 1965 (Nahm 1989:378–420). After about 1958 Kim Il-sung ceased to address religious people in his speeches. Between 1966 and 1970 the seongbun or ideologically based caste system was strengthened. With few exceptions, the small number of religious people who remained in North Korea were put in the lowest category on the basis that their religion was a threat to the state (Kim Heung-soo and Ryu 2002:81–83, 101). References to Christians by the North Korean regime were from then on entirely negative, and any positive memory of Christianity was erased. For example, the church and memorial to Robert Thomas in Pyongyang were replaced with a monument commemorating the burning of the ship *General Sherman*.

In the 1970s, as North Korea's international relations became more strained and internal conditions began to deteriorate, the ideology of the state was strengthened (P. Finch 2007:38). This system consisted not only of a personality cult but also of the philosophy of Juche (Juche Sasang), essentially a nationalist ideology (Cumings 2005:414; Shin Gi-wook 2006:88). The term 'juche' simply means 'self-reliance' and has its origins in the 1919 independence movement and, in particular, in the economic and Gandhian nationalism of the 1920s and 1930s, several leaders of which were, or became, Socialists or Marxists (Wells 1990:163). It expressed the aspirations of the colonised for independence and opposition to any form of sadae. In North Korea it took on the meaning of freedom, 'the freedom to be Korean', independent of foreign predators (Cumings 2004:151–58). It was further developed as a Korean humanism in which human beings were the 'subjects' (or agents) of their own history and the masters of their destiny (Shin Eun-hee 2007:518; Shin Gi-wook 2006:89). Juche was contrasted with materialism as a form of life-centrism, a holistic approach which emphasised harmony between spirit and matter. It justified the corporatist nature of North Korean society by an organic understanding of the nation as a family hierarchy animated by a common spirit which owed a great deal to the ideas of Shin Chae-ho and Yi Kwang-su and to pre-war Japan (Shin Gi-wook 2006:95; cf. Cumings 2005:408–12). Kim Jong-il further built up the cult of personality around Kim Il-sung and his dynasty, and his advisors fused it with Juche thought to make a complete world-view and philosophical system (Shin Gi-wook 2006:89). After 1975, indoctrination into the thought of the 'Great Leader' became an integral part of education and re-education in the North and North Korean academics actively promulgated it internationally (Kim Hyun-sik 2008:22–23).

Juche-Kimilsungism drew on indigenous East Asian religious ideas from Dangun and Donghak to Shinto and Confucianism and took on religious dimensions (Shin Eun-hee 2007:518). At the same time, it also appeared in many ways to be 'a counterfeit of the Christian vision', for example, in its use of dates, locations and symbols associated with the 'Great Leader', and also in its moral requirements and thought structures (Kim Hyun-sik 2008:24). There are several reasons why the parallels between Juche and Christianity should not be surprising: first, Juche was constructed as an antidote to Christianity, which was perceived to be the chief ideology of North Korea's arch enemies, the United States, and the regime in the South, and posed the most significant religious threat to Kim's power when he took over the leadership in North Korea. Second, many of the first generation of North Korean intellectuals would have studied Christian theology and some of the party leaders were, or had been, Christian ministers. Therefore, there was a 'large element of ideological competition between Juche and Christianity' (Beal 2005:146). Conceptually, Juche thought showed a similarity to Christian doctrine: for example, in the use of the Father and Son to describe a mutual relationship of leader and people and also in the description of a 'non-subordinationist perichoretic unity' between leader, people and party (or state), a kind of Korean Trinity (Shin Eun-hee 2007:521–23). Although Juche-Kimilsungism was consistently defined as atheistic, its leadership cult, messianic expectation and corporatism gave it much in common with other Korean new religions, and particularly with that other notable Korean religious product of the 1950s, the Unification Church. Even if not considered a religion, it was at least a functional substitute for traditional Korean religious activity, especially for the Protestant Christianity originating in pre-war Pyongyang.

Meanwhile Christians in the South continued to believe that 'a faithful remnant is working underground' in the North which would emerge once repression was removed (Han Kyung-chik 2002:362–71). Mission organisations tried to maintain contact with the underground church. They received support from international missions working covertly in the Soviet Bloc, including Pastor Richard Wurmbrand's Voice of the Martyrs, which began sending balloons with messages across the border in 1968 and radio broadcasts in 1972. Mission to North Korea, not merely propaganda, was first organised in 1971 as a result of a decision of the Tonghap General Assembly. This was in the brief period of rapprochement between South and North which led to an extraordinary joint North–South communiqué, issued pointedly on US Independence Day, 4 July 1972, stating that national unity should be achieved by the two Koreas independently of other powers and by peaceful means, and that it should be promoted above ideology or systems (S. C. H. Kim 2008b:179–80; Hoare and Pares 2005:116–20). Other denominations followed the Tonghap lead and started the interdenominational North Korea Mission in 1972. It organised prayer meetings and services for unification, provided education and publications about persecution, smuggled in Bibles and disseminated information on human rights abuses to world organisations (Kang In-cheol 2006:309–27). Attempts were made to befriend North Koreans working outside the country either as diplomats or as experts in Third World countries, and Christians entering North Korea from countries that had diplomatic ties with it were asked to help. From 1976 US citizens could visit the North, and by 1987 about three thousand Korean-Americans had been there. Some took the opportunity to proselytise among North Koreans or make contact with any underground churches (Yi Mahn-yol 2006:243; IHCK 1996:453; Lee Jong-yun 1983:75–76).

In the late 1970s, as the activists for democracy came to see the division of the peninsula as the chief hindrance to freedom in both South and North, they began to give serious consideration to reunification. A series of South Korean–German Christian conferences considered the possibilities, and after the fourth meeting, in 1981, the German churches gave practical support to an NCCK committee set up to pursue the issue; however, little concrete political progress was made toward reunification (Yi Mahn-yol 2006:238–44). The North, unable to unify the peninsula by war while the United States remained, and unsuccessful in inciting revolution in the South or winning over international opinion, sensed that there could be some advantage in religious contact. First, religious groups could be used to indicate social plurality and encourage interest in the country; second, through the WCC and other global bodies, religion could offer a point of contact in relating to the South; and third, South Korean Christians involved in anti-government movements were open to the North. Confident that the remaining religious people in the North were now supportive of Communist ideology and posed no threat to the regime, Kim Il-sung made some speeches which were positive about religion and in particular about the potential Christianity had for the liberation of the minjung (Hoare and Pares 2005:90; IHCK 1996:442–43).

The North Korean government then took several steps to legitimise religion. First, the new constitution of 1972 guaranteed religious freedom, although at the same time it asserted the right to use anti-Christian propaganda. Second, the CCF was re-established, its activities were reported in the media and its status was upgraded, with its chairperson, Kang Yang-uk, becoming a national vice-president or deputy of the state. A seminary, Pyongyang Theological Institute, was started in 1972, and between 1974 and 1980 it graduated about twenty-five pastors. Christians were allowed to meet in homes in the evening led by the pastors who were otherwise employed during the day. In 1980 government sources claimed that there were about five thousand Christians in five hundred house churches. In 1983 a new hymnbook was published, followed by a Bible in 1984 which was an adaptation of the 1977 South Korean Common Bible (IHCK 1996:444–46). Third, North Korean Christian leaders began to reach out internationally. In 1974, staff at the WCC headquarters in Geneva received two letters from the CCF, thanking them for their 1972 statement welcoming peace talks between North and South and expressing interest in attending WCC activities. The same year a representative of the North Korean observer mission at the United Nations in Geneva approached the WCC asking about membership. The WCC requested direct contact with the churches or the CCF, but none was forthcoming at this stage. Meanwhile, the CCF continued to mail international Christian organisations regularly with demands that they take action against the South. In 1975 and 1976 the CCF sent representatives to the Asian conference of the World Conference for Peace, an initiative of Christians in the Eastern Bloc (IHCK 1996:449–50).

About this time, North Korean fortunes began to be eclipsed by the South and by the early 1980s the international community viewed the North with increasing suspicion (Hoare and Pares 2005:120–23). In 1981 the WCC was approached by the Council of [Korean] Christians Overseas for National Unification, who wished to hold a meeting in Geneva and visit the WCC. This group was led mainly by South Korean expatriates – Hong Dong-geun, Seonwoo Hak-won, Kang Wi-jo and Kim Dong-su – and Koh Gi-joon, an official of the CCF. Rhee Syng-man (no relation to the former president), general secretary of the mission department of the PCUSA, who had first visited North Korea in 1978, was the chief facilitator of the meetings (IHCK 1996:454). However, when conservative South Korean Christians heard about this, they protested strongly at the WCC's talking to a group which did not represent them and put pressure on the Swiss Reformed churches not to support the meeting. A meeting nevertheless took place but in Vienna in November of that year between North and South Korean Christians and overseas South Korean Christians from the United States and Europe, with observers, mostly from German churches (AKCSNA 1993:9–27). The overseas Christians were impressed with the genuineness of the faith of the North Koreans and by the fact that one North Korean pastor carried a well-thumbed 1930s Bible and hymnbook. The meeting issued a statement, but many South Korean Christians were incensed that, as they had feared, it condemned only South Korea and nothing critical was stated about the situation in the North (Kim Heung-soo 2003b:69–73). Further meetings of this council were held in Helsinki, Finland, in 1982, in Pyongyang in 1983, and in other cities, but their declarations were rejected by the South Korean media and the general public, and pleased only the North, even though from 1988 the South Korean authorities allowed its religious leaders to join.

After having observed the problems of the Council of Christians Overseas, and also having the benefit of the experience of Eastern European Christians to help them understand the situation of the North Koreans, WCC staff initiated their own North–South meeting taking a different approach. The Ecumenical Consultation on Peace and Justice in North East Asia was organised with the help of the Japanese churches and held in Tozanso, Japan, in 1984. The CCF was invited to the meeting but sent only greetings (Kim Heung-soo 2003b:89–108). There were signs of renewed interest from the North in 1985 when a CCF delegation visited the China Christian Council in Beijing and the first delegation for over ten years attended the Christian Peace Conference in Prague (IHCK 1996:450–51). In November 1985, two WCC staff members visited Pyongyang at the invitation of the CCF and the powerful government Committee for Peaceful Reunification of the Fatherland. In between sight-seeing, education about Juche philosophy and denunciations of the regime in the South – including video footage of the events in Gwangju in 1980 – they were told that religion had weakened in post-war North Korea because of disillusionment with the United States on the one hand and the power of Juche thought to fulfil spiritual needs on the other. They heard that there were now ten thousand Christians in North Korea, including about eight hundred Roman Catholic believers, but no Catholic priests. Neither were there any functioning church buildings, although Christians said that they did not need any, preferring to meet in family or house churches. The WCC representatives were taken to visit such a meeting in a private apart-ment where they shared a simple service of worship led by a pastor, together with four women and four men, all apparently over the age of thirty-five. It was explained that there was no longer any infant baptism and that Christian marriages were rare, but that the Eucharist was celebrated when ministers were available (Weingärtner 1985; IHCK 1996:452–62; Kim Heung-soo 2003b:89–108, 112–13).

Following the WCC visit to Pyongyang, the North Koreans accepted an invitation to a seminar with representatives of the South on 2–6 September 1986 at Glion, Switzerland (Yi Mahn-yol 2001:382–88). This was the first North–South meeting of any non-governmental agency (Kim Heung-soo 2003b:116). Four representatives came from the North – two pastors, one elder and a layman. The South Korean government did not oppose participation in the event. The meeting reached an emotional climax during the worship, when all the participants embraced one another and took the Eucharist together. The North Korean Christians were not much interested in questions of doctrine and faith but showed a conservative spirituality together with enthusiasm for the social and political functions of the church, which they regarded as compatible with Juche philosophy. Asked about the theological position of the CCF, Rev. Koh Gi-joon replied, 'Of course we Christians believe in the Almighty Creator God but . . . we do not leave everything to God' (IHCK 1996:458–59). The North Koreans explained that ever since the Korean War there had been no denominationalism (although some clergy did identify themselves as Presbyterian or Methodists), that they had deliberately cut themselves off from the Western churches and that they did not want any advice. When a second, larger WCC delegation visited North Korea in 1986, they found a Protestant church under construction (IHCK 1996:506–16).

In February 1988 as the WCC Tozanso process was continuing, the NCCK issued the 'Declaration of the Churches of Korea on National Reunification and Peace', which had a significant impact both nationwide and within the churches. The NCCK declaration drew on liberation theological themes, especially on Jesus' message of 'good news to the poor' and proclamation of the year of jubilee. The declaration acknowledged and confessed the sins of mutual hatred, of justifying the division of Korea and of accepting each ideology as absolute. This, the NCCK declared, was 'a betrayal of the ultimate sovereignty of God' and 'a sin'. While affirming the three aims of the North–South Joint Declaration of 1972, the NCCK added the priority of humanitarian practice and the participation of the minjung – the victims of the divided Korea – in the unification discussions. The document made practical suggestions to both governments for a change from 'ceasefire' to 'peace' guaranteed by the international community, including the withdrawal of the US army and the dismantling of the UN head office. It then proclaimed the year 1995 – the fiftieth anniversary of the Liberation – a jubilee year for peace and unification which the two Koreas could celebrate together. It urged the churches to renewal ahead of the jubilee year by working together and employing all possible means for peace and reconciliation (NCCK 1988; Yi Mahn-yol 2001:389–414).

The NCCK declaration was welcomed by many South Korean churches and was endorsed by the Council of Chosŏn Christian Church in the North at the second North–South meeting at Glion in 1988. However, it provoked severe criticism from conservative sections of the churches because of their strongly anti-Communist stance (Suh Kwang-sun 1991:185). They expressed deep concern over what they saw as naïve views towards the North with regard to the proposed peace treaty, the suggested withdrawal of US troops from South Korea and the recognition of the official church in the North, which the conservatives regarded as a part of the Communist Party (Chung Shung-han 2003:276–80). Nevertheless, the declaration put the issue of reunification onto the main agenda of Korean Christians, even conservatives. Furthermore, it articulated the prevailing concerns of the nation on the issue and set the future direction of South Korean churches towards unification (S. C. H. Kim 2008b).

CHAPTER 7

Missions, Reconciliation and Public Life, 1988–Present

The year 1988 was a watershed in South Korea not only in its transition to democracy but also in its opening to the world as it hosted a highly successful Olympic Games. The 1988 games were the first occasion since 1976 that both the Americans and the Russians competed. The thaw in the Cold War enabled South Korea to establish diplomatic and economic links with Soviet and Eastern Bloc countries for the first time, while rebuffing North Korea's efforts to co-host the games and thus isolating its neighbor. Hosting the games stimulated intense national pride in the South and great interest in other nations and cultures. There were a few concerns about the revival of Korean 'pagan' customs and culture for the opening ceremony, but most Christians welcomed the Olympics as confirmation of God's blessing on Korea. In preparation for the games the Protestant churches held what was to be the last great mass evangelism event: the '88 World Evangelization Crusade or 'Soulympics' on 15–18 August on Yoido Plaza. Although the total attendance was not the highest, the event surpassed all the others in its rhetoric about Korea as a chosen nation. With the world coming to Seoul, an outstanding opportunity for world evangelisation presented itself. Korea Sports Evangelism (founded in 1982) was responsible for the operation of the Protestant Chapel in the athletes' village, which was attended by chaplains from all over the world and visited by thousands of athletes, including hundreds of Russians, Chinese and Arabic speakers. Furthermore, because of their familiarity with Western culture and the English language, and the exhortations of their pastors, many of the volunteers and interpreters for the Olympics were Christians who took the opportunity to share their faith and pass on literature. Local churches were matched to particular countries; some congregations attended events to cheer the competitors from those countries and even hosted entire teams (Cho Chong-nahm 1995).

Now embraced by the 'international community', South Korea grew in confidence on the world stage. Global participation meant opening up domestic markets, new cultural influences, travel opportunities and diversification in the expatriate community in Korea which had been dominated by US troops to this point. The new foreigners included business people and tourists from all over the world and also migrant workers from poorer Asian countries. After 1988 economic development continued apace. Manufacturers, supported by research and development, produced increasingly sophisticated and high-tech goods for global export. Over just half a century what had been in 1953 one of the world's poorest nations became numbered among its richest. South Korea became a developed and urbanised country with a thriving middle class enjoying leisure pursuits and social networking. Women's participation in the labour market shot up; they gained an increasing voice in the public sphere, and in 2012 the first woman president, Park Geun-hye, was elected. Changes in family life were also profound. Into the twenty-first century, the birth rate dropped alarmingly and the divorce rate mounted. South Korea became a rapidly aging society but increasing wealth made nationwide medical insurance possible, together with pension and education schemes and welfare provision (Kim Jin-wung 2012:544–54; Tudor 2012). The political front saw increasing democratisation and burgeoning growth of civil society. Although when he was elected as the president in 1988, Roh Tae-woo was technically a civilian; it was the election of Kim Young-sam in 1993 that really brought an end to military administrations, and in 1997 the election of the veteran dissident Kim Dae-jung marked the first peaceful transfer of power to the opposition. South Korean politics now resembled that of other developed nations with distinct left and right wings, although the National Security Law was still in place (Chang Yun-shik 2009). When the Berlin Wall fell, the DMZ stayed firmly in place but the population was only rarely reminded of the threat from the North and at the end of the twentieth century the government was confident enough to transform its great showground, Yoido Plaza, into a city park, signalling also an end of the mass mobilisations of the twentieth century.

UNIFICATION, AID AND CHRISTIANITY IN NORTH KOREA

The building of churches in Pyongyang was probably in expectation of receiving foreign visitors for the Olympics and other world events (Hoare and Pares 2005:88–91; Kim Heung-soo 2003b:166–68). The first Protestant church to be built in the North since the Korean War, Bongsu Church in Pyongyang was completed with funds raised by South Koreans, channelled through the World Council of Churches, on land provided by the government in Mangyeondae district. In 1988, Park Kyung-seo, the Asia secretary of the WCC, went to Pyongyang to help with arrangements for the opening of the church in cooperation with the main pastor there, Lee Seong-bong (Kim Heung-soo 2003b:166–74). Bongsu Church was a showcase and received many foreign visitors who reported a congregation of one hundred to three hundred mostly older people and families with children. The children received baptism, although wider evangelistic activity was not allowed. The service followed the familiar Presbyterian order with lay participation (Beal 2005:146). In 2008 the church was rebuilt and extended to seat one thousand two hundred with funds from South Korean Presbyterians (Tonghap denomination). In 1992 a second Protestant church was built at Chilgol, in South Pyeongan province, in honour of Kim Il-sung's mother (IHCK 1996:478). However, the majority of registered Protestants continued to meet in several hundred house churches.

Overseas Korean Catholics also travelled to the North in the 1980s; one of the first was Bishop Chi Hak-soon. North Koreans made direct contact with the Vatican as well. In 1987 the Vatican sent a delegation to visit the Chosŏn Catholic Association in North Korea and its chair, Jang Jae-cheol. Jangchung Church was built and consecrated a year later. Unlike the Catholic Church in China, the Koreans had not set up an alternative hierarchy, so when the first mass was celebrated there on 31 October 1988, it was by special representatives from the Vatican: Chang Ik (son of former prime minister Chang Myon) and Jeong Hui-cheol. The elderly in the Korean congregation needed to be taught the new mass in the vernacular and other post-Vatican II forms. However, no regular arrangement for ministry was made and, without a resident priest, mass could be held only when there were visiting clergy (IHCK 1996:485–91). In 1995 Seoul Diocese founded the National Reconciliation Committee to prepare for reunification and reconciliation. After the visit of its president, Bishop Choi Chang-mou, to Pyongyang in May 1998, clergy and lay members from South Korea were able to go there more easily (RFKCH 2010:163).

Building churches allowed the regime to claim that there was freedom of religion, attract Christian support and secure economic aid from Christians. The government also organised conferences through the Protestant seminary to spread the ideology of the 'Great Leader' to the world. In 2002, after Kim Jong-il had visited Russia and seen newly rebuilt and refurbished churches there, he commissioned the building of an Orthodox church, and two Koreans – Theodor Kim and John Ra – were sent to study theology in Moscow. Holy Trinity Church was consecrated in 2006 by Metropolitan Kirill of Smolensk and Kaliningrad, and the Koreans were appointed priests there (Kim Heung-soo and Ryu 2002:155–64; Kim Hyun-sik 2008:22–26).

Since the activists for democracy in South Korea had come to see the division of the peninsula as the flip side of the suppression of civil and human rights, it was natural that, having ousted the military regime, they should turn their attention to unification. The 1988 NCCK declaration resulted in a flurry of activity by student movements and civil society. It influenced President Roh Tae-woo's July 7 declaration which espoused a reconciliatory approach to the North, and almost all of the key points made by the NCCK were incorporated into the North–South Korean Agreement on Reconciliation and Non-aggression and Exchange and Cooperation adopted by both Koreas in 1992 and in the Joint Declaration on De-Nuclearization of the Peninsula of 1991 (Yi Mahn-yol 2006).

At Korean New Year 1989, Kim Il-sung took advantage of the new democratic climate in the South when he issued a public invitation to Rev. Moon Ik-hwan, Cardinal Kim Sou-hwan and other leaders of the democrat-isation movement and opposition politicians to visit North Korea. Under the National Security Law, South Koreans were forbidden to travel from the South to the North, or even to the border, but Moon accepted the invitation. Moon argued that unification should be a natural consequence of democrat-isation and put forward a plan for a unified Korea as a neutral nation guaranteed by the other four powers involved – China, Japan, the USSR and the United States (Moon Ik-hwan 1984:29–44). He had already written a well-known poem, 'I Will Go to Pyongyang' (Moon Ik-hwan 1990:18–19). To the ire of South Korean politicians and the shock of the South Korean public, Moon appeared in Pyongyang on 25 March. He met Kim Il-sung twice, and, in the name of a new coalition for democracy, he made a joint statement with North Korean officials which was strongly biased towards the North's concerns. Not surprisingly, he was arrested on his return home.

Later the same year (1989), Lim Su-kyung, a young Catholic woman and member of a radical student group, responded to an invitation to the World Festival of Youth and Students in Pyongyang. She was received as a heroine, and one hundred and fifty thousand people in the new stadium chanted 'Our nation is one'. Lim took part with four hundred North Koreans in an international peace march south to Panmunjom on the border, where she was joined by Moon Gyu-hyeon, a representative of the Priests' Association sent (illegally) to assist her. On 27 July the group tried to cross the border into South Korea but was prevented by South Korean troops, while twenty priests who had started from Seoul to welcome them were arrested. Lim, Moon and a hundred others began a fast, and eventually, on 15 August, Liberation Day, Lim and Moon alone were allowed into the South; sym-bolically, they walked hand in hand across the border. Both were arrested and sentenced, but their actions encouraged Catholics to embrace reunification as an agenda (Yi Mahn-yol 2006:248–49). The CPAJ organised a series of masses and other activities to campaign for the repeal of the National Security Law and for unification.

Many older Christians in the South, especially those who had fled from the North, were worried by what they saw as the naïveté of youth who had not experienced Communism first-hand. Since the NCCK was now aligned with radical democratisation groups who tended to take North Korea's side, Han Kyung-chik seized the initiative in January 1989 to call leading representatives of Tonghap and other denominations, and they agreed to form the Christian Council of Korea (CCK) to represent the conservative evangelical churches. Nine out of ten of these elder statesmen were, like Han, originally from the North. They were strongly opposed to any compromise with North Korea and were actively anti-Communist (Kang In-cheol 2006:280–91).

Between 1989 and 1992 a series of discussions about unification and the compatibility of Juche philosophy with Christianity took place between North Korean leaders and South Korean and Korean-American theologians which were organised by the Association of Korean Christian Scholars in North America (AKCSNA). Leading figures included Kang Wi-jo, a Lutheran professor, and Rhee Syng-man, who in 1990 became president of the US National Council of Churches. Park Seung-deok, the director of the Research Centre on Juche Ideology, Pyongyang Institute of Social Sciences, introduced 'a new perspective of Juche Sasang on Christianity'. He concluded that Christianity shared common goals and values with Juche thought. Both were concerned about the people (minjung and minjok) and the destiny of humanity, and therefore the two could work together (AKCSNA 1993:80–86). Meanwhile, the North Korean government dealt with both the ideological challenge of South Korea's trade links with China and the USSR and the collapse of the Soviet Union by adopting 'Socialism of our style' and increasingly appealing to racial and ethnic populist ideas to justify its continued existence (Shin Gi-wook 2006:89–95). The death of Kim Il-sung in 1994 caused a mass outpouring of grief and great uncertainty for the future, but plans for the succession were successfully implemented and Kim Jong-il took power (Oberdorfer and Carlin 2014:274).

From the late 1980s poor growing conditions, long-term overuse of fertilizers and loss of subsidised imports from Communist allies caused growing food shortages in North Korea, which became public in 1995 when the country took the unprecedented step of appealing to the United Nations for aid. This situation finally opened up opportunities to reach out to the people of the North such as churches and mission organisations in the South had been praying and preparing for. The first occasions for Christian mission agencies to make direct contact with North Korean citizens were through the outflow of refugees which came about as the Public Distribution System inside the country broke down and people were forced to obtain necessities by other means. Many evangelical agencies worked along the border area to evangelise North Koreans, despite evidence that those who had had contact with religious groups were punished on their return (Hoare and Pares 2005:77). Some evangelical groups even actively encouraged defections through agents inside the North. As conditions grew more severe, more North Koreans migrated into China. Usually with the help of Chinese Koreans, these Christian agencies were involved in receiving refugees, shielding them from the Chinese authorities whose official policy was to return them and arranging for their transfer to South Korea (Verdier 2014). There churches received them, and some had special programmes to enable them to access information, enter business and education, address issues of physical and psychological health, adjust to differences in the language, and so on (Park Yeong-shin 2010). Under its pastor Lee Chul-shin, Youngnak Church, which had been established by Han Kyung-chik and other early migrants from the North, placed particular emphasis on caring for recent defectors. Many of those contacted in this way became Christians. One survey (2008) found that of 444 North Korean refugees in the South, 66 per cent had become Protestants while in China or a third country soon after leaving North Korea (Cheong Jae-yeong 2010). The reasons they converted were complex (Jung Jin-heon 2013). One factor was to satisfy the expectation of or bow to pressure from the Christians who were their means of escape. Another was that, arguably, North Koreans found in the Protestant churches the community support, moral leadership and reverence for a saviour-figure for which Juche-Kimilsungism substituted (cf. Oberdorfer and Carlin 2014:144). For Christians in the South, the arrival of the refugees was an opportunity to practise Christ-like forgiveness of their enemies (albeit not without condescension and triumphalism). One observer commented that the extent to which South Korean Christians were ready to show genuine compassion to North Koreans in their circumstances of need laid bare the ground on which to build any future unification (Yi Beom-seong 2010).

As news emerged of a contracting economy in the North, South Korean Protestants were the first to send aid. In 1989, already aware of food shortages, Han Kyung-chik had initiated the nationwide Rice of Love campaign. In 1993 this expanded to become the South–North Sharing Campaign. It was led by Presbyterians – including both the Tonghap and Hapdong denominations. A series of natural calamities in 1995–1997 further contributed to a severe famine in the North in which two to three million people are estimated to have died (Cumings 2005:442–43). As the crisis deepened, the Sharing Campaign gained increasing support from across the Protestant spectrum. Since the progressive churches were few in numbers, it was conservatives and Pentecostals who bankrolled most of the Protestant aid effort. The Reconciliation Committee of the South Korean Catholic Church's Help North Korea campaign also sent millions of US dollars in aid to the North (RFKCH 2010:163).

Although the largest donors of food aid to North Korea in the 1990s became China and the United States (through various different agencies), South Korea also contributed up to a third of humanitarian assistance, through both government channels and church-related NGOs (Schloms 2003:135). The South Korean Christian aid operation suffered from frequent setbacks according to the relations between North and South, but it continued for more than a decade. The Korean branch of World Vision, which became self-supporting in 1991, was the largest Korean Faith-Based Organisation (FBO) involved. Campus Crusade for Christ's Global Aid Network was another major contributor. Korean-American agencies also participated, such as the Korean-American Sharing Movement, Samaritan's Purse (led by Franklin Graham, son of Billy and Ruth) and the Eugene Bell Foundation, set up by the great-grandson of the Southern Presbyterian missionary of that name. By the mid-1990s many South Korean Protestant organisations were operating independently to aid the North, and CBS was broadcasting appeals. Almost every denomination and many large churches plus youth, student and other organisations directly supported projects. They provided cows and goats for dairy production, seeds and fertilisers, and clothing. Evangelicals saw this aid as a means of reviving the church in the North, and in 1995 the CCK formed the North Korean Church Reconstruction Council which aimed to cooperate ecumenically in ministry to North Korea, build a single denomination in the North to protect it from the denominationalism of the South and enable the churches of North Korea to be independent and self-reliant without domination by South Korean churches.

After the devastating rains of August 1995, the Chosŏn Christian Federation (CCF; now renamed Joseon Geurisdogyo Yeonmaeng) contacted the ACT Alliance of the WCC directly with an unprecedented request for five million US dollars for food, medicines, and so on. The alliance responded positively with contributions from the NCCK and other non-WCC member churches in Korea along with Western and Japanese FBOs. The World Food Program and Caritas Hong Kong distributed the aid on the ground. Aid agencies were assured of the 'implementing capacity' of the CCF because it was closely related to the state (Kim Heung-soo 2003b:277–330). In South Korea, the Korean Sharing Movement was founded in 1996 by a coalition of WCC-related churches and other faiths to work directly with the CCF to coordinate and streamline efforts, but also to overcome the South Korean government's monopoly on the aid supply, which they feared was being manipulated for political purposes (Yi Mahn-yol 2006:254–55). It continued its work despite criticism from the South Korean government that it and other agencies were channelling aid illegally through China (Schloms 2003:163–64). The response to its request greatly enhanced the profile of the CCF in North Korea and that of Kang Yeong-seop, its chairperson. South Korean aid to the North continued for more than a decade despite continued incursions and provocations by the North's regime. Eventually, however, the election in 2008 of a South Korean government with a tougher policy towards the North and the first test-firing of a missile by North Korea in 2009 led to aid and other activities by the South and other outside agencies in the North being scaled back severely.

The impact of Christian relief activities in North Korea is difficult to assess. Undoubtedly the majority of the aid workers, who worked under very difficult conditions, were genuine in their aim to help starving North Koreans. But some were accused of triumphalism, paternalism and misusing aid to pursue an 'aggressive' conversion agenda (D. Clark 1997:211–12 n.32). The question of whether aid should be conditional on the implementation of human rights, peace or regime change was much debated among NGO workers (e.g. Flake and Snyder 2003; Schloms 2003). Christians were divided between those who opposed food aid and those who promoted it. Conservative Protestants – including President Lee Myung-bak, who took office in 2008 – were among the more hard-line, first, for the political reason that propping up the regime was simply delaying reunification. They also questioned the credibility of CCF members, the required concessions to the 'idolatrous' regime and the lack of opportunity for conversion and church planting. Other Christians countered that at the very least relief work changed the North Koreans' perception of Christians from 'threatening enemies' to 'loving brothers' and that Christian generosity also challenged their belief in the unique benevolence of Kim Il-sung (Kim Hyun-sik 2008:25; cf. Bluth 2011:209). The South Korean aid agencies were mostly new, worked only in North Korea and lacked a non-political tradition of supplying aid. The longer the Northern regime remained unchanged, the less the enthusiasm in the South for supplying aid unconditionally, the greater the suspicion that their generosity was being cynically manipulated by the regime and the stronger the fear that aid might be helping to fuel future aggression from the North (Schloms 2003:148).

Other Christians and agencies sought more long-term engagement with the North through development work in agriculture, medicine and education. After 1991, when North Korea created several free economic zones and tourist resorts on its borders, beginning with Rajin-Seonbong (Rason) in the far north-east, some Christians saw in such commercial ventures a chance to share the Christian message with their employees (cf. Hoare and Pares 2005:46–83). Others set up businesses inside the North. The shortages made it possible for different agencies to gain access to support factories producing basic foodstuffs such as noodles and soymilk, and medical supplies. Bongsu Church, for example, operated a welfare programme funded by Presbyterian churches from the South, the United States and New Zealand. Some built hospitals and orphanages in North Korea: with the support of the Benedictines of St Ottilien, Rason International Catholic Hospital was opened in 2005. Such development work was less susceptible to changing political climates.

The various Christian processes for a political solution to the division of the peninsula continued in the 1990s. The Catholic Church held a series of exchanges between priests from the South and the North which were hosted in Japan from 1993 (Rivé-Lasan 2013:134–35). The Tozanso process resulted in a WCC policy document on Korean reunification in 1989 – the first of any international body since 1946 (Kim Heung-soo 2003b). A practice was established in WCC-related churches of marking the Sunday immediately before 15 August (Liberation Day) as Korean Reunification Sunday. A liturgy and common prayer for the occasion was written jointly by the NCCK and the CCF in 1991. Despite a delay in the process due to the period of mourning for Kim Il-sung, in 1995 the hoped-for 'jubilee' was marked with a North–South meeting in Kyoto, Japan, supported by the Japanese Council of Churches. However, the plan to hold a joint worship service at Panmunjom on Sunday 13 August could not go ahead. It was strongly supported by North Korea but (partly for this reason) disallowed by the government in the South (Suh Kwang-sun 1991:177–88). In 2009, the WCC organised a conference in Hong Kong to celebrate twenty-five years of the Tozanso process, at which Kang Yeong-seop, chair of the CCF, and Bae Tae-jin, general secretary of the NCCK, co-celebrated communion and the hope was expressed that they would send a delegation to the tenth WCC General Assembly to be held in Busan, South Korea, in late 2013. However, the process was dealt a serious blow at the end of 2012 when Kang, a member of Kim Il-Sung's mother's family who had led the CCF since late 1989, passed away.

The efforts for peace on the peninsula in the 1990s took place against the backdrop of the North's development of nuclear capability and the widening international concern about the stability of North-east Asia. In the United States, both the first Bush and the Clinton administrations took advantage of visits of Billy Graham to the North in 1992 and 1993 in their efforts to improve relations (Oberdorfer and Carlin 2014:234). The necessary coalescence of internal and external circumstances for a breakthrough on the peninsula appeared to have arrived in 1997 when Kim Dae-jung, the veteran opposition leader, was elected president in the South. On taking office Kim adopted an attitude of 'reconciliation and cooperation', which was expressed in his Sunshine Policy towards North Korea. This was partly inspired by Catholic social teaching and was strongly supported by the Catholic Church (Chérel-Riquier 2013:85). It aimed to change the rhetoric on the peninsula by recognising the humanity and dignity of the North Korean people and softening attitudes through the building of a warm relationship (Cumings 2003:132). It rejected any military solution, or the absorption of one Korea by the other, proposing instead a period of peaceful co-existence of the two states in a federation before their eventual reunification. To this end, and regardless of progress on intergovernmental relations, the policy encouraged economic deals and reunions of separated families (Moon Chung-in 1999). It resulted in the first ever North–South summit, held in Pyongyang in June 2000, for which Kim Dae-jung received the Nobel Peace Prize. However, these conditions did not last, especially because, during the presidency of George W. Bush, international discussion of North Korea tended to focus on terror and weapons questions. Because of the widened threat, six parties became involved in talks: the United States, China, Russia, Japan and the two Koreas. Since it was unlikely that the regime in the North would ever give up its weapons programme, which it regarded as essential to its survival, little progress was made. The already existing commitments of North and South to a path to unification arguably offer a better basis for international efforts for peace than focusing on weapons does (Bluth 2011:209). In view of the initiatives already shown by Christians in the South and the North in framing such commitments to unification, it seems that they will continue to have an important role to play.

Christian approaches to reunification can be summarised in three positions: unification as part of an anti-Communist campaign and mission agenda (conservative Christians), promoting dialogue between the two nations (progressive Christians) and involvement in a supportive and sharing humanitarian campaign (some conservative and most progressive Christians) (S. C. H. Kim 2008b:166). The third approach was described earlier. The first translates politically into conquest or absorption of the North by the South. However, this is not regarded as a likely or desirable scenario, first, because North Korea would not admit any kind of military defeat and, second, because absorption would be extremely costly for the South (S. S. Kim 2006:302–7), although opinion is divided on this second point. On the one hand, their strongly anti-Communist stance has prevented conservative Christians from any dialogue with North Korea and therefore from engaging in the political process. On the other hand, they have always upheld the hope that unification is possible; they have prayed for it, supported it and worked by whatever means available to disseminate the gospel in North Korea (Suh Kwang-sun 1991:185). Considering the strength of Christianity in North Korea before the partition, it is not inconceivable that a religious revival may play a part in a peaceful reunification process (cf. Kim Hyun-sik 2008:24), although the opposite possibility that religion could contribute to the ideological division between the two nations is also possible. The ecumenical and Catholic approach of promoting dialogue between the two nations is more willing to countenance a political compromise such as the federal system of unity envisaged in Kim Dae-jung's Sunshine Policy. However, the difficulty of dialogue with the regime in the North is well recognised. Moreover, the more dialogically minded Christians will have to convince their more conservative co-religionists who have been so stridently opposed to the regime since its inception (Choo Chai-yong 1998:413–21).

The on-going division of the peninsula and its rival political and economic polarisations aggravated tendencies towards dualism rooted in traditional Korean cosmologies (yin–yang and inner–outer – see Chapter 1). These were re-expressed in Korean Christianity as church versus world, Christian truth versus untruth, spiritual versus material, sacred versus secular, faith versus works and personal versus communal life. Despite a growing sense of the enormity of the task and evidence that the younger generation lacked interest in unification, the churches continued to hold out hope of reconciliation which would be not only political but also holistic and based on truth and justice (Torrey 2008:21; Shin Gi-wook 2006:185–203; S. C. H. Kim 2008b:161–78; Yi Beom-seong 2010:66–94).

THE CHURCHES IN SOUTH KOREA

In the early twenty-first century South Korea was on the surface quite unrecognisable compared to the 1980s and showed 'all the traits of a mature post-industrial society' (Kim Jin-wung 2012:549). Issues for the churches were as much to do with affluence and new technologies as with poverty and human rights. But in its religious statistics, South Korean society went against the trend in other similarly developed countries towards an increase in the category 'no religion'. Religious affiliation in Korea was negligible when it was first measured by the Japanese. It grew throughout the twentieth century, and in the 2005 census for the first time a majority of Koreans (53 per cent) identified with a particular religion (D. Baker 2006c). Furthermore, in South Korea having 'no religion' did not mean 'non-practising' or 'non-religious' because Confucian and shamanistic rituals continued to be performed but without any affiliation. By all measures, in the early twenty-first century South Korea was a highly religious country and repeated Weberian predictions of disenchantment were not fulfilled (D. Baker 2008). The combined Christian membership in 2005 was 29.2 per cent, outstripping Buddhism at 22.8 per cent. Christianity was the majority religion in every region, although in Gyeongsang-do Buddhism retained a much stronger presence than elsewhere. However, the two main forms of Christianity fared differently in terms of numerical growth. In 1989–1997 both Protestant and Catholic proportions increased slightly, but after the mid-1990s, Protestant numbers began to decline slightly (by 1.6 per cent in 1995–2005), while Catholic affiliation increased by almost three-quarters between 1995 and 2005 (IHCK 2009:116; Jang Suk-man 2004:154–55; Han Gil-soo, Han and Kim 2009:333–34) (Table 1).

Despite stagnating numbers of adherents, in the 1990s, especially under Kim Young-sam (1993–1998), the political influence of Protestants was strong. They constituted half the members of the Assembly and more than 40 per cent of the administration. Even under the Catholic Kim Dae-jung, Protestants were a majority in central government although regional officials were more likely to be Buddhist. Conservative Protestant credentials did not ensure election, but they could be very advantageous. Politicians wooed the Protestant vote, and for Kim Young-Sam's election in 1992 evangelicals across the country were mobilised. In 1997 both main contenders – Kim Dae-jung and Yi Hoe-chang – were Catholics but all the candidates canvassed the evangelical vote and courted Cho Yong-gi, Kim Jang-hwan (president of the Far East Broadcasting Company) and other prominent leaders. In that decade also, Protestants were among the

Table 1. *Table of demographic changes in South Korean Christian membership (1950–2005)*

Year	Total South Korean population	Protestant membership	Percentage of total population	Catholic membership	Percentage of total population	Ratio of Protestant to Catholic membership
1950	20,188,641 (1949 figure)	500,198[a]	2.5	158,000[d] (1949 figure)	0.8	1:0.3
1960	24,989,241	623,072[a]	2.5	450,200[d]	1.8	1:0.7
		1,524,258[b]	6.1			1:0.3
1970	31,435,252	3,192,621[a]	10.2	751,217[a]	2.4	1:0.2
1980	37,406,815	7,180,627[c]	19.2	1,321,393[a]	3.5	1:0.2
1985	40,419,652	6,489,282	16.0	1,865,397	4.6	1:0.3
1995	44,553,710	8,760,336 (+35%)	19.7	2,950,730 (+58.2%)	6.6	1:0.4
2005	47,041,434	8,616,438 (−1.6%)	18.3	5,146,147 (+74.4%)	10.9	1:0.6

[a] Korea Jonggyosahoe Research Institute.
[b] Korea National Council of Churches.
[c] Ministry of Culture and Information.
[d] Research Foundation of Korean Church History (RFKCH) (2010), *Inside the Catholic Church of Korea*. Seoul: The Research Foundation of Korean Church History.
If not otherwise indicated, results are from the South Korean government census.
    Based on table in Institute of the History of Christianity in Korea (IHCK) (2009), *A History of Korean Church* III. Seoul: Institute of Korean Church History Studies, p. 116.

wealthiest of the population and disproportionately held top executive posts in business and industry (T. S. Lee 2010:142–46; 2006:337–40).

    At Protestantism's apex in the late 1980s and early 1990s, mainline Presbyterian-Methodist-Holiness churches had several distinguishing characteristics. The first was an evangelical conservative faith with its emphasis on biblical inerrancy, exclusive belief in the Cross and suffering of Christ for redemption, the necessity of conversion and assurance of salvation, activism – especially in the form of proclamation – and a practical approach to believing which worked hard at devotion in the expectation of blessing. To these features should be added a premillennialist outlook and a conservative personal morality with regard to abortion, premarital sex, adultery, smoking, drinking, gambling and dancing. The second characteristic was independency – a legacy of the Three-self method. Protestantism's primary expression was the local church, whereas denominational structures remained weak. Churchgoers' tithes and offerings were the sole source of income for local congregations and their pastors. In 2004 the Gallup Poll found that nearly 50 per cent of Protestants gave 10 per cent or more of their income to the church (Han Gil-soo et al. 2009:347–48). Third, Protestantism was marked by its competitiveness and preoccupation with growth. Protestant churches tended to operate as businesses rather than as voluntary societies or social service organisations; there was no parish system and market rules applied. Growth was maintained by the fierce loyalty of members to their local church and to their religion, and it was carried out by mutual and sometimes aggressive proselytising. Although churches cooperated for specific purposes, notably evangelisation, there was no significant movement for structural unity. Fourth, traditional leadership patterns predominated. Public leadership was overwhelmingly, or even exclusively, male in most denominations. However, churches were sustained by strong women's movements whose activities were separate from the men's but generated substantial income. Fifth, Korean Protestants guarded their doctrine of exceptionalism. The remarkable story of Korean church growth was taken as evidence that Korean Christianity was unique and should be taught and exported globally through mission activity (Kim Kwang-ok 1997:231–32). Sixth, the churches were at home in the modern world. Christianity was still seen as a modernising force, and it was arguably more modernising than Christianising (Park Chang-won 2011:106–7). The larger churches kept pace with technological developments, which were on display in their sound and video systems, sophisticated websites and communications' infrastructures. Lastly, Protestants were extensively involved in providing social welfare in Korea and in delivering relief and development aid elsewhere. In the mid-1990s, Protestant educational institutions far outnumbered those of Catholics or Buddhists and Protestants were estimated to have operated up to two-thirds of all faith-based social welfare agencies (T. S. Lee 2006:337).

Sabbath-keeping was a key tenet of Protestant belief – not in the sense of abstaining from commerce but by attending at least one Sunday service. Across the denominations the main Sunday morning service consisted of a combination of prayers, traditional hymns and Bible readings; it incorporated an offering and culminated in a thematic sermon by the be-robed pastor, followed by another hymn and stirring blessing. The preaching of the word was almost invariably the climax of the service in all the major denominations except when communion was celebrated, which was usually only between two and four times a year. Its rarity made it a special occasion requiring careful preparation, and its interpretation dwelt on the physical suffering and sacrifice of Christ as the means of salvation. In most urban churches only adults attended the main services and there was no adult Sunday school. Children, youth and students were catered to in separate, age-delineated services, Sunday schools and activities. Although women made up the majority of the congregation, in most churches they officiated only as greeters, ushers and collectors of the offering, and then demurely wearing traditional dress. Churches produced a weekly bulletin along with the order of service giving contacts, details of forthcoming activities, items for prayer and often a list of those who had given offerings for birthdays and other special occasions. In larger churches, a digest of the previous week's sermon or pastor's reflections would also be included. Many people attended more than one service on a Sunday or attended other activities. And churches provided cafeterias where they could eat with other members.

By the early twenty-first century, five strands of Korean Protestant theology were distinguishable (S. C. H. Kim 2008a:129–53). Bible Christianity was reflected in the centrality of preaching on Sundays, in the expository preaching in services on Sunday and Wednesday evenings, in cell group meetings, and also in the culture of regular and sustained Bible-reading and love of the scriptures. Korean Christians set great store by reading the whole Bible as a spiritual exercise, and in the late 1980s the spiritual discipline of hand copying the Bible emerged, mainly among older people (Park Chang-won 2011:57–90). Revival Christianity and gibok sinang remained central to Protestant Christianity. Under the influence of Pentecostalism, petitions for forgiveness of sins and salvation for the nation were heard less often and the emphasis was more on the need for the power of the Holy Spirit, especially in the form of wealth and success. In contrast to revivalism, folk Christianity was mainly an elite expression through theology of religions, interfaith dialogue, eco-feminism and other movements which sought consciously to indigenise the Christian faith. But these innovative approaches were usually rejected by mainline churches. The fourth strand of Korean Protestantism, minjung theology, emerged during the labour and democratisation movements. Both gibok sinang and minjung theology addressed the problems of poverty and injustice in the second half of the twentieth century. After the achievement of democracy and the cooling of ideological standpoints, the division between progressive and conservative, between humanisation and evangelisation, social commitment and salvation of souls became less evident. The more obvious gap was between those churches which had achieved prosperity and the rest, which included the minjung churches.

After democracy was achieved, a fifth strand of Korean Christianity was born. 'Reconciling Christianity' emerged out of the movements for

North–South unity and further reflection on the theology of jubilee articulated in the 1988 declaration, which proved to have many dimensions. The identification of the year of jubilee in 1995 brought the issue of reunification to the fore and challenged even conservatives to move from evangelism to humanitarian work and peacemaking. Furthermore, as a call for redistribution of the land, jubilee was linked to the on-going struggle for justice for the poor which, after democratisation, became the concern of evangelical as well as progressive churches. Simultaneously, the jubilee theme matched the growing concern for eco-justice. Against the background of dualistic cosmologies, feminist responses to the declaration exposed not only the need for gender reconciliation but also the importance of tackling the gap between the conservative and progressive theologies, the competition between churches and the tensions between religions, especially between Protestants and Buddhists (Park Jong-chun 1998:131; cf. Yi Mahn-yol 2001:351–58). A final dimension of the jubilee theme was its challenge to the Christian community to reform itself, the need for which became painfully evident in the next decade (Chai Soo-il 2003). Despite these theological developments, in the early twenty-first century, the evangelical and charismatic characteristics of Protestant Christianity predominated.

In the Catholic Church too, distinctive Korean theology now began to emerge. Shim Sang-tae, a systematician, founded the Korean Christian Thought Institute in 1992 to promote inculturation with regard to both Korean traditions and contemporary contexts. The liberation strand of Korean Catholic theology was represented by Chong Ho-kyong, who developed a pastoral theology for farmers that addressed social inequalities, and by Kim Sung-hae, a religious sister, who has expounded a contemplative theology of interreligious dialogue (Adams 2012:229–46). Korean theology, written mainly in Korean for domestic consumption, was a burgeoning field (England, Kuttianimattathil and Prior 2004:475–651; K. Kim 2006). In the early twenty-first century, there were at least fifty major Christian publishing houses and hundreds of smaller ones and the theological book trade was thriving.

In 1991, following reconciliation work led by Park Jeong-geun, most of the three factions into which the Korean Assemblies of God had split came together as the Assemblies of God of Korea. Yoido Full Gospel Church and Cho's theology were dominant in the united denomination. Cho founded a theological institute which diverted attention from prosperity and material blessing to focus instead on the power of the Holy Spirit to effect change in people's lives and, in interaction with theologians of the minjung tradition, to bring about ecological well-being, holism and harmony (Ma Won-suk et al. 2004:260–61; Bae Hyoen-sung 2005). The overarching role of 'the fourth dimension' was now described as a 'holistic approach' that deals with people's han (Jeong Chong-hee 2005:551–71). Cho Yong-gi's relationship with the US Assemblies of God was restored, and in 1992 he became the first non-American chair of World Assemblies of God Fellowship. The Assemblies of God now took a more ecumenical and socially concerned stance and positioned itself within the mainstream of Korean Protestant churches. This was signalled in 1992 when it became a member of the NCCK and in 1994 when a committee of the Presbyterian General Assembly that had been investigating Cho's theology pronounced it to be basically sound (Kim Ig-jin 2003:176–81). Far from the church's origins among the poor, the Pew Forum reported in 2006 that 63 per cent of Korean Full Gospel Christians were in the upper two income categories, compared with only 49 per cent of the general population. However, YFGC operated extensive social welfare ministries, including Elim Welfare Town, which offered services for unemployed youth and elderly people living alone. By the end of the twentieth century, the Assemblies of God denomination had become similar in size to Tonghap or Hapdong, overtaking the Methodist Church, which now ranked in numbers with the combined Holiness churches and the Baptist Convention. Presbyterianism remained the largest single Protestant grouping, and Tonghap and Hapdong were still by far the largest Presbyterian denominations (Barrett, Kurian and Johnson 2001:682–87). Tonghap and the Methodist Church had many institutions of long standing that were founded by missionaries, including leading universities, such as Yonsei (which had its origins in Joseon Christian College), Soongsil and Ewha, and hospitals, such as Severance Hospital in Seoul and Ilsin Hospital in Busan.

In the first decade of the twentieth century, the General Council of Evangelical Missions in Korea had been keen to develop one united Protestant church in Korea, but at the beginning of the twenty-first century, Korean Protestantism had a reputation for separatism and was split into more than seventy different groups. The missionaries did not succeed, partly because of the divisiveness of their own comity arrangement and the Nevius method. Furthermore, South Korean Protestants did not develop a strong movement towards structural church unity like those which were at their height in many other countries in the 1950s to 1980s. These were resisted in South Korea, first, because structural unity had been imposed by the Japanese in the form of the Joseon Gyodan and by North Korea in the CCF as part of the restriction of religious freedom; second, because the leading ecumenical body, the NCCK was linked to the WCC, which was in dialogue with church leaders from the Communist Bloc; and third, because the NCCK became linked with the radical politics of the 1970s–1980s so that the more conservative denominations stayed outside it and later formed the CCK. Nevertheless, there were many organisations which crossed Protestant denominational boundaries – women's organisations (Lee Yeon-ok 2011:234–45), mission agencies, FBOs and so on – and evangelistic activities were often interdenominational.

Despite competition between churches and the lack of ecumenical structures, one thing that the Protestant churches had shared through most of their history was the same Bible. But when in 1993, after ten years of work, the Korean Bible Society brought out the New Korean Standard Version intended for interdenominational Protestant use, it was rejected by Hapdong and other conservatives, partly because it sounded too unfamiliar – for example, the name Jehovah was replaced with LORD following global practice – and partly because in places the interpretation was too liberal – for instance, in Genesis 1.2 the Hebrew word 'ruah' was translated as 'wind' (baram) rather then 'spirit' and inclusive language was used (Lim Hee-kuk 2013:217–19). A revision of the 1961 version produced in 1998 proved more acceptable and became the one most commonly used, except by Hapdong, which continued using the 1961 version, preferring the solemnity of the old verb forms.

Mega- and very large congregations continued to grow numerically. These churches were wealthy, sophisticated in their organisation and centred on a powerful senior pastor whose sermons were disseminated through tapes and books, and later online. They embraced the new information technologies of the 1990s, defining themselves through their websites in ways which enhanced the status and profile of the pastor and their businesslike organisation. They also grasped the possibilities of new technologies as tools for evangelism, using aggressive websites and SMS messaging systems as means of strengthening the church networks and of penetrating deeper into members' lives (K. Kim 2007a). YFGC still ranked as the largest church not only in Korea but in the world. It had successfully negotiated the transition from founder-minister Cho Yong-gi to second-generation pastor Lee Young-hoon and developed a sophisticated and corporate business-style organisational structure. It continued its extensive national evangelistic and media work, and its educational work included a university in Korea (Hansei) and another in California. In 2013 YFGC offered its twenty satellite or regional churches autonomy as 'disciple churches'. Membership of the Seoul congregation was given as five hundred thousand and of the others as three hundred thousand. Cho Yeong-muk, younger brother of Cho Yong-gi, was the senior minister of

Grace and Truth Church in Anyang City. Incheon Full Gospel Church, pastored by Choi Sung-kyu, was also a megachurch at sixty thousand members. Choi made a point of relating Christian ethics to filial piety and established Sungsan Hyo (Filial Piety) University.

The largest Presbyterian church was Myungsung Church in Myeongil-dong, Seoul, a member of Tonghap. Ninety thousand were registered there in 2010, and forty thousand attended regularly. The congregation was predominately young – 80 per cent were below forty years of age – and its worship style was charismatic. Pastor Kim Sam-whan began the church in 1980 on the then fringes of urban development. As the area developed, three churches were built successively on the same site in 1983, 1990 and 2011 to cater to the growing numbers. The church was known especially for its early morning prayer meetings which started every hour on the hour from 5:00 AM until 9:00 AM and were said to attract fifty thousand in total per day. Kim Sam-whan's message was popular and intended to encourage the congregation in their personal and daily life, and like most megachurches, Myungsung had a large social work and mission programme, including supporting the foundation of Somang Correctional Institution, an initiative for a more humane prison which opened in 2010. Another very large and prominent Tonghap church was Somang Church, which was President Lee Myung-bak's home church and situated in the elite Gangnam area of Seoul. In contrast to Myungsung Church, under the ministry of Kwak Sun-hee (succeeded by Kim Jie-chul), the worship was restrained and the church purposely did not engage in evangelistic or revival meetings. The largest single congregation in the Hapdong denomination was Sarang Community Church, Seoul, founded by Ok Han-hum, who was succeeded by Oh Jung-hyun. In 2009 it claimed eighty thousand registered members. It put a particular emphasis on training lay people as disciples in an evangelistic way. Of the Methodist churches, the largest was Kumnan Church in Seoul, which had grown out of a tent church started in 1957 by Kim Hwal-ran in a poor area north of Seoul. Kim Hong-do, who joined in 1968 as main pastor, was the second of four brothers, all of whom were in ministry. Two of them, Kim Sun-do and Kim Guk-do, pastored two other Methodist mega-churches. Kumnan Church had one hundred thirty thousand registered members, and the new church building completed in 2000 was designed to seat ten thousand, making it the largest Methodist church building in the world. In 2012 the claim to the largest church building in the world was with Yonsei Central Baptist Church in Seoul, founded in 1986 by Yoon Seok-jeon, whose sanctuary seated twenty-eight thousand, although its member-ship was probably about half the size of Kumnan's.

Evangelical dominance was not received as a blessing by all. In celebrating their liberation from the Egypt of religious and social oppression, Korean Protestants were accused of neglecting the rights of and oppressing the Canaanites in the promised land (cf. Kim Won-il 2006:232). Protestantism's political and ecclesial success led to jingoism and claims that demographic advantages and political power were a blessing from God. Many had a survival-of-the-fittest theology which celebrated the victory of ideological Christianity over Communism, its religious supremacy over other contenders and its political dominance. The CCK celebrated 'Korean church power' in a photo book, without any hint of reticence, intertwining the history of the church with modern Korean history and making little distinction between the two (Shine Yun-shik 2006).

However, the rise of both civil society and the media encouraged criticism of religion in general and of alleged Protestant extremism, power wielding and corruption. A major cause of Protestant unpopularity was their zealous evangelism. Non-Christians were more likely to be targeted by Protestant evangelists than by any of the other faiths, and those most frequently approached were least inclined towards them. Furthermore, examples of aggressive proselytising practices gave rise to the impression that Christians were more interested in church growth than in truth and love, and campaigns against heresy made it appear that Protestants lacked compassion (Hong Young-gi 2007; Jang Suk-man 2004:149–50). In August 2007, Seoul Union Church, the foreign congregation which had been worshipping in the new premises provided by the Korean churches at Yanghwajin, was forced to cease its morning worship by the more recently established, and rapidly growing, Centenary Memorial Church, a Korean congregation which was using the premises and also meeting the expenses of the surrounding foreigners' cemetery. This led to a complicated dispute about the ownership of the land and rights to the church building, which was seen by many as ungracious towards the missionaries and their descendants (Shin Ho-cheol 2008; Centenary Memorial Church 2010). In the context of such incidents, a former deputy prime minister criticised his own Protestant tradition as 'the Church of Jesus without Jesus', or at least with only a dogmatic Jesus but lacking his body and heart (Han Wan-sang 2008:7). Some fundamentalist elements condemned people holding other points of view as evil, and despised or even cursed other religious groups. There were instances of violence against other religionists and of Protestant extremists setting fire to old wooden Buddhist temples and defacing Buddhist images, village spirit posts and statues of Dangun (T. S. Lee 2010:149–50). In a climate of plurality and critical thinking, the accusation of conservatism was levelled against the Protestant churches in theological, cultural and political senses. With the growth of progressive and left-wing politics, the mainstream Protestant churches' pro-American stance, which was manifest when some Protestants took a leading role in pro-US demonstrations in the early 2000s, was out of step with the prevailing mood (Jang Suk-man 2004:148–53; Shin Gi-wook 2006:175–76). 'Mammonism' was another key allegation, particularly as in many cases giving to the church was regarded as a key measure of faith and there appeared to be a transactional relationship between members and the church which was motivated more by business than by religious considerations (Lee Won-gue 1998:237–43). Whereas churches had earlier been seen as means of community support and development, their traditions and prosperity theology increasingly appeared 'inward looking' and their preoccupation with numerical growth and raising funds for their own congregational support or to build new premises appeared self-centred (Han Wan-sang 2008:7–10). The wider society now demanded tolerance and social service of religious organisations, and the apocalypticism and lack of constructive engagement in political processes of conservative Protestant churches further isolated them (Han Gil-soo 2009:341–44).

In the early twenty-first century, South Korea was the most internet-penetrated country in the world (Janelli and Janelli 2005). As well as facilitating Christian outreach, the internet made possible the emergence of a distinct anti-Christian movement. This movement was initially a response to Christians taking advantage of opportunities for online comment to post biblical verses and Christian slogans, but it widened to include anyone who considered themselves victims of Protestant mission or who wished to promote atheism or recruit for other religions. Participants saw suppression of autonomy and superstition as the essence of Christianity and instead emphasised freedom of conscience, secular humanism and cultural pluralism (Lee Jin-gu 2004:223–45; Kim Young-dong 2010:357–79; Lee Won-gue 2000:236–55). Legal attempts were made to erode religious privileges that benefited Protestants especially, such as the exemption of Christian ministers from paying taxes. A new law in 2005 introduced greater transparency in the running of private schools and universities, and in 2010 a student won his case against expulsion for refusing to take a mandatory religious education class in a Christian school on grounds of religious freedom (Jang Suk-man 2004:145–56; Chang Dong-min 2009).

The continued growth of megachurches belied the downward trend in membership in other Protestant churches and the fact that many congregations were merely surviving. Urbanisation had left rural churches struggling, the activities of the minjung churches were limited by dependence on the larger churches for funds and church plants (gaecheok gyohoe) in poorer suburbs could barely afford to support their pastors (Chai Soo-il 2003:542–43; T. S. Lee 2010:89; Kim Kwang-ok 1997:230–31). The decline in numerical growth provoked a widespread crisis of theology and identity in the churches, which had become so oriented to such growth as the measure of God's favour and an incontrovertible sign of church health. Much soul-searching was generated by surveys showing, for example, that 55 per cent of non-believers had at some time attended a Protestant church. The focus on numerical growth was replaced in the early twentieth century with preoccupation about the reasons for decline. Critical voices were raised from within the mainstream churches themselves about aggressive evangelism, conservative theology, materialist outlooks and failures of leadership, and multiple reasons were advanced for this turnaround in Protestant fortunes, including sociological and ecclesial (Lee Won-gue 1998:186–201; 2000:69–91).

Korean social patterns changed hugely in the two decades either side of the millennium owing to democratisation and growing wealth, and some of these changes particularly impacted church life. For example, leisure pursuits became 'a functional alternative to religions', and with so many alternatives, the church was no longer the centre of social activity, especially for the youth. Because of a rapidly aging population, there were fewer young people and this sapped the churches of their vitality. Another factor was that women's support of church life was affected by the increase in their employment, which lessened their availability. In these conditions, it could be argued, the growth strategy had simply reached its limit since the social conditions that had promoted it no longer pertained (Park Joon-sik 2012:60–64; but cf. Kim Byong-suh 2006:325–26; Jang Suk-man 2004:143–44). However, most commentators, noting the continued growth of Catholicism, tended to blame the Protestant churches themselves for the slowdown. Two major causes were identified: leadership and ethics.

With the advent of civil society the churches became public institutions, and following democratisation new standards of accountability began to be expected in public life and merit tended to be preferred over inheritance (Han Gil-soo et al. 2009:348). From the 1990s there were many scandals surrounding high-profile clergy and prominent church elders accused of corruption, extravagance, nepotism and hypocrisy (T. S. Lee 2010:148; Lee Won-gue 1998:241–43; Han Gil-soo et al. 2009:350). But although the press seized on examples of wrong-doing, there were many more counter-examples of ordinary Protestant ministers serving their congregation and community faithfully.

In 2000, Han Kyung-chik died at the age of ninety-eight. He had been the elder statesman of Protestant Christianity and was highly respected for his simple lifestyle, humble attitude, vision for working together and concern for the people of North Korea. His service to society was recognised in 1992 by the award of the prestigious Templeton Prize. Another revered figure was Bang Ji-il, who had served as a Presbyterian missionary in Shandong province in China for twenty years (1937–1957) and was known for his kindness, wisdom and devotion. The poor quality of leadership of some of the younger generation was blamed by some on an oversupply of theology graduates. In 2009 there were estimated to be four hundred Protestant seminaries producing seven thousand graduates per year, whereas Catholic seminaries produced only three hundred. Limited curricula left graduates with few other career options; many founded welfare institutions which could obtain government subsidies, and while the vast majority were engaged in valuable social service, a few were charged with irregularities (Han Gil-soo et al. 2009:350–53). However, the free market ethos of the Protestant churches left few means to address such problems. Nor could much be done to limit the growth of megachurches, although democratic processes tempered the power of megachurch pastors within their respective denominations.

Around the turn of the millennium the problems of the Protestant churches were identified as primarily ethical (see Yim Sung-bhin 2002). Surveys repeatedly found that the churches lacked social credibility, and even that they ranked with the media, judiciary and parliament as the most distrusted groups in society (CEMK 2008:8–39; see also Tyrannus 1999:41–47). From the beginning of its introduction to Korea, Protestantism had promoted personal devotion, corporate worship and acts of service but paid less attention to conduct in public life. This dualism had tolerated clergy abuse of their authority in areas such as the handling of finance and personnel as long as the minister was demonstrating the desired 'spiritual' leadership. Now churches saw a need to address this issue not by curbing enthusiasm, nor merely by building social capital, but by renewal of faith as a commitment to living out the values of the kingdom of God (S. C. H. Kim 2013).

As a sign of the Korean Catholic Church's significance within the world church, Seoul was chosen to host the 44th International Eucharistic Congress which took place in October 1989. Pope John Paul II came for the second time in five years, and noting South Korea's global fame for material progress, he urged that this should 'go hand in hand with authentic spiritual sensitivity and growth'.[1] In the face of the division of the peninsula,

---

[1] Address of His Holiness John Paul II, Seoul, Saturday, 7 October 1989.

he urged the people to draw on their spiritual resources of reconciliation and he prayed especially for the people of North Korea under the congress theme, 'Christ our Peace' (Kim Sou-hwan 2009:377–82). The Pope found a lively, Korean-led church, with oversized urban parishes, a thriving market in devotional literature – much of it translated – and a wide variety of activities and institutions. Parish-based activities included base communities, Bible study and charismatic renewal groups, local branches of lay organisations, and business, academic and professional groups. Furthermore, despite their history of deprivation, Catholics were now above average in social and economic status (Park Moon-su 2012:92). In 2006 Archbishop Cheong Jin-seok (Nicholas), the successor to Cardinal Kim, was also elevated to cardinal. The church had nineteen dioceses, including a military ordinariate and three dioceses in North Korea (RFKCH 2010:168). Despite this, in 2012 the Korean Catholic Church was not yet recognised as fully mature; it remained under the Congregation for the Evangelization of Peoples instead of under the Congregation for Bishops and still maintained mission stations.

The census results of 2005 giving the number of Catholics as five million were a surprise even to the church, which put the figure at half a million lower because the Bishops' Conference excluded people who were non-practising (Moon Young-seok 2011:165–66). Between 1995 and 2005 the Catholic Church was the only organised religious group that increased its membership and it grew to be about 40 per cent of the Christian population. By 2012 Catholics had exceeded 10 per cent of the South Korean population as a whole. By other measures also the church was growing: congregational sizes continued to increase; the number of priests and religious had expanded rapidly and continued to grow, although growth was not as rapid as before; and there was a noticeable lessening of interest in religious vocations among women (Park Moon-su 2012:94–95).

The reasons commonly suggested for Catholic numerical growth were mostly the opposite of those given for the Protestant decline. The main one was that the church realised the values expected by the Korean public: 'trustworthiness and integrity of clergy', 'consideration for the weak in society', 'harmony between religions' and 'faithfulness to proper religious missions' (Park Moon-su 2012:95). Furthermore, Catholics were more confident than any other group in their religious leaders (CEMK 2008:31). Certainly, Cardinals Kim and Cheong had a much higher leadership stature nationally than any contemporary Protestant or Buddhist leader. The esteem in which Cardinal Kim was held was demonstrated when he died in February 2009 and more than four hundred thousand people queued in the bitter cold to pay him homage. The Catholic Church was much less implicated than Protestants in corruption and scandal, perhaps because of the strict education, formation and regulation of its clergy and lay leadership (Moon Young-seok 2011). Moreover, owing to the parish system, Catholic clergy and churches were not in direct competition with each other as Protestant churches were. In 1998, Archbishop Cheong, a canon lawyer, divided up large parishes and instituted a 'common pastoral care system' to encourage collaboration and resource sharing between local deaneries (RFKCH 2010:168–69). The Catholic Church was perceived to have other advantages over Protestantism in the more plural society of the 1990s and 2000s. Since it did not demand a tithe, it did not appear to be mercenary, although about 15 per cent of Catholics were estimated to tithe their income (Han Gil-soo et al. 2009:347–48). Catholic evangelistic activities were less aggressive than Protestant ones; whereas Protestants were regarded as exclusive, the Catholic Church was regarded as open to other faiths. Another factor in its favour was that, because of its permission for ancestor rites, its ordered spirituality and its sense of the sacred, it was visibly connected with the Confucian heritage of Korea, which was undergoing something of a revival (Yang Jong-hoe 2008; Moon Young-seok 2011:161–64; A. Min 2009:213).

The Catholic Church's social commitment to all regardless of difference seemed to be the main reason for its high credibility, and pejorative contrasts were made with Protestantism. In 1998, after the economic crash, Catholics were reportedly the most active religious denomination in providing social services and programmes for those who had lost their jobs. The network of educational and medical institutions maintained by the church was not as extensive as in Western Europe for Catholic communities of a similar size, but in 2012 the Bishops' Conference listed eleven universities, twenty-five general hospitals and hundreds of welfare institutions. In addition, many public social welfare institutions had been transferred to the church – a tenfold increase between 1976 and 1999 and more than a 1,000 per cent rise between 2000 and 2012. In 2012 it was delivering about half of the government's social welfare facilities, although these projects were mostly reliant on the state for their funding (Park Moon-su 2012:102–3).

Because of the rapid influx of new members, the church took pastoral measures to bring qualitative growth up to the level of quantitative growth through increasing catechesis, Bible study and lay theological education (RFKCH 2010:163–64). In 2005 the Catholic Bishops' Conference published a new translation of the Bible, in process since the bicentenary, to replace the one Catholics shared with Protestants. In addition, the church increased the number of priests by nearly a half in the first decade of the twenty-first century (D. Baker 2006b:302–3). Improvements were also made in pastoral care of members and in pastoral services such as Marriage Encounter and ministry for the aged (Park Moon-su 2012:98).

At the same time, distinctively Catholic lay spirituality movements developed with attendant publications and the latest practices. The cult of the martyrs continued strong, and in 2007 a process was begun for the beatification of the martyrs of Deokwon and other Catholics who died in North Korea. Around the country, there was a pilgrimage network of holy sites dedicated to the martyrs. Their graves were marked by statues of them, monuments or even mausoleums with information about their suffering. In addition, ancestor memorial services were a regular part of Korean religiosity (Rausch and Baker 2007:383–92). Korean Catholicism had a strong charismatic movement within the church; however, other popular religious practices – mostly among women – gave cause for concern (Park Moon-su 2012:100). The church moved to discourage several movements which focused on local stories of the miraculous that were not verified by its processes. The most prominent example was the devotion to Our Lady of Naju (a city in South Jeolla province), which began in the 1980s. It was one of a number of instances of Marian revelations in Korea stretching back to the 1950s. Yun Hong-seon (Julia Kim) claimed to have a statue of the Virgin which wept blood, that she herself suffered the stigmata and that the host turned into bloody flesh in her mouth. Yun was a convert from Protestantism and a charismatic with a reputation as a healer through her touch and urine (Julia Kim 1992). Devotion centred on a chapel and Blessed Mother's Mountain, where retreats were held. These attracted an international congregation, and Yun developed a global ministry. In January 2008, the archbishop of Gwangju, with the support of the Bishops' Conference, attempted to excommunicate Yun and anyone participating in these activities, and a priest – Jang Hong-bin (Aloysius) – was expelled from the diocese.

In 2012, the Catholic Church in Korea was largely untainted by the scandals of sexual and other abuse by priests and nuns that rocked the Catholic Church in the West, and it was outperforming its main religious rivals, but the Korean church was not without its critics. The first concern identified was nominalism. Although the figure of 25 per cent attending Sunday mass compared favourably with many Western countries, the number of non-practising Catholics had increased significantly since the 1980s, particularly among youth. This was seen to adversely affect both the vitality of the church and the solidarity of congregations. Second, the upward mobility of Catholics and the high regard in which the church was held give it an aura of respectability and made it susceptible to accusations that it was accommodating to middle-class demands and acting as a 'religious power'. On the one hand, major social campaigns were being led more by official church bodies rather than by voluntary groups like the Priests' Association and the Catholic Farmers' Movement. But on the other hand, participation of Catholic-based organisations in social movements appeared to have decreased and Catholics looked more conservative than before (Park Moon-su 2012:105). The focus on the pastoral care and teaching of the church members themselves led to fears that the church was turning inward, and its extensive charitable activities made it seem to be the 'church of the privileged'. Third, the increasing number of priests was perceived to be making the laity passive and giving them less reason for commitment to the church. The priests themselves were accused of clericalism and of doing little to implement the wishes of the laity. Educated lay people tended not to be given responsibility and there was no permanent diaconate in Korea through which married people could exercise ministry. The rise of the middle class had the potential to undermine the authority of priests and the male-dominated, authoritarian and undemocratic organisation, but the church offered little public forum for debate and criticism of the hierarchy. The two Catholic newspapers – *Pyeonghwa Shinmun* and *The Catholic Times* – were controlled by the church authorities and did not print criticism; however, the Catholic internet news *Jigeum Yeogi*, established in 2007 by a number of priests and lay people, campaigned for a more open church (Moon Young-seok 2011; Park Moon-su 2012).

The continued presence of the Orthodox and Anglican churches in Korea, although small, was a reminder that Korean Christianity could not be neatly divided into Protestant and Catholic. The Orthodox Church founded the Holy Monastery of the Transfiguration, Gapyeong, in 1986 and, although it was under the Ecumenical Patriarchate, after the end of the Cold War, Seoul became a centre for Russian Orthodox mission to other parts of Asia. In 1996 St Nicholas Seminary was established in Seoul to train students from Korea and abroad. The patriarch of Constantinople visited Korea in 1995, and centenary celebrations were held in 2000. In 2004 the Korean Orthodox Church was raised to the status of metropolis under Metropolitan Sotirios. It had six parishes in the South, nine clergy (seven Koreans) and about three thousand parishioners and supporters. The Anglican Church had an estimated sixty-five thousand members in 120 parish and mission churches in 2013, and by its Anglo-Catholic ethos, which combined attention to liturgy and social action, it had made a distinctive contribution. It was elevated to a province in 1992 and thus finally became an independent national church with its own primate. St Michael's Theological Institute eventually became Sungkonghoe University in the early 1990s. Kim Song-su, who became archbishop in 2000, was known for his pioneering work as head of St Peter's School, in Seoul, the first school, when it was founded in 1975, to provide special education for children with learning disabilities (Lee Jae-jeong 1990:308–10). This work expanded into rehabilitation facilities, continuing the Anglican tradition in Korea of concern for the marginalised.

The diversity of Korean Christianity, its varied expression and the multiple groupings within it, was another sign that Christianity really had become Korean. Participation in the WCC General Assembly in Busan in 2013 demonstrated that Korean Christianity included most of the global church families: representatives of Korean Orthodox, Lutheran, Presbyterian, Anglican, Methodist, Holiness, Evangelical and Pentecostal churches and the Salvation Army, all attended as members, and there was a Catholic delegation as well. However, the planning for the assembly also re-exposed the fault lines in Korean Presbyterianism particularly, going back to the splits of the 1950s. While Tonghap and Kijang enthusiastically supported the event, Hapdong and Koshin declined to participate. Many other conservative denominations – some of them very large such as Hapdong and Baptists – stayed away, and some fundamentalist groups, who were strongest in the Busan area, publically protested against the event.

CHRISTIANS IN SOUTH KOREAN PUBLIC LIFE

Both Protestants and Catholics as individuals and the churches as organisations were prominent in South Korean public life in the decades on either side of the millennium. Between the end of military rule in 1993 and 2013 three out of the four presidents were Christians: Kim Young-sam (1993–1998), a moderate Presbyterian; Kim Dae-jung, a Catholic emphasising social justice (1998–2003); and Lee Myung-bak (2008–2013), a more conservative Presbyterian.

In the era of civil society, Christian activist support for labour movements declined, partly because these became more militant and also because the churches became more middle class (Koo Ha-gen 2007:82–83). Minjung activists gravitated instead towards social movements on environmental, life, justice and peace issues. Global environmental concerns resonated especially strongly in South Korea as the damage done by decades of rapid industrialisation began to tell, and from the 1990s the Green movement expanded rapidly (Kim Sun-hyuk 2007:61–62). The campaigns included several religious groups: Catholic, Protestant and Buddhist. For Christians they represented, in some respects, a return to rural mission. This was particularly so for the Catholic Church, whose support for rural communities affected by environmental changes, for cooperatives and for the farmers' movement, especially where food quality and security were concerned, had always been strong. However, more radical actions did not gain the support of the whole church. Both the Bishops' Conference and the Priests' Association supported campaigns against state-sponsored large-scale environmental projects – particularly the Four Rivers project – on both environmental and human rights grounds. But in 2010 their actions were opposed by Cardinal Cheong, with the support of prominent lay Catholics, on the basis that the church should not interfere in state matters (Park Moon-su 2012:112).

Progressive Protestants developing the jubilee principle also joined environmental campaigns and blamed Protestantant premillennialism for ecological neglect (Cho Han-sik 2010). Eco-theologies developed from 1988 as the NCCK began linking the jubilee and reconciliation motifs with the WCC agenda for Justice, Peace and the Integrity of Creation, which was launched in Seoul in 1990. Some of these portrayed the minjung as the people of the land and celebrated aspects of Korean indigenous religions (Yi Mahn-yol 2006:247). One of eco-theology's most radical expressions was the 'eco-feminism' represented by Chung Hyun-kyung, a young Methodist woman theologian who gave a plenary presentation at the WCC General Assembly in Canberra, Australia, in 1991. Chung couched her theological argument in terms of a shaman's gut (Chung Hyun-kyung 1991a; K. Kim 2007b:viii–xiv), and she was vilified by Korean conservatives for syncretism and heresy (Ro Bong-rin 1993:54, 55–58; Han Soong-hong 1996b:517). However, as environmental awareness spread in the twenty-first century, mainline churches also engaged in campaigning and a more moderate eco-theology became widespread among Korean Christians. In 2003 Tonghap Presbyterians adopted a new confession of faith which emphasised God as creator and named the destruction of creation as the primary expression of sin (Hwang Jae-buhm 2007).

Although the affirmation of life in the sense of nature struck a chord in a rapidly post-industrialising Korea with a Buddhist heritage and recent memory of an agrarian past, this concern did not on the whole apply to foetal life. The number of abortions was notoriously high, and pro-life movements did not gain widespread support in South Korea. But the issue began to be raised in the 1990s as Korean scientists came to prominence in stem-cell research. The Catholic Church's pro-life agenda benefited from the revelation in 2005 that research results had been fabricated. After that the church had an active bioethics committee led by Cardinal Cheong. This committee campaigned strongly against stem-cell research, abortion and the death penalty and on other life issues such as the high suicide rates (RFKCH 2010:169–70).

In 1996 the South Korean economy reached eleventh in the world economic rankings and achieved a milestone of economic development when it joined the Organisation for Economic Cooperation and Development (OECD). But a year later, near the end of Kim Young-sam's presidency, economic crisis engulfed South Korea, leading to International Monetary Fund (IMF) intervention and restructuring pro-grammes. These policies undermined the still minimal welfare provision and caused severe social strains (Yang Jong-hoe 2008). The intervention of the IMF was seen by South Koreans as a national humiliation and a loss of sovereignty comparable to the Japanese protectorate or another trusteeship (Cumings 2005:331–34, 398). As they had done in the early twentieth century, Christians collected gold jewellery to pay off the debt and obtain foreign currency. A Catholic initiative raised twenty billion US dollars, and the National Association of Korean Presbyterian Women held a similar campaign (Yoon In-shil 2007:365; Lee Yeon-ok 2011:407). Although it might be thought that the crisis would be a test of faith in a gospel of prosperity, it was interpreted rather as a challenge to pray and to work harder to defeat the IMF and other perceived enemies who would wreck what had been achieved. In the meantime even the megachurches were forced to rein in their budgets and activities. Church building plans were scaled back, with renovation preferred to rebuilding. Churches supported government initiatives by 'economizing, sharing, exchanging, recycling' (Chai Soo-il 2003:547). They also raised special collections for relief work and did practical service for unemployed and homeless people. The min-jung churches briefly came into their own again as welfare providers (Hwang Hong-eyoul 2003:88). Both Protestant and Catholic churches cooperated with NGOs to address structural problems and initiated actions by small shareholders and the monitoring of business corporations. They campaigned against the sale and privatisation of public utilities and initiated a movement for social and ethical investment. The scrutiny given to church finances in this period partly accounts for the revelations of various scandals in Protestant churches.

Arguably the moral denunciation of corruption brought about by the strong religio-moral traditions of Korea was a contributing factor in the country's rapid reformation and recovery (Pratt 2006:291). Within two years, South Korea returned to growth and in 2002–2003 it briefly regained its former ranking before being overtaken by other emerging economies. However, the income gap had widened significantly and the South Korean economy was now further entwined with the global economic system (Kim Jin-wung 2012:546–47). Reflection on the economic crisis and its effect provoked among more radical Christians basic questions about the nature of globalisation and its role in global oppression. A leading figure in this development was Kim Yong-bock, Tonghap minister and former president of Hanil University (Kijang denomination), who insisted on the need for transformative encounters with the principalities and powers. Using his ideas, Korean progressive Christians globalised minjung theology when they called for a restructuring of the world economy towards sangsaeng or a 'sharing community' (*IRM* 2008:129–34).

In the context of the Sunshine Policy towards the North, there were various peace movements linked to the hope of reunification and concern about peninsular security and environmental issues, many of which were intertwined with questions of ROK–US relations (S. Chung 2011). The extent of religious support for the peace activists was shown by the prevalence of candle-lit vigils as part of their demonstrations (cf. Cumings 2005:401–2). They campaigned against the presence of military bases, especially US bases, and for their relocation outside Seoul, as well as for the rights of the people affected by them. The Catholic Priests' Association led actions against the annual joint exercises of the ROK and US militaries and against President Bush's anti–North Korea 'axis of evil' rhetoric, which created a real fear that war on the Korean peninsula would be next. In 2007, Kang U-il (Peter), the Catholic bishop of Jeju Diocese, with the support of Jesuit priests, spearheaded public opposition to a proposed new naval base on Jeju Island (S. Chung 2011; Kim Sun-hyuk 2007). When the government proposed sending troops to Iraq in 2004, progressive Protestants joined other peace activists in opposing the measure, in marked contrast to Korean participation in the Vietnam War, which Christians had unanimously supported (Ryu Dae-young 2004:219).

Although both Catholic and Protestant traditions had initially made significant contributions to women's education, self-identity and empowerment, women's struggle for liberation had been largely eclipsed by the struggle for national liberation and reconstruction and by the expectation that women would service the industrial growth of the nation as carers and providers of welfare (Hoffman 1995:117–19). Women who converted to Protestantism in the 1990s frequently reported that they had been seriously ill or experiencing a breakdown as a result of pressures on them attributable to being caught between modernity and tradition, or between husband and mother-in-law, and had found that the church offered one of the few places where they could unburden themselves. Churches functioned for women as a spiritual and institutional vehicle for coping with, and seeking liberation from, domestic or marital distress and suffering, although they engaged somewhat less in action to tackle the underlying social issues (K. Chong 2006:352–66).

The position of women in the Protestant churches can be illustrated by the National Association of Korean Presbyterian Women (Yeojeondohoe) belonging to Tonghap. In its jubilee year 1978, the organisation made a plan to build a new headquarters building on land donated by the PCUSA and conducted massive national fund-raising efforts (Lee Yeon-ok 2011:157–75). When completed in 1987, this twenty-two-storey office and conference block dwarfed the nearby headquarters of the denomination itself which had been constructed for the Protestant centenary three years earlier. But despite their obvious gifts and power, few women held office in the centenary building. At that time they could not rise above the level of jipsa (deacon), jeondosa (evangelist or trainee pastor) or gweonsa (a term translated as 'woman elder'; earlier, a 'Bible woman'), which was not an ordained position. It was in 1933 that the issue of women's ordination had first been raised in the General Assembly, and the Presbyterian women continued to petition the denomination annually. In 1953 representatives of the Presbyterian Church Women Evangelists Association issued a declaration of 'the permanent character of the priesthood of women' (Rhie and Cho 1997:250–51), but although the Methodists began ordaining Korean women in 1955 and Kijang first ordained women elders in 1957 and pastors in 1974, the Presbyterian General Assembly was unmoved. In 1975 the women's movement changed tack and campaigned instead for the 'democratization of the church', producing a report on discriminatory practices and starting a conscientization programme (Lee Yeon-ok 2011:140–57). However, it took another two decades before, in 1994, ordination was finally approved, after a sixty-year struggle. In 1996 the first woman elder, Park Seok-ran, was ordained at Andong Church and the first woman pastor, Park Jin-sook, at Dongshin Church, Ulsan Presbytery (Lee Yeon-ok 2011:195–228, 294–95; Yi Hyo-jae 1985:93–102; Lee Sun-ai and Ahn 1992:272–73). In 1996 the Korean Assemblies of God agreed to ordain women pastors, and in 2003–2004 the two main Holiness churches did the same, but most other Presbyterian denominations did not. Even in denominations which allowed ordination for women, relatively few received it, and women ordained as pastors were rarely appointed to churches. This was because in most cases the power of appointment was with the local church; few congregations would call a woman pastor and few men would be content to serve under one. Often the only clergy posts open to women were in specialist ministries in large churches, generally in education, music or youth work (cf. Kim Myong-hi 1992).

While women exercised significant power in domestic and financial affairs, the public sphere in South Korea remained androcentric and hostile because of the Confucian legacy, the pervasiveness of physical violence and the reinvented patriarchal tradition in the context of modernisation (Hoffman 1995:119). Although the 1970s labour movement was largely a women's movement, there was no explicit feminist agenda until the later 1980s (Koo Ha-gen 2001:96–98). Korea Church Women United started campaigning against male sex tourism in 1973 and with the encouragement of the Christian Academy, a women's studies programme began at Ewha University in 1977 (Moon Seung-sook 2007:126), but feminist consciousness began to emerge only in the 1980s among progressive women in the minjung theology movement. The Korean Association of Women Theologians was established in 1980 by Park Soon-kyung and encouraged the development of Korean feminist theology (e.g. Lee Sun-ai Park 1992; Chung Mee-hyun 2006). In the 1990s Church Women United engaged in the movement for peace and unification around the year of jubilee, campaigned with others for justice for the 'comfort women' who had been abused by the Japanese military during the Pacific War and supported reform of family law (Lee Yeon-ok: 2011:229–34). Catholic women, encouraged by the Maryknoll Sisters, also established feminist networks in the 1990s. These included in 1993 the (New World Opening) Catholic Women's Fellowship, which worked on behalf of the comfort women and against all rape, sexual harassment and domestic violence, and also the Catholic Female Community and the Female Theologians Society (1996). But these organisations weakened in the early twenty-first century because of the increase of clericalism and the decreased social role of the church (Park Moon-su 2012:113–14). Nevertheless, although they might not be openly feminist, the early twenty-first century Catholic Church had powerful women's organisations which were represented in the Bishops' Conference.

Before the modern period, different organised religions had successively dominated Korea in alliance with the state. First was Buddhism and then

Confucianism. In the colonial period, Shinto practices were imposed, and between 1945 and the end of the twentieth century Christianity – particularly Protestantism – came close to being the latest in this line of state religions. Such was its influence that other religions modelled themselves on its 'confessional and congregational' form, for example, by meeting regularly for worship in special buildings and giving faith-based doctrines and monotheism a more significant place (D. Baker 2006c:255–57; Jang Suk-man 2004:154). Christian influence on Buddhism, in particular, is seen in the emergence of movements of laity from the 1910s onwards. Buddhists in Korea used hymns with borrowed Christian tunes, said prayers in daily life (e.g. for meals), worshipped in Sunday morning services, had robed choirs and youth and high school associations, offered counselling and ran charitable institutions. They also utilised Christian methods of evangelism, which included from the 1990s the Buddhist Broadcasting System and overseas missionary work (Grayson 2001). The growth of Christianity, together with the not-unrelated growth of feminist consciousness, and the spread of urban lifestyles 'threatened' and 'transformed' many aspects of Confucian practice (Moon Ok-pyo 1998), and the new religions which emerged in the 1950s derived much of their theology and organisation from Christianity (D. Baker 2009).

After democratisation, however, South Korea entered a new context of religious plurality in which not just Protestantism but the big three organised religions as counted in the census – Buddhism, Protestantism and Catholicism – dominated the landscape. In 2005 much smaller numbers (0.2%) were committed to Confucianism as a religion, although about half of Korean families were estimated to practise ancestor veneration, and Confucian decorum, aspirations to sagehood and patterns of social relations remained integral to Korean culture (Bell and Chaibong 2003:1–28). Shamanism, including attendant practices of geomancy, divination, and so on, was not recognised as a religion in the census. During Park Chung-hee's New Village Movement, village shrines were torched, ceremonies known as gut were raided and shamans were fined or imprisoned, with the result that shamans regarded the policy as driving Koreans to embrace Christianity (Kendall 2009:10). But in the late twentieth century, shamanism was recognised as part of Korea's folk heritage and its informal practice became more open. With the presence of several world religions and strong indigenous movements, South Korea was one of the most religiously diverse nations in the world. At the same time it was argued that Koreans share a common 'spirituality' (D. Baker 2008:1–5). This is true insofar as we have shown that Christianity in Korea had become distinctively Korean, and the same might be said of other religions, especially those which had existed in the peninsula for much longer. But defining a common essence of Korean spirituality was fraught with difficulty, especially considering the tensions we have observed between Confucian-type and shamanistic spirituality – paternal and maternal.

Religious pluralism in the sense of the influence of traditional religions – including Buddhism – on the Korean people was undeniable. Other religions were not on the 'outside' but on the 'inside' of Koreans in that they were the heritage of the people because they were 'the cultural and philosophical mentors of the past' (Park Jong-chun 1998:41; Ahn Sang-jin 2001:132). But Koreans were not pluralistic in the sense of individuals picking and mixing their religious practice (Lee Moon-jang 1999:409–12). Each of the organised religions was seen to be unique, and fixed boundaries were perceived between one faith and another. Each was seen to offer a distinctive teaching, which Koreans aimed to master rather than dilute with other schools of thought. Although Koreans might be influenced by several religions, the value they placed on loyalty meant that their religious identity was single. Since each was fully immersed in his or her own religion, it was difficult to cross over for an in-depth encounter with another faith (Han Gil-soo et al. 2009:352). This was true as much for relations between Catholics and Protestants as it was for Christians' relations with other religions. In the context of polarised ideologies, although some Christians – more likely Catholics – were willing to have dialogue with other faiths, most – and especially Protestants – were unwilling to risk the perception that they were softening their resolve and believed that compromise implied capitulation. An interfaith movement was hosted from the 1960s by the Christian Academy and led by Kim Sou-hwan (Catholic), Kang Won-yong (NCCK) and Beop Jeong (Buddhist) (Yeohae Ecumenical Forum 2013). It had limited success, and since then dialogues have tended to be bilateral (e.g. Kim Sung-hae and Heisig 2008b). The Korean Conference of Religions for Peace was founded in 1998, but interfaith and ecumenical activity for its own sake continued to be rare in South Korea.

Perhaps one reason why, at the turn of the twenty-first century, most religious people did not problematize the discreteness of one religion from another was that, although South Korea was a religiously plural society, the country's faith differences had not been a major cause of societal conflict; indeed, they were celebrated as a sign of religious freedom. The over-riding sense of Korean identity and South Korean solidarity against the North may also have been reasons why not, as well as the overwhelming power of one religion over the others at different periods. However, to fully appreciate

Korean attitudes towards Christianity and Christian attitudes towards other faiths, it should be noted that even in the early twenty-first century Christianity, despite its rapid growth, was still a minority religion (cf. Biernatzki et al. 1975:89). Furthermore, South Korean society could not be described, as could Western societies, as post-Christian; rather, it was post-Buddhist or post-Confucian. In the twenty-first century, conversion still caused family difficulties and Christians continued to seek freedom for their faith on a day-to-day practical level. Because Christianity was a new and minority religion which other religions had found difficult to tolerate, Korean Christians did not feel the same guilt towards other religions that was detectable in Western theologies of religion which carried with them a history of colonial domination (Lee Moon-jang 1999). Although Christians might be triumphalist, this should not always be misconstrued as jingoism; their triumph was born out of suffering and struggle.

By the millennium, the Christian Korea many strove to establish had not been realised, and in religiously plural South Korea, Christian – especially Protestant – dominance began to be strongly challenged. In this context, conservative Protestants found it hard to adjust their 'Cold War logic' that South Korea should be Christianised and were in conflict with the new Korean religions and with Buddhism (Han Wan-sang 2008:9). From presidents downwards, Christians often failed to show sensitivity to Korean religious plurality. The Protestant presidents tended to favour their co-religionists for government posts. President Lee Myung-bak particularly antagonised other religions, especially Buddhists. In August 2008, tens of thousands of them, led by monks, staged a protest against Lee's 'anti-Buddhist bias' and alleged intention to turn the country into a 'medieval Christian kingdom'. Specific complaints included the regular Christian service he started in the Cheongwadae (presidential residence) and the perceived influence on his policies of certain megachurch pastors.

Protestants consistently opposed attempts by Dangunists and Buddhists to have their religions recognised. Conservative Christians had mobilised against attempts to erect statues to Dangun in 1966 and 1985. In 1987 they objected to a revision of school history books which they believed implied that Dangun was a national god and that they feared would lead to Dangunism being established as a state religion. Their protests were also in part against minjung Christian association with Dangun symbols in the contemporary democratisation struggle. In 1999 they clashed with the Korean Cultural Campaigns Association, which was systematically erecting statues of Dangun on the premises of willing schools and other public institutions. However, because conservative Christians resisted the incorporation of the Dangun myth into their theology, except negatively, their Korean-ness was bound to be questioned and an important part of their shared ethnic identity with the North, which also proclaimed the Dangun myth, was also being denied (cf. T. S. Lee 2009).

Historically, Korea had had little contact with the other two Abrahamic religions but in the early twenty-first century there was growing Korean Christian awareness of, and involvement in, some of the tensions between Christianity, Judaism and Islam. In 2010 Korea was second in the world in the number of pilgrims to the Holy Land – both Protestants and Catholics (Park Moon-su 2012:114). Although progressives took on the Palestinian cause, the tendency of Korean Protestants to have a literal and historical approach to the Bible, together with their premillennial eschatological expectations and triumphalism, made most of them natural allies of Zionist movements (Kim Sung-gun 2011:85–95). For example, in 2005, Cho Yong-gi and the mayor of Seoul hosted the second Jerusalem Summit Asia, a pro-Israel gathering of more than a thousand Asian Christians in the 'Holy City', and in 2007 the Korea World Mission Conference and the Middle East Mission Organization co-organised a 'Back to Jerusalem' march which aimed to visit Jerusalem as well as 440 Arab villages for evangelism.

Koreans had had only limited contact with Islam until, from the 1960s, Korean workers undertook construction and business contracts in the Middle East, which led to some conversions. In addition, after 1990 there was an influx into South Korea of migrant workers from Muslim countries. Koreans have had no history of negative relations with Muslims. Church leaders, however, tended to see Islam as anti-Christian, and Cho Yong-gi and Gil Ja-yeon, the president of the CCK, resisted any accommodation to it in South Korea, such as a plan for Islamic banking in 2011. Conservative Christians generally regarded Muslims in Korea as targets for proselytising, and the activities of Christian missionaries in Muslim countries caused tensions and embarrassment for the Korean government (D. Baker 2006a; Grayson 2002:195–97; see the next section).

CHRISTIAN DIASPORA, GLOBAL INTERACTIONS AND OVERSEAS MISSIONS

Following the Seoul Olympics, Korea's foreign relations became increasingly multi-lateral and South Koreans more freely explored the rest of the world through trade, travel and mission activities. At the same time, factors such as the growth of the Korean economy and an aging population led to increasing numbers of foreign visitors, migrant workers and other immigration. Korean Christianity increasingly embraced an international vision, and the worldwide Korean networks and activities began to have significant global impact.

By 2009, emigration had resulted in seven million Koreans living abroad in 176 countries (Kim Gui-ok 2004:50–60, 70–72). From the 1960s the South Korean government had encouraged emigration as part of its economic policy, and from the 1990s globalising forces accelerated it further. It was now seen as permanent or long-term rather than a temporary escape from famine or oppression. It resulted in the establishment of Korean populations in Latin America and Western Europe, and the community in North America substantially increased. These were in addition to the older diaspora populations in China, Japan, Russia and Central Asia. The post-1960 diaspora was mainly Protestant, first, because those Koreans who were in the best position to emigrate to the West were often Protestants because of the higher standard of education they enjoyed in that period, and because they were more likely to have English-language skills and be positively inclined towards the West. Second, although Korean migrant communities formed a Haninhoe or Korean Committee which connected the community with the government, it was a general pattern that a Protestant church became the focal point of each Korean migrant community. In some cases the church was founded before any other association, for example, the Korean United Presbyterian Church in São Paulo in 1965 (Chun Do-myung 2011). The church functioned as a social centre, offered welfare services, disseminated news from home and ran the Korean school. It often had dedicated personnel for this purpose since churches at home sent out pastors or chaplains to minister to diaspora communities. So even those individuals who were not Christian in Korea tended to identify as Christian in diaspora. The diaspora was held together and connected with Korea itself by church links, as much as by business and government. Korean Catholics generally joined the local Catholic parish, but when the community grew sufficiently, they might form a Korean congregation within the local diocese. There were exceptions such as the Korean Catholic Church in the Philippines, which was begun by lay people for gathering and sharing and was tied to a diocese in Korea from which priests were sent every year. In 2009–2010 there were estimated to be more than 5,500 Korean diaspora churches around the world. About 4,000 of these were in the United States; about 300 were in Canada, 200 in Japan, 175 in Australia, 100 in Germany, 55 in the United Kingdom, and 50 each in Brazil and Argentina (D. Oh 2011; Lee Soon-keun 2011:199).

In 2009 there were perhaps two million Korean Chinese, mostly settled in north-east China since before 1945 but from the late 1980s many had relocated to large cities and to Russia, South Korea, Japan, the United States and Canada (Lee Soon-keun 2011:197–98). Christians had been among the many migrants to north-east China from the late nineteenth century onwards, and in 1949 there were 162 Protestant churches in North Gando with nearly thirty-two thousand members (Kang Wi-jo 1990). In this period Korean Protestants were especially enthusiastic about the Three-self Movement in the Chinese Church because it drew on the Nevius method (Wickeri 2011) and some were equally supportive of the Chinese campaign to 'oppose America, support Korea'. But before long, Christians were being persecuted, especially during the Cultural Revolution. After the churches were officially reopened and the China Christian Council was formed (1980), Korean Chinese were active in the revival of Chinese Christianity. For example, in Shenyang, the church founded by John Ross had thirty thousand members in 2010 and was led largely by Koreans. Many of the South Koreans who began to visit and do business in Chinese cities after the liberalisation of the economy in 1978 were Protestants eager to use their business contacts to evangelise Chinese. They discouraged Korean Christians from being part of the Three-self Movement because of its Communist links and encouraged instead 'underground', 'unregistered' or 'independent' churches which they tied to their own churches or missions (Kang Wi-jo 1990). By the late 1980s they were able to get permission to found Korean churches, first in Beijing and then in Qingdao, Shanghai and other cities. There were estimated to be several hundred unofficial churches throughout China by 2010 (D. Oh 2011:191).

The Korean community in Russia, which had been forcibly deported by Stalin, included many church communities who now found themselves in Kazakhstan, Uzbekistan, Russia or other Central Asian states. They were under strong pressure to assimilate in the Soviet period and to cease their Christian practice. Numbering about half a million by the millennium, Koreans in Soviet Central Asia referred to themselves as Goryo-saram and in the post-Soviet era they revived aspects of Korean culture (G. Kim 2003). From the late 1980s the Goryo-saram had increasing contact with South Koreans who came both as business people and as missionaries (e.g. Song Min-ho 2011:117–18) and generally welcomed them as a way of rediscovering their Korean past. Korean churches engaged in cultural activities with the people, for example, by sending out choirs which sang old folk songs that they could recognise. Although Russian Protestant missionaries had had little success in converting them, Kazakhs and other ethnic groups also became Christians in the Korean churches which multiplied rapidly in the cities. But by the late 1990s the churches had largely stopped growing and there were complaints of Korean missionary colonialism (McNeill 2012:79–80).

The Korean diaspora of about one and one-half million residents in Japan in 2010 included Korean-Japanese who had emigrated to Japan in the colonial period and whose bitter history posed continued difficulties for them there (Kawashima 2009). The Korean Christian Church in Japan, which began as a student group in 1908, had had a painful history (Park Heon-wook 1995). Korean missionaries were sent to Japan from 1909, and some of these planted other separate denominations. After the Liberation, Yi In-ha put forward Giryumin Theology (Theology of Diaspora) to protest against the perception that Koreans in Japan were 'aliens and exiles' and to restore their dignity, neither rejecting nor assimilating with Japanese culture (Yang Hyeon-hye 2009:241–48). After Japanese–Korean relations were normalised, newer migrants from South Korea settled in Japan. As Korean churches there grew, they increased their evangelistic efforts towards the Japanese, whose percentage of Christians remained stubbornly low. From the 1990s Korean megachurches were very active in trying to 'revive' Japanese Christianity, although they did not always work in consultation with the Japanese churches. They arranged large praise and worship gatherings, and they organised and funded other activities, such as the Tokyo 2010 conference.

Of the two-million-strong Korean community in the United States in the early twenty-first century, 98 per cent were migrants or descendants of migrants who arrived after 1968 when Korean emigration to the United States was regularised (Patterson and Kim 1992). It was estimated that more than 70 per cent of them were affiliated with Korean churches. Forty per cent of these had gravitated towards the church and become Christians after arriving in the United States; four out of five attended church more than once a week and generously supported it (H. Kim 2008:27–41; S. Kang and Hackman 2012). Korean churches mushroomed from about forty Protestant congregations and a single Catholic one in 1972 to more than four thousand spread out from California across the nation. The largest churches – Youngnak Presbyterian Church and Sa-rang Community Church, both in Los Angeles, and New York Presbyterian Church – numbered several thousand members, but most Korean Protestant churches were small – between twenty and fifty adults. Their pastors were mostly theologically conservative. Forty per cent of Protestant churches were Presbyterian, and other significant denominational groups were Baptist,

Methodist, Full Gospel and Holiness. Other churches were independent or interdenominational (S. Kang and Hackman 2012). Some churches existed as Korean congregations within US denominations – notably in the PCUSA, which recorded 430 Korean-American churches with their own synodical structure in 2012, and in the Catholic Church, where there were 130 parishes with a specific ministry to Korean communities in 2010 (Gray et al. 2013:22).

If the second generation dropped out of the Korean-medium congregations of their parents, they might move to English-speaking congregations or, in the case of Protestants, Christian young people – often church youth groups – might set up new churches themselves. Despite their high rates of education, income and mobility, second-generation Korean-Americans were still marginalised because of their race and were observed to develop a distinctive 'hybrid' Christian expression of their own (Sharon Kim 2010:160–65). Second-generation Korean Protestants were less conservative than the first generation and keen to become good citizens. They used the church as a platform for community development and outreach, including social service programmes to non-Koreans (Ecklund 2006:70, 117, 137; S. Kang and Hackman 2012:74–75). Some of their churches were multi-ethnic congregations mainly made up of other Asians, in which Koreans played the leading role (Ecklund 2006:39–44). This might be partly a recognition by other Asians of the unique history of Korean Protestantism, and it was probably also bolstered by the spread of Korean popular culture (Sharon Kim 2010:161). In this context Korean-Americans developed a distinctive theology which was directed not at issues on the Korean peninsula but at the questions of identity raised in the North American situation (e.g. P. Chung, Kärkkäinen and Kim 2007). Korean-Americans formed the largest non-white group in American evangelical seminaries, and some were in the leadership of national or international evangelical organisations (Sharon Kim 2010:5).

Korean migration to Europe was negligible until 1963 when miners and nurses were invited as guest workers to West Germany. They planted Korean churches there in the early 1970s. At about the same time the first Korean church was established in London. By the year 2000 most other major European cities also had Korean communities and churches (S. Hun Kim 2011:150–51). Whereas in the urban areas of the United States, where most Koreans settled, their churches tended to blend into the religious marketplace, in Europe their relationship with existing churches was more of an issue because Europeans tended to expect ecumenical working. Although some formed no relationship at all with ethnically European churches, a number of other patterns emerged. These ranged from simply renting premises to becoming Korean congregations within an existing local church and to making formal partnerships at the denominational level, such as the one facilitated in 1998 by the United Evangelical Mission (UEM) with seventeen Korean churches in North Rhein-Westphalia (K. Kim 2012:271–76; S. Hun Kim 2011:150–51). A similar pattern emerged in Australia, where by 2011 three different Korean denominations were in partnership with the Uniting Church and thereby experiencing ecumenical relations which they could not enjoy in South Korea (cf. Yang Myong-duk 2009).

By their nature, the priorities of diaspora churches were to minister to the local Korean community and to serve its interest vis-à-vis that of the wider society in a particular country or region. But diaspora churches might also be self-consciously missionary within their context, at least in the sense that they saw themselves as a chosen people exercising a leavening and even salvific effect on their surroundings, particularly where these were dominated by another faith or ideology (Lee Soon-keun 2011:202–3). Some diaspora churches actively engaged in outreach to the local people. For example, Abidjang Korean Church, Côte d'Ivoire, which was founded in 1980, claimed by 2010 to have planted eleven urban churches and forty-five rural ones and to have helped found the local Presbyterian seminary. The Full Gospel Korean Church in Quito, Ecuador, had planted fifteen self-supporting churches around the country (Song Min-ho 2011:126–27). Grace Korean Church in Fullerton, California, began a mission to the former Soviet Union in the early 1990s and established contacts with five hundred ethnic Koreans at Dushanbe in Tajikistan and drew in local Tajiks as well. Their impact may be judged by the fact that the church was bombed in 2000 (Ma Won-suk 2012).

Whether conscious of it or not, diaspora churches were part of wider Korean expansion, exploration and missionary movements. They were inseparable from the projection of South Korean products and cultures onto the world stage and the reception of Western ideas in Korea and its development. The diaspora churches supported business ventures, overseas studies, and diplomatic and outreach activities. They were part of South Korea's soft power which had been greatly enhanced since the 1990s by the transformation of its image from war-torn, unstable dictatorship to stylish democracy. In the 1990s the government saw the economic potential of Korean culture for export, and much of its diffusion – known as the Hallyu or 'Korean wave' – was through the diaspora communities (Kim Jin-wung 2012:553–54). Insofar as Korean culture had been Christianised, the Hallyu also spread Christian influences, including into areas like China and the Middle East, which were otherwise culturally resistant to Christianity, and so it was seen as advantageous to world evangelisation (D. Oh 2011:195).

South Korean society is often described as 'mono-cultural' in that it appears to be entirely composed of ethnic Koreans who share a common language and culture, but from the 1990s it began to host increasing numbers of migrants. By 2009 more than 2 per cent of the population of South Korea, or one million residents, was foreign, and the figure was rising (Kim Jin-wung 2012:549). A lively nationwide discussion ensued, which was to a large extent stimulated by the churches, on multiculturalism and issues such as the treatment of foreign workers, international marriage and the status of children of such marriages, relations with overseas Koreans and the assimilation of North Korean migrants. The mistreatment and lack of rights of migrant workers in Korea's burgeoning factories was first raised as an issue by minjung activists as a continuation of their action for workers' rights and social justice (Hwang Hong-eyoul 2003:92–93). In general, the churches encouraged a multiculturalism that contrasted with the government's assimilationist approach (Yun In-jin 2008; Jun Chul-han 2011:209–11). Cross-cultural marriage reached one in ten of the total marriages in 2007 (Kim Jin-wung 2012: 549). Christians – as part of global church families – tended to have a more open attitude about such marriages than some other sectors of the population. From the mid-2000s significant mistreatment of female marriage immigrants was exposed, leading some Christians to campaign for the reform of immigration and naturalisation procedures, to open shelters for battered women and to provide legal and counselling services (Yun In-jin 2008). Whereas progressive Christians were concerned mainly about the human rights aspects of migration, conservatives focused on evangelisation, including various practical and compassionate measures. A typical evangelical model of ministry to migrant workers consisted of inviting them to church and to a meal afterwards, and then offering assistance with medical, physical and legal needs. Some churches hired foreign pastors to minister to migrant workers in separate services and ministries according to language groups. Nationwide missions to migrants were set up, and in some instances foreign workers, especially those from countries otherwise closed to Christian mission, were trained and supported to be missionaries to their own people when they returned (Jun Chul-han 2011:212–22).

The revivalist evangelicalism dominant in Korea placed strong emphasis on world mission in the sense of reaching all nations and peoples as an obligation placed on all Christians in obedience to Christ's command. From the early twentieth century, Protestants had sent workers abroad to minister to diaspora Koreans and they had also maintained missions to other peoples from the Presbyterian mission to Shandong, China, in 1913 onwards. There was never a sharp distinction between serving the diaspora and missionary activity: first, because diaspora communities themselves were sometimes missional towards those around them, and second, because diaspora congregations provided important support bases and staging posts for missionaries. Koreans found innovative ways of fulfilling the Great Commission when overseas travel was restricted. In 1974, for example, Korea Harbor Evangelism (KHE) was founded by church leaders Han Kyung-chik, Kim Eui-min, Yi Gi-hyeok, Choi Hun-ok and Choi Ki-man in Incheon as an indigenous, interdenominational mission to seamen, both through evangelism and welfare. In the port missionaries encountered a range of nationalities, including Russians and others from the Eastern Bloc which was otherwise closed to Christian mission. In 1978 KHE linked up with Operation Mobilisation, an international youth mission organisation, for which it recruited Koreans, and in 1982 it formed World Concern Korea, the Korean branch of an international relief and development agency, to recruit professionals, mainly medical, for Africa and for other parts of Asia.

In the early 1980s, Han Chul-ha, the president of ACTS, insisted that Korea would evangelise the world, not according to the Western model of 'triumphalistic missionary sending', but by an ethical mission of demonstrating a righteous national life like 'Jerusalem of old' (Han Chul-ha 1983:51–68). But by the end of that decade, there was great enthusiasm for cross-cultural mission, which was considered more prestigious than pastoral work among diaspora communities (cf. D. Clark 1997:185). The main reasons for this development were first the energy behind the 'explosive' growth of Korean churches in the 1960s and 1970s which was then channelled into overseas mission in the 1980s. This development was reflected in the great crusades of that era and articulated particularly in the pronouncements of Kim Joon-gon (1983:36–37). Like the Korean church growth movement, the missionary movement was a way of demonstrating South Korean success and demanding respect from other nations, and it was also a global strategy to hold back Communism (cf. D. Clark 1997:187). Second, leading Western evangelicals saw a huge potential of hundreds of thousands of Korean Christians for the goal of world evangelisation, especially for evangelising the rest of Asia and also 'restricted' parts of the world that Westerners could not penetrate. This idea was bolstered by church growth theorists' 'unreached people group' approach, according to which Koreans, being closer culturally, would be more effective in evangelism there (Winter and Hawthorne 1981). Third, in the late 1980s restrictions were lifted on overseas travel and residence, and foreign-exchange laws were relaxed. These measures, together with the growing wealth of Koreans, made an overseas mission movement and short-term mission easier. Fourth, there was a surplus of Christian ministers and church workers graduating from seminaries and other Christian institutions and, at the same time, there were fewer non-evangelised areas or pastoral vacancies in Korea. These factors combined to encourage graduates to move overseas. Similarly, after the economic downturn in 1997–1998, lack of opportunity at home led to an increase in the numbers of missionaries (cf. Moon Sang-cheol 2008:59–64; Han Gil-soo et al. 2009:350–53).

The growth of the Korean Protestant missionary movement was very rapid. In 1979 there were just ninety-three Korean cross-cultural missionaries. A decade later, this figure had climbed to over a thousand. It rose by an average of 25 per cent per year through the 1990s to more than eight thousand in 2000 and nearly fifteen thousand in 2006 (Moon Sang-cheol 2008). In 2011 there were more than nineteen thousand Korean missionaries serving overseas who had been sent out by a recognised agency, a figure which included slightly more men than women (Moon Sang-cheol 2012). In 2006 it was widely reported that South Korea was second only to the United States in the total number of missionaries sent. If global Catholic sending is also taken into account, in 2010 South Korea ranked fifth in both total missionary numbers and missionaries per capita (Moll 2006; Johnson and Ross 2009:259). In 2012 the number of Protestant missionaries was still rising but the rate of growth was slowing. This was partly the inevitable result of declining church numbers and partly due to a diminishing number of young people in the population. Undaunted, some mission agencies were already making efforts to mobilise retired people to maintain the movement (P. Chang 2011: 237).

In 2011 Korean missionaries were active in 177 countries (Moon Sang-cheol 2012). More than half were serving in other parts of Asia, including the Middle East, with the main destinations being China, Japan and the Philippines. Russia, Thailand, Indonesia and India were also large fields, and there were several hundred Korean missionaries involved in campus ministries in the United States, Germany and Canada. The average missionary was married and middle-aged. For the purposes of statistics, wives were counted as missionaries but in practice it was the husband who was called and salaried, especially if he was ordained, as were about half of male missionaries. Most served for at least five years and a few for a lifetime. Three-quarters of the missionaries were engaged full time in mission work.

Table 2. *Table of Korean Protestant missions by region*

Region	Number of missionaries
North-east Asia	6,167
South-east Asia	4,641
South Asia	1,612
Central Asia	1,087
Middle East	1,158
North America	3,116
Latin America	1,151
Caribbean	86
Western Europe	1,265
Eastern Europe	1,049
South-east Africa	1,008
North Africa	461
West-central Africa	337
South Pacific	837
South Korea (home base)	1,690
Total	25,665

From Korea World Missions Association, 'Current Statistics of Korean Missionaries', December 2012.

The remainder were 'tent making', that is, doing other work to support themselves after the example of the Apostle Paul. Often they were using another profession or occupation to gain entry to a place where full-time missionaries were not welcomed or supported (Moon Sang-cheol 2008). In different regions of the world, Protestants from various Korean denominations networked among themselves. Korean missionaries in India and in Europe, for example, held annual conferences to discuss their work and the common issues they faced in each context (Table 2).

Korean Protestant missionaries used a variety of different methods but broadly followed the agenda of the nineteenth-century Euro-Americans who had evangelised Korea; like them, they did not usually consider it necessary to work with existing churches in the field (cf. Park Seong-won 1997:331–32). In 2006 nearly 40 per cent were extending the primary mission activity of Korean churches: growing Christian numbers by church planting; another 4–5 per cent were itinerant evangelists, and a few were specialised in Bible translation. All kinds of activities were employed to attract people to join churches, from organised campaigns of evangelism, where permissible, to personal evangelism. Aspects of Korean culture were also used to draw people's interest and attention, such as Taekwondo classes (the World Taekwondo Mission was founded in 1990), acupuncture and other traditional medicine, church music and 'worship dance' and computer and internet skills. Missionaries in the field might receive back-up through 'mission trips' from their sending churches, including choirs, groups of young people to do evangelism or other acts of service, and parties of professionals, like medical personnel, who offered their skills for a few days or weeks. Other missionaries were spreading Korean church growth methods by discipleship training or were engaged in education and theological education or social welfare and community development, including through medical services, business and information technology (cf. Moon Sang-cheol 2008). The figures show that the Korean missionary movement was primarily a religious movement and was not co-opted for purposes of international development as happened with many European mission, or former mission, agencies. Nevertheless, Korean missionaries were building institutions and supporting existing ones. Institutions founded by Koreans included theological seminaries such as Moscow Presbyterian Theological Seminary, universities such as Mongolia International University, and hospitals like Goli Medical Center in Uganda and Myungsung Christian Medical College in Ethiopia. These initiatives were supported almost entirely with funds raised from churches (Fig. 10).

In 2011 the missionary movement was supported by about 170 mission agencies, most of Korean foundation (Moon Sang-cheol 2012). They included the largest, the Global Mission Society, which was the mission agency of Hapdong. Claiming second place was the University Bible Fellowship, the largest of the campus ministries, which was founded in 1961, although the fact that many of its missionaries were not full time but were students and migrants disqualified it in the eyes of some (P. Chang 2011:223). Other large agencies were Campus Mission International, the Global Missionary Fellowship (originally the Korean branch of the Overseas Missionary Fellowship), and the mission boards of the Presbyterian Church of Korea, the Methodist Church, the Assemblies of God, and the Baptist Convention. Not all the agencies were large; in fact, in 2006, nearly two-thirds of them had fewer than fifty missionaries (Moon Sang-cheol 2008). A number of umbrella bodies brought the multiple mission organisations together: Mission Korea linked campus mission organisations and other mission-sending bodies and hosted a large gathering biannually from 1988. It played a major role in challenging and recruiting young people for overseas mission (see Han Chul-ho 2011:164–70). The Korea World Mission Council for Christ had been formed in the United States in 1988 with the help of Billy Graham. It organised the quadrennial

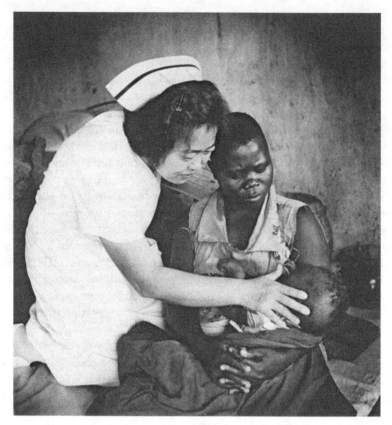

10. Kim Chung-youn, medical missionary at work at Goli Health Centre, Nebbi, Uganda, 1989. World Concern Korea.

Korean World Mission Conferences at Wheaton College, Chicago. These brought together Korean missionaries having US sponsorship with Korean-American ministers and youth. The Korea-based Korea World Missions Association (KWMA) was initiated in 1990 by Park Chong-soon, founder-pastor of Choongshin Presbyterian Church, and other leading pastors. In 2013 it had four hundred member bodies and functioned as the main forum for mission organisations. Other major bodies included the Korean Association of Tentmakers, the Korea Council of Christian Mission Organizations and Torch Mission.

Although missionaries were generally sent through agencies, they were funded by churches, usually their home church with additional support from others as required. The agencies provided a support structure for the missionary enterprise of travel arrangements, health care, insurance, pensions, communications and children's education (cf. D. Clark 1997:187). Missionaries were trained at a number of different specialist institutes, such as the Global Missionary Training Institute, a ministry of the Global Missionary Fellowship, or on courses run by mission boards. The quality and content of training varied considerably from those which were mainly intended to motivate and inspire missionaries and raise their level of English and Bible knowledge to others which included instruction in cultural studies, mission history and world religions. Teaching about global politics, poverty, social issues or critical approaches to mission history was rare. The Philippines became from the 1970s one of the major mission fields for Korean Protestants, who did not consider its overwhelmingly Catholic population evangelised. Because it was relatively close and accessible and used an English medium, it became a popular centre for training and orientation to mission in Asia.

The Korean missionary movement was primarily an activist movement addressing itself to the 'unfinished' task of world evangelisation. There was little self-conscious reflection on mission until the twenty-first century. But there was a Korean world mission theology which had several components. The first was to 'repay the debt of the gospel', that is, to fulfil the obligation arising in Confucian culture on receipt of a gift (e.g. Kim Myung-hyuk 1983:133). The grace received from Christ's suffering on the Cross and the sacrifice made by the missionaries to Korea together represented a gift which demanded a generous response. Furthermore, to be able to 'repay the debt' was a matter of national pride and a duty to the martyrs whose blood should be the seed of the church (CPCK 2000). Second, Korean Christians regarded the growth of the Korean church and the economic miracle of twentieth-century Korea as a unique blessing from God which gave them a particular responsibility, especially for the evangelisation of Asia. It was explained that their Christ-like experience of suffering and their transformation from depravity to prosperity meant that they could identify with Asia's poor and gave them the burden to share their resources (Kim Myung-hyuk 1983:133). Their participation in evangelisation was regarded as all the more urgent because of the widespread perception that the churches in Europe and North America, which had once led world mission, were dying or even 'dead'. It was argued that the torch that had once been relayed from Europe to the United States was now being passed on to Asia (Park Cho-choon 1983:206; D. Oh 2011:181). Third, Korean mission theology inherited the theology of church growth in the power of the Spirit and extended it on a global scale. The Great Commission to 'go and make disciples' was interpreted to mean the conversion of as many as possible from all the different ethnicities to explicit faith in Christ and membership in the Christian community. The church was more or less identified with the kingdom of God, and so this was also an agenda for global social and political transformation in the longer term. Two more eschatological factors were important in mission motivation and partly explained its sense of urgency: first was the conviction that without Christ, people are lost eternally in hell and therefore, whatever they or others might think, presenting them with the gospel message is the best way to help them. The second factor was the expectation that 'this gospel of the kingdom will be preached in the whole world as a testimony to all nations, and then the end will come' (Matthew 24:14, New International Version), which was understood to mean that the fulfilment of the project of world evangelisation would precipitate the arrival of salvation (for Christians) and judgement. In the 1990s, the premillennialist AD 2000 movement which took this view flourished in Korea.

In the 1980s missionary work was seen as enhancing the national reputation by pioneering regions where Korea was unknown, but even as early as 1983 attempts at overseas mission were being criticised by some church leaders. It was said that churches and denominations were competing with each other to send more missionaries, that there was no consistent and comprehensive mission policy, and that leaders were too ambitious considering that missionaries who were able and willing to work cross-culturally were few. Missionary attitudes were also criticised as 'imperialistic' and paternalistic towards other Asians, too readily singing the praises of the Korean church and replicating its methods without cultural sensitivity. Mission organisations lacked policies, qualifications for mission work were unclear, missionaries were not offered proper training and there was little study of the field or steady relationship with it. Missionaries, it was said, found out what to do when they got to the field and were not accountable to the senders (Kim Myung-hyuk 1983). By 1999, such problems were recognised by the churches themselves, as they were, for example, by the Council of Presbyterian Churches in Korea in 2000 (CPCK 2000:233–38; cf. Chai Soo-il 2003).

In celebration of religious freedom, all the religions in South Korea were 'exclusive in their religious commitment and missionary in their practice' (Lee Moon-jang 1999:408). However, missionaries were not always conscious that they were on a public, or even a world, stage. In the first decade of the twentieth century, the activities of some Korean missionaries overseas drew public attention and embarrassed the Korean government. The most serious incident occurred in 2007 when twenty-three Korean short-term missionaries from Saemmul Presbyterian Church, in Bundang, south of Seoul, were kidnapped in Afghanistan. The incident ended tragically with the execution of two members of the team. The release of the captured missionaries was secured with a reiteration of the South Korean promise to withdraw its troops by the end of 2007 and, it was claimed, payment in exchange for their safe return. The actions of the group in ignoring a warning from the government not to travel to Afghanistan drew widespread criticism both from within and outside the churches. The missionaries by their ill-judged actions were accused of putting other Korean lives at risk. However, they could not be dismissed as a fundamentalist group engaging in aggressive evangelism. Saemmul Church had a large suburban congregation which was not especially conservative by Korean standards. The group was intending to do evangelism and some medical work. Their fault was only a naïve focus on their own vision and ministry without regard for risk or political considerations. Being ready to sacrifice themselves, they were not able to understand why their fellow citizens were so alarmed and also apparently so willing to accept Taliban restrictions on religious freedom.

In 1975 Bishop Choi Jae-sun (John), who was concerned about the decrease in vocations in Europe, founded the Catholic Foreign Mission Society of Korea, now the Korean Mission Society (KMS). It was established with the permission of the Bishops' Conference and the encouragement of the Congregation for the Evangelization of Peoples. Like the Protestants, Catholics described their initiative as 'a sign of a mature Korean Church' and expressed similar motives of gratitude and responsibility, to which they added compassion. However, Catholic missionaries naturally did not convey the same sense that the church in Europe was 'dead' but looked to play their part in the 'world church', and they stressed unity as an outcome of mission. Entrusting themselves to the care of the Blessed Mother and calling on the martyr spirit of Korean Catholicism, they dedicated themselves for self-sacrifice after the model of St Paul. A house of formation for mission was established to prepare for mission in 'poverty, gratitude, and charity'. The first KMS priest, Kim Dong-Gi (Michael), was ordained in 1981 and left that same year for Papua New Guinea. Between then and 2012, the KMS trained and sent out about seventy priests. The society also opened work in Taiwan in 1990, China in 1996 and also Cambodia, Mozambique, the Philippines, Mexico and the United States.

Several reasons could be suggested why the Catholic Church in Korea came later to world evangelisation than did the Protestant churches. First, since the Korean Christian diaspora was predominantly Protestant,

Catholics by and large lacked this important support and intelligence base for overseas mission. Second, until recently the Catholic Church was very short of Korean priests to send overseas, and despite its foundation as a lay community, on the whole its laity was not encouraged to take such initiative. Third, Korean Catholics did not have the same sense of obligation to overseas service as Protestants since Korea itself was still classed as a mission field. However, from 1990 onwards, the Congregation for the Evangelization of Peoples began to pressure the Korean Church to evangelise the rest of Asia because Korea was a relatively wealthy country with one of the largest percentages of Catholics in Asia and its citizens enjoyed freedom of movement. One way in which the church contributed was by training seminarians from other countries – mostly in Asia, especially at the seminary in Daejeon. Altogether in 2012, according to the Bishops' Conference, 183 Korean priests were engaged in mission to foreign nations and a further 400 were serving the diaspora. The number of Koreans serving overseas with missionary congregations had risen to around 700 – the vast majority sisters. This figure was increasing by about 10 per cent annually, and overseas service in the missions was becoming another distinguishing feature of Korean Catholicism.

Both the Korean diaspora and the missionary movements were pioneering ventures in which Koreans explored and mapped the world after many centuries of isolation. In the beginning Christianity was instrumental in bringing Koreans into the global system; now it encouraged globalisation from Korea. Aspects of Korean culture, Korean models of development and church growth, were exported by missionaries, and Korean Christianity was being stamped on the character of churches and organisations around the world. Korean Christianity was deeply marked by its history of suffering, including both the religious persecution of the martyrs who opposed ancestor veneration, Shinto shrine worship, Communism and military dictators, and also the national traumas of loss of nationhood, foreign occupation, economic deprivation, partition, civil war and social oppression. These experiences engendered resilience, a strong sense of justice and an urgent desire for peace and security. The incubation of Christianity in such turbulent times had moulded it into a strong, national movement providing a new identity for Koreans. It had instilled a sense of responsibility to honour the martyrs and a willingness to work hard and make sacrifices for the cause of freedom and national prosperity. The characteristic response of Korean Christians to suffering had not been withdrawal or victimhood but repentance for past failure, a spirit of defiance and a determination to overcome adversity and to remodel their lives and society so that their tragic history would not be repeated. Christianity had been actively sought as a resource, and it was received as a gift of grace which gave grounds for optimism, means for change and vision for the future. Christians played a leading role in the Korean Enlightenment, the modernisation of Korea, the independence movement, nationalist activities, nation-building and the struggle for democracy and human rights. The churches, their institutions and their organisations had functioned as supportive and enabling communities which had been a haven of help, a beacon of education, a means of self-development and a source of humanitarian aid for millions of people.

By the twenty-first century Korean churches had grown in maturity, developed distinctive theologies and gained confidence in public life and in global affairs. Korean Christians had a sense of calling to repay the debt of the gospel by sharing what they had received with other nations and peoples. They were known for their commitment, enthusiasm, initiative and determination, but contemporary Koreans also carried with them the burden of a divided nation. Christians were expected to love their kin on the other side of the border, yet they struggled to reconcile themselves with the ideology of the other. Whatever they achieved, their lives and livelihoods were overshadowed by threats and uncertainty. While the future of the peninsula remained unresolved and unknown, they could not rest content. Yet this eschatological reality was a source of inspiration for their faith and motivation to action. Apart from the on-going division of North and South, there were other challenges and opportunities, which included economic and gender inequality and the excesses of late-modern capitalism in the South and Communist totalitarianism in the North. There were issues to be dealt within the churches themselves as well: threats of divisive sectarian movements, criticism of standards of conduct in public life, accusations of abuse of power and complaints of exclusive attitudes to others. It remains to be seen how the Korean Christians will respond to these challenges, but this history suggests that they will continue to be active in articulating and actualising Christian models for their lives and society and that, whatever the future holds, the potential of Korean churches to influence events at home and even shape global developments should not be underestimated.

Glossary

Anbang	the women's quarters of a traditional Korean house
Buheunghoe	revival meeting
Chaebol	Korean industrial conglomerate
Cheon	heaven (derived from Chinese)
Cheondogyo	Korean religion emerging from the late nineteenth-century Donghak movement and based on the thought of Choi Je-u
Cheonju	Lord of Heaven
Cheonjugyo	Roman Catholicism
Cheonmin	bonded servants or outcastes
Chudoyebae	Christian ritual substituted for ancestor veneration
Chulok seongdo	'released believers' who served a gaol term for refusing to worship at Shinto shrines
Daejonggyo	Korean religion established in 1909 by Na Cheol
Dangun	legendary founder of the first Korean kingdom
Donghak	'Eastern learning'; the thought of Choi Je-u which gave rise to the Donghak Peasant Revolution in 1894
Eonhaeng sillok	*Written Records of Words and Acts* composed by Yuhandang Gwon
Gibok sinang	'faith seeking blessings'; a form of Korean spirituality
Gidokgyo	Protestant Christianity
Goryeo	the first unified Korean kingdom (918–1392)
Gut	exorcism performed by a shaman (mudang)
Gweonsa	'woman elder' but not an ordained office
Gyoan	'struggles' or local disturbances involving Catholics in the late nineteenth and early twentieth centuries
Gyodan	the united Korean Protestant church created by the Japanese in 1945

Gyouchon	'believers' villages; communities of Catholics in remote areas during the period of persecution in the nineteenth century
Hallyu	the 'Korean wave' or Korean cultural influence abroad from the late 1990s
Han	'just indignation' or 'feeling of repression'; a Korean term used by minjung theologians
Hananim	God; possibly derived from 'hana' meaning 'one' and 'nim' meaning 'lord'
Haneul	heaven (Korean word)
Haneunim	God; possibly derived from 'haneul' meaning 'heaven' and 'nim' meaning 'lord'
Hangul	the Korean alphabet devised in the fifteenth century
Hapdong	the Presbyterian Church in Korea and one of the two largest Presbyterian denominations
Jangno	church elder
Jeondosa	evangelist or trainee pastor
Jeonggamrok	the record of Jeonggam, which prophesied the imminent fall of the Joseon dynasty and the appearance of a deliverer, Jeong Do-ryang
Jipsa	church deacon
Joseon	the Korean state founded by the Yi dynasty in 1392 which lasted until 1897
Joseon Gyodan	*see* Gyodan
Juche	literally, 'self-reliance' and 'self-sufficiency'; the political philosophy of North Korea
Juche-kimilsungism	*see* Juche and Kimilsungism; the combined political philosophy and personality cult of North Korea
Jungin	the middle class
Kijang	Daehan Gidokgyo Jangnohoe; Presbyterian Church in the Republic of Korea
Kimilsungism	the North Korean cult of personality around the 'Great Leader', Kim Il-sung
Koshin	the Presbyterian Church in Korea
Minjok	the people or race
Minjung	the people or masses
Moksa	pastor
Mudang	shaman

Myeongdohoe	Society for Illumination of the Way; early Catholic leadership organisation
Namin	the 'Southerners' faction in the Korean court in late Joseon
Noron	the 'Old-learning' faction in the Korean court in late Joseon
Sadae	the attitude of 'serving the great'
Sangje	Lord on High
Sarangbang	outer quarters of a traditional Korean house where the men of the house entertained
Seongbun	'attitude'; a system of social division based on ideological purity in North Korea
Silhak	'true philosophy', 'practical learning' or 'relevant scholarship'; a school of thought in late Joseon
Sinbu	priest
Singanhoe	New Shoot Society; a Korean nationalist movement, 1927–1931
Sinminhoe	New People's Association founded by Ahn Chang-ho in 1907
Sunbogeum	'full' or 'pure gospel'; a term used by Holiness and Pentecostal Christians
Tonghap	the Presbyterian Church of Korea and one of the two largest Presbyterian denominations
Tongilgyo	the Unification Church (Moonies), founded in 1954 by Sun Myung Moon
Uibyeong	resistance armies; literally, 'righteous armies'
Yangban	aristocracy
Yushin	'Restoration' constitution imposed by President Park Chung-hee in October 1972

Bibliography

Adams, Daniel J. (1995), 'Church Growth in Korea: A Paradigm Shift from Ecclesiology to Nationalism', in Mark R. Mullins and Richard Fox Young (eds.), *Perspectives on Christianity in Korea and Japan*. Lewiston, NY: Edwin Mellen Press, 13–28.

Adams, Daniel J. (2012), *Korean Theology in Historical Perspective*. Delhi: ISPCK.

Ahn, Byung-mu (1981), 'Jesus and Minjung', in CTCCCA (Commission on Theological Concerns of the Christian Conference of Asia) (ed.), *Minjung Theology: People as the Subjects of History*. Singapore: Christian Conference of Asia, 138–52.

Ahn, Byung-mu (1989), 민중사건속의 그리스도 (*Christ in the Midst of the Minjung Event*). Seoul: Korea Theological Study Institute.

Ahn, Byung-mu (1990), *The Story of Minjung Theology*. Seoul: Korea Institute of Theology.

Ahn, Jong-cheol (2010), 미국선교사와 한미관계, 1931–1948 (*American Missionaries and Korean-American Relations, 1931–1948*). Seoul: Institute of the History of Christianity in Korea.

Ahn, Sang-jin (2001), *Continuity and Transformation: Religious Synthesis in East Asia*. New York: Peter Lang.

AKCSNA (Association of Korean Christian Scholars in North America) (ed.) (1993), 기독교와 주체사상: 조국통일을 위한 남북 해외 기독인과 주체사상가의 대화 (*Christian Faith and Juche Philosophy: Christian and Juchean Dialogue for Reunification of Motherland*). Seoul: Faith and Reason.

Anderson, Allan (2004a), *An Introduction to Pentecostalism: Global Charismatic Christianity*. Cambridge: Cambridge University Press.

Anderson, Allan (2004b), 'The Contextual Theology of David Yonggi Cho', in Wonsuk Ma, William W. Menzies and Hyeon-sung Bae (eds.), *David Yonggi Cho: A Close Look at His Theology and Ministry*. Baguio, Philippines: APTS Press, 133–59.

Armstrong, Charles K. (2004), *The North Korean Revolution, 1945–1950*. Ithaca, NY: Cornell University Press.

Armstrong, Charles K. (2007a), 'Introduction', in Charles K. Armstrong (ed.), *Korean Society: Civil Society, Democracy and the State*. 2nd edition. London: Routledge, 1–8.

Armstrong, Charles K. (2007b), 'Beyond the DMZ: The Possibility of Civil Society in North Korea', in Charles K. Armstrong (ed.), *Korean Society: Civil Society, Democracy and the State.* 2nd edition. London: Routledge, 187–203.

Bae, Hyeon-sung (2011), 'Full Gospel Theology and a Korean Pentecostal Identity', in Allan Anderson and Edmond Tang (eds.), *Asian and Pentecostal: The Charismatic Face of Christianity in Asia.* 2nd edition. Oxford: Regnum Books, 445–64.

Baird, Annie Laurie Adams (1909), *Daybreak in Korea: A Tale of Transformation in the Far East.* New York: Young People's Missionary Movement of the United States and Canada.

Baker, Don (1979), 'The Martyrdom of Paul Yun: Western Religion and Eastern Ritual in Eighteenth-Century Korea', *Transactions of the Royal Asiatic Society, Korea Branch*, no. 54, 33–58.

Baker, Don (1979–1980), 'A Confucian Confronts Catholicism: Truth Collides with Morality in Eighteenth-Century Korea', *Korean Studies Forum*, no. 6, 1–44.

Baker, Don (1981), 'The Use and Abuse of the Sirhak Label: A New Look at Sin Hu-dam and His Sŏhak Pyŏn', *Gyohoesa Yeongu*, no. 3, 183–254.

Baker, Don (1994), 'Monks, Medicine, and Miracles: Health and Healing in the History of Korean Buddhism', *Korean Studies*, vol. 18, 50–75.

Baker, Don (1997), 'From Pottery to Politics: The Transformation of Korean Catholicism', in Lewis R. Lancaster and Richard K. Payne (eds.), *Religion and Society in Contemporary Korea.* Berkeley: University of California Institute of East Asian Studies, 127–68.

Baker, Don (1999), 'Catholicism in a Confucian World', in JaHyun Kim Haboush and Martina Deuchler (eds.), *Culture and the State in Late Chosŏn Korea.* London: Harvard University Press, 199–230.

Baker, Don (2002), 'Hananim, Hanŭnim, Hanullim, and Hanŏllim: The Construction of Terminology for Korean Monotheism', *Review of Korean Studies* 5/1 (June), 105–31.

Baker, Don (2004), 'Tasan between Catholicism and Confucianism: A Decade under Suspicion, 1791 to 1801', *Tasan Hak*, no. 5, 55–86.

Baker, Don (2006a), 'Islam Struggling for a Toehold in Korea: Muslims in a Land Dominated by Monks and Ministers', *Harvard Asia Quarterly* X/1, 25–30.

Baker, Don (2006b), 'Sibling Rivalry in Twentieth-Century Korea', in Robert E. Buswell Jr. and Timothy S. Lee (eds.), *Christianity in Korea.* Honolulu: University of Hawaii, 283–308.

Baker, Don (2006c), 'The Religious Revolution in Modern Korean History: From Ethics to Theology and from Ritual Hegemony to Religious Freedom', *Review of Korean Studies* 9/3, 249–75.

Baker, Don (2007a), 'Introduction', in Robert E. Buswell Jr. (ed.), *Religions of Korea in Practice.* Princeton, NJ: Princeton University Press, 1–31.

Baker, Don (2007b), 'International Christian Network for Korea's Democratization', in *Democratic Movements and Korean Society: Historical Documents and Korean Studies*, Kim Dae-Jung Presidential Library and Museum. Seoul: Yonsei University, 133–61.

Baker, Don (2008), *Korean Spirituality*. Honolulu: University of Hawaii Press.

Baker, Don (2009), 'Tradition Modernized: Globalization and Korea's New Religions', in Chang Yun-shik, Hyun-ho Seok and Donald L. Baker (eds.), *Korea Confronts Globalization*. New York: Routledge, 206–24.

Baker, Kevin (2006), *A History of the Orthodox Church in China, Korea and Japan*. Lewiston, NY: Edwin Mellen Press.

Bang, Sang-keun (2006), 19 세기 중반 한국 교회사 연구 (*A Study of Mid-19th Century Korean Church History*). Seoul: Institute of Korean Church History.

Barrett, David B., George T. Kurian and Todd M. Johnson (2001), *World Christian Encyclopedia*, 2nd edition. Vol. 1: *The World by Countries: Religionists, Churches, Ministries*. Oxford: Oxford University Press.

Bautista, Julius and Francis Khek Gee Lim (eds.) (2009), *Christianity and the State in Asia: Complicity and Conflict*. London: Routledge.

Beal, Tim (2005), *North Korea: The Struggle against American Power*. London and Ann Arbor, MI: Pluto Press.

Belke, Thomas J. (1999), *Juche: A Christian Study of North Korea's State Religion*. Bartlesville, OK: Living Sacrifice Book.

Bell, Daniel A. and Hahm Chaibong (2003), *Confucianism for the Modern World*. Cambridge: Cambridge University Press.

Bergsten, C. Fred and Inbom Choi (eds.) (2003), *Korean Diaspora in the World Economy*. Washington, DC: Institute for International Economics.

BFBS (British and Foreign Bible Society) (1907). *The Leaves of the Tree: A Popular Illustrated Report of the British and Foreign Bible Society for the Year, 1906–1907*. London: Bible House.

BFMMEC (Board of Foreign Mission of the Methodist Episcopal Church) (2001), *Annual Report: Korea Mission, 1884–1942*. Seoul: IHCK.

Biernatzki, William E., Luke Jin-Chang Im and Anselm K. Min (1975), *Korean Catholicism in the 70s: A Christian Community Comes of Age*. Maryknoll, NY: Orbis Books.

Bierne, Paul (2009), *Su-un and His World of Symbols: The Founder of Korea's First Indigenous Religion*. Farnham: Ashgate.

Blair, William and Bruce Hunt (1977), *The Korean Pentecost and the Sufferings which Followed*. Edinburgh: Banner of Truth Trust.

Bluth, Christoph (2011), *Crisis on the Korean Peninsula*. Washington, DC: Potomac Books.

Bossy, John (1975), *English Catholic Community, 1570–1850*. London: Darton, Longman and Todd.

Briggs, John, Mercy Amba Oduyoye and Georges Tsetsis (eds.) (2004), *A History of the Ecumenical Movement*. Vol. 3: *1968–2000*. Geneva: World Council of Churches.

Brouwer, Steve, Paul Gifford and Susan D. Rose (1996), *Exporting the American Gospel: Global Christian Fundamentalism*. New York: Routledge.

Brown, Arthur Judson (1919), *The Mastery of the Far East: The Story of Korea's Transformation and Japan's Rise to Supremacy in the Orient*. New York: C. Scribner's Sons.

Brown, Frank L. (1916), 'The Sunday School Situation in China, Korea and Japan', *IRM* 5/4, 614–27.

Brown, G. Thompson (2008), *How Koreans Are Reconverting the West*. Philadelphia: Xlibris.

Brown, John (2009), *Witnessing Grace*, trans. Byun Joon-chang. Seoul: Presbyterian Church of Korea Publishing House.

Brunner, Edmund de Schweinitz (1928), 'Rural Korea: A Preliminary Survey of Economic, Social and Religious Conditions', in IMC (ed.), *The Christian Mission in Relation to Rural Problems: Report of the Jerusalem Meeting of the IMC*, vol. 6. London: Oxford University Press, 100–208.

Buswell Jr., Robert E. (ed.) (2007), *Religions of Korea in Practice*. Princeton, NJ: Princeton University Press.

Buswell Jr., Robert E. and Timothy S. Lee (eds.) (2006), *Christianity in Korea*. Honolulu: University of Hawaii.

Buzo, Adrian (2002), *The Making of Modern Korea*. London: Routledge.

Campbell, Arch (1957), *The Christ of the Korean Heart*. London: Christian Literature Crusade.

CCA (Churches of Christ in America) (1919), *The Korean Situation: Authentic Accounts of Recent Events by Eye Witnesses*. New York: Commission on Relations with the Orient of the Federal Council of the Churches of Christ in America.

CCA (Churches of Christ in America) (1920), *The Korean Situation*, vol. 2. New York: Commission on Relations with the Orient of the Federal Council of the Churches of Christ in America.

CEMK (Christian Ethics Movement of Korea) (2008), 2008년 한국교회의 사회적신뢰도 여론조사결과 발표세미나 (*Social Credibility of the Korean Churches, 2008: Seminar Revealing the Results of the Survey*). Seoul: Christian Ethics Movement of Korea.

Centenary Memorial Church (2010), 양화진의 진실I (*The Truth about Yanghwajin*). Seoul: Centenary Memorial Church.

Chai Soo-il (2003), 'Missio Dei – Its Development and Limitation in Korea', *IRM* 92/367, 538–49.

Chandra, Vipan (1988), *Imperialism, Resistance, and Reform in Late Nineteenth Century Korea: Enlightenment and the Independence Club*. Berkeley: Institute of East Asian Studies, University of California.

Chang, Dong-ha (2005), 개항기 한국사회와 천주교회 (*Korean Society and the Catholic Church in the Period of Opening*). Seoul: Catholic Publishing House.

Chang, Dong-ha (2006), 한국근대사와 천주교회 (*Korean Modern History and the Catholic Church*). Seoul: Catholic Publishing House.

Chang Dong-ha, Lee Ki-baek and Choe Ching-young (1972), *The Rule of the Taewŏn'gun, 1864–1873: Restoration in Yi Korea*. Cambridge, MA: East Asian Research Center, Harvard University.

Chang, Dong-min (2009), 'Crises and Prospects of Mission Schools in Contemporary Korea', in Jan A. B. Jongeneel, Peter Tze Ming Ng, Chong Ku Paek, Scott W. Sunquist and Yuko Watanabe (eds.), *Christian Mission and Education in Modern China, Japan, and Korea: Historical Studies*. Frankfurt-am-Main: Peter Lang, 141–53.

Chang, Paul Yun-sik (2006), 'Carrying the Torch in the Darkest Hours: The Sociopolitical Origins of Minjung Protestant Movements', in Robert E. Buswell Jr. and Timothy S. Lee (eds.), *Christianity in Korea*. Honolulu: University of Hawaii, 195–220.

Chang, Peter (2011), 'International Evangelical Student Mission Movement: UBF Case Study', in S. Hun Kim and Wonsuk Ma (eds.), *Korean Diaspora and Christian Mission*. Oxford: Regnum Books, 223–41.

Chang, Peter H. (2007), *The Salvation Army in Korea*. Seoul: Salvation Army Korea Territory.

Chang, Sung-jin (2005), 'Korean Bible Women: Their Vital Contribution to Korean Protestantism, 1895–1945', PhD thesis, University of Edinburgh.

Chang, Yun-shik (2009), 'Left and Right in South Korean Politics', in Chang Yun-shik, Hyun-ho Seok and Donald L. Baker (eds.), *Korea Confronts Globalization*. New York: Routledge, 173–91.

Chang, Yun-shik, Hyun-ho Seok and Donald L. Baker (eds.) (2009), *Korea Confronts Globalization*. New York: Routledge.

Cheong, Jae-yeong (2010), '탈북자의 사회의식' (Social Consciousness of North Korean Defectors), in Park Yeong-shin, Park Jong-so, Lee Beom-seong, Chung Jae-yeong and Cho Seong-don (eds.), 통일, 사회통합, 하나님나라 (*Unification, Social Integration and the Kingdom of God*). Seoul: Christian Literature Society, 113–40.

Cheong, Yak-jong (1986), 주교요지 (*Jukyeo Yeoji*). Seoul: St Joseph Press.

Chérel-Riquier, Evelyne (2003), 'Les Eglises chrétiennes et l'Etat en Corée du Sud (1945–1950): Naissance d'un lien de type symbiotique', paper presented at 1st Congress of Réseau Asie, 24–25 September, Paris.

Chérel-Riquier, Evelyne (2013), 'The South Korean Catholic Church's Attitude towards North Korea: From Antagonism to Development of Dialogue and Cooperation', *Journal of Korean Religions* 4/2, 67–92.

Cho, Chong-nahm John (1995), 'Sports Evangelism', in Ro Bong-rin and Marlin L. Nelson (eds.), *Korean Church Growth Explosion*, 2nd edition. Seoul: Word of Life Press, 156–69.

Cho, Dong-jin (1983), 'The Growth of Korean Missions and Its Contribution to World Evangelization', in Ro Bong-rin and Marlin L. Nelson (eds.), *Korean Church Growth Explosion*. Seoul: Word of Life Press, 103–26.

Cho, Kwang (1996a), 'The Chosŏn Governments's Measures against Catholicism', in Yu Chai-shin (ed.), *The Founding of Catholic Tradition in Korea*. Mississauga, ON: Korea and Related Studies Press, 103–13.

Cho, Kwang (1996b), 'The Meaning of Catholicism in Korean History', in Yu Chai-shin (ed.), *The Founding of Catholic Tradition in Korea*. Mississauga, ON: Korea and Related Studies Press, 115–40.

Cho, Kwang (2006), 'Human Relations as Expressed in Vernacular Catholic Writings of the Late Chosŏn Dynasty', trans. Timothy S. Lee, in Robert E. Buswell Jr. and Timothy S. Lee (eds.), *Christianity in Korea*. Honolulu: University of Hawaii, 29–37.

Cho, Kwang (2010a), 조선후기 사회와 천주교 (*Society and Catholicism in Late Joseon*). Seoul: Kyeungin Munhwsa.

Cho, Kwang (2010b), 한국 근현대 천주교사 연구 (*The Study on Modern Korean Catholic Christianity*). Seoul: Kyung-in Publishing.

Cho, Kwang, Jang Jeong-ran, Kim Jeong-suk and Song Jong-rye (2007), 순교자 강 완숙 역사를 위해 일어나다 (*Martyr Kang Wan-suk, Raised for History*). Seoul: Catholic Publishing.

Cho, Paul Han-sik (2010), *Eschatology and Ecology: Experiences of the Korean Church*. Oxford: Regnum Books.

Cho, Yong-gi (1977), *Threefold Blessing*. Seoul: Youngsan Publications.

Cho, Yong-gi (1979), *The Fourth Dimension*. Seoul: Logos.

Cho, Yong-gi (1989), *The Holy Spirit, My Senior Partner: Understanding the Holy Spirit and His Gifts*. Milton Keynes, Eng.: Word Publishing.

Choe, Ching-young (1972), *The Rule of the Taewŏn'gun, 1864–1873: Restoration in Yi Korea*. Cambridge, MA: East Asian Research Center, Harvard University.

Choi, Anne-soon (2008), 'To Determine Our Own Course': The Wilsonian Moment, Protestant Christianity, and Korean Students in the United States', *Acta Koreana* 11/3 (Dec.), 29–45.

Choi, Hee-an (2005), *Korean Women and God: Experiencing God in a Multi-religious Colonial Context*. Maryknoll, NY: Orbis Books.

Choi, Hyae-weol (2009), *Gender and Mission Encounters in Korea: New Women, Old Ways*. Berkeley: University of California Press.

Choi, Jai-keun (2006), *The Origin of the Roman Catholic Church in Korea: An Examination of Popular and Governmental Responses to Catholic Missions in the Late Chosôn Dynasty*. Cheltenham: Hermit Kingdom Press.

Choi, Jai-keun (2007), *The Korean Church under Japanese Colonialism*. Seoul: Jimmundang.

Choi [Ch'oe], Ki-bok (1988), 'Ancestor Worship: From the Perspective of Confucianism and Catholicism', in Jung-young Lee (ed.), *Ancestor Worship and Christianity in Korea*. Lewiston, NY: Edwin Mellen Press, 35–43.

Choi, Mee-saeng [Meesaeng] Lee (2008), *The Rise of Korea Holiness Church in Relation to the American Holiness Movement: Wesley's Scriptural Holiness and the Fourfold Gospel*. Lanham, MD: Scarecrow Press.

Choi, Seok-u [Ch'oe, Sŏk-u] (1967), 'Catholic Church and Modernization in Korea', *Korea Journal* 7/1, 4–9.

Choi, Seok-u [Ch'oe Sŏk-u] (1984), 'Korean Catholicism Yesterday and Today', *Korea Journal* 24/8, 4–13.

Choi, Seok-u (1991), 한국교회사의 탐구 II (*Research on Korean Church History* II). Seoul: Institute of Korean Church History.

Choi, Seok-u [Ch'oe, Sŏk-u] (1996), 'Korean Catholicism Yesterday and Today', in Yu Chai-shin (ed.), *The Founding of Catholic Tradition in Korea*. Mississauga, ON: Korean and Related Studies Press, 141–60.

Choi, Seok-u (2000), 한국교회사의 탐구 III (*Research on Korean Church History* III). Seoul: Institute of Korean Church History.

Choi, Sung-kyu (2004), *Hyo Theology*. Seoul: Sungsanseowon.

Choi, Young-keun (2010), 'The Great Revival in Korea, 1903–1907: Between Evangelical Aims and the Pursuit of Salvation in the National Crisis', *Korean Journal of Christian Studies* 72, 129–49.

Choi, Young-keun (2012), 'The Significance of Protestant Nationalism in Colonial Korea', *Korea Presbyterian Journal of Theology* 44/3, 11–35.

Choi, Young-woong (2002), 'The Mission of the Presbyterian Church of Korea in Shandong, North China, 1913–1957', in Klaus Koschorke (ed.), *Transcontinental Links in the History of Non-Western Christianity*. Wiesbaden: Harrassowitz Verlag, 117–30.

Chong, Kelly H. (2006), 'In Search of Healing: Evangelical Conversion of Women in Contemporary South Korea', in Robert E. Buswell Jr. and Timothy S. Lee (eds.), *Christianity in Korea*. Honolulu: University of Hawaii, 351–70.

Choo, Chai-yong (1998), 한국그리스도교 신학사 (*A History of Christian Theology in Korea*). Seoul: Christian Literature Society of Korea.

Chou, Fan-lan (1995), 'Bible Women and the Development of Education in the Korean Church', in Mark R. Mullins and Richard Fox Young (eds.), *Perspectives on Christianity in Korea and Japan*. Lewiston, NY: Edwin Mellen Press, 29–45.

Chryssides, George D. (1991), *The Advent of Sun Myung Moon: The Origins, Beliefs and Practices of the Unification Church*. London: Macmillan.

Chun, Chae-ok (2009), 'Rediscovering Ewha Mission and Its Contribution to Education', in Jan A. B. Jongeneel, Peter Tze Ming Ng, Chong Ku Paek, Scott W. Sunquist and Yuko Watanabe (eds.), *Christian Mission and Education in Modern China, Japan, and Korea: Historical Studies*. Frankfurt am Main: Peter Lang, 115–29.

Chun, Do-myung (2011), 'Kingdom-centred Identity: The Case of Bicultural Korean-Brazilians', in S. Hun Kim and Wonsuk Ma (eds.), *Korean Diaspora and Christian Mission*. Oxford: Regnum Books, 242–59.

Chung, Byeong-jun (2007), 호주장로회 선교사들의 신학사상과 한국선교, 1889–1942 (*Theology and Mission in Korea of Missionaries from the Australian Presbyterian Church, 1889–1942*). Seoul: Institute of the History of Christianity in Korea.

Chung, Chin-hwang (1983), 'Bible Studies and Laymen's Witness' in Ro Bong-rin and Marlin L. Nelson (eds.), *Korean Church Growth Explosion*. Seoul: Word of Life Press, 318–30.

Chung, David (2001), *Syncretism: The Religious Context of Christian Beginnings in Korea*. Albany: State University of New York Press.

Chung, Hyun-kyung (1988), '"Han-pu-ri": Doing Theology from a Korean Women's Perspective', *Ecumenical Review* 40/1 (Jan.), 27–36.

Chung, Hyun-kyung (1991a), 'Come, Holy Spirit – Renew the Whole Creation', in Michael Kinnamon (ed.), *Signs of the Spirit: Official Report of the Seventh Assembly of the WCC, Canberra*. Geneva: WCC, 37–47.

Chung, Hyun-kyung (1991b). *Struggle to Be the Sun Again: Introducing Asian Women's Theology*. London: SCM Press.

Chung, Mee-hyun (2006), 'Introducing Korean Feminist Theology', in Chung Mee-hyun (ed.), *Breaking Silence: Theology from Asian Women*. Delhi: ISPCK, 77–89.

Chung, Paul S., Veli-Matti Kärkkäinen and Kim Kyoung-Jae (eds.) (2007), *Asian Contextual Theology for the Third Millennium: Theology of Minjung in Fourth-Eye Formation*. Cambridge: James Clarke and Co.

Chung, Shung-han (2003), 한국기독교 통일 운동사 (*A History of Unification Movements in Korean Churches*). Seoul: Grisim.

Chung, Steve Lok-wai (2011), 'Peace Movements in South Korea and Their Impacts on the Politics of the Korean Peninsula', *Journal of Comparative Asian Development* 10/2, 253–80.

Clark, Allen D. (1971), *A History of the Church in Korea*. Seoul: Christian Literature Society.

Clark, Charles Allen (1930), *The Korean Church and the Nevius Methods*. New York: Fleming H. Revell.

Clark, Charles Allen (1934), 'The Missionary Work of the Presbyterian Church of Korea', in PCUSA (Presbyterian Church in the United States of America), *The Fiftieth Anniversary Celebration of the Korea Mission of the Presbyterian Church in the USA*. Seoul: John D. Wells School, 201–6.

Clark, Charles Allen (1937), *The Nevius Plan for Mission Work in Korea*. Seoul: CLS.

Clark, Donald N. (1986), *Christianity in Modern Korea*. Lanham, MD: University Press of America.

Clark, Donald N. (ed.) (1988), *The Kwangju Uprising: Shadows over the Regime in South Korea*. Boulder, CO: Westview Press.

Clark, Donald N. (1997), 'History and Religion in Modern Korea: The Case of Protestant Christianity', in Lewis R. Lancaster and Richard K. Payne (eds.), *Religion and Society in Contemporary Korea*. Berkeley: University of California Institute of East Asian Studies, 169–214.

Clark, Donald N. (2003), *Living Dangerously in Korea: The Western Experience, 1900–1950*. Norwalk, CT: EastBridge.

Clark, Donald N. (2006), 'Mothers, Daughters, Biblewomen, and Sisters: An Account of "Women's Work" in the Korea Mission Field', in Robert E. Buswell Jr. and Timothy S. Lee (eds.), *Christianity in Korea*. Honolulu: University of Hawaii, 167–92.

Clark, Donald N. (2007), 'Protestant Christianity and the State: Religious Organizations as Civil Society', in Charles K. Armstrong (ed.), *Korean Society: Civil Society, Democracy and the State*, 2nd edition. London: Routledge, 167–86.

Considine, John J. (1949), 'Missions of the Catholic Church, 1948', *IRM* 38/150, 165–80.

Corfe, C. J. (1905), *The Anglican Church in Corea*. Seoul: Seoul Press.

Cox, Harvey (1996), Fire from Heaven: *The Rise of Pentecostal Spirituality and the Reshaping of Religion in the Twenty-first Century*. London: Cassell.

CPCK (Council of Presbyterian Churches in Korea) (2000), 'Statement on the Mission of the Korean Churches in the New Millennium', *IRM* 89/353 (Apr.), 233–38.

CTCCCA (Commission on Theological Concerns of the Christian Conference of Asia) (ed.) (1981), *Minjung Theology: People as the Subjects of History*. Singapore: Christian Conference of Asia.

Cumings, Bruce (1988), *Korea: The Unknown War*. New York: Pantheon Books.

Cumings, Bruce (2003), 'Cold War Structures and Korea's Regional and Global Security', in Jang Jip Choi (ed.), *Post-Cold War and Peace: Experiences, Conditions and Choices*. Seoul: Asiatic Research Centre, 129–50.

Cumings, Bruce (2004), *North Korea: Another Country*. New York: New Press.

Cumings, Bruce (2005), *Korea's Place in the Sun: A Modern History*, 2nd edition. New York: W. W. Norton.

Cynn, Hugh Heung-woo (1920), *The Rebirth of Korea: The Awakening of the People, Its Causes, and the Outlook*. New York: Abingdon Press.

Dallet, Charles (1874a), Histoire de l'Église de Corée (*A History of the Church of Korea*), vol. 1. Paris: V. Palmé.

Dallet, Charles (1874b), Histoire de l'Église de Corée (*A History of the Church of Korea*), vol. 2. Paris: V. Palmé.

De Medina, Juan G. Ruiz (1991), *The Catholic Church in Korea: Its Origins, 1566–1784*. Rome: Istituto Storico.

Deuchler, Martina (1992), *The Confucian Transformation of Korea: A Study of Society and Ideology*. Cambridge, MA: Council on East Asian Studies, Harvard University.

Deuchler, Martina (1999), 'Despoilers of the Way – Insulters of the Sages: Controversies over the Classics in Seventeenth-Century Korea', in JaHyun Kim Haboush and Martina Deuchler (eds.), *Culture and the State in Late Chosŏn Korea*. London: Harvard University Press, 91–133.

Dixon, David N. (2012), 'The Second Text: Missionary Publishing and Bunyan's Pilgrim's Progress', *IBMR* 36/2 (Apr.), 86–90.

Eckert, Carter J., Ki-baik Lee, Young Ick Lew, Michael Robinson and Edward W. Wagner (eds.) (1990), *Korea, Old and New: A History*. Seoul: Ilchokak.

Ecklund, Elaine Howard (2006), *Korean American Evangelicals: New Models for Civic Life*. Oxford: Oxford University Press.

Elliott, Charles (1989), *Sword and Spirit: Christianity in a Divided World*. London: BBC Books.

England, John C. (1996), *The Hidden History of Christianity in Asia: The Churches of the East before the Year 1500*. Delhi: ISPCK and CCA.

England, John C., Jose Kuttianimattathil and John M. Prior (2004), *Asian Christian Theologies: A Research Guide to Authors, Movements, Sources*. Vol. 3: *Northeast Asia*. Delhi: ISPCK.

Fairbank, John K. (ed.) (1968), *The Chinese World Order: Traditional China's Foreign Relations*. Cambridge, MA: Harvard University Press.

Farhadian, Charles E. (2007), *Christian Worship Worldwide: Expanding Horizons, Deepening Practices*. Grand Rapids, MI: Wm B. Eerdmans.

Fey, Harold E. (ed.) (1993), *The Ecumenical Advance: A History of the Ecumenical Movement*. Vol. 2: *1948–1968*. Geneva: World Council of Churches.

Finch, Andrew J. (2000), 'A Persecuted Church: Roman Catholicism in Early Nineteenth-Century Korea', *Journal of Ecclesiastical History* 51/3 (July), 556–80.

Finch, Andrew J. (2008), 'A Necessary and Fruitful Labour: The Société des Missions Étrangères de Paris and the Formation of a Native Clergy in Korea', *Historical Research* 81/212, 280–91.

Finch, Andrew J. (2009), 'The Pursuit of Martyrdom in the Catholic Church in Korea before 1866', *Journal of Ecclesiastical History* 60/1, 95–118.

Finch, Paul (2007), *North Korea: The Paranoid Peninsula: A Modern History.* London: Zed Books.

Fisher, James Earnest (1928), 'Democracy and Mission Education in Korea'. PhD diss., Columbia University.

Flake, L. Gordon and Scott Snyder (eds.) (2003), *Paved with Good Intentions: The NGO Experience in North Korea.* Westport, CT: Praeger.

Foley, James A. (2003), *Korea's Divided Families: Fifty Years of Separation.* London: Routledge.

Gale, James Scarth (1909), *Korea in Transition.* New York: Eaton and Mains.

Gale, James Scarth (1924), *A History of the Korean People.* Seoul.

Gibson, Ralph (1989), *A Social History of French Catholicism, 1989–1914.* London: Routledge.

Gil, Soo-han (1994), *Social Sources of Church Growth: Korean Churches in the Homeland and Overseas.* Lanham, MD: University Press of America.

Goh, Moo-song (2001), 토마스와 함께 떠나는 순례여행: 토마스목사의 생애와 선교사역에 관한 연구 (*A Study of the Life and Missionary Work of Robert J. Thomas*). Seoul: Qumran.

Gordon, E. A. (1921), *Asian Christology and the Mahayana.* Tokyo: Maruzen.

Gray, Mark, Melissa Cidade, Mary Gautier and Thomas Gaunt (2013), *Cultural Diversity in the Catholic Church in the United States.* Washington DC: Center for Applied Research in the Apostolate (CARA) at Georgetown University.

Grayson, James H. (1985), *Early Buddhism and Christianity in Korea: A Study in the Emplanatation of Religion.* Leiden: E. J. Brill.

Grayson, James H. (1995), 'Dynamic Complementarity: Korean Confucianism and Christianity' in Richard H. Roberts (ed.), *Religion and the Transformations of Capitalism: Comparative Approaches.* London: Routledge, 76–87.

Grayson, James H. (1999), 'The Legacy of John Ross', *IBMR* 23/4, 167–72.

Grayson, James H. (2001), 'Cultural Encounter: Korean Protestantism and Other Religious Traditions', *IBMR* 25/2, 66–72.

Grayson, James H. (2002), *Korea – A Religious History*, revised edition. Abingdon, Oxon: RoutledgeCurzon.

Grayson, James H. (2006), 'A Quarter-Millennium of Christianity in Korea', in Robert E. Buswell Jr. and Timothy S. Lee (eds.), *Christianity in Korea.* Honolulu: University of Hawaii, 7–25.

Grayson, James H. (2007), 'The Grieving Rite: A Protestant Response to Confucian Ancestral Rituals', in Robert E. Buswell Jr. (ed.), *Religions of Korea in Practice.* Princeton, NJ: Princeton University Press, 434–45.

Grayson, James H. (2011), 'Montanism and the "Empire of Mount Sion": Lessons from the Early Church and the Early Korean Church', *Journal of Korean Religions* 2/2, 83–110.

Griffis, William Elliot (1894), *Corea the Hermit Nation*. New York: American Book Co.

Gützlaff, Karl Friedrich (1834), *Journal of Three Voyages along the Coast of China in 1831, 1832 and 1833, with Notices of Siam, Corea, and the Loo-Choo Islands*. London: Frederick Westley and A. H. Davis.

Haboush, JaHyun Kim (1999), 'Constructing the Center: The Ritual Controversy and the Search for a New Identity in Seventeenth-Century Korea', in JaHyun Kim Haboush and Martina Deuchler (eds.), *Culture and the State in Late Chosŏn Korea*. London: Harvard University Press, 46–90.

Haboush, JaHyun Kim and Martina Deuchler (eds.) (1999), *Culture and the State in Late Chosŏn Korea*. London: Harvard University Press.

Ham, Sok-hon (1985), *Queen of Suffering: A Spiritual History of Korea*, trans. E. Sang Yu. London: Friends World Committee for Consultation.

Hamilton, Ian (1990), *The Erosion of Calvinistic Orthodoxy*. Edinburgh: Rutherford House.

Han, Chul-ha (1983), 'Involvement of the Korean Church in the Evangelization of Asia', in Ro Bong-rin and Marlin L. Nelson (eds.), *Korean Church Growth Explosion*. Seoul: Word of Life Press, 51–68.

Han, Chul-ho (2011), 'Mission Korea: The Contribution of Global Youth Mobilization', in S. Hun Kim and Wonsuk Ma (eds.), *Korean Diaspora and Christian Mission*. Oxford: Regnum Books, 164–70.

Han, Gil-soo, Joy J. Han and Andrew Eun-gi Kim (2009), '"Serving Two Masters": Protestant Churches in Korea and Money', *International Journal for the Study of the Christian Church* 9/4, 333–60.

Han, Gyu-mu (1997), 일제하 한국기독교농촌운동 1925–1937 (*Korean Christian Farmers Movement under Japanese Occupation, 1925–1937*). Seoul: Institute of the History of Christianity in Korea.

Han, Kyung-chik (1983), 'The Present and Future of the Korean Church', in Ro Bong-rin and Marlin L. Nelson (eds.), *Korean Church Growth Explosion*. Seoul: Word of Life Press, 348–70.

Han, Kyung-chik (2002), *May the Words of My Mouth*. Seoul: Youngnak Church.

Han, Kyung-chik (2010a), 한경직구술 자서전: 나의 감사 (*Autobiography of Han Kyung-chik: My Thanksgiving*). Seoul: Duranno.

Han, Kyung-chik (2010b), 'Christianity and the Foundation of the Nation', in Kim Eun-seop (ed.), *Kyung-chik Han Collection: Sermons 1*. Seoul: Kyung-chik Han Foundation, 408–20.

Han, Soong-hong (1996a), 한국신학사상의 흐름 (상) (*Trends of Korean Theological Thought I*). Seoul: PCTS Press.

Han, Soong-hong (1996b), 한국신학사상의 흐름 (하) (*Trends of Korean Theological Thought II*). Seoul: PCTS Press.

Han, Wan-sang (1981), 한국교회 이대로 좋은가 (*What's the Problem with the Korean Church?*). Seoul: Korean Christian Press.

Han, Wan-sang (2008), 예수없는 예수교회 (*The Jesus Church without Jesus*). Pajusi, Kyeunggi-do: Gimmyyoungsa.

Hanson, Eric O. (1980), *Catholic Politics in China and Korea*. Maryknoll, NY: Orbis Books.

Hardacre, Helen (1989), *Shintō and the State, 1868–1988*. Princeton, NJ: Princeton University Press.

Harvey, Young-sook Kim (1979), *Six Korean Women: The Socialization of Shamans*. St Paul, MN: West Publishing.

Heo, Ho-ik (2009a), 귀츨라프의생애와 조선선교활동 (*The Life of Gützlaff and His Mission Activities in Joseon*). Seoul: Institute of the History of Christianity in Korea.

Heo, Ho-ik (2009b), 길선주목사의 목회와 신학사상 (*The Ministry and Theological Thought of Gil Seon-ju*). Seoul: Christian Literature Society of Korea.

Heo, Myung-sup (2009), 허명섭, 해방이후 한국교회의 재형성 1945–1960 (*The Restructuring of the Korean Church after the Liberation of Korea, 1945–1960*). Seoul: Institute for the Study of Modern Christianity.

Hoare, J. E. and Susan Pares (2005), *North Korea in the 21st Century: An Interpretive Guide*. Folkestone: Global Oriental.

Hoffman, Diane M. (1995), 'Blurred Genders: The Cultural Construction of Male and Female in South Korea', *Korean Studies* 19, 112–38.

Hogarth, Hyun-key Kim (1999), *Korean Shamanism and Cultural Nationalism*. Seoul: Jimoondang.

Hong, Sung-wook (2008), *Naming God in Korea: The Case of Protestant Christianity*. Oxford: Regnum.

Hong, Young-gi (2007), 'Evangelism and Church Growth: Research on Non-Believers for Developing an Evangelizing Strategy in the Korean Context and the Diamond Evangelistic System', *IRM* 96/382–83, 221–47.

Hulbert, Homer B. (1905), *A History of Korea*, in 2 vols. Seoul: Curzon Press.

Hulbert, Homer B. (1906), *The Passing of Korea*. New York: Doubleday, Page and Co.

Hulbert, Homer B. (1907), *The Japanese in Korea: Extracts from the Korea Review*. Seoul.

Hunt Jr., Everett N. (1980), *Protestant Pioneers in Korea*. Maryknoll, NY: Orbis Books.

Huntley, Martha (1984), *Caring, Growing, Changing: A History of the Protestant Mission in Korea*. New York: Friendship Press.

Hurston, John W. and Karen L. Hurston (1977), *Caught in the Web: The Home Cell Unit System at Full Gospel Central Church, Seoul, Korea*. Seoul: Church Growth International.

Hutchison, Wm R. (1987), *Errand to the World: American Protestant Thought and Foreign Missions*. Chicago: University of Chicago Press.

Hwang Hong-eyoul (2003), 'Searching for a New Paradigm of Church and Mission in a Secularized and Postmodern Context in Korea', *IRM* 92/364, 84–97.

Hwang, Jae-buhm (2007), 'A New Confession of Faith with an Eco-Theology and a Father-Centred Trinitarianism: A Critical Study of the 21st Century

Confession of Faith of the Presbyterian Church of Korea', *IRM* 96/380–81, 128–41.

Hwang, Sa-yeong (1998), 황사영백서 (*Hwang Sa-yeong Letter*), trans. Kim Yeong-su. Seoul: St Joseph Press.

IHCK (Institute of the History of Christianity in Korea) (1996), 북한교회사 (*A History of the North Korean Church*). Seoul: Institute of the History of Christianity in Korea.

IHCK (Institute of the History of Christianity in Korea) (2009), 한국기독교의역사 III (*A History of Korean Church* III). Seoul: Institute of Korean Church History Studies.

IKCH (Institute of Korean Church History) (2009), 한국천주교회사 1 (*Korean Catholic History* 1). Seoul: Institute of Korean Church History.

IKCH (Institute of Korean Church History) (2010a), 한국천주교회사 2 (*Korean Catholic History* 2). Seoul: Institute of Korean Church History.

IKCH (Institute of Korean Church History) (2010b), 한국천주교회사 3 (*Korean Catholic History* 3). Seoul: Institute of Korean Church History.

IKCH (Institute of Korean Church History) (2011), 한국천주교회사 4 (*Korean Catholic History* 4). Seoul: Institute of Korean Church History.

IKCHS (Institute of Korean Church History Studies) (1989), 한국기독교의역사 I (*A History of Korean Church* I). Seoul: Christian Literature Press.

IKCHS (Institute of Korean Church History Studies) (1990), 한국기독교의역사 II (*A History of Korean Church* II). Seoul: Christian Literature Press.

Im, Hyug-baeg (2006), 'Christian Churches and Democratization in South Korea', in Tun-Jen Cheng and Deborah A. Brown, *Religious Organizations and Democratization: Case Studies from Contemporary Asia*. New York: M. E. Sharpe, 136–56.

IMC (International Missionary Council) (1932), 'The Missionary Significance of the Last Ten Years: A Survey', *IRM* 21/1, 3–105.

IMC (International Missionary Council) (1937), 'Survey of the Year 1936', *IRM* 26/1, 3–106.

IMC (International Missionary Council) (1938), 'Survey of the Year 1937', *IRM* 27/1, 3–101.

IMC (International Missionary Council) (1942), 'Survey of the Year 1941', *IRM* 31/1, 3–97.

IMC (International Missionary Council) (1949), 'Survey of the Year 1948', *IRM* 38/149, 3–74.

IMC (International Missionary Council) (1951), 'Survey of the Year 1950' *IRM* 40/157, 3–78.

Iraola, Antton Egiguren (2007), *True Confucians, Bold Christians: Korean Missionary Experience – A Model for the Third Millennium*. Amsterdam: Rodopi.

IRM (*International Review of Mission*) (1953), 'Survey of the Year 1952', *IRM* 42/1, 3–70.

IRM (*International Review of Mission*) (2008), 'Bringing Together Ubuntu and Sangsaeng: A Journey Towards Life-Giving Civilization, Transforming Theology and the Ecumenism of the 21st Century', *IRM* 97/384–85, 129–34.

Janelli, Roger L. and Dawnhee Yim Janelli (1982). *Ancestor Worship and Korean Society*. Stanford, CA: Stanford University Press.

Janelli, Roger L. and Dawnhee Yim Janelli (2005), 'The Cyberspace Frontier in Korean Studies', Association for Korean Studies in Europe 2005 Biennial Conference Keynote Address.

Jang, Suk-man (2004), 'Historical Currents and Characteristics of Korean Protestantism after Liberation', *Korea Journal*, 133–56.

Jeong, Chong-hee (2011), 'The Korean Charismatic Movement as Indigenous Pentecostalism', in Allan Anderson and Edmond Tang (eds.), *Asian and Pentecostal: The Charismatic Face of Christianity in Asia*. 2nd edition. Oxford: Regnum Books, 465–82.

Jeong, Ha-sang (1999), 상재상서 (*Defence of the Catholic Faith*), trans. Yun Min-gu. Seoul: St Joseph Press.

Ji, Won-yong (1965), 'Christian Church and Sects in Korea', *Korea Journal*, 4–11.

Ji, Won-yong (1991), *A History of Lutheranism in Korea: A Personal Account*. St Louis, MO: Concordia Seminary.

Jo, Yoong-hee (2006), 'The Relationship between Joseon Envoys and Western Missionaries in Beijing in the Early 18th Century: Focusing on Lee Gi-ji's Iramyeon-gi', *Review of Korean Studies* 9/4, 33–43.

Johnson, Todd M. and Kenneth R. Ross (eds.) (2009), *Atlas of Global Christianity*. Edinburgh: Edinburgh University Press.

Jorgensen, John (1998), 'Who Was the Author of the Tan'gun Myth?', in Sang-Oak Lee and Duk-soo Park (eds.), *Perspectives on Korea*. Sydney: Wild Peony, 222–55.

Jun, David Chul-han (2011), 'A South Korean Case Study of Migrant Ministries', in S. Hun Kim and Wonsuk Ma (eds.), *Korean Diaspora and Christian Mission*. Oxford: Regnum Books, 207–22.

Jung, Jin-heon (2013), 'North Korean Refugees and the Politics of Evangelical Mission in the Sino-Korean Border Area', *Journal of Korean Religions* 4/2, 147–73.

Kang, David C. (2010), *East Asia before the West: Five Centuries of Trade and Tribute*. New York: Columbia University Press.

Kang, Don-ku (1999), 'The Transmission of Christianity and Reception of Western Philosophy in Korea', *Korea Journal* 39/1, 198–223.

Kang, In-cheol (2004), 'Protestant Church and Wolnamin: An Explanation of Protestant Conservatism in South Korea', *Korea Journal* (Winter), 157–90.

Kang, In-cheol (2006), 한국의 개신교와 반공주의 (*Korean Protestant Church and Anti-Communism*). Seoul: Jungsim.

Kang, Man-gil (2005), *A History of Contemporary Korea*. Folkestone: Global Oriental.

Kang, S. Steve and Megan A. Hackman (2012), 'Toward a Broader Role in Mission: How Korean Americans' Struggle for Identity Can Lead to a Renewed Vision for Mission', *IBMR* 36/2, 72–76.

Kang, Sa-moon (1995), 'The Problem of the Application of Jubilee Law to 50th Anniversary of Liberation', in Korean Association for Christian Studies (ed.), *50th Anniversary of Liberation and Jubilee*. Seoul: Kamshin, 47–82.

Kang, Wi-jo (1987), *Religion and Politics in Korea under the Japanese Rule*. Lewiston, NY: Edwin Mellen Press.

Kang, Wi-jo (1990), 'Korean Minority Church-State Relations in the People's Republic of China', *IBMR* 14/2, 77–82.

Kang, Wi-jo (1997), *Christ and Caesar in Modern Korea: A History of Christianity and Politics*. New York: State University of New York.

Kang, Wi-jo (2006), 'Church and State Relations in the Japanese Colonial Period', in Robert E. Buswell Jr. and Timothy S. Lee (eds.), *Christianity in Korea*. Honolulu: University of Hawaii, 97–115.

Kang, Woong-jo (2005), *The Korean Struggle for International Identity in the Foreground of the Schufeldt Negotiation, 1866–1882*. Lanham, MD: University Press of America.

Karlsson, Anders (2000), *The Hong Kyŏngnae Rebellion, 1811–1812: Conflict Between Central Power and Local Society in 19th-Century Korea*. Stockholm: Stockholm University.

Katsiaficas, George (2012), *Asia's Unknown Uprisings*. Vol. 1: *South Korean Social Movements in the 20th Century*. Oakland, CA: PM Press.

Kawashima, Ken C. (2009), *The Proletarian Gamble: Korean Workers in Interwar Japan*. Durham, NC: Duke University Press.

KDF (Korea Democracy Foundation) (2009), 한국민주화운동사 2 (*A History of Democracy Movement in Korea* 2). Seoul: Dolbegae.

KDF (Korea Democracy Foundation) (2010), 한국민주화운동사 3 (*A History of Democracy Movement in Korea* 3). Seoul: Dolbegae.

Kendall, Laurel (1985), *Shamans, Housewives, and Other Restless Spirits: Women in Korean Ritual Life*. Honolulu: University of Hawaii Press.

Kendall, Laurel (2009), *Shamans, Nostalgias, and the IMF: South Korean Popular Religion in Motion*. Honolulu: University of Hawaii Press.

Keum, Jang-tae (1996), 'The Doctrinal Disputes between Confucianism and Western Thought in the Late Chosŏn Period', in Yu Chai-shin (ed.), *The Founding of Catholic Tradition in Korea*. Mississauga, ON: Korean and Related Studies Press, 7–44.

Keum, Jang-tae (2000), *Confucianism and Korean Thoughts*. Seoul: Jimoondang.

Kim, Byong-suh (1985), 'The Explosive Growth of the Korean Church Today: A Sociological Analysis', *IRM* 74/293, 59–72.

Kim, Byong-suh (2006), 'Modernization and the Explosive Growth and Decline of Korean Protestant Religiosity', in Robert E. Buswell Jr. and Timothy S. Lee (eds.), *Christianity in Korea*. Honolulu: University of Hawaii Press, 309–29.

Kim, Byoung-lo Philo (1992), *Two Koreas in Development: A Comparative Strategy of Principles and Strategies of Capitalist and Communist Third World Development*. New Brunswick, NJ: Transaction Publishers.

Kim, Chang-in (1983), 'A Church in Middle Class Suburbia: Secrets of Growth in the Chung Hyeon Presbyterian Church', in Ro Bong-rin and Marlin L. Nelson (eds.), *Korean Church Growth Explosion*. Seoul: Word of Life Press, 245–58.

Kim, Chi-ha (1978), *The Gold-Crowned Jesus and Other Writings*. Maryknoll, NY: Orbis Books.

Kim, Chong-bum (2006), 'Preaching the Apocalypse in Colonial Korea: The Protestant Millennialism of Kil Sŏn-ju', in Robert E. Buswell Jr. and Timothy S. Lee (eds.), *Christianity in Korea*. Honolulu: University of Hawaii, 149–66.

Kim, Chong-bum (2008), 'For God and Home: Women's Education in Early Korean Protestantism', *Acta Koreana* 11/3, 9–28.

Kim, Chong-ho (2003), *Korean Shamanism: The Cultural Paradox*. Aldershot, Hants: Ashgate.

Kim, Djun-kil (2005), *The History of Korea*. London: Greenwood Press.

Kim, German (2003), 'Koryo Saram, or Koreans of the Former Soviet Union', *Amerasia Journal* 29/3, 23–29.

Kim, Gui-ok (2004), 이산가족: 이산가족 문제를 보는 새로운 시각 (*Separated Families: New Perspective on the Problem*). Seoul: Yeoksa Bipyeongsa.

Kim, Ha-gen (2001), *Korean Workers: The Culture and Politics of Class Formation*. Ithaca, NY: Cornell University Press.

Kim, Henry (2008), *Ethno-religious Perpetuity? Religious Internalization and Second-Generation Korean Americans*. Saarbrücken: DDM Merlag Dr. Müller.

Kim, Heung-soo (ed.) (1992), 해방후북한교회사 (*A History of the North Korean Church since 1945*). Seoul: Dasangeulbang.

Kim, Heung-soo (2003a), *Documents of the WCC Library: The Korean War*. Seoul: Institute for Korean Church History.

Kim, Heung-soo (2003b), *Documents of the WCC Library: Chosŏn Christian Federation*. Seoul: Institute for Korean Church History.

Kim, Heung-soo (2005), '한국전쟁시기 기독교 외인단체의 구호활동' (Relief Activities of Foreign Christian Voluntary Agencies during the Korean War), 한국기독교와 역사 (*Korean Christianity and History*), vol. 23, 97–124.

Kim, Heung-soo and Ryu Dae-young (2002), 북한종교의 새로운 이해 (*Religion in North Korea: A New Understanding*). Seoul: Dasan Press.

Kim, Hyun-sik (2008), 'Reflections on North Korea: The Psychological Foundation of the North Korean Regime', *IBMR* 32/1, 22–26.

Kim, Ig-jin (2003), *History and Theology of Korean Pentecostalism: Sunbogeum (Pure Gospel) Pentecostalism*. Zoetermeer: Uitgeverij Boekencentrum.

Kim, In-soo (1996), *Protestants and the Formation of Modern Korean Nationalism, 1885–1920: A Study of the Contributions of Horace G. Underwood and Sun Chu Kil*. New York: Peter Lang.

Kim, In-soo (1997), 한국 기독교회의 역사 (*History of the Christian Church in Korea*). Seoul: PCTS Press.

Kim, Jin-wung (2012), *A History of Korea: From 'Land of the Morning Calm' to States in Conflict*. Bloomington: Indiana University Press.

Kim, Jonah N. (1992), 일사각오 (*A Determination to Risk One's Life*). Seoul: Research Mission of Christians' Biographies in Korea.

Kim, Joon-gon (1983), 'Korea's Total Evangelization Movement', in Ro Bong-rin and Marlin L. Nelson (eds.), *Korean Church Growth Explosion*. Seoul: Word of Life Press, 17–50.

Kim, Joseph Chang-mun and John Jae-sun Chung (eds.) (1964), *Catholic Korea: Yesterday and Today*. Seoul: Catholic Korea Publishing.

Kim, Julia (1992), *Miracle in Naju, Korea: Heaven Speaks to the World*, trans. Sang M. Lee. Gresham, OR: Mary's Touch By Mail.

Kim, Jung-ha (1997), *Bridge-Makers and Cross-Bearers: Korean-American Women and the Church*. Atlanta: Scholars Press.

Kim, Kirsteen (2006), 'Holy Spirit Movements in Korea – Paternal or Maternal? Reflections on the Analysis of Ryu Tong-Shik (Yu Tong-Shik)', *Exchange* 35/2, 147–68.

Kim, Kirsteen (2007a), 'Ethereal Christianity: Reading Korean Church Websites', *Studies in World Christianity* 13/3, 208–24.

Kim, Kirsteen (2007b), *The Holy Spirit in the World: A Global Conversation*. Maryknoll, NY: Orbis Books.

Kim, Kirsteen (2008), 'Reconciliation in Korea: Models from Korean Christian Theology: Humanization, Healing, Harmonization, Hanpuri', *Missionalia* 35/1, 15–33.

Kim, Kirsteen (2010), 'Christianity's Role in the Modernization and Revitalization of Korean Society in the Twentieth-Century', *International Journal of Public Theology* 4/2, 212–36.

Kim, Kirsteen (2012), *Joining in with the Spirit: Connecting World Church and Local Mission*. London: SCM Press.

Kim, Kwang-ok (1997), 'Ritual Forms and Religious Experiences: Protestant Christians in Contemporary Korean Political Context', in Lewis R. Lancaster and Richard K. Payne (eds.), *Religion and Society in Contemporary Korea*. Berkeley: University of California Institute of East Asian Studies, 215–48.

Kim, Kwan-sik (1947), 'The Christian Church in Korea', *IRM* 36/2, 125–40.

Kim, Kyeong-jin (2012), 'The Context, Contour and Contents of the Worship of the Korean Church', *Korea Presbyterian Journal of Theology* 44/3, 65–92.

Kim, Myeong-bae (2009), 해방후 한국기독교사회운동사 (*Social Movements of the Korean Church Post-Independence*). Seoul: Book Korea.

Kim, Myong-hi (1992), 'The Situation and Problems of Korean Women Ministers', *In God's Image* 11/2 (Summer), 10–18.

Kim, Myung-hyuk (1983), 'Korean Mission in the World Today and Its Problems', in Ro Bong-rin and Marlin L. Nelson (eds.), *Korean Church Growth Explosion*. Seoul: Word of Life Press, 127–34.

Kim, Myung-hyuk (1988), 'Ancestor Worship: From the Perspective of Korean Church History', in Jung-young Lee (ed.), *Ancestor Worship and Christianity in Korea*. Lewiston, NY: Edwin Mellen Press, 21–34.

Kim, Nyung (1993), 'The Politics of Religion in South Korea, 1974–1989: The Catholic Church's Political Opposition to the Authoritarian State'. PhD diss., University of Washington.

Kim, Ok-hy (1984), 'Women in the History of Catholicism in Korea', *Korea Journal*, 28–40.

Kim, S. Hun (2011), 'Migrant Workers and "Reverse Mission" in the West', in S. Hun Kim and Wonsuk Ma (eds.), *Korean Diaspora and Christian Mission*. Oxford: Regnum Books, 146–52.

Kim, S. Hun and Wonsuk Ma (eds.) (2011), *Korean Diaspora and Christian Mission*. Oxford: Regnum Books.

Kim, Samuel S. (2006), *The Two Koreas and the Great Powers*. Cambridge: Cambridge University Press.

Kim, Sebastian C. H. (2007), 'The Problem of Poverty in Post-war Korean Christianity: Kibock Sinang or Minjung Theology?', *Transformation* 24/1, 43–50.

Kim, Sebastian C. H. (2008a), 'The Word and the Spirit: Overcoming Poverty, Injustice and Division in Korea', in Sebastian C. H. Kim (ed.), *Christian Theology in Asia*. Cambridge: Cambridge University Press, 129–53.

Kim, Sebastian C. H. (2008b), 'Reconciliation Possible? The Churches' Efforts toward the Peace and Reconciliation of North and South Korea', in Sebastian C. H. Kim, Pauline Kollontai and Greg Hoyland (eds.), *Peace and Reconciliation: In Search of Shared Identity*. Aldershot, Hants: Ashgate, 161–95.

Kim, Sebastian C. H. (2013), 'Contemporary Korean Christianity in Economics, Politics and Public Life', *Theologia Viatorum* 37/1, 26–49.

Kim, Sebastian C. H. and Kirsteen Kim (2008), *Christianity as a World Religion*. London: Continuum.

Kim, Seong-tae (ed.) (1991), 한국 기독교와 신사참배문제 (*The Korean Church and the Problem of Shinto Worship*). Seoul: Institute of the History of Christianity in Korea.

Kim, Seong-tae (1994), 한국기독교의 역사적반성 (*Historical Reflection of Korean Church*). Seoul: Dasan Geulbang.

Kim, Seong-tae (2006), 한말. 일제 강점기 선교사 연구, 1884–1942 (*Protestant Missionaries in Korea during Japanese Occupation, 1884–1942*). Seoul: Institute of the History of Christianity in Korea.

Kim, Seung-jin (2000), 'The Beginning of Southern Baptist Work in Korea', *Korea Journal of Theology*, vol. 2, 269–87.

Kim, Sharon (2010), *A Faith of Our Own: Second-Generation Spirituality in Korean American Churches*. New Brunswick, NJ: Rutgers University Press.

Kim, Sou-hwan (2009), 추기경 김수환 이야기 (*The Story of Cardinal Kim Sou-hwan*). Seoul: Pyeonghwa Broadcasting.

Kim, Su-jin and Noh Nam-do (2007), 어둠을 밝힌 한국교회와 대각성운동 (*The Emerging Korean Church and the Great Revival Movement*). Seoul: Qumran.

Kim, Sung-gun (2011), 'Korean Christian Zionism: A Sociological Study of Mission', *IRM* 100/1, 85–95.

Kim, Sung-hae (2008), 'The New Religions of Korea and Christianity', in Kim Sung-hae and James Heisig (eds.), *Encounters: The New Religions of Korea and Christianity*. Seoul: Royal Asiatic Society, 1–29.

Kim, Sung-hae and James Heisig (eds.) (2008a), *Encounters: The New Religions of Korea and Christianity*. Seoul: Royal Asiatic Society.

Kim, Sung-hae and James W. Heisig (eds.) (2008b), *Monasticism – Buddhist and Christian: The Korean Experience*, English translation. Leuven: Peeters.

Kim, Sun-hyuk (2007), 'Civil Society and Democratization in South Korea', in Charles K. Armstrong (ed.), *Korean Society: Civil Society, Democracy and the State*. 2nd edition. London: Routledge, 53–72.

Kim, Won-il (2006), 'Minjung Theology's Biblical Hermeneutics: An Examination of Minjung Theology's Appropriation of the Exodus Account', in Robert E. Buswell Jr. and Timothy S. Lee (eds.), *Christianity in Korea*. Honolulu: University of Hawaii, 221–37.

Kim, Yang-sun (1956), 한국기독교해방십년사 (*A History of the First Ten Years of the Korean Church Post-Independence*). Seoul: General Assembly of the Presbyterian Church of Korea.

Kim, Yang-sun (2004), 'Compulsory Shinto Shrine Worship and Persecution', in Chai-shin Yu (ed.), *Korea and Christianity*. Seoul: Korean Scholar Press, 87–120.

Kim, Yeong-myeong (2008), 정경옥: 한국감리교신학의 개척자 (*Jeong Gyeong-ok: Pioneer of Korean Methodist Theology*). Seoul: Sallim Books.

Kim, Yeong-su (ed.) (2000), 천주가사자료집 (상) (*Collection of Catholic Hymns I*), Seoul: Catholic University Press.

Kim, Yong-bock (1981a), 'Korean Christianity as a Messianic Movement of the People', in CTCCCA (Commission on Theological Concerns of the Christian Conference of Asia) (ed.), *Minjung Theology: People as the Subjects of History*. Singapore: Christian Conference of Asia, 80–119.

Kim, Yong-bock (1981b), 'Messiah and Minjung: Discerning Messianic Politics Over Against Political Messianism', in CTCCA (Commission on Theological Concerns of the Christian Conference of Asia (ed.), *Minjung Theology: People as the Subjects of History*. Singapore: Christian Conference of Asia, 183–93.

Kim, Young-dong (2010), '반기독교운동의 도전과 선교' (The Challenge of the Anti-Christian Movement and Its Missiological Countermeasure of the Korean Church), *Janshin Nondan* 38, 357–79.

Kim, Young-Jae (1992), 한국교회사 (*A History of Korean Church*). Suwon: Hapshin University Press.

Kim, Yung-Jae (2008), 되돌아보는 한국기독교 (*Korean Church and Theology*). Suwon: Hapdong Theological Seminary Press.

Koo, Ha-gen (2001), *Korean Workers: The Culture and Politics of Class Formation*. Ithaca, NY: Cornell University Press.

Koo, Ha-gen (2007), 'Emerging Civil Society: The Role of the Labor Movement', in Charles K. Armstrong (ed.), *Korean Society: Civil Society, Democracy and the State*. 2nd edition. London: Routledge, 73–94.

Korean Hymnal Society (2007), *Hymnal*. Seoul: Korean Hymnal Society.

Ku, Sang (2005), *Eternity Today: Selected Poems*, trans. Brother Anthony of Taizé. Seoul: Seoul Selection.

Küster, Volker (1994), 'Minjung Theology and Minjung Art', *Mission Studies* XI/1, 108–29.

Küster, Volker (2010), *A Protestant Theology of Passion: Korean Minjung Theology Revisited*. Leiden: Brill.

Kwon, Ok-yun (2003), *Buddhist and Protestant Korean Immigrants: Religious Beliefs and Socioeconomic Aspects of Life*. New York: LFB Scholarly Pub.

Ladd, George Trumbull (1908), *In Korea with Marquis Ito*. London: Longmans, Green and Co.

Lancashire, Douglas and Peter Hu Kuo-chen (1985), 'Translators' Introduction', in Edward Malatesta (ed.), *Matteo Ricci, The True Meaning of the Lord of Heaven (T'ien-chu Shih-i)*, trans. Douglas Lancashire and Peter Hu Kuo-chen. St Louis, MO: Institute of Jesuit Sources, 3–53.

Latourette, Kenneth Scott (1944), *A History of the Expansion of Christianity VI*. New York: Harper and Row.

Launay, Adrien (1925), *Martyrs français et coréens (1838–1846) béatifiés en 1925*. Paris: Société des Missions Étrangères de Paris.

Ledyard, Gari (2006), 'Kollumba Kang Wansuk, an Early Catholic Activist and Martyr', in Robert E. Buswell Jr. and Timothy S. Lee (eds.), *Christianity in Korea*. Honolulu: University of Hawaii, 38–71.

Lee, Chul-woo (1999), 'Modernity, Legality, and Power in Korea under Japanese Rule', in Gi-wook Shin and Michael Robinson (eds.), *Colonial Modernity in Korea*. Cambridge, MA: Harvard University Asia Center, 21–51.

Lee, Eok-ju (Jeremiah) (2010), 한국교회사 I, 1884–1945 (*Korean Ecclesiastical History I, 1884–1945*). Seoul: Sejul.

Lee, Graham (1907), 'How the Spirit Came to Pyeng Yang', *KMF*, vol. 3, 33–37.

Lee, Hong-jung (1999), '*Minjung* and Pentecostal Movements in Korea', in Allan H. Anderson and Walter Hollenweger (eds.), *Pentecostals after a Century: Global Perspectives on a Movement in Transition*. Sheffield: Sheffield Academic Press, 138–60.

Lee, Jae-jeong (1990), 대한성공회 백년사, 1890–1990 (*A History of a Century of the Korean Anglican Church, 1890–1990*). Seoul: Korean Anglican Church Press.

Lee, Jin-gu (2004), 'Korean Protestantism as Viewed by Netizens: A Focus on Recent Activities of Anti-Christian Sites', *Korea Journal* 44 (Winter), 223–45.

Lee, Jong-yun (1983), 'North Korea: Mission Impossible?', in Ro Bong-rin and Marlin L. Nelson (eds.), *Korean Church Growth Explosion*. Seoul: Word of Life Press, 69–76.

Lee, Jung-bae (2003), 한국 개신교 전위 토착신학연구 (*A Study on Transposition of Indigenous Theology of Korean Protestant Church*). Seoul: Christian Literature Society of Korea.

Lee, Jung-young (ed.) (1988a), *Ancestor Worship and Christianity in Korea*. Lewiston, NY: Edwin Mellen Press.

Lee, Jung-young (ed.) (1988b), *An Emerging Theology in World Perspective: Commentary on Korean Minjung Theology*. Mystic, CT: Twenty-third Publications.

Lee, Ki-baik (1984), *A New History of Korea*, trans. Edward W. Eagner with Edward J. Shultz. Cambridge, MA: Harvard University Press.

Lee, Kwang-soon (2005), 한국교회의 성장과 저성장 (*Growth and Undergrowth of the Korean Church*). Seoul: Missionacademy.

Lee, Moon-jang (1999), 'Experience of Religious Plurality in Korea', *IRM* 88/351, 399–413.

Lee, Nam-hee (2007), 'The South Korean Student Movement: Undongkŏn as a Counterpublic Sphere', in Charles K. Armstrong (ed.), *Korean Society: Civil Society, Democracy and the State*. 2nd edition. London: Routledge, 95–120.

Lee, Soon-keun (2011), 'The Founding and Development of the Korean Diaspora Forum', in S. Hun Kim and Wonsuk Ma (eds.), *Korean Diaspora and Christian Mission*. Oxford: Regnum Books, 197–206.

Lee, Sun-ai and Ahn Sang-nim (eds.) (1988), *Let the Weak Be Strong: A Woman's Struggle for Justice – Cho Wha Soon*. Bloomington, IN: Meyer-Stone Books.

Lee, Sun-ai Park (1992), 'Asian Women in Mission', *IRM* 81/322, 265–80.

Lee, Sung-jeon (2009), 'Empire, Moral Superiority and Mission Schools: The Establishment of Sungsil School and College in Early 20th Century Pyeongyang, Korea', in Jan A. B. Jongeneel, Peter Tze Ming Ng, Chong Ku Paek, Scott W. Sunquist and Yuko Watanabe (eds.), *Christian Mission and Education in Modern China, Japan, and Korea: Historical Studies*. Frankfurt am Main: Peter Lang, 131–40.

Lee, Theresa J. (2005), *The Divided Land: A Tale of Survival in War-Torn Korea*. New York: iUniverse.

Lee, Timothy S. (2000), 'A Political Factor in the Rise of Protestantism in Korea: Protestantism and the 1919 March First Movement', *Church History* 69/1, 116–42.

Lee, Timothy S. (2006), 'Beleaguered Success: Korean Evangelicalism in the Last Decade of the Twentieth Century', in Robert E. Buswell Jr. and Timothy S. Lee (eds.), *Christianity in Korea*. Honolulu: University of Hawaii, 330–50.

Lee, Timothy S. (2009), 'What Should Christians Do about a Shaman-Progenitor?: Evangelicals and Ethnic Nationalism in South Korea', *Church History* 78/1, 66–98.

Lee, Timothy S. (2010), *Born Again: Evangelicalism in Korea*. Honolulu: University of Hawaii Press.

Lee, Won-gue (1998), 한국교회 무엇이 문제인가? (*What Is It All about the Korean Church?*). Seoul: Methodist Theological Seminary Publishing.

Lee, Won-gue (2000), 한국교회 어디로 가고있나 (*Where Is the Korean Church Going?*). Seoul: Christian Literature Society.

Lee, Won-gue (2010), 종교사회학적 관점에서 본 한국교회의 위기와 희망 (*The Crisis and Hope of Korean Church from the Perspective of Religio-Sociology*). Seoul: Korean Methodist Church.

Lee, Won-soon (1986), 한국천주교회사 연구 (*A Study of the Korean Catholic Church*). Seoul: Institute of Korean Church History.

Lee, Won-soon (2004), 한국천주교회사 연구 II (*A Study of the Korean Catholic Church* II). Seoul: Institute of Korean Church History.

Lee, Won-sul, Lee Seung-joon and Han Joong-sik (2005), *Just Three More Years to Live! The Story of Rev. Kyung-Chik Han*. Seoul: Rev. Kyung-Chik Han Foundation.

Lee, Yeon-ok (1983), 'The Role of Women in Korean Church Growth', in Ro Bong-rin and Marlin L. Nelson (eds.), *Korean Church Growth Explosion*. Seoul: Word of Life Press, 231–44.

Lee, Yeon-ok (2011), *100 Years of the National Organization of the Korean Presbyterian Women*, trans. Park Myung-woo and Hong Ji-yeon. Seoul: Publishing House of the Presbyterian Church of Korea.

Lee, Young-hee (2006), 'Gender Specificity in Late-Choson Buddhist Kasa', *Sungkyun Journal of East Asian Studies* 6/1, 61–88.

Lee, Young-hoon (2004), 'The Life and Ministry of David Yonggi Cho and the Yoido Full Gospel Church', *Asian Journal of Pentecostal Studies* 7/1, 3–20.

Lee, Young-hoon (2009), *The Holy Spirit Movement in Korea: Its Historical and Theological Development*. Oxford: Regnum.

Lee Park, Sun-ai (1992), 'Asian Women in Mission', *IRM* 81/322, 265–80.

Lewis, James B. (2004), 'The Trade with Japan and the Economy of Kyŏngsang Province', *Acta Koreana* 7/1, 47–68.

Lewis, James B. (2006), 'Accounting Techniques in Korea: 18th Century Archival Samples from a Non-profit Association in the Sinitic World', *Accounting Historians Journal* 33/1, 53–87.

Lewis, Linda (1988), 'The "Kwangju Incident" Observed: An Anthropological Perspective on Civil Uprisings', in Donald N. Clark (ed.), *The Kwangju Uprising: Shadows over the Regime in South Korea*. Boulder, CO: Westview Press, 15–27.

Lewis, Linda (2002), *Laying Claim to the Memory of May: A Look Back at the 1980 Kwangju Uprising*. Honolulu: University of Hawai'i Press.

Lim, Hee-kuk (ed.) (2013), *Christianity in Korea: Historical Moments of Protestant Churches*. Seoul: NCCK.

Linden, Ian (2009), *Global Catholicism: Diversity and Changes since Vatican II*. London: Hurst and Co.

Ma, Won-suk (2012), 'Grace Korean Church, Fullerton, California: Mission from the Margins', *IBMR* 36/2, 65–71.

Ma, Won-suk, William W. Menzies and Hyeon-sung Bae (2004), *David Yonggi Cho: A Close Look at His Theology and Ministry*. Seoul: Hansei University Press.

McCann, David R. (1988), 'Confrontation in Korean Literature', in Donald N. Clark (ed.), *The Kwangju Uprising: Shadows over the Regime in South Korea*. Boulder, CO: Westview Press, 28–51.

McGavran, Donald A. and C. Peter Wagner (1990), *Understanding Church Growth*, 3rd edition. Grand Rapids, MI: Wm B. Eerdmans.

McKenzie, Frederick Arthur (1908), *The Tragedy of Korea*. London: Hodder and Stoughton.

McKenzie, Frederick Arthur (1920), *Korea's Fight for Freedom*. New York: Fleming H. Revell.

McNeill, John (2012), 'Lessons from Korean Mission in the Former Soviet Region', *IBMR* 36/2, 78–82.

Memorial Committee (2002), *May the Words of My Mouth: A Memorial Collection of Rev. Kyung-chik Han's Sermons*. Seoul: Youngnak Church.

MEP (Société des Missions Étrangères de Paris) (1924), *The Catholic Church in Korea*. Hong Kong: Société des Missions Étrangères de Paris.

Miller, Owen (2010), 'The Idea of Stagnation in Korean Historiography', *Korean Histories* 2/1, 3–12.

Min, Anselm Kyong-suk (2009), 'Between Indigenization and Globalization: Korean Christianity after 1989'. In Klaus Koschorke (ed.), *Falling Walls:*

The Year 1989/90 as a Turning Point in the History of World Christianity. Wiesbaden: Harrassowitz, 195–214.

Min, Kyoung-bae (1982), 한국기독교회사 (*A History of the Korean Church*). Seoul: Korea Christian Publication.

Min, Kyoung-bae (1996), 'National Identity in the History of the Korean Church', in Chai-shin Yu (ed.), *Korea and Christianity*. Seoul: Korean Scholar Press, 121–43.

Min, Kyoung-bae (2008), 한국민족교회 형성사론 (*The Establishment of an Indigenous Korean Church*). Seoul: Yonsei University Press.

Mitchell, Donald W. (2008), *Buddhism*, 2nd edition. Oxford: Oxford University Press.

Moffett, Samuel Hugh (1988), *A History of Christianity in Asia*. Vol. I: *Beginnings to 1500*. Maryknoll, NY: Orbis Books.

Moffett, Samuel Hugh (2005), *A History of Christianity in Asia*, Vol. II: *1500 to 1900*. Maryknoll, NY: Orbis Books.

Moll, Rob (2006), 'Missions Incredible', *Christianity Today* (24 Feb.).

Moon, Chung-in (1999), 'Understanding the DJ Doctrine: The Sunshine Policy and the Korean Peninsula', in Chung-in Moon and David I. Steinberg, *Kim Dae-jung Government and Sunshine Policy: Promises and Challenges*. Seoul: Yonsei University Press, 35–56.

Moon, Cyris H. S. (1985), *A Korean Minjung Theology: An Old Testament Perspective*. Maryknoll, NY: Orbis Books.

Moon, Ik-hwan (1984), 통일은 어떻게 가능한가 (*How Can Unification Be Achieved?*). Seoul: Hakminsa.

Moon, Ik-hwan (1990), *I Shall Go Even on Foot*. Seoul: Muneumsa.

Moon, Ok-pyo (1998), 'Ancestors Becoming Children of God: Ritual Clashes between Confucian Tradition and Christianity in Contemporary Korea', *Korea Journal* (Autumn), 148–77.

Moon, Sang-cheol Steve (2008), 'The Protestant Missionary Movement in Korea: Current Growth and Development', *IBMR* 32/2, 59–64.

Moon, Sang-cheol Steve (2012), 'Missions from Korea 2012: Slowdown and Maturation', *IBMR* 36/2, 84–85.

Moon, Seung-sook (2007), 'Women and Civil Society in South Korea', in Charles K. Armstrong (ed.), *Korean Society: Civil Society, Democracy and the State*. 2nd edition. London: Routledge, 121–44.

Moon, Young-seok (2011), 'Sociological Implications of the Roman Catholic Conversion Boom in Korea', *Korea Journal* (Spring), 143–75.

Mooney, Paul G. (2011), 'The Anglican Church of Korea', *Anglo-Korean Society Newsletter*.

Mott, John R. (1910), *The Decisive Hour of Christian Missions*. Edinburgh: Foreign Mission Committee of the Church of Scotland.

Mullins, Mark R. (1995), 'Christianity Transplanted: Toward a Sociology of Success and Failure', in Mark R. Mullins and Richard Fox Young (eds.), *Perspectives on Christianity in Korea and Japan*. Lewiston, NY: Edwin Mellen Press, 61–77.

Mullins, Mark R. (1998), *Christianity Made in Japan: A Study of Indigenous Movements*. Honolulu: University of Hawai'i Press.

Mullins, Mark R. and Richard Fox Young (eds.) (1995), *Perspectives on Christianity in Korea and Japan*. Lewiston, NY: Edwin Mellen Press.

Murabayashi, Duk Hee Lee (ed.) (2004), *Hawai'i Contributors to the Defense of An Chunggŭn*. Honolulu: Center for Korean Studies, University of Hawai'i Press.

Myeongdong Cathedral (1984), 한국 가톨릭 인권운동사 (*A History of the Catholic Human Rights Movements in Korea*). Seoul: Myeongdong Cathedral.

Nahm, Andrew C. (1989), *Korea: Tradition and Transformation: A History of the Korean People*. Elizabeth, NJ: Hollym.

NCCK (National Council of Churches in Korea) (1988), 'Declaration of the Churches of Korea on National Reunification and Peace', in Sebastian C. H. Kim, Pauline Kollontai and Greg Hoyland (eds.), *Peace and Reconciliation: In Search of Shared Identity*. Aldershot, Hants: Ashgate, 185–95.

Neill, Stephen (1990), *A History of Christian Missions*. London: Penguin.

Nelson, Marlin L. (1983), 'Korean Church Mission Growth', in Ro Bong-rin and Marlin L. Nelson (eds.), *Korean Church Growth Explosion*. Seoul: Word of Life Press, 88–102.

Nevius, John L. (1899), *The Planting and Development of Missionary Churches*. 3rd edition. Shanghai: Presbyterian Press.

Noh, Chi-joon (1993), 일제하 한국기독교의 민족운동연구 (*A Study of the Korean Protestant Nationalistic Movement under the Japanese Rule*). Seoul: Institute for Korean Church History.

Noh, Gil-myeong (2005), 민족사와 천주교회 (*History of the Korean People and the Catholic Church*). Seoul: Institute of Korean Church History.

Noh, Jong-sun (1994), *Liberating God for Minjung*. Seoul: Hanul Publishing.

Noh, Yong-pil (2008), 한국천주교회사의 연구 (*A History of Korean Catholic Church*). Seoul: Korean History.

O, Mun-hwan (1928), 도마스목사전 (*The Life of R. J. Thomas (Who was Killed at Pyeng Yang in 1866)*). Pyongyang: Thomas Memorial Association.

Oak, Sung-deuk (2001), 'Shamanistic Tan'gun and Christian Hanănim: Protestant Missionaries' Interpretation of the Korean Founding Myth, 1895–1934', *Studies in World Christianity*, vol. 7, 42–57.

Oak, Sung-deuk (2004), *Sources of Korean Christianity, 1832–1945*. Seoul: Institute of Korean Church History Studies.

Oak, Sung-deuk (2006), 'Chinese Protestant Literature and Early Korean Protestantism', in Robert E. Buswell Jr. and Timothy S. Lee (eds.), *Christianity in Korea*. Honolulu: University of Hawaii, 72–93.

Oak, Sung-deuk (2009), 'Edinburgh 1910, Fulfillment Theory, and Missionaries in China and Korea', *Journal of Asian and Asian American Theology*, vol. IX, 29–51.

Oak, Sung-deuk (2010a), 'Healing and Exorcism: Christian Encounters with Shamanism in Early Modern Korea', *Asian Ethnology* 69/1, 95–128.

Oak, Sung-deuk (2010b), 'Images of the Cross in Early Modern Korea: The Geomantic Prophecy of the Chŏnggam-nok and the Protestant Flag of the Red Cross', *Journal of Korean Religions* 1/1, 117–61.

Oak, Sung-deuk (2013), *The Making of Korean Christianity: Protestant Encounters with Korean Religions, 1876–1915*. Waco, TX: Baylor University Press.

Oberdorfer, Don and Robert Carlin (2014), *The Two Koreas: A Contemporary History*, 3rd edition. New York: Basic Books.

O'Connor, Daniel et al. (2000), *Three Centuries of Mission: The United Society for the Propagation of the Gospel, 1701–2000*. London: Continuum.

Ogle, George E. (1977), *Liberty to the Captives: The Struggle against Oppression in South Korea*. Atlanta: John Knox Press.

Oh, Dough K. (2011), 'History of the Korean Diaspora Movement', in S. Hun Kim and Wonsuk Ma, (eds.), *Korean Diaspora and Christian Mission*. Oxford: Regnum Books, 181–96.

Oh, Pyeng-seh (1983), 'Keeping the Faith Pure', in Ro Bong-rin and Marlin L. Nelson (eds.), *Korean Church Growth Explosion*. Seoul: Word of Life Press, 211–30.

Paik, Lak-geoon George (1970 [1929]), *The History of Protestant Missions in Korea, 1832–1910*, 2nd edition. Seoul: Yonsei University Press.

Pak, Jacqueline (2006), 'Cradle of the Covenant: Ahn Changho and the Christian Roots of the Korean Constitution', in Robert E. Buswell Jr. and Timothy S. Lee (eds.), *Christianity in Korea*. Honolulu: University of Hawaii, 116–48.

Pak, Ung-kyu (2005), *Millennialism in the Korean Protestant Church*. New York: Peter Lang.

Palais, James B. (1975), *Politics and Policy in Traditional Korea*. Cambridge, MA: Harvard University Press.

Palmer, Spencer J. (1967), *Korea and Christianity: The Problem of Identification with Tradition*. Seoul: Hollym.

Paramore, K. N. (2009), 'Anti-Christian Ideas and National Ideology: Inoue Enryo and Inoue Tetsujiro's Mobilization of Sectarian History in Meiji Japan', *Sungkyun Journal of East Asian Studies* 9/1, 107–44.

Park, Chang-won (2011), *Cultural Blending in Korean Death Rites: New Interpretive Approaches*. London: Continuum.

Park, Cho-choon (1983), 'The Dynamics of Young Nak Presbyterian Church Growth', in Ro Bong-rin and Marlin L. Nelson (eds.), *Korean Church Growth Explosion*. Seoul: Word of Life Press, 201–10.

Park, Chung-shin (2003), *Protestantism and Politics in Korea*. Seattle: University of Washington Press.

Park, Heon-wook (1995), 'The Korean Christian Church in Japan: A Study of the Gospel, Indigenization, and Nationalism', in Mark R. Mullins and Richard Fox Young (eds.), *Perspectives on Christianity in Korea and Japan*. Lewiston, NY: Edwin Mellen Press, 47–59.

Park, Hyung-kyu (1985), 'The Search for Self-Identity and Liberation', *IRM* 74/293, 37–48.

Park, Jae-soon (2000), 'Ham Sŏk-hŏn's National Spirit and Christian Thought', *Korea Journal* (Summer), 134–74.

Park, Jong-chun (1998), *Crawl with God, Dance in the Spirit! A Creative Formation of Korean Theology of the Spirit*. Nashville, TN: Abingdon Press.

Park, Joon-sik (2012), 'Korean Protestant Christianity: A Missiological Reflection', *IBMR* 36/2, 59–64.

Park, Keun-won (1985), 'Evangelism and Mission in Korea: A Reflection from an Ecumenical Perspective', *IRM* 74/293, 49–58.

Park, Moon-su (2012), 'Urgent Issues Facing Modern Korean Catholicism and Their Subtext', *Korea Journal* 52/3 (Autumn), 91–118.

Park, Seong-won (1997), 'A Survey on Mission Work in the Korean Churches', *IRM* 86/342, 329–33.

Park, Seong-won (2001), *Worship in the Presbyterian Church in Korea: Its History and Implications*. New York: Peter Lang.

Park, Yeong-shin (2010), '사회구조, 통일, 사회통합' (Social Structure, Unification and Social Integration), in Park Yeong-shin, Park Jong-so, Lee Beom-seong, Chung Jae-yeong and Cho Seong-don (eds.), 통일, 사회통합, 하나님나라 (*Unification, Social Integration and the Kingdom of God*). Seoul: Christian Literature Society, 13–40.

Parratt, John (2011), 'Barth and Buddhism in the Theology of Katsume Takizawa', *Scottish Journal of Theology* 64/2, 195–210.

Patterson, Wayne and Hyung-chan Kim (1992), *Koreans in America*, 2nd edition. Minneapolis, MN: Lerner.

PCUSA (Presbyterian Church in the United States of America) (1934), *The Fiftieth Anniversary Celebration of the Korea Mission of the Presbyterian Church in the USA*. Seoul: John D. Wells School.

Piacentini, Arthur (1890), *Mgr Ridel, Évéque des Philippopolis, Vicaire Apostolique de Corée: d'après sa correspondence*. Lyon: Librairie Générale Catholique et Classique.

Poitras, Edward W. (1994), 'The Legacy of Henry G. Appenzeller', *IBMR* 18/4 (1994), 177–80.

Pozdnyaev, Denis A. (ed.) (2012), 러시아 정교회 한국선교 이야기 (*A Mission History of Russian Orthodox Church in Korea*), trans. Yi Yo-han and Yi Jeong-gwon. Seoul: Hongsungsa.

Pratt, Keith (2006), *Everlasting Flower: A History of Korea*. London: Reaktion Books.

Pyun, Young-tai (1988), 'Ancestor Worship: From the Perspective of an Early Protestant Christian', in Jung-young Lee (ed.), *Ancestor Worship and Christianity in Korea*. Lewiston, NY: Edwin Mellen Press, 45–60.

Ra, Dong-kwang (2003), 'Ch'ondogyo's Preparation for the March First Independence Movement', *Donghak Yeongu*, vol. 14–15, 167–184.

Rausch, Franklin (2008), 'Saving Knowledge: Catholic Educational Policy in the Late Chosŏn Dynasty', *Acta Koreana* 11/3, 47–85.

Rausch, Franklin and Don Baker (2007), 'Catholic Rites and Litergy', in Robert E. Buswell Jr. (ed.), *Religions of Korea in Practice*. Princeton, NJ: Princeton University Press, 376–92.

RFKCH (Research Foundation of Korean Church History) (2010), *Inside the Catholic Church of Korea*. Seoul: Research Foundation of Korean Church History.

Rhee, Syng-man [Syngman Rhee] (1993 [1904]), 독립정신 (*The Spirit of Independence*). Seoul: Jeondong Publication.

Rhie, Deok-joo (2001), 한국 토착교회 형성사 연구 (*A Study on the Formation of the Indigenous Church in Korea, 1903–1907*). Seoul: Institute for Korean Church History.

Rhie, Deok-joo and Cho Yee-jei (eds.) (1997), 한국그리스도인들의 신앙고백 (*Creeds and Confessions of Korean Church*). Seoul: Han Deul.

Ricci, Matteo S. (1985 [1594]), *True Meaning of the Lord of Heaven*, trans. Douglas Lancashire and Peter Hu Kuo-chen, St Louis, MO: Institute of Jesuit Sources.

Rim, Gol (2010), 'Kyung-Chik Han (1902–2000)'s Faith Theory of Church', in Kim Eun-seop (ed.), *Kyung-chik Han Collection: Theses 1*, Seoul: Kyung-chik Han Foundation, 265–314.

Rivé-Lasan, Marie-Orange (2013), 'Korean Christian Churches, the Ibuk Ch'ulsin Minority and the Perception of the North', *Journal of Korean Religions* 4/2, 123–46.

Ro, Bong-rin (1983a), 'Non-Spiritual Factors in Church Growth', in Ro Bong-rin and Marlin L. Nelson (eds.), *Korean Church Growth Explosion*. Seoul: Word of Life Press, 159–70.

Ro, Bong-rin (1983b), 'The Korean Church: God's Chosen People for Evangelism', in Ro Bong-Rin and Marlin L. Nelson (eds.) (1983), *Korean Church Growth Explosion*. Seoul: Word of Life Press, 11–44.

Ro, Bong-rin (1993), 'Theological Debates in Korea after Canberra', in Ro Bong-rin and Bruce J. Nicholls (eds.), *Beyond Canberra: Evangelical Responses to Contemporary Ecumenical Issues*. Oxford: Regnum Books, 53–59.

Ro, Bong-rin and Marlin L. Nelson (eds.) (1983), *Korean Church Growth Explosion*. Seoul: Word of Life Press.

Ro, Bong-rin and Marlin L. Nelson (eds.) (1995), *Korean Church Growth Explosion*, 2nd edition. Seoul: Word of Life Press.

Ro, Young-chan (1988), 'Ancestor Worship: From the Perspective of Korean Tradition', in Jung-young Lee (ed.), *Ancestor Worship and Christianity in Korea*. Lewiston, NY: Edwin Mellen Press, 7–19.

Robert, Dana (ed.) (2002), *Gospel Bearers, Gender Barriers: Missionary Women in the Twentieth Century*. Maryknoll, NY: Orbis Books.

Robinson, Michael Edson (1988), *Cultural Nationalism in Colonial Korea, 1920–1925*. Seattle: University of Washington Press.

Robinson, R. H., W. L. Johnson and B. Thanissaro (2005), *Buddhist Religions: A Historical Introduction*, 5th edition. Belmont, CA: Wadsworth/Thomson Learning.

Ross, John (1877), *Corean Primer, Being Lessons in Corean on All Ordinary Subjects*. Shanghai: American Presbyterian Mission Press.

Ross, John (1890), 'The Christian Dawn in Korea', *Missionary Review of the World*, vol. 4, 241–48.

Ross, John (1891), *History of Corea, Ancient and Modern with Description of Manners and Customs, Language and Geography*. London: Elliot Stock.

Ross, John (1903), *Mission Methods in Manchuria*. London: Fleming H. Revell Co.

Roux, Pierre-Emmanuel (2012), 'The Great Ming Code and the Repression of Catholics in Chosŏn Korea', *Acta Korea* 15/1, 73–106.

Rutt, Richard (1973), *Korean Works and Days*. 2nd edition. Seoul: Taewon Publishing Co.

Rutt, Richard (1979), 'An Early Koreanologist: Eli Barr Landis, 1865–1898', *Transactions of the Royal Asiatic Society Korea Branch* 54/4, 59–100.

Ryu, Dae-young (2003), 'Treaties, Extraterritorial Rights, and American Protestant Missions in Late Joseon Korea', *Korea Journal* 43/1 (Spring), 174–203.

Ryu, Dae-young (2004), 'Korean Protestant Churches' Attitude towards War: With a Special Focus on the Vietnam War', *Korea Journal*, 191–222.

Ryu, Dae-young (2008), 'The Origin and Characteristics of Evangelical Protestantism in Korea at the Turn of the Twentieth Century', *Church History* 77/2, 371–98.

Ryu, Dae-young (2009), 한국 근현대사와 기독교 (*Christianity and Modern Korean History*). Seoul: Pureun Yeoksa.

Ryu, Dong-sik (2000), 한국신학의 광맥 (*The Mineral Veins of Korean Theology*), 2nd edition. Seoul: Dasan Geulbang.

Ryu, Dong-sik (2005a), 한국감리교회의 역사 I, 1884–1992 (*History of Korean Methodist Church I, 1884–1992*). Seoul: Korean Methodist Church.

Ryu, Dong-sik (2005b), 한국감리교회의 역사 II, 1884–1992 (*History of Korean Methodist Church II, 1884–1992*). Seoul: Korean Methodist Church.

Ryu, Geum-ju (2005), 이용도의 신비주의와 한국교회 (*The Mysticism of Yi Yong-do and the Korean Church*). Seoul: Christian Literature Society of Korea.

Ryu, Hong-ryeol (1992), 한국천주교회사 (*History of the Catholic Church in Korea*), Seoul: Catholic Publishing.

Sandler, Stanley (1999), *The Korean War: No Victors, No Vanquished*. London: UCL Press.

Schloms, Michael (2003), *North Korea and the Timeless Dilemma of Aid: A Study of Humanitarian Action in Famines*. Münster: LIT.

Schmid, Andre (2002), *Korea between Empires, 1895–1919*. New York: Columbia University Press.

Schmid, Andre (2010), 'Two Americans in Seoul: Evaluating an Oriental Empire', *Korean Histories* 2/2, 7–23.

Schwekendiek, Daniel (2011), *A Socioeconomic History of North Korea*. Jefferson, NC: McFarland and Co.

SCKCM (Special Committee of Korean Christian Ministers) (1952), Letter to President-elect Dwight D. Eisenhower, in Kim Heung-soo (ed.) (2003a), *Documents of the WCC Library: The Korean War*. Seoul: Institute for Korean Church History, 326–27.

Scott, William (1916), *Report of the British and Foreign Bible Society*. London: BFBC.

Shearer, Roy E. (1965), 'The Evangelistic Missionary's Role in Church Growth in Korea', *IRM* 54/216, 462–70.

Shim, Il-sup (1985), 'The New Religious Movements in the Korean Church', *IRM* 74/293, 103–8.

Shin, Eun-hee (2007), 'The Sociopolitical Organism: The Religious Dimensions of Juche Philosophy', in Robert E. Buswell Jr. (ed.), *Religions of Korea in Practice*. Princeton, NJ: Princeton University Press, 517–33.

Shin, Gi-wook (1996), *Peasant Protest and Social Change in Colonial Korea*. Seattle: University of Washington Press.

Shin, Gi-wook (2006), *Ethnic Nationalism in Korea: Genealogy, Politics, and Legacy*. Stanford, CA: Stanford University Press.

Shin, Gi-wook (2010), *One Alliance, Two Lenses: U.S.-Korea Relations in a New Era*. Stanford, CA: Stanford University Press.

Shin, Gi-wook and Michael Robinson (eds.) (1999), *Colonial Modernity in Korea*. Cambridge, MA: Harvard University Asia Center.

Shin, Ho-cheol (ed.) (2008), 양화진 외국인묘지: 토지소유권의 역사적 진실 (*Yanghwajin Foreign Cemetery: Historical Truth of Land Ownership*). Seoul: Yanghwajin Missionary Society.

Shin, Ik-cheol (2006), 'The Experiences of Visiting Catholic Churches in Beijing and the Recognition of Western Learning Reflected in the Journals of Travel to Beijing', *Review of Korean Studies* 9/4, 11–31.

Shin, Jong-cheol (2003), 한국장로교회와 근본주의 (*The Korean Presbyterian Church and the Fundamentalism*). Seoul: Grisim Publishing.

Shin, Michael D. (2011), 'Pyeongan Province and the Origins of Modern Society', *Papers of the British Association for Korean Studies*, vol. 23, 59–88.

Shin, Yun-hyoung Michael (2011), 'Avalokteśvara's Manifestation as the Virgin Mary: The Jesuit Adaptation and the Visual Conflation in Japanese Catholicism after 1614', *Church History* 80/1, 1–39.

Shine, Yun-shik (2006), *Korea Church Power I and II*. Seoul: Christian Council of Korea.

Smith, D. Frank Herron (1920), *The Other Side of the Korean Question*. Seoul: Seoul Press.

Smith, John C. (1961), 'Policy Lessons from Korea', *IRM* 50/199, 320–24.

Sohn, Hak-kyu (1989), *Authoritarianism and Opposition in South Korea*. London: Routledge.

Song, Jong-rye Gratia (2003), 'Martyrdom and the Autonomy of Korean Catholic Women', *Asia Journal of Theology* 17/2, 364–77.

Song, Min-ho (2011), 'The Diaspora Experience of the Korean Church and Its Implications for World Missions', in S. Hun Kim and Wonsuk Ma (eds.), *Korean Diaspora and Christian Mission*. Oxford: Regnum Books, 117–28.

Strawn, Lee-Ellen (2012), 'Korean Bible Women's Success: Using the Anbang Network and the Religious Authority of the Mudang', *Journal of Korean Religions* 3/1, 117–49.

Suh, David Kwang-sun (1981), 'A Biographical Sketch of an Asian Theological Consultation', in CTCCCA (Commission on Theological Concerns of the Christian Conference of Asia) (ed.), *Minjung Theology: People as the Subjects of History*. Singapore: Christian Conference of Asia, 15–37.

Suh, David Kwang-sun (1986), 'American Missionaries and a Hundred Years of Korean Protestantism', *IRM* 74/293 (1986), 5–18.

Suh, David Kwang-sun (1991), *The Korean Minjung in Christ*. Hong Kong: Christian Conference of Asia.

Suh, Nam-dong (1983), 'Toward a Theology of Han', in CTCCCA (Commission on Theological Concerns of the Christian Conference of Asia) (ed.), *Minjung Theology: People as the Subjects of History*. Singapore: Christian Conference of Asia, 51–65.

Sunquist, Scott W. (2009), 'American Christian Mission and Education: Henry W. Luce, William R. Harper, and the Secularization of Christian Higher Education', in Jan A. B. Jongeneel, Peter Tze Ming Ng, Chong Ku Paek, Scott W. Sunquist and Yuko Watanabe (eds.), *Christian Mission and Education in Modern China, Japan, and Korea: Historical Studies*. Frankfurt am Main: Peter Lang, 1–14.

T. K. [Chi Myeong-gwan] (1976), *Letters from South Korea by T. K.*, trans. David L. Swain. Tokyo: Iwanami Shoten.

Tahk, Myeong-hwan (1986), 기독교이단연구 (*The Research on Christian Cults*). Seoul: International Religions Research Institute.

Tao, Xinzhong (2000), *An Introduction to Confucianism*. Cambridge: Cambridge University Press.

Torrey, Ben (2008), 'The Mission to North Korea', *IBMR* 32/1, 20–22.

Trollope, Mark Napier (1915), *The [Anglican] Church in Corea*, London: A. R. Mowbray.

Tudor, Daniel (2012), *Korea: The Impossible Country*. Tokyo: Tuttle Publishing.

Turner, John G. (2008), *Bill Bright and Campus Crusade for Christ: The Renewal of Evangelicalism in Postwar America*. Chapel Hill, NC: University of North Carolina Press.

Tyrannus (1999), 한국개신교인의 교회활동과 신앙의식 (*Report on Church Activities and Attitudes to Faith of Korean Protestant Christians*). Seoul: Tyrannus.

Underwood, Horace G. (1908), *The Call of Korea, Political – Social – Religious, by Horace G. Underwood, for Twenty-Three Years a Missionary in Korea*. New York and Chicago: Fleming H. Revell Co.

Underwood, Horace G. (1910), *The Religions of Eastern Asia*. New York: Macmillan.

Underwood, Lillias H. (1904), *Fifteen Years among the Top-knots, or Life in Korea*. Boston: American Tract Society.

Underwood, Lillias H. (1918), *Underwood of Korea; Being an Intimate Record of the Life and Work of the Rev. H. G. Underwood, D. D., LL. D., for Thirty-one years a Missionary of the Presbyterian Board in Korea*. New York: Fleming H. Revell Co.

Vanderbilt, Gregory (2009), 'Post-war Japanese Christian Historians, Democracy, and the Problem of the "Emperor-System" State', in Julius Bautista and Francis Khek Gee Lim (eds.), *Christianity and the State in Asia: Complicity and Conflict*. London: Routledge, 59–78.

Verdier, Marie-Laure (2014), 'Contextualised Mission: The South Korean Evangelical Responses to the Humanitarian Crisis in North Korea (1995–2012)', PhD thesis, School of Oriental and African Studies, University of London.

Walraven, Boudewijn (1999), 'Popular Religion in a Confucianized Society', in JaHyun Kim Haboush and Martina Deuchler (eds.), *Culture and the State in Late Chosŏn Korea*. London: Harvard University Press, 160–98.

Walraven, Boudewijn (2009), 'Cheju Island, 1901: Records, Memories and Current Concerns', *Korean Histories* 1/1, 3–24.

Weber, Max ([1905] 1974), *The Protestant Ethic and the Spirit of Capitalism*, trans. Talcott Parsons. London: Unwin University Books.

Weingärtner, Erich (1985), 'The Tozanzo Process', Address to the North American Conference on the Unification of Korea, Stoney Point, NY, 9–12 December, in Kim Heung-soo (ed.), *Documents of the WCC Library: Korean Christian Federation*. Seoul: Institute for Korean Church History, 2003, 89–108.

Welch, Herbert (George) (1922), 'The Missionary Significance of the Last Ten Years: A Survey III in Korea', *IRM* 11/3, 337–59.

Wells, Kenneth M. (1990), *New God, New Nation: Protestants and Self-reconstruction Nationalism in Korea, 1896–1937*. Honolulu: University of Hawai'i Press.

Wells, Kenneth M. (1999), 'The Price of Legitimacy: Women and the Kŭnuhoe Movement, 1927–1931', in Gi-Wook Shin and Michael Robinson (eds.), *Colonial Modernity in Korea*. Cambridge, MA: Harvard University Asia Center, 191–220.

Wells, Kenneth M. (2009), 'The Failings of Success', *Korean Histories* 1/1, 60–80.

Wheeler, W. Reginald (ed.) (1950), '6: Korea: War Torn and Divided', in Sung-deuk Oak, *Selected Materials of the Korea Mission of the PCUSA, 1886–1950*. Seoul: Institute of Korean Church History Studies, 320–38.

Whelan, John B. (1960), 'The Anglican Church in Korea', *IRM* 49/194, 157–66.

Wickeri, Philip L. (2011), *Seeking the Common Ground: Protestant Christianity, the Three-self Movement and China's United Front*, 2nd edition. Eugene, OR: Wipf and Stock.

Williamson, Alexander (1870), *Journeys in North China, Manchuria, and Eastern Mongolia, with Some Account of Corea*, vol. II. London: Smith, Elder and Co.

Winter, Ralph D. and Steven C. Hawthorne (eds.) (1981), *Perspectives on the World Christian Movement*. Pasadena, CA: William Carey Library.

WMC (World Missionary Conference) (1910), *Report of Commission I: Carrying the Gospel to All the Non-Christian World*. Edinburgh and London: Oliphant, Anderson and Ferrier.

Won, Yong-ji (1988), *A History of Lutheranism in Korea*. St Louis, MO: Concordia Seminary.

Yang, Hyeon-hye (2009), 근대 한.일 관계사 속의 기독교 (*Christianity in the Context of Modern Korean-Japanese Relations*). Seoul: Ehwa University Press.

Yang, Jong-hoe (2008), 'Globalization and Value Change in Korea: With a Special Emphasis on the Impact of the Recent Economic Crisis and Neoliberal Reform on the Confucian Value System', in Chang Yun-shik, Hyun-ho Seok and Donald L. Baker (eds.), *Korea Confronts Globalization*. New York: Routledge, 192–205.

Yang, Myong-duk (2009), *Toward a Multicultural Church*. Seoul: Presbyterian Church of Korea.

Yang, Yong-sun (2009), *Korean Methodist Church in Australia and New Zealand: History and Character*. Highland Park, NJ: Hermit Kingdom Press.

Yee, Chan-sin (2003), 'The Confucian Conception of Gender in the Twenty-first Century', in Daniel A. Bell and Hahm Chaibong (eds.), *Confucianism for the Modern World*. Cambridge: Cambridge University Press, 312–33.

Yeohae Ecumenical Forum (2013), *The Voice of One Crying in the Wilderness: Remembering Yeohae Kang Won-Yong, Pioneer of Ecumenical Movement, 1917–2006*. Seoul: Christian Literature Society of Korea.

Yi, Beom-seong (2010), '통일, 하나님나라운동' (Unification and the Kingdom of God), in Park Yeong-shin, et al. (eds.), 통일, 사회통합, 하나님나라 (*Unification, Social Integration and the Kingdom of God*). Seoul: Christian Literature Society, 66–94.

Yi, Byeok (1986 [1785]), 성교요지 (*Seongkyo Yoji*), trans. Ha Seong-re. Seoul: St Joseph Press.

Yi, Hyo-jae (1985), 'Christian Mission and the Liberation of Korean Women', *IRM* 74/293, 93–102.

Yi, Ik (1999), 성호 사설 (*Seongho Saseol*), trans. Choi Seok-ki. Seoul: Hangilsa.

Yi, Ku-yeol [Ku-yŏl] (1984), '200 Years of Catholic Art in Korea', *Korea Journal*, 53–59.

Yi, Mahn-yol (1991), 한국기독교와 민족의식 (*Korean Christianity and People's Consciousness*). Seoul: Jisik Saneopsa.

Yi, Mahn-yol (1998), 한국기독교 수용사 연구 (*Study on the Korean Reception of Christianity*). Seoul: Durae Side.

Yi, Mahn-yol (2001), 한국기독교와 민족통일운동 (*Korean Christianity and the National Unification Movement*). Seoul: Institute of the History of Christianity in Korea.

Yi, Mahn-yol (2004), 'The Birth of the National Spirit of the Christians in the Late Chosŏn Period', trans. Ch'oe Ŭn-a, in Chai-shin Yu (ed.), *Korea and Christianity*. Fremont, CA: Asian Humanities Press, 39–72.

Yi, Mahn-yol (2006), 'Korean Christianity and Unification Movement', in Robert E. Buswell Jr. and Timothy S. Lee (eds.), *Christianity in Korea*. Honolulu: University of Hawaii Press, 238–57.

Yi, Mahn-yol (2007), 역사에 살아있는 그리스도인 (*Christians Who Live in History*). Seoul: Institute of the History of Christianity in Korea.

Yi, Won-sun (1996), 'The Sirhak Scholars' Perspectives of Sŏhak in the Late Chosŏn Society', in Chai-shin Yu (ed.), *The Founding of Catholic Tradition in Korea*. Mississauga, ON: Korea and Related Studies Press, 45–102.

Yim, Sung-bhin (2002), 21세기 책임윤리의 모색 (*Search for More Responsible Ethics in the 21st Century*). Seoul: PCTS Press.

Yoo, Boo-woong (1986), 'Response to Korean Shamanism by the Pentecostal Church', *IRM* 75/297, 70–74.

Yoo, David K. (2010), *Contentious Spirits: Religion in Korean American History, 1903–1945*. Stanford, CA: Stanford University Press.

Yoo, Jang-choon (2010), 'Social Service of Rev. Han Who Served Korean Society beyond Youngnak Church', in Kim Eun-seop (ed.), *Kyung-hik Han Collection: Theses 2*. Seoul: Kyung-chik Han Foundation, 181–249.

Yoon, In-shil Choe (2007), 'Martyrdom and Social Activism: The Korean Practice of Catholicism', in Robert E. Buswell Jr. (ed.), *Religions of Korea in Practice*. Princeton, NJ: Princeton University Press, 355–75.

Yoon, Min-kyung (2012), 'North Korean Art Works: Historical Paintings and the Cult of Personality', *Korean Histories* 3/1, 53–72.

Youngnak Church (1998), 영락교회 50년사, 1945–1995 (*Fifty Years of History of Youngnak Church, 1945–1995*). Seoul: Youngnak Church.

Yu, Chai-shin (ed.) (1996), *The Founding of Catholic Tradition in Korea*. Mississauga, ON: Korea and Related Studies Press.

Yu, Chai-shin (ed.) (2004), *Korea and Christianity*. Fremont, CA: Asian Humanities Press.

Yun, In-jin (2008), '한국적 다문화주의의 전개와 특성: 국가와 시민사회의 역할을 중심으로' (The Development and Characteristics of Multiculturalism in South Korea: Focusing on the Relationship of the State and Civil Society), *Hanguk sahoehak* 42/2, 72–103.

Yun, Kyeong-no [Kyŏng-no] (1996), 'The Relationship between Korean Catholics and Protestants in the Early Mission Period', in Chai-shin Yu (ed.), *Korea and Christianity*. Seoul: Korean Scholar Press, 7–37.

Yun, Sung-bum (1998a), 한국종교문화와 한국적 기독교 (*Korean Religious Culture and Korean Christianity*). Seoul: Gamsin.

Yun, Sung-bum (1998b), 한국유교와 한국적 신학 (*Korean Confucianism and Korean Theology*). Seoul: Gamsin.

Zoh, Byoung-ho (2005), 한국기독청년학생운동 100 년사 (*A History of the Christian Student Movements in Korea*). Seoul: Ttanesseungeulssi.

Index